UNCANNY X-FORCE

THE DARK ANGEL SAGA
BOOK 2

UNCANNY X-FORCE: THE DARK ANGEL SAGA BOOK 2. Contains material originally published in magazine form as UNCANNY X-FORCE #14-18. First printing 2012. ISBN# 978-0-7851-5887-5. Published by MARVEL WORLDWIDE, INC., a subsidiary of MARVEL ENTERTAINMENT, LLC. OFFICE OF PUBLICATION: 135 West 50th Street, New York, NY 10020. Copyright © 2011 and 2012 Marvel Characters, Inc. All rights reserved. $24.99 per copy in the U.S. and $27.99 in Canada (GST #R127032852); Canadian Agreement #40668537. All characters featured in this issue and the distinctive names and likenesses thereof, and all related indicia are trademarks of Marvel Characters, Inc. No similarity between any of the names, characters, persons, and/or institutions in this magazine with those of any living or dead person or institution is intended, and any such similarity which may exist is purely coincidental. Printed in the U.S.A. ALAN FINE, EVP - Office of the President, Marvel Worldwide, Inc. and EVP & CMO Marvel Characters B.V.; DAN BUCKLEY, Publisher & President - Print, Animation & Digital Divisions; JOE QUESADA, Chief Creative Officer; DAVID BOGART, SVP of Business Affairs & Talent Management; TOM BREVOORT, SVP of Publishing; C.B. CEBULSKI, SVP of Creator & Content Development; DAVID GABRIEL, SVP of Publishing Sales & Circulation; MICHAEL PASCIULLO, SVP of Brand Planning & Communications; JIM O'KEEFE, VP of Operations & Logistics; DAN CARR, Executive Director of Publishing Technology; SUSAN CRESPI, Editorial Operations Manager; ALEX MORALES, Publishing Operations Manager; STAN LEE, Chairman Emeritus. For information regarding advertising in Marvel Comics or on Marvel.com, please contact John Dokes, SVP Integrated Sales and Marketing, at jdokes@marvel.com. For Marvel subscription inquiries, please call 800-217-9158. Manufactured between 1/16/2012 and 2/13/2012 by R.R. DONNELLEY, INC., SALEM, VA, USA.

10 9 8 7 6 5 4 3 2 1

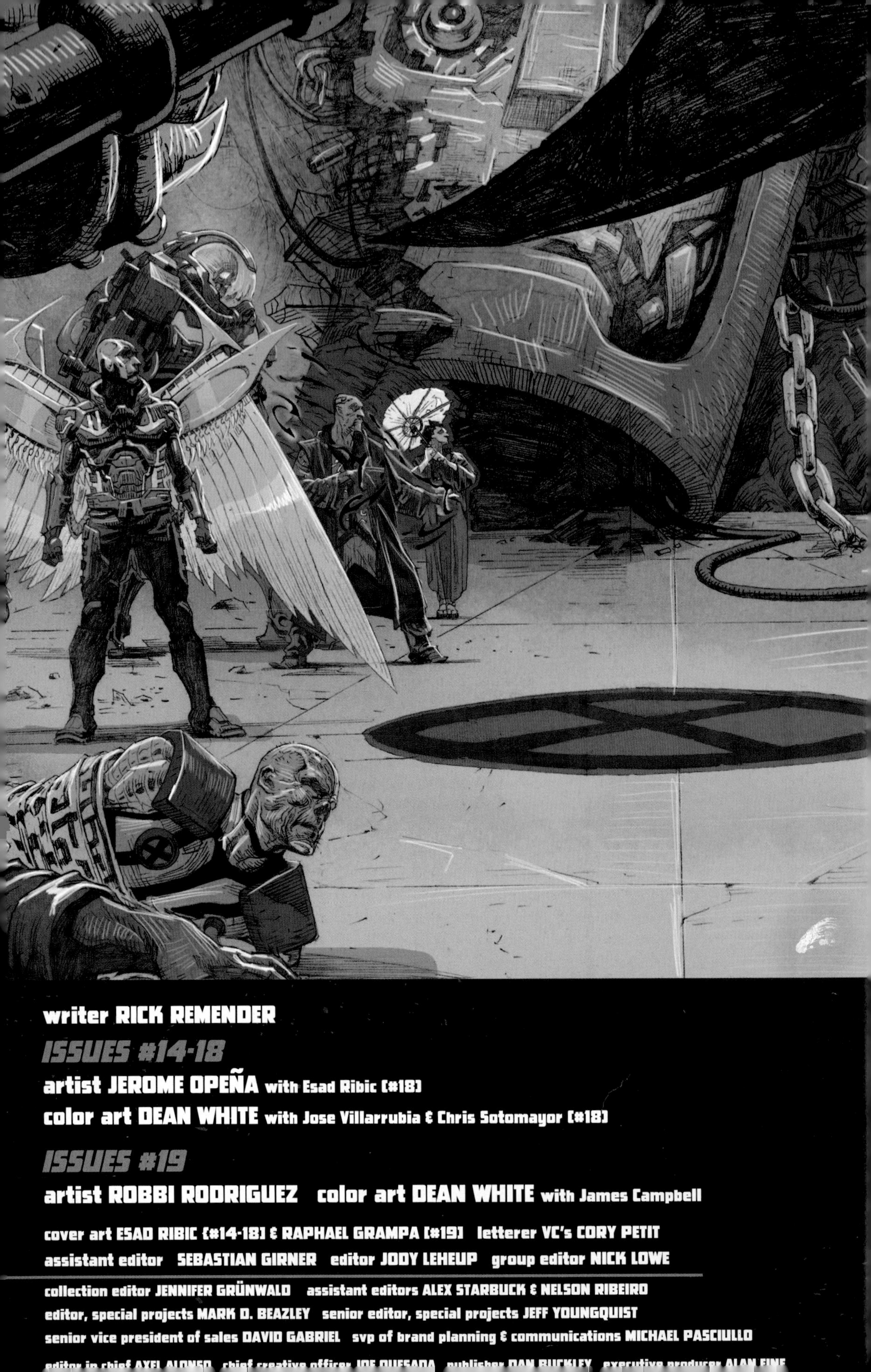

writer **RICK REMENDER**

ISSUES #14-18

artist JEROME OPEÑA with Esad Ribic (#18)

color art DEAN WHITE with Jose Villarrubia & Chris Sotomayor (#18)

ISSUES #19

artist ROBBI RODRIGUEZ **color art DEAN WHITE** with James Campbell

cover art ESAD RIBIC (#14-18) & RAPHAEL GRAMPA (#19) letterer VC's CORY PETIT

assistant editor SEBASTIAN GIRNER editor JODY LEHEUP group editor NICK LOWE

collection editor JENNIFER GRÜNWALD assistant editors ALEX STARBUCK & NELSON RIBEIRO

editor, special projects MARK D. BEAZLEY senior editor, special projects JEFF YOUNGQUIST

senior vice president of sales DAVID GABRIEL svp of brand planning & communications MICHAEL PASCIULLO

editor in chief AXEL ALONSO chief creative officer JOE QUESADA publisher DAN BUCKLEY executive producer ALAN FINE

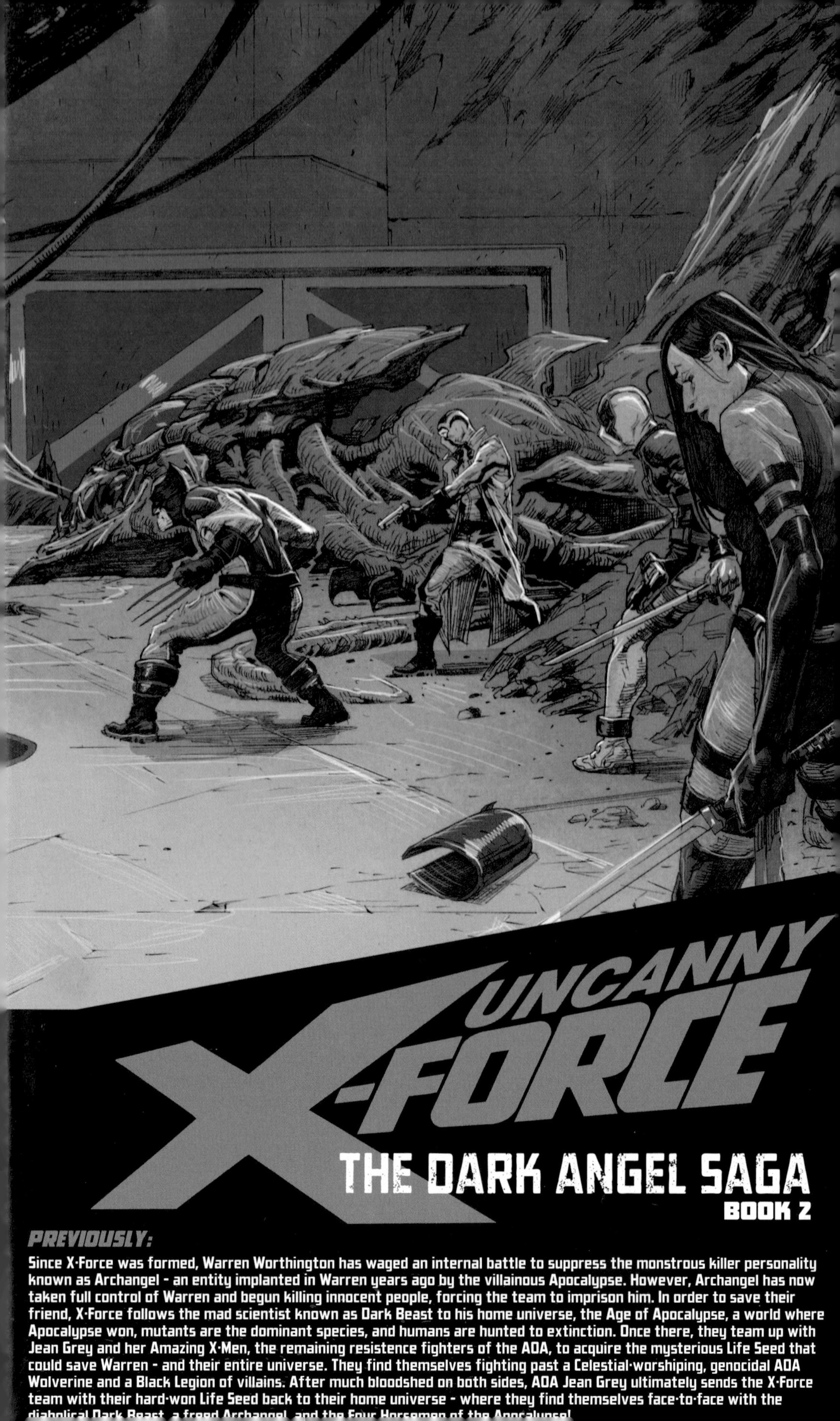

UNCANNY X-FORCE

THE DARK ANGEL SAGA

BOOK 2

PREVIOUSLY:

Since X-Force was formed, Warren Worthington has waged an internal battle to suppress the monstrous killer personality known as Archangel - an entity implanted in Warren years ago by the villainous Apocalypse. However, Archangel has now taken full control of Warren and begun killing innocent people, forcing the team to imprison him. In order to save their friend, X-Force follows the mad scientist known as Dark Beast to his home universe, the Age of Apocalypse, a world where Apocalypse won, mutants are the dominant species, and humans are hunted to extinction. Once there, they team up with Jean Grey and her Amazing X-Men, the remaining resistence fighters of the AOA, to acquire the mysterious Life Seed that could save Warren - and their entire universe. They find themselves fighting past a Celestial-worshiping, genocidal AOA Wolverine and a Black Legion of villains. After much bloodshed on both sides, AOA Jean Grey ultimately sends the X-Force team with their hard-won Life Seed back to their home universe - where they find themselves face-to-face with the diabolical Dark Beast, a freed Archangel, and the Four Horsemen of the Apocalypse!

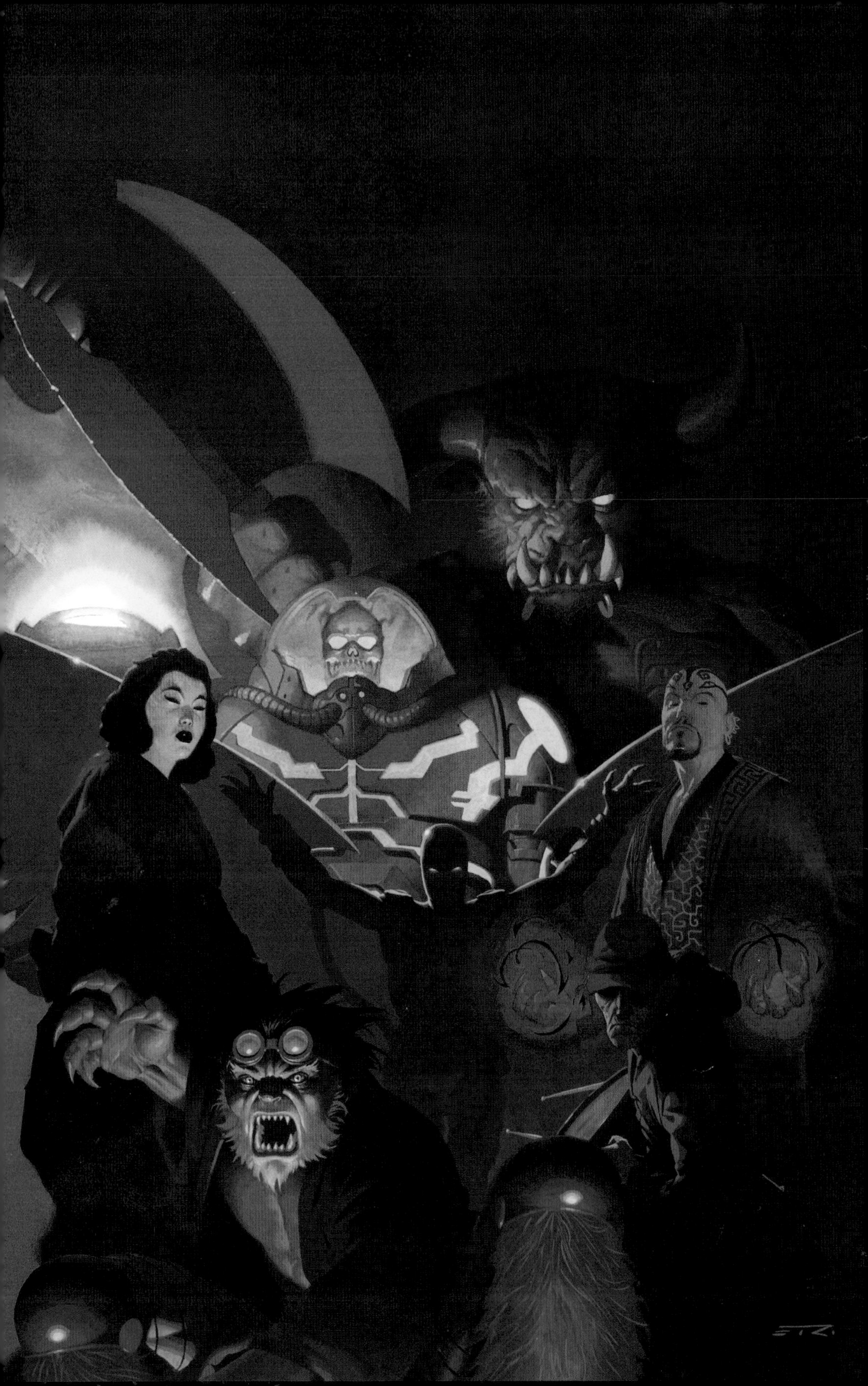

THUNDER FOR THE NEXT WORLD

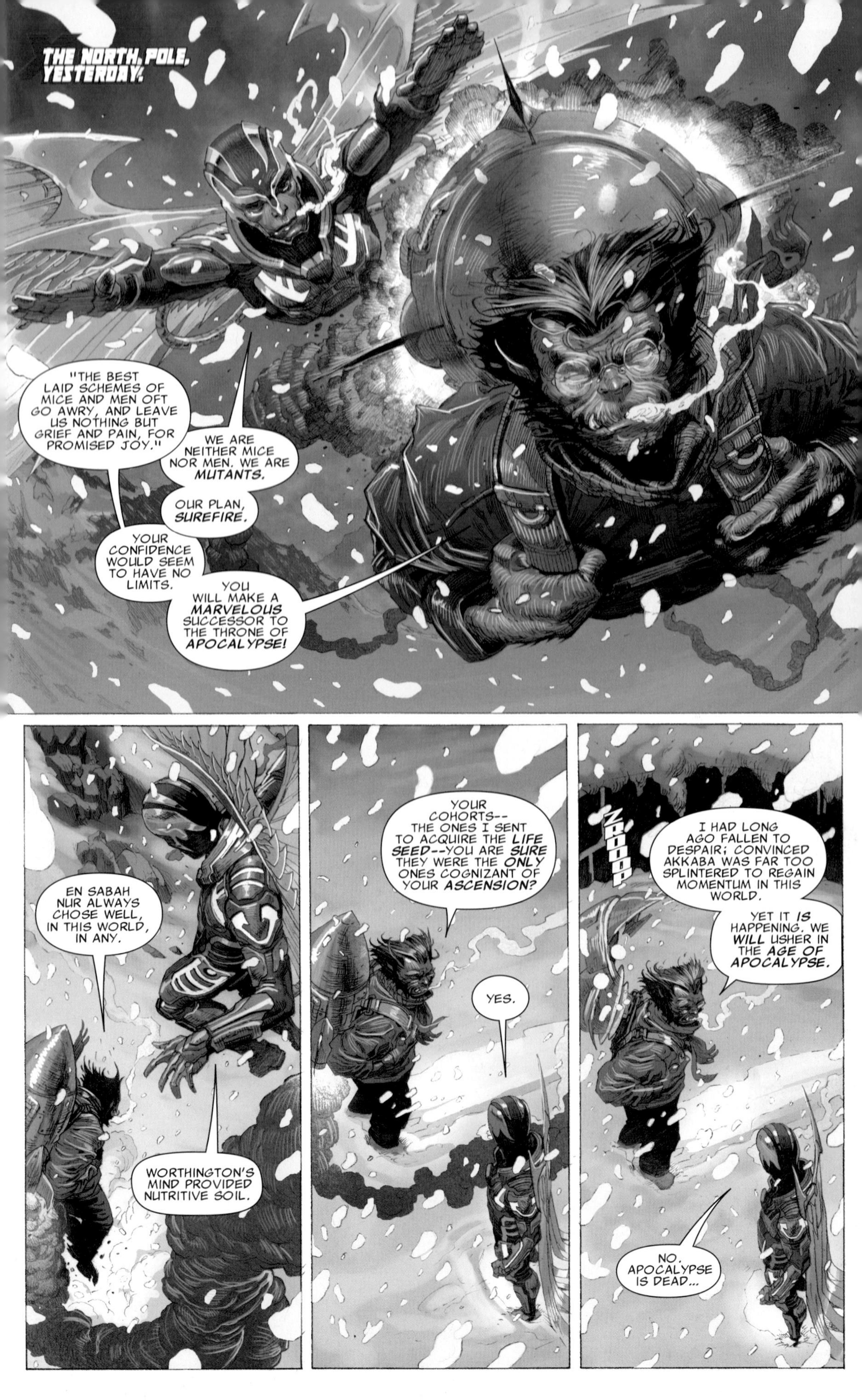
THE NORTH POLE, YESTERDAY:
"THE BEST LAID SCHEMES OF MICE AND MEN OFT GO AWRY, AND LEAVE US NOTHING BUT GRIEF AND PAIN, FOR PROMISED JOY."
WE ARE NEITHER MICE NOR MEN. WE ARE MUTANTS.
OUR PLAN, SUREFIRE.
YOUR CONFIDENCE WOULD SEEM TO HAVE NO LIMITS.
YOU WILL MAKE A MARVELOUS SUCCESSOR TO THE THRONE OF APOCALYPSE!
EN SABAH NUR ALWAYS CHOSE WELL, IN THIS WORLD, IN ANY.
WORTHINGTON'S MIND PROVIDED NUTRITIVE SOIL.
YOUR COHORTS-- THE ONES I SENT TO ACQUIRE THE LIFE SEED--YOU ARE SURE THEY WERE THE ONLY ONES COGNIZANT OF YOUR ASCENSION?
YES.
ZOOOOP
I HAD LONG AGO FALLEN TO DESPAIR; CONVINCED AKKABA WAS FAR TOO SPLINTERED TO REGAIN MOMENTUM IN THIS WORLD.
YET IT IS HAPPENING. WE WILL USHER IN THE AGE OF APOCALYPSE.
NO. APOCALYPSE IS DEAD...

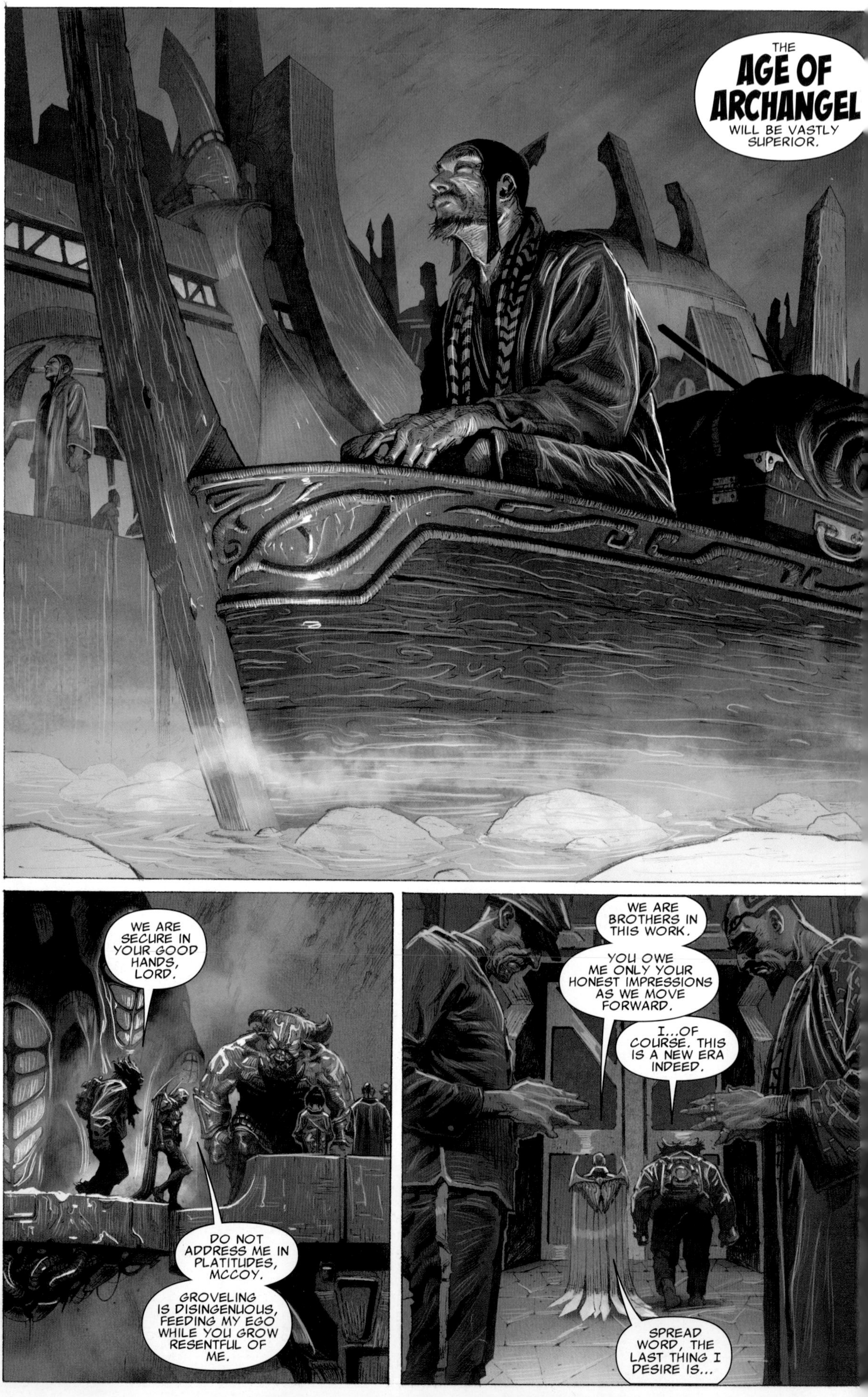
THE AGE OF ARCHANGEL WILL BE VASTLY SUPERIOR.
WE ARE SECURE IN YOUR GOOD HANDS, LORD.
DO NOT ADDRESS ME IN PLATITUDES, MCCOY.
GROVELING IS DISINGENUOUS, FEEDING MY EGO WHILE YOU GROW RESENTFUL OF ME.
WE ARE BROTHERS IN THIS WORK.
YOU OWE ME ONLY YOUR HONEST IMPRESSIONS AS WE MOVE FORWARD.
I...OF COURSE. THIS IS A NEW ERA INDEED.
SPREAD WORD, THE LAST THING I DESIRE IS...

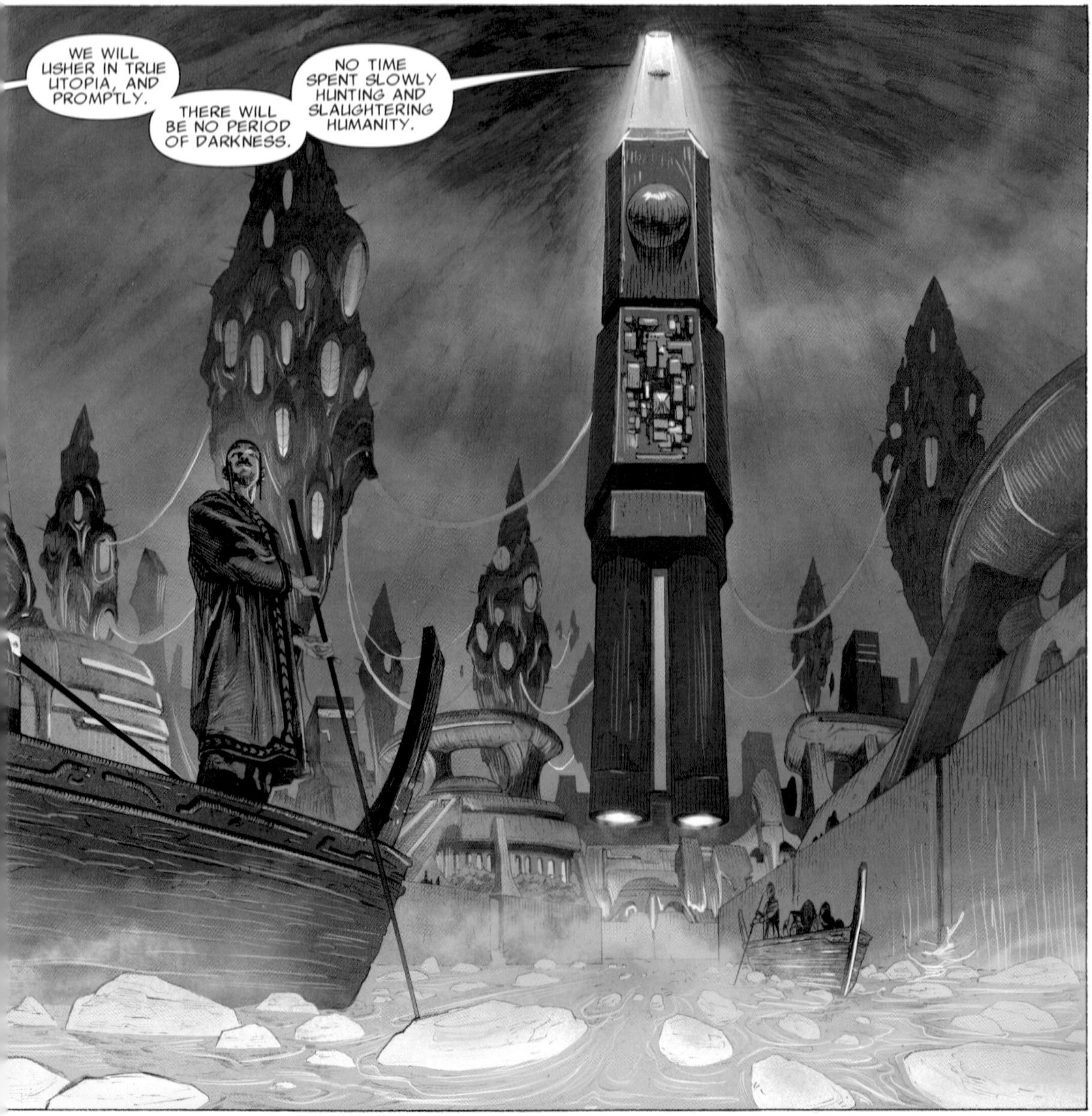
WE WILL USHER IN TRUE UTOPIA, AND PROMPTLY.
THERE WILL BE NO PERIOD OF DARKNESS.
NO TIME SPENT SLOWLY HUNTING AND SLAUGHTERING HUMANITY.

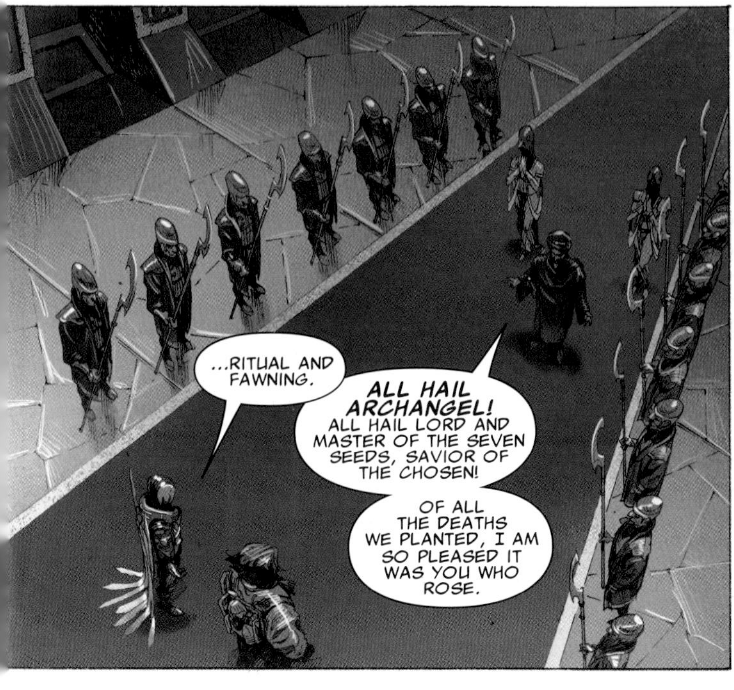
...RITUAL AND FAWNING.
ALL HAIL ARCHANGEL! ALL HAIL LORD AND MASTER OF THE SEVEN SEEDS, SAVIOR OF THE CHOSEN!
OF ALL THE DEATHS WE PLANTED, I AM SO PLEASED IT WAS YOU WHO ROSE.

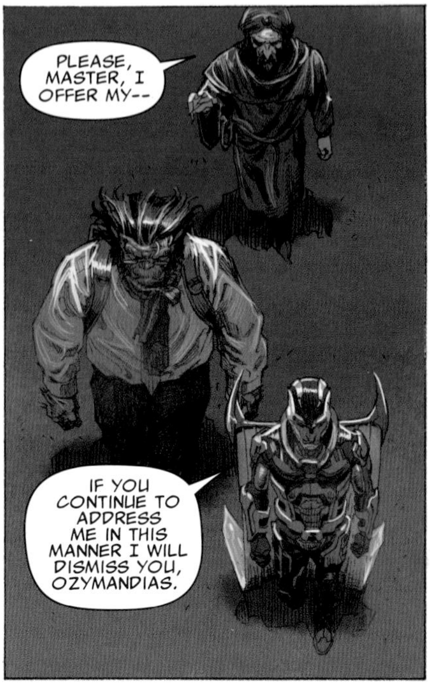
PLEASE, MASTER, I OFFER MY--
IF YOU CONTINUE TO ADDRESS ME IN THIS MANNER I WILL DISMISS YOU, OZYMANDIAS.

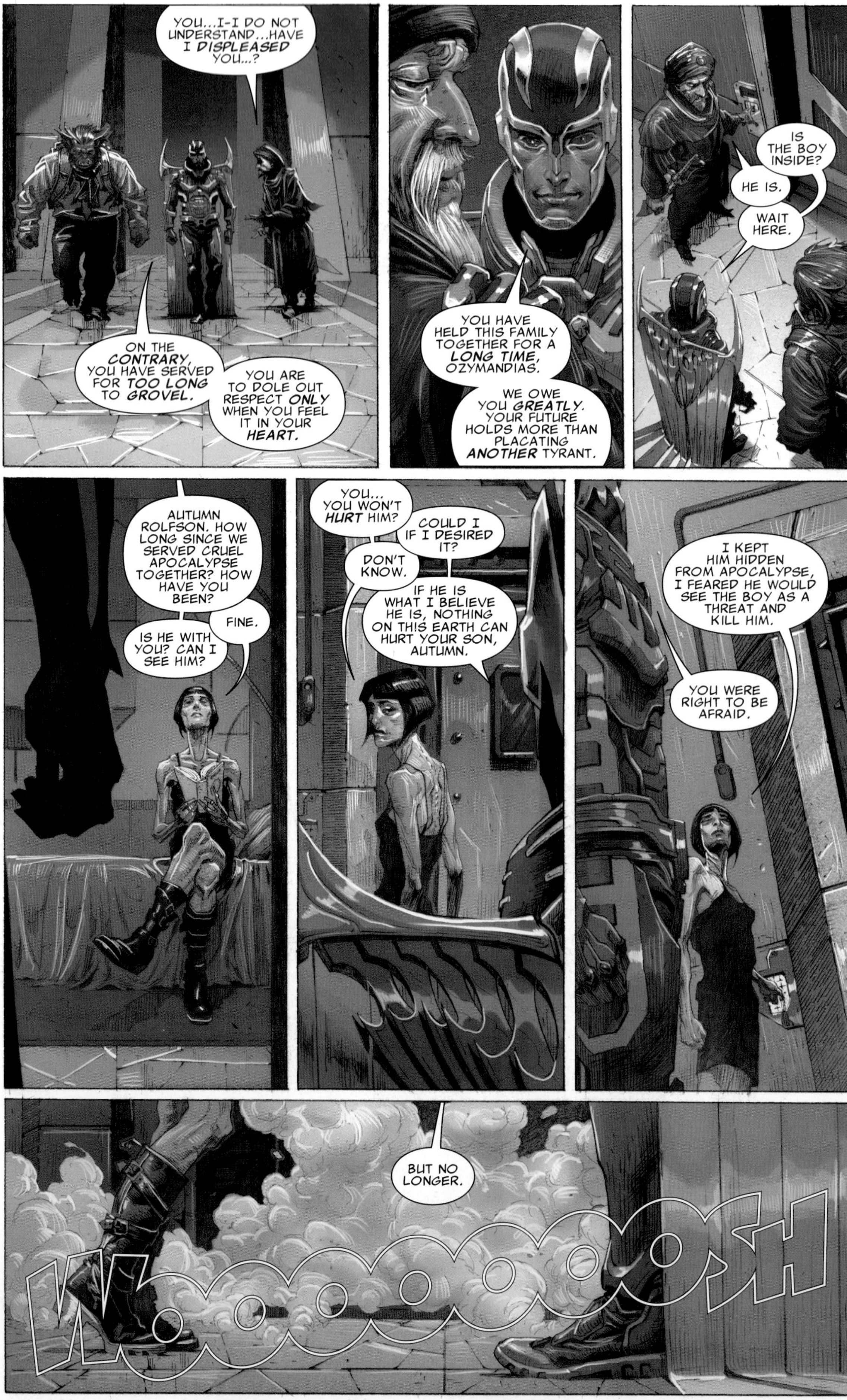
YOU...I-I DO NOT UNDERSTAND...HAVE I DISPLEASED YOU...?
ON THE CONTRARY, YOU HAVE SERVED FOR TOO LONG TO GROVEL.
YOU ARE TO DOLE OUT RESPECT ONLY WHEN YOU FEEL IT IN YOUR HEART.
YOU HAVE HELD THIS FAMILY TOGETHER FOR A LONG TIME, OZYMANDIAS.
WE OWE YOU GREATLY. YOUR FUTURE HOLDS MORE THAN PLACATING ANOTHER TYRANT.
IS THE BOY INSIDE?
HE IS.
WAIT HERE.
AUTUMN ROLFSON. HOW LONG SINCE WE SERVED CRUEL APOCALYPSE TOGETHER? HOW HAVE YOU BEEN?
FINE.
IS HE WITH YOU? CAN I SEE HIM?
YOU... YOU WON'T HURT HIM?
COULD I IF I DESIRED IT?
DON'T KNOW.
IF HE IS WHAT I BELIEVE HE IS, NOTHING ON THIS EARTH CAN HURT YOUR SON, AUTUMN.
I KEPT HIM HIDDEN FROM APOCALYPSE, I FEARED HE WOULD SEE THE BOY AS A THREAT AND KILL HIM.
YOU WERE RIGHT TO BE AFRAID.
BUT NO LONGER.
WHOOOOOOOOSH

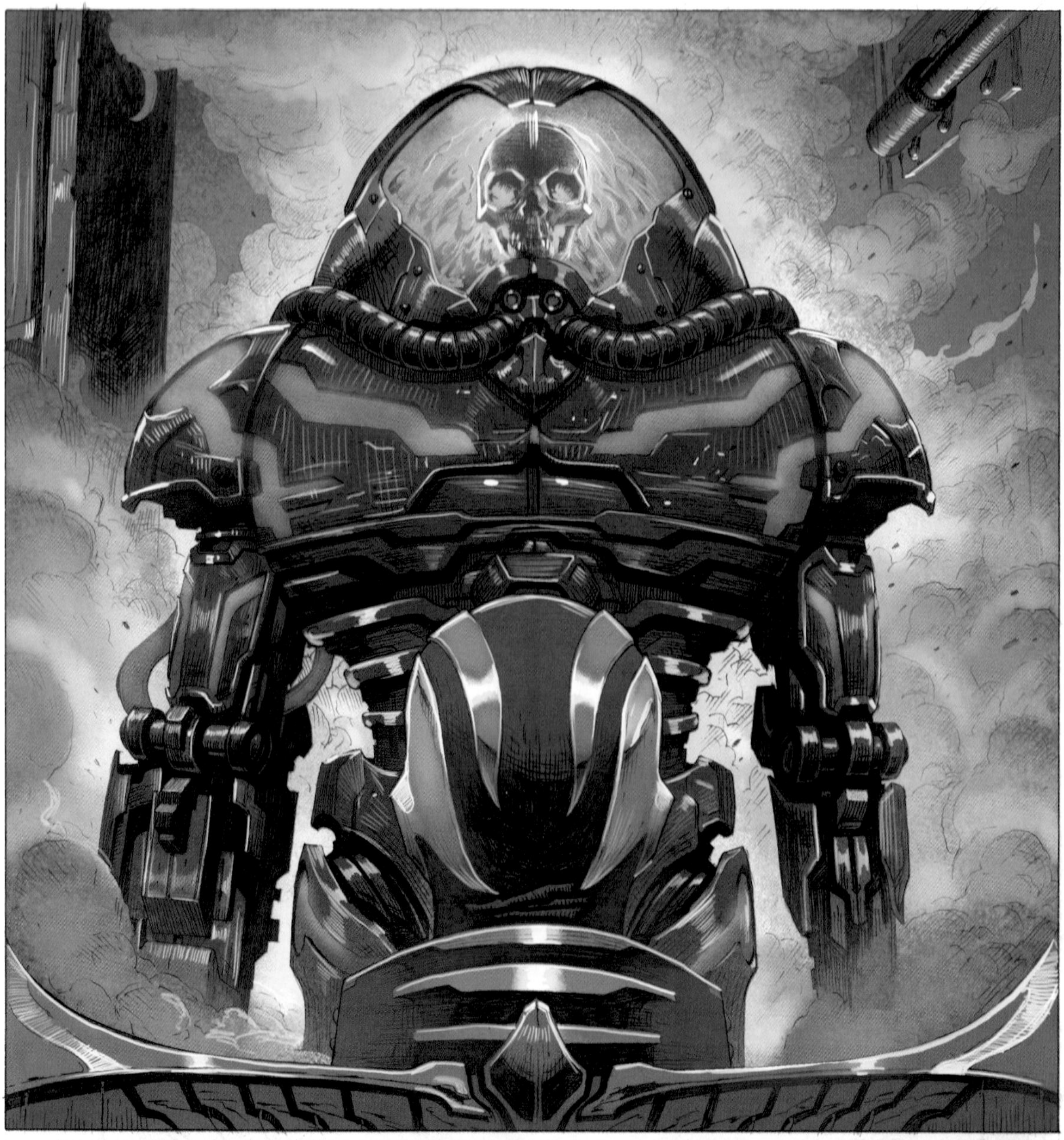

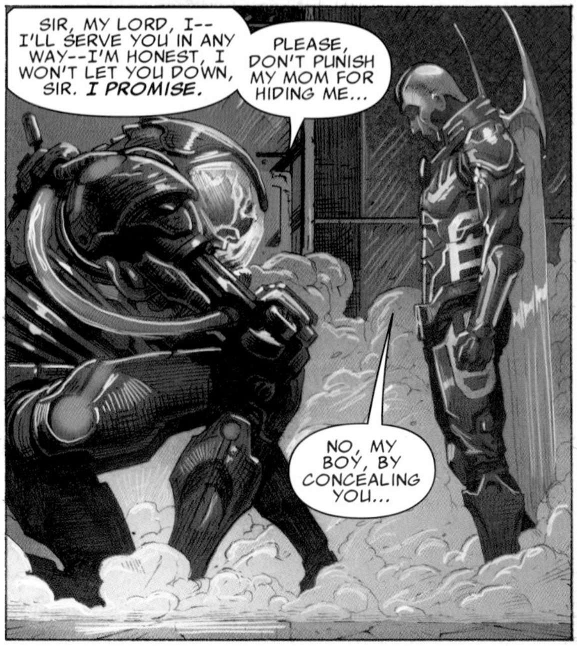
SIR, MY LORD, I-- I'LL SERVE YOU IN ANY WAY--I'M HONEST, I WON'T LET YOU DOWN, SIR. ***I PROMISE.***
PLEASE, DON'T PUNISH MY MOM FOR HIDING ME...
NO, MY BOY, BY CONCEALING YOU...

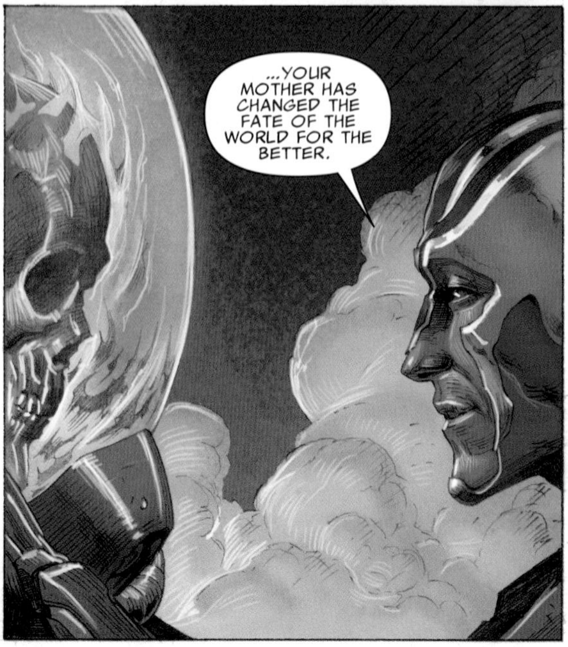
...YOUR MOTHER HAS CHANGED THE FATE OF THE WORLD FOR THE BETTER.

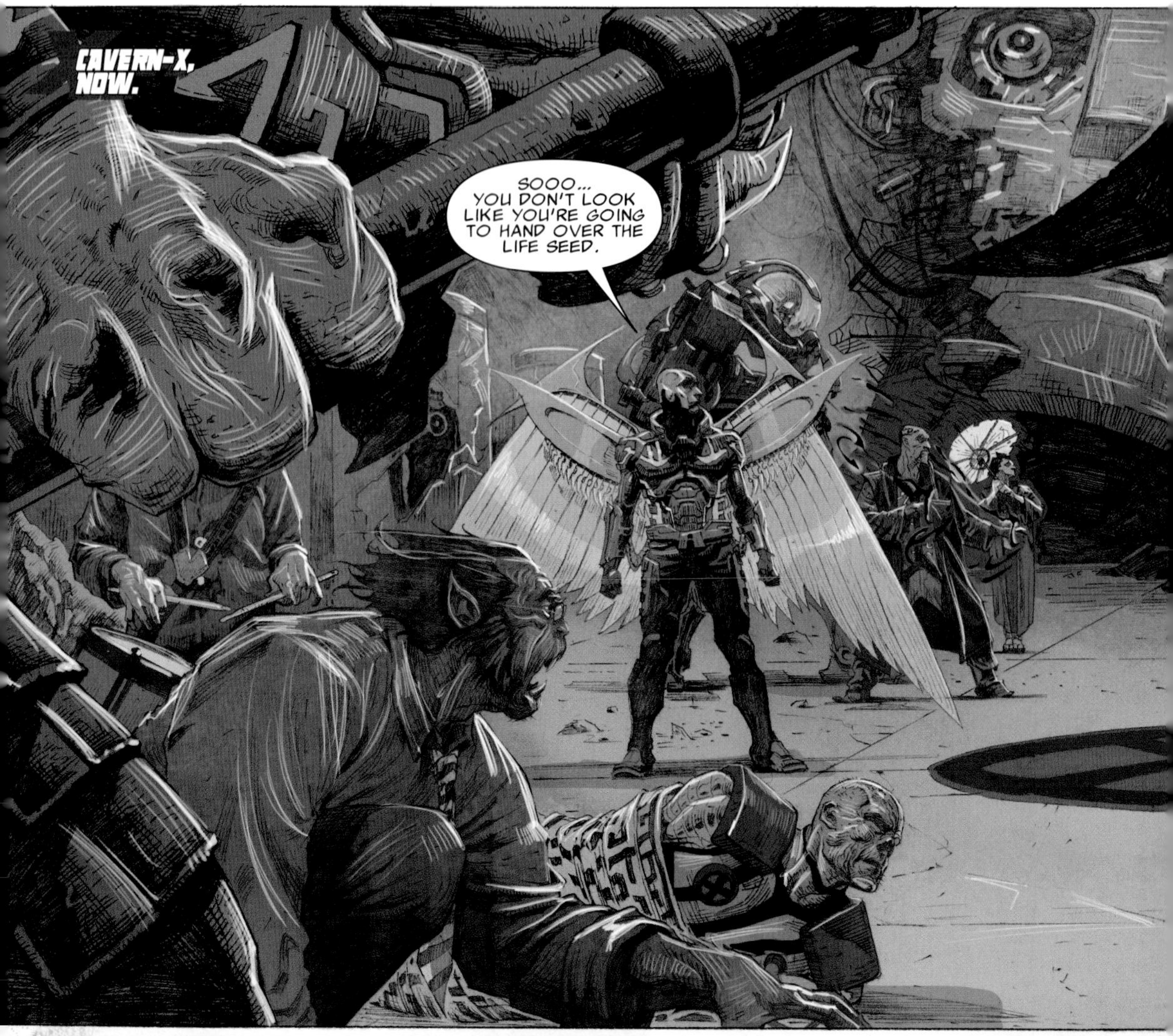
CAVERN-X, NOW.
SOOO... YOU DON'T LOOK LIKE YOU'RE GOING TO HAND OVER THE LIFE SEED.

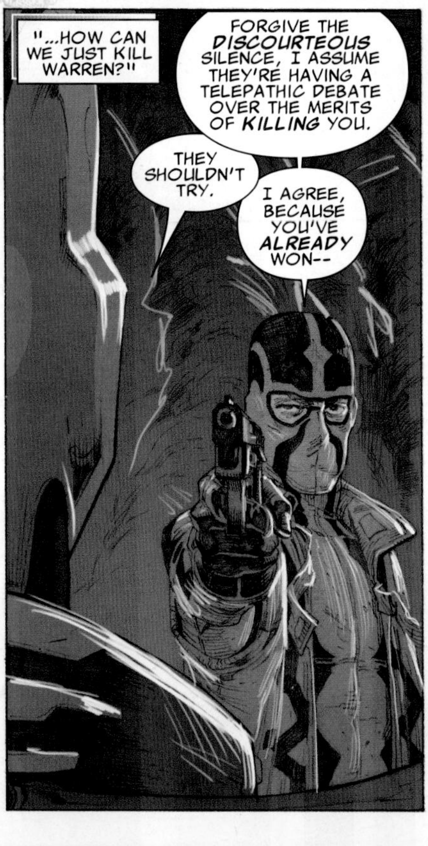
"...HOW CAN WE JUST KILL WARREN?"
FORGIVE THE DISCOURTEOUS SILENCE, I ASSUME THEY'RE HAVING A TELEPATHIC DEBATE OVER THE MERITS OF KILLING YOU.
THEY SHOULDN'T TRY.
I AGREE, BECAUSE YOU'VE ALREADY WON--

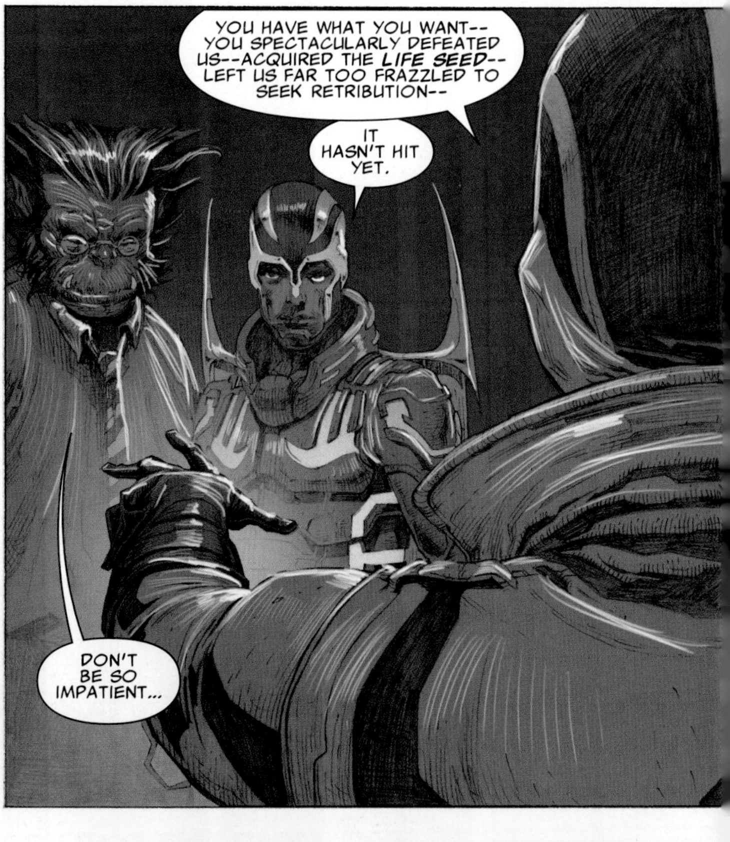
YOU HAVE WHAT YOU WANT-- YOU SPECTACULARLY DEFEATED US--ACQUIRED THE LIFE SEED-- LEFT US FAR TOO FRAZZLED TO SEEK RETRIBUTION--
IT HASN'T HIT YET.
DON'T BE SO IMPATIENT...

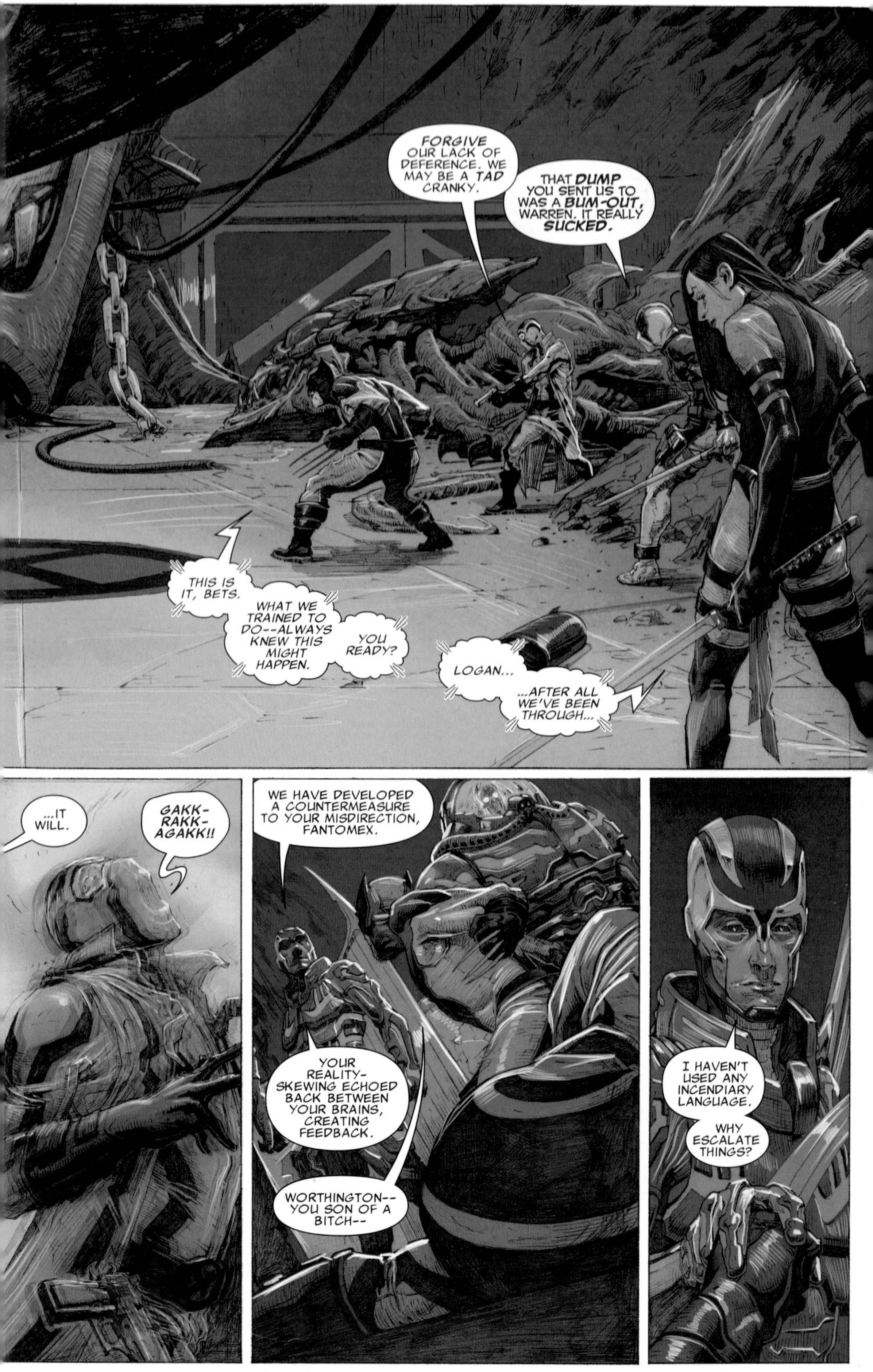
FORGIVE OUR LACK OF DEFERENCE. WE MAY BE A TAD CRANKY.
THAT DUMP YOU SENT US TO WAS A BUM-OUT, WARREN. IT REALLY SUCKED.
THIS IS IT, BETS.
WHAT WE TRAINED TO DO--ALWAYS KNEW THIS MIGHT HAPPEN.
YOU READY?
LOGAN...
...AFTER ALL WE'VE BEEN THROUGH...
...IT WILL.
GAKK-RAKK-AGAKK!!
WE HAVE DEVELOPED A COUNTERMEASURE TO YOUR MISDIRECTION, FANTOMEX.
YOUR REALITY-SKEWING ECHOED BACK BETWEEN YOUR BRAINS, CREATING FEEDBACK.
WORTHINGTON--YOU SON OF A BITCH--
I HAVEN'T USED ANY INCENDIARY LANGUAGE.
WHY ESCALATE THINGS?

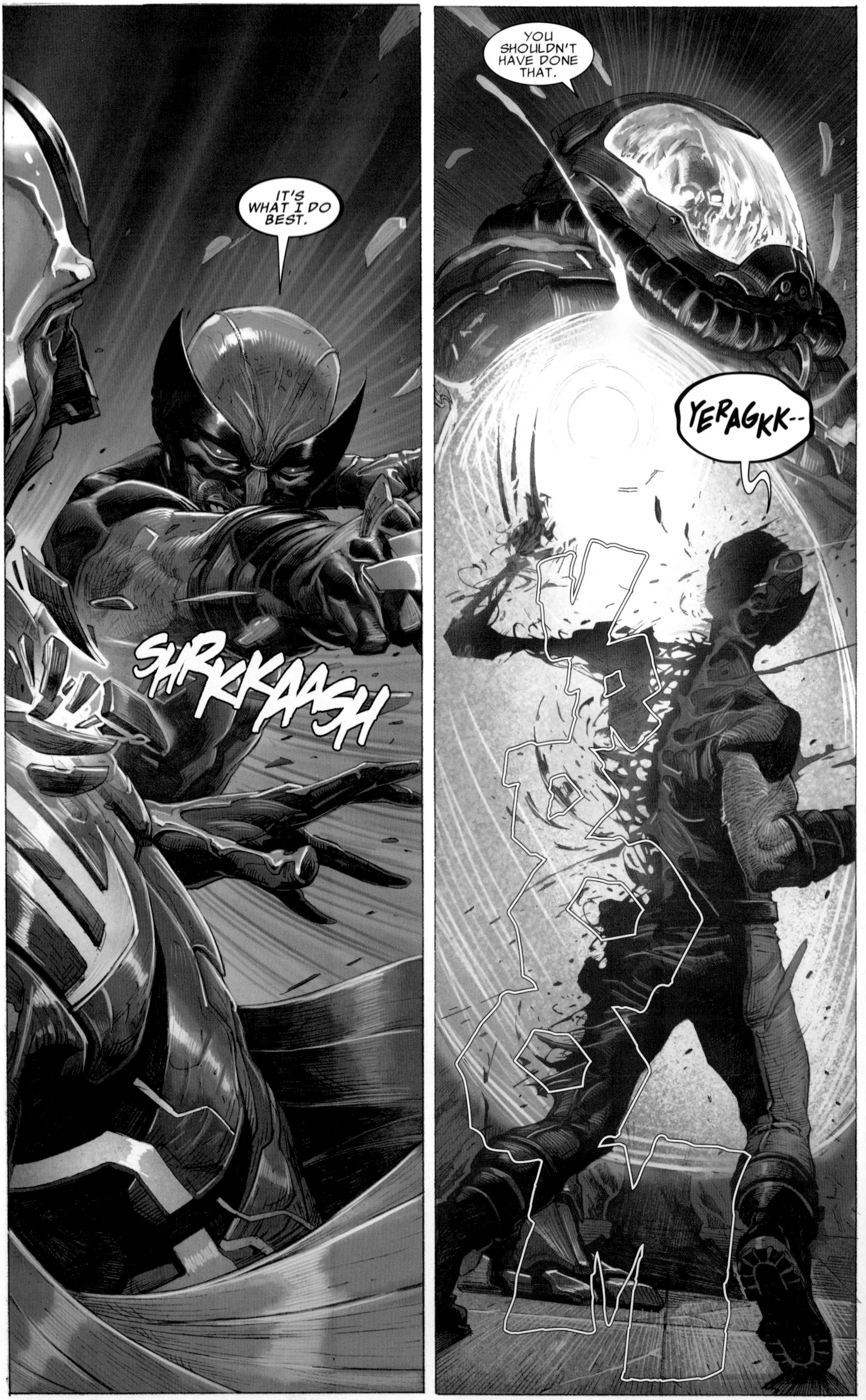
IT'S WHAT I DO BEST.
SHRKKAASH
YOU SHOULDN'T HAVE DONE THAT.
YERAGKK--

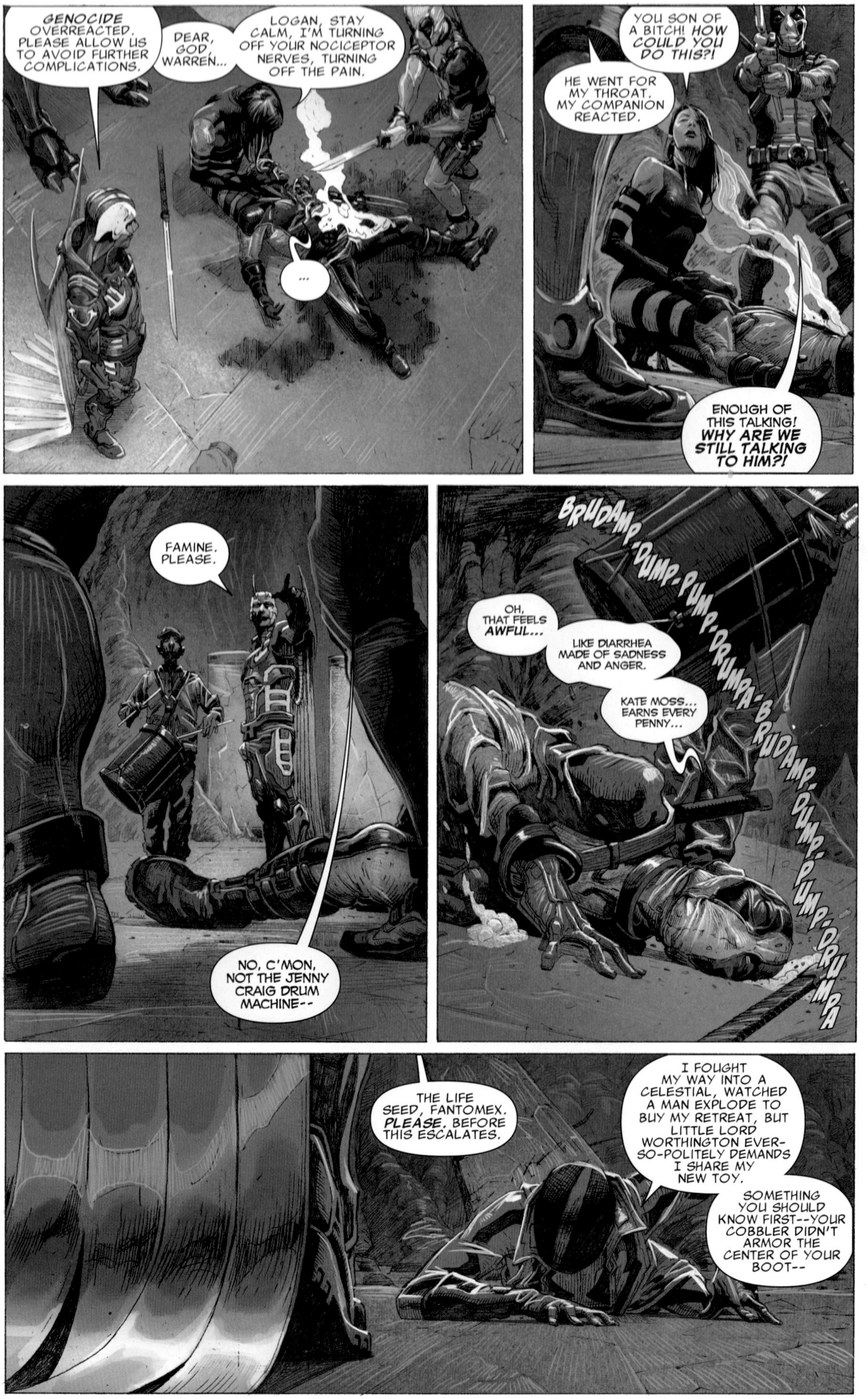
GENOCIDE OVERREACTED. PLEASE ALLOW US TO AVOID FURTHER COMPLICATIONS.
DEAR, GOD, WARREN...
LOGAN, STAY CALM, I'M TURNING OFF YOUR NOCICEPTOR NERVES, TURNING OFF THE PAIN.
...
YOU SON OF A BITCH! HOW COULD YOU DO THIS?!
HE WENT FOR MY THROAT. MY COMPANION REACTED.
ENOUGH OF THIS TALKING! WHY ARE WE STILL TALKING TO HIM?!
FAMINE. PLEASE.
NO, C'MON, NOT THE JENNY CRAIG DRUM MACHINE--
BRUDAMP-DUMP-PUMP-DRUMPA-BRUDAMP-DUMP-PUMP-DRUMPA
OH, THAT FEELS AWFUL...
LIKE DIARRHEA MADE OF SADNESS AND ANGER.
KATE MOSS... EARNS EVERY PENNY...
THE LIFE SEED, FANTOMEX. PLEASE. BEFORE THIS ESCALATES.
I FOUGHT MY WAY INTO A CELESTIAL, WATCHED A MAN EXPLODE TO BUY MY RETREAT, BUT LITTLE LORD WORTHINGTON EVER-SO-POLITELY DEMANDS I SHARE MY NEW TOY.
SOMETHING YOU SHOULD KNOW FIRST--YOUR COBBLER DIDN'T ARMOR THE CENTER OF YOUR BOOT--

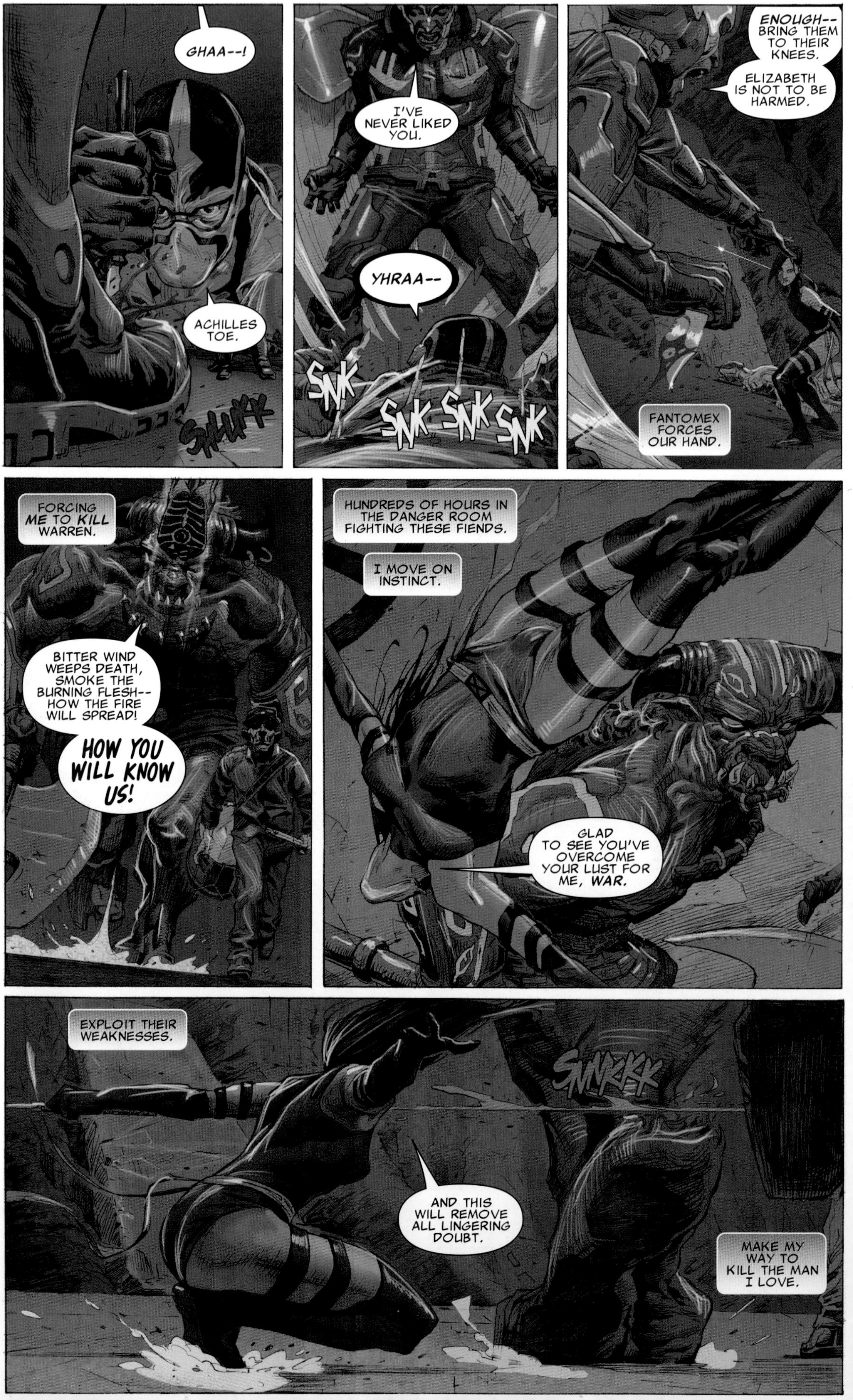
GHAA--!
ACHILLES TOE.
SHUKK
I'VE NEVER LIKED YOU.
YHRAA--
SNK
SNK SNK SNK
ENOUGH-- BRING THEM TO THEIR KNEES.
ELIZABETH IS NOT TO BE HARMED.
FANTOMEX FORCES OUR HAND.
FORCING ME TO KILL WARREN.
BITTER WIND WEEPS DEATH, SMOKE THE BURNING FLESH-- HOW THE FIRE WILL SPREAD!
HOW YOU WILL KNOW US!
HUNDREDS OF HOURS IN THE DANGER ROOM FIGHTING THESE FIENDS.
I MOVE ON INSTINCT.
GLAD TO SEE YOU'VE OVERCOME YOUR LUST FOR ME, WAR.
EXPLOIT THEIR WEAKNESSES.
SNIKKK
AND THIS WILL REMOVE ALL LINGERING DOUBT.
MAKE MY WAY TO KILL THE MAN I LOVE.

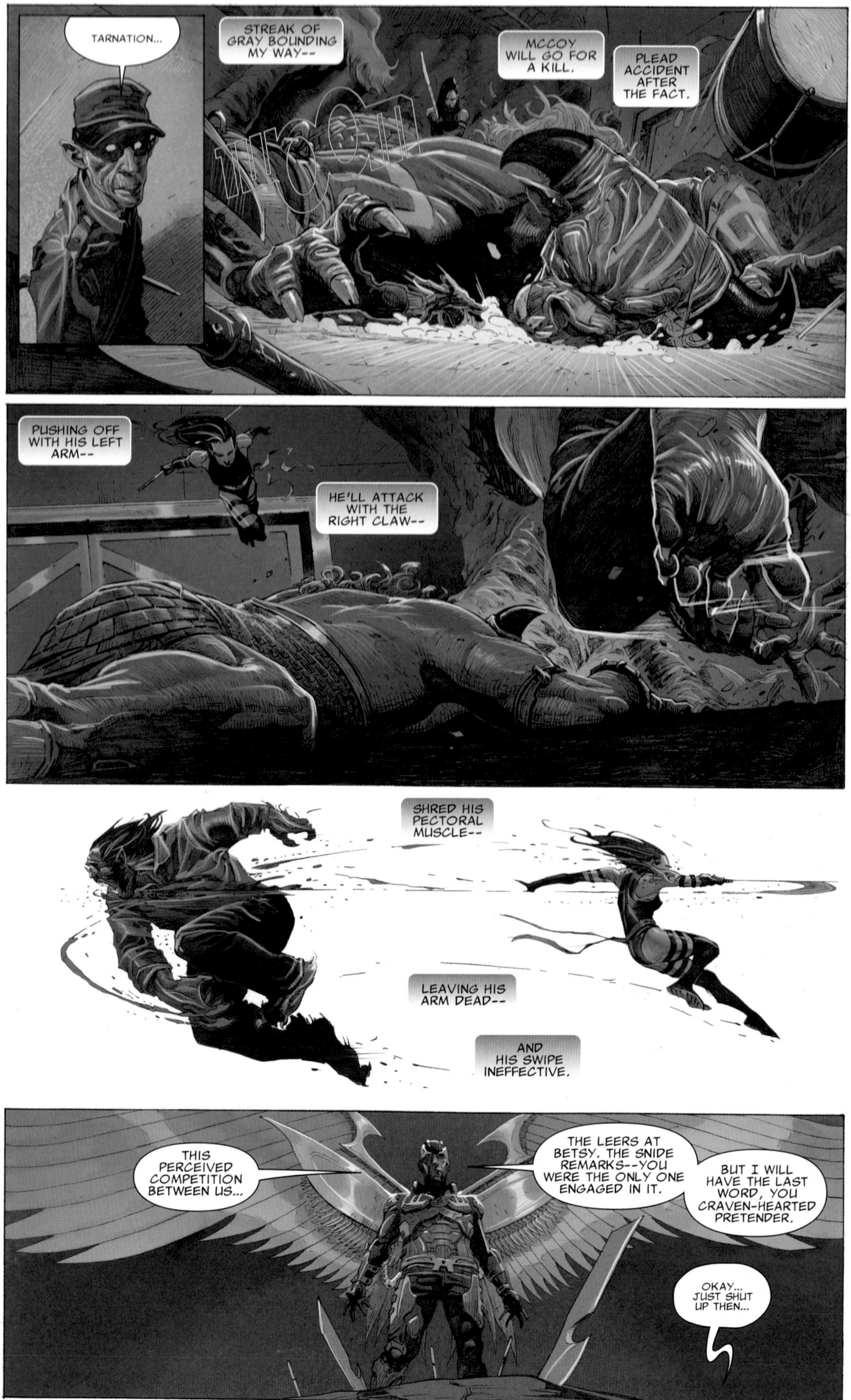
TARNATION...
STREAK OF GRAY BOUNDING MY WAY--
MCCOY WILL GO FOR A KILL.
PLEAD ACCIDENT AFTER THE FACT.
PUSHING OFF WITH HIS LEFT ARM--
HE'LL ATTACK WITH THE RIGHT CLAW--
SHRED HIS PECTORAL MUSCLE--
LEAVING HIS ARM DEAD--
AND HIS SWIPE INEFFECTIVE.
THIS PERCEIVED COMPETITION BETWEEN US...
THE LEERS AT BETSY. THE SNIDE REMARKS--YOU WERE THE ONLY ONE ENGAGED IN IT.
BUT I WILL HAVE THE LAST WORD, YOU CRAVEN-HEARTED PRETENDER.
OKAY... JUST SHUT UP THEN...

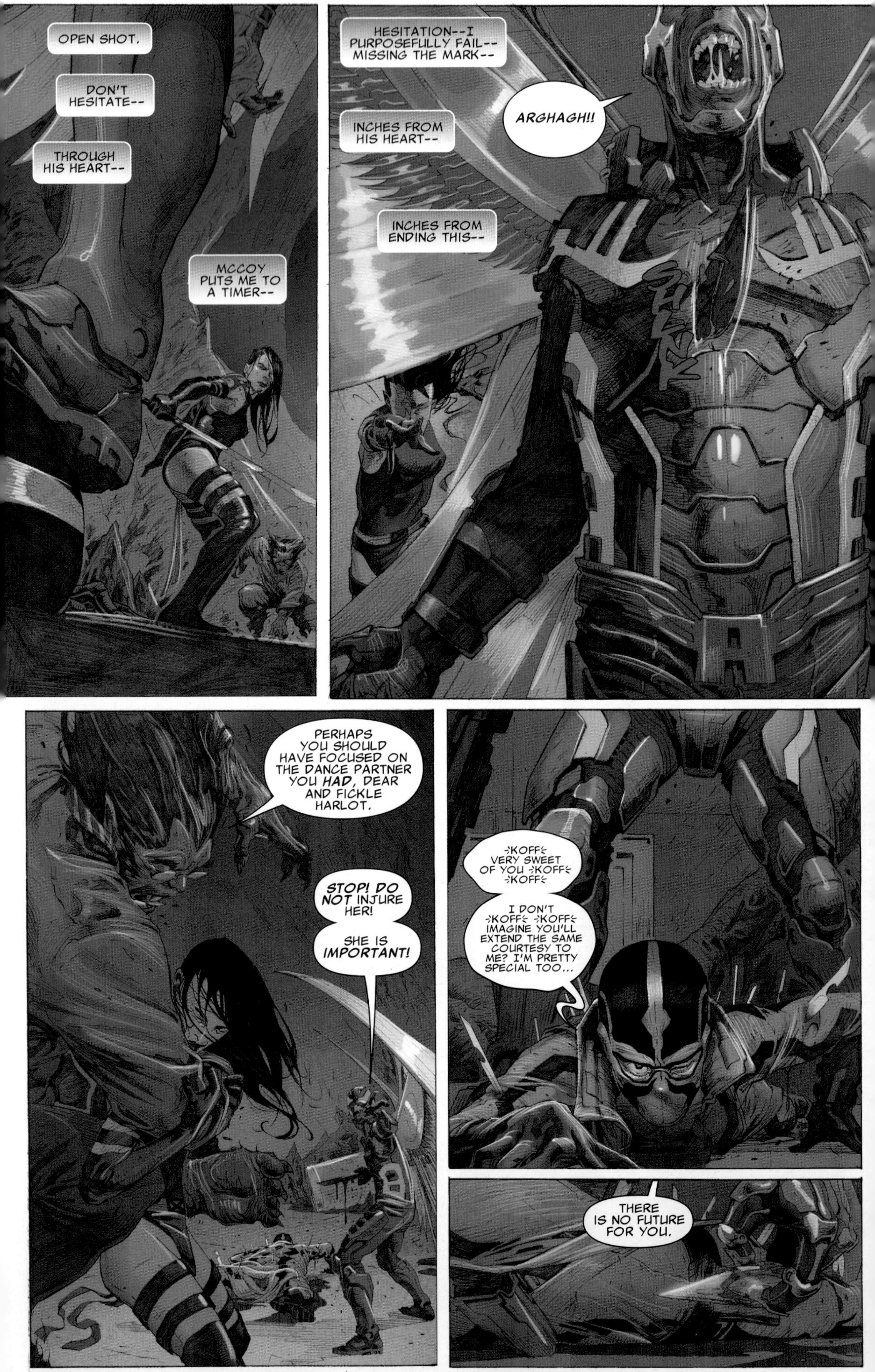
OPEN SHOT.
DON'T HESITATE--
THROUGH HIS HEART--
MCCOY PUTS ME TO A TIMER--
HESITATION--I PURPOSEFULLY FAIL--MISSING THE MARK--
ARGHAGH!!
INCHES FROM HIS HEART--
INCHES FROM ENDING THIS--
SHUKK
PERHAPS YOU SHOULD HAVE FOCUSED ON THE DANCE PARTNER YOU HAD, DEAR AND FICKLE HARLOT.
STOP! DO NOT INJURE HER!
SHE IS IMPORTANT!
KOFF VERY SWEET OF YOU KOFF KOFF
I DON'T KOFF KOFF IMAGINE YOU'LL EXTEND THE SAME COURTESY TO ME? I'M PRETTY SPECIAL TOO...
THERE IS NO FUTURE FOR YOU.

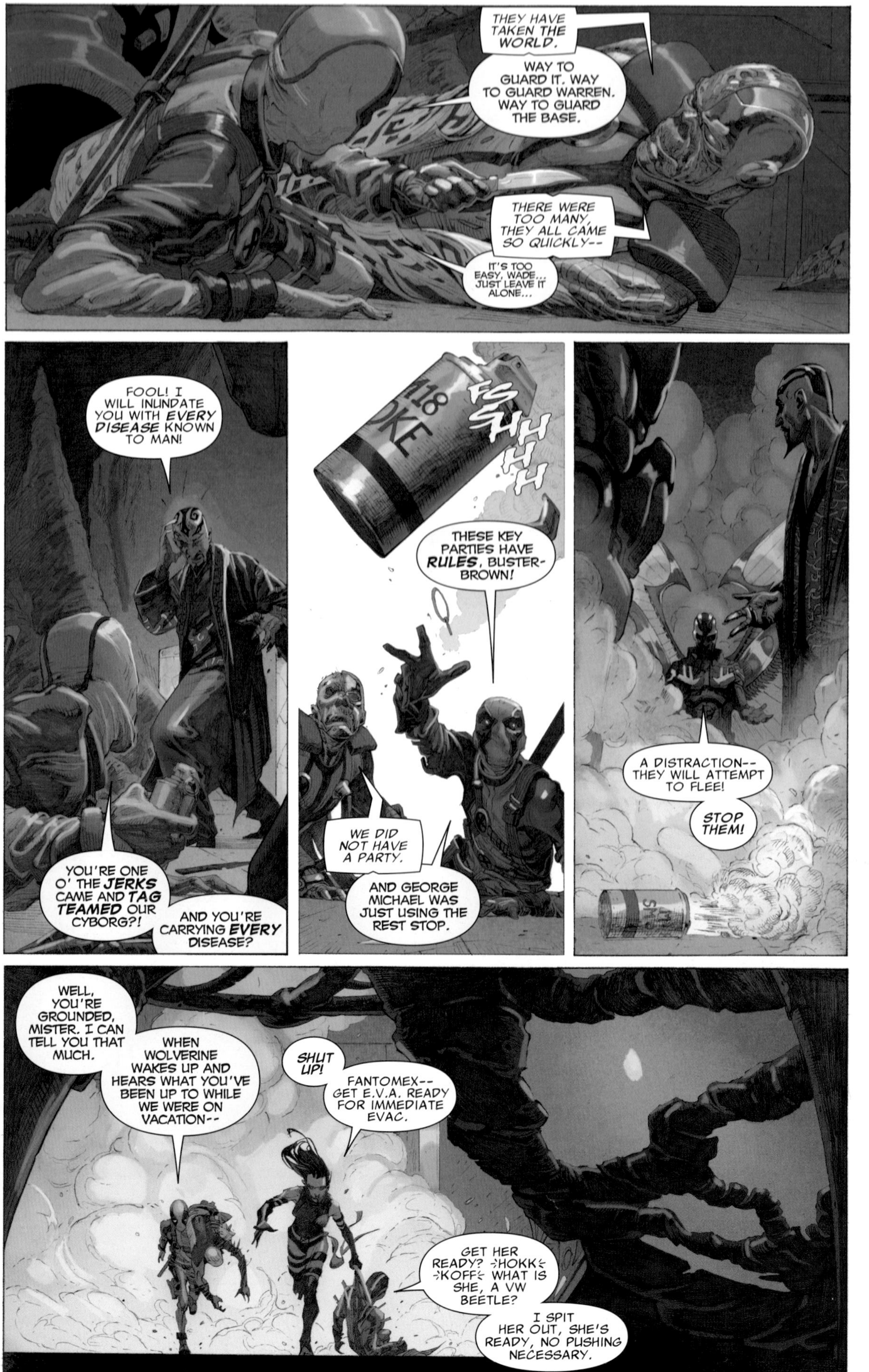
THEY HAVE TAKEN THE WORLD.
WAY TO GUARD IT. WAY TO GUARD WARREN. WAY TO GUARD THE BASE.
THERE WERE TOO MANY, THEY ALL CAME SO QUICKLY--
IT'S TOO EASY, WADE... JUST LEAVE IT ALONE...
FOOL! I WILL INUNDATE YOU WITH EVERY DISEASE KNOWN TO MAN!
YOU'RE ONE O' THE JERKS CAME AND TAG TEAMED OUR CYBORG?!
AND YOU'RE CARRYING EVERY DISEASE?
FSSHHHH
THESE KEY PARTIES HAVE RULES, BUSTER-BROWN!
WE DID NOT HAVE A PARTY.
AND GEORGE MICHAEL WAS JUST USING THE REST STOP.
A DISTRACTION-- THEY WILL ATTEMPT TO FLEE!
STOP THEM!
WELL, YOU'RE GROUNDED, MISTER. I CAN TELL YOU THAT MUCH.
WHEN WOLVERINE WAKES UP AND HEARS WHAT YOU'VE BEEN UP TO WHILE WE WERE ON VACATION--
SHUT UP!
FANTOMEX-- GET E.V.A. READY FOR IMMEDIATE EVAC.
GET HER READY? HOKK KOFF WHAT IS SHE, A VW BEETLE?
I SPIT HER OUT, SHE'S READY, NO PUSHING NECESSARY.

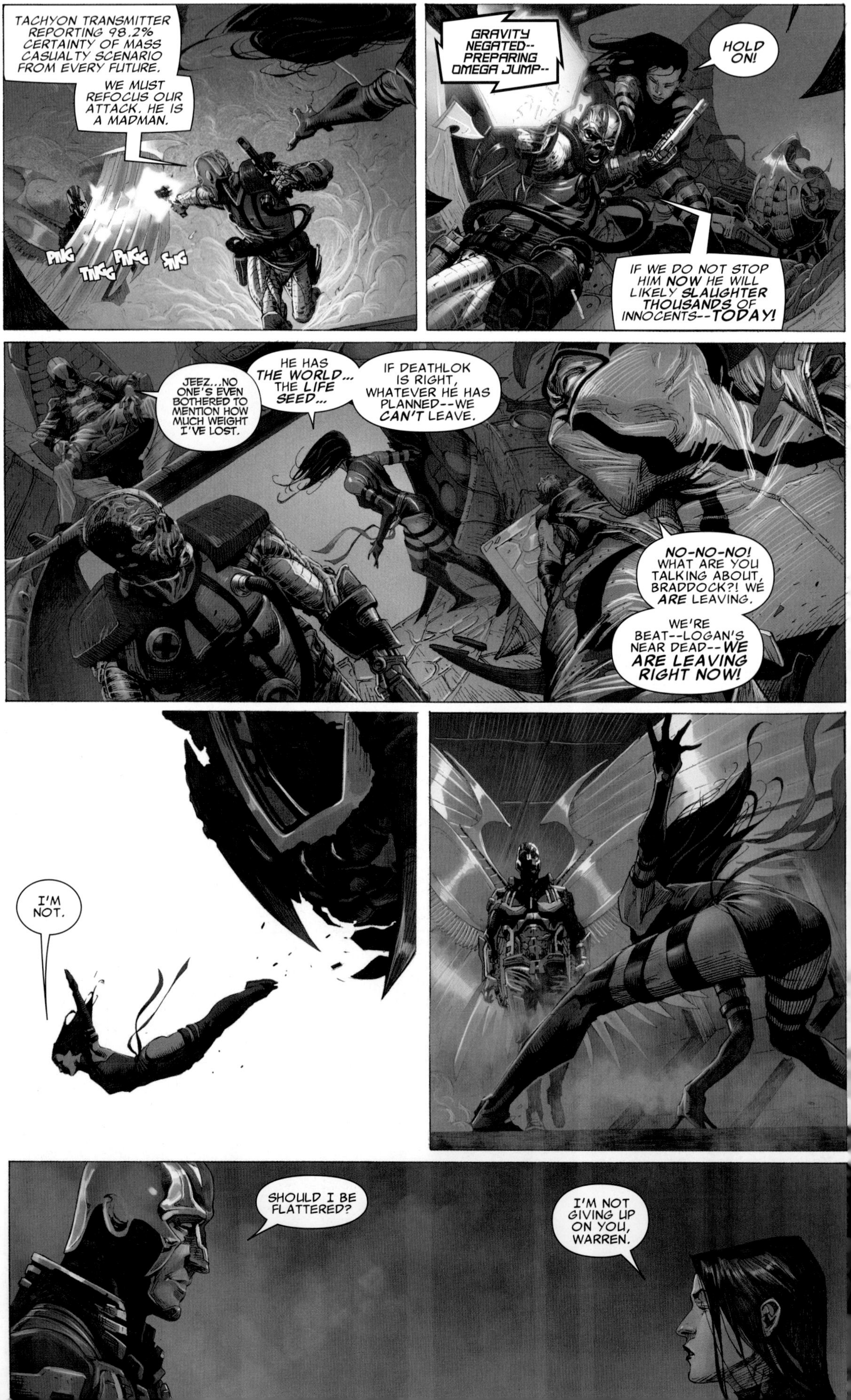
TACHYON TRANSMITTER REPORTING 98.2% CERTAINTY OF MASS CASUALTY SCENARIO FROM EVERY FUTURE.
WE MUST REFOCUS OUR ATTACK. HE IS A MADMAN.
PING TINGG PINGG SNG
GRAVITY NEGATED-- PREPARING OMEGA JUMP--
HOLD ON!
IF WE DO NOT STOP HIM NOW HE WILL LIKELY SLAUGHTER THOUSANDS OF INNOCENTS--TODAY!
JEEZ...NO ONE'S EVEN BOTHERED TO MENTION HOW MUCH WEIGHT I'VE LOST.
HE HAS THE WORLD... THE LIFE SEED...
IF DEATHLOK IS RIGHT, WHATEVER HE HAS PLANNED--WE CAN'T LEAVE.
NO-NO-NO! WHAT ARE YOU TALKING ABOUT, BRADDOCK?! WE ARE LEAVING.
WE'RE BEAT--LOGAN'S NEAR DEAD--WE ARE LEAVING RIGHT NOW!
I'M NOT.
SHOULD I BE FLATTERED?
I'M NOT GIVING UP ON YOU, WARREN.

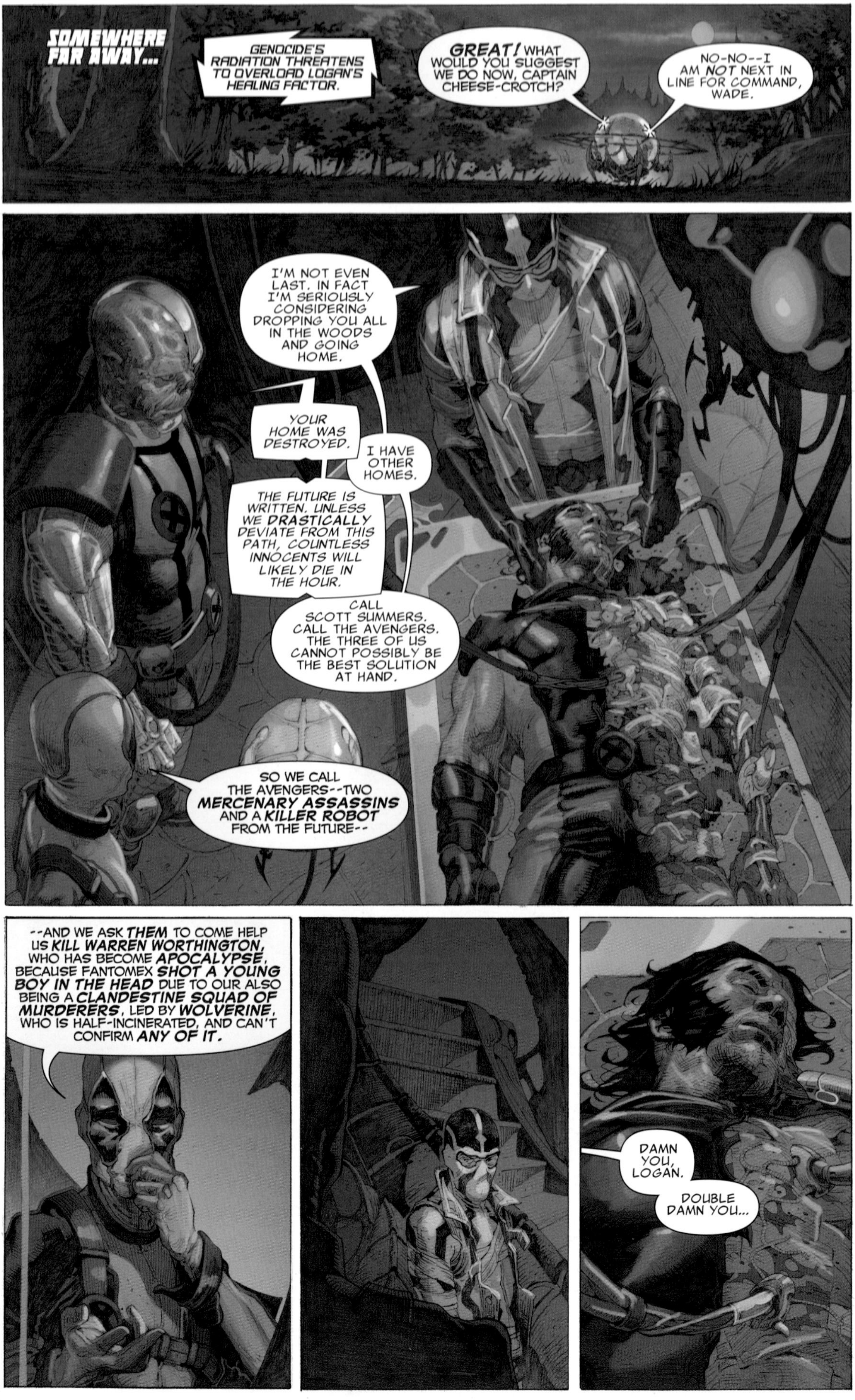
SOMEWHERE FAR AWAY...
GENOCIDE'S RADIATION THREATENS TO OVERLOAD LOGAN'S HEALING FACTOR.
GREAT! WHAT WOULD YOU SUGGEST WE DO NOW, CAPTAIN CHEESE-CROTCH?
NO-NO--I AM NOT NEXT IN LINE FOR COMMAND, WADE.
I'M NOT EVEN LAST. IN FACT I'M SERIOUSLY CONSIDERING DROPPING YOU ALL IN THE WOODS AND GOING HOME.
YOUR HOME WAS DESTROYED.
I HAVE OTHER HOMES.
THE FUTURE IS WRITTEN. UNLESS WE DRASTICALLY DEVIATE FROM THIS PATH, COUNTLESS INNOCENTS WILL LIKELY DIE IN THE HOUR.
CALL SCOTT SUMMERS. CALL THE AVENGERS. THE THREE OF US CANNOT POSSIBLY BE THE BEST SOLUTION AT HAND.
SO WE CALL THE AVENGERS--TWO MERCENARY ASSASSINS AND A KILLER ROBOT FROM THE FUTURE--
--AND WE ASK THEM TO COME HELP US KILL WARREN WORTHINGTON, WHO HAS BECOME APOCALYPSE, BECAUSE FANTOMEX SHOT A YOUNG BOY IN THE HEAD DUE TO OUR ALSO BEING A CLANDESTINE SQUAD OF MURDERERS, LED BY WOLVERINE, WHO IS HALF-INCINERATED, AND CAN'T CONFIRM ANY OF IT.
DAMN YOU, LOGAN.
DOUBLE DAMN YOU...

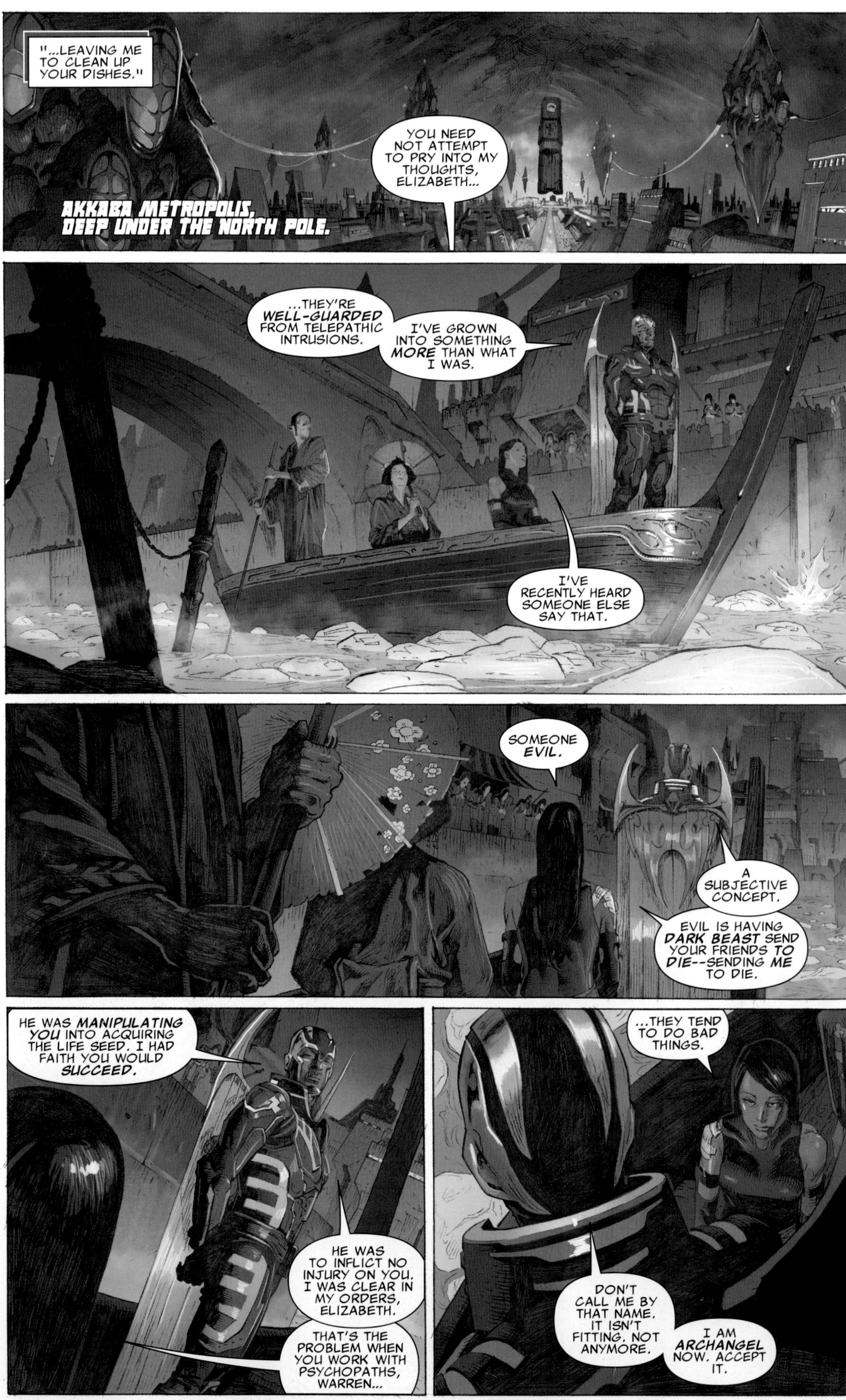
"...LEAVING ME TO CLEAN UP YOUR DISHES."
AKKABA METROPOLIS, DEEP UNDER THE NORTH POLE.
YOU NEED NOT ATTEMPT TO PRY INTO MY THOUGHTS, ELIZABETH...
...THEY'RE WELL-GUARDED FROM TELEPATHIC INTRUSIONS.
I'VE GROWN INTO SOMETHING MORE THAN WHAT I WAS.
I'VE RECENTLY HEARD SOMEONE ELSE SAY THAT.
SOMEONE EVIL.
A SUBJECTIVE CONCEPT.
EVIL IS HAVING DARK BEAST SEND YOUR FRIENDS TO DIE--SENDING ME TO DIE.
HE WAS MANIPULATING YOU INTO ACQUIRING THE LIFE SEED. I HAD FAITH YOU WOULD SUCCEED.
HE WAS TO INFLICT NO INJURY ON YOU. I WAS CLEAR IN MY ORDERS, ELIZABETH.
THAT'S THE PROBLEM WHEN YOU WORK WITH PSYCHOPATHS, WARREN...
...THEY TEND TO DO BAD THINGS.
DON'T CALL ME BY THAT NAME. IT ISN'T FITTING. NOT ANYMORE.
I AM ARCHANGEL NOW. ACCEPT IT.

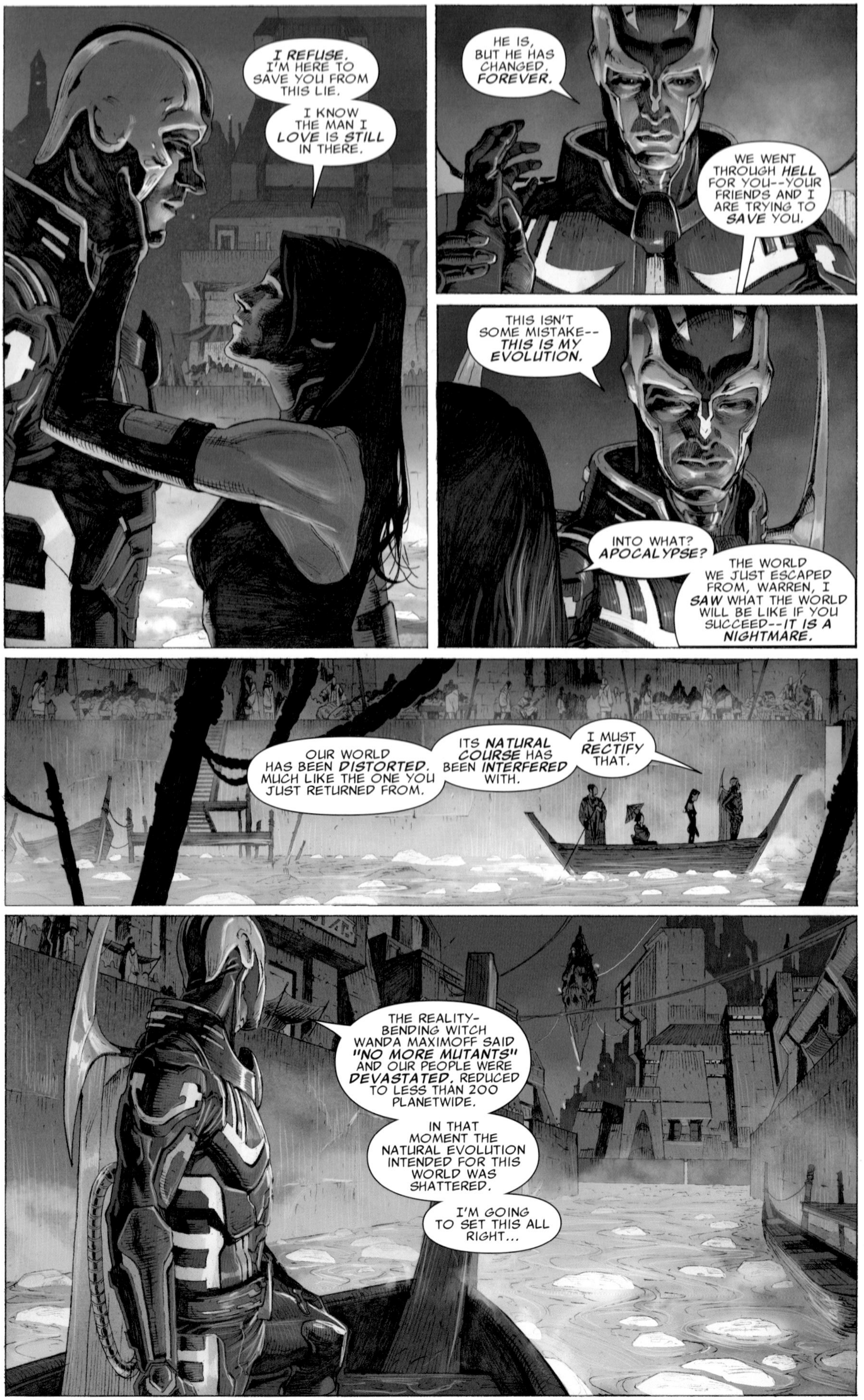
I REFUSE. I'M HERE TO SAVE YOU FROM THIS LIE.
I KNOW THE MAN I LOVE IS STILL IN THERE.
HE IS, BUT HE HAS CHANGED. FOREVER.
WE WENT THROUGH HELL FOR YOU--YOUR FRIENDS AND I ARE TRYING TO SAVE YOU.
THIS ISN'T SOME MISTAKE--THIS IS MY EVOLUTION.
INTO WHAT? APOCALYPSE?
THE WORLD WE JUST ESCAPED FROM, WARREN, I SAW WHAT THE WORLD WILL BE LIKE IF YOU SUCCEED--IT IS A NIGHTMARE.
OUR WORLD HAS BEEN DISTORTED. MUCH LIKE THE ONE YOU JUST RETURNED FROM.
ITS NATURAL COURSE HAS BEEN INTERFERED WITH.
I MUST RECTIFY THAT.
THE REALITY-BENDING WITCH WANDA MAXIMOFF SAID "NO MORE MUTANTS" AND OUR PEOPLE WERE DEVASTATED. REDUCED TO LESS THAN 200 PLANETWIDE.
IN THAT MOMENT THE NATURAL EVOLUTION INTENDED FOR THIS WORLD WAS SHATTERED.
I'M GOING TO SET THIS ALL RIGHT...

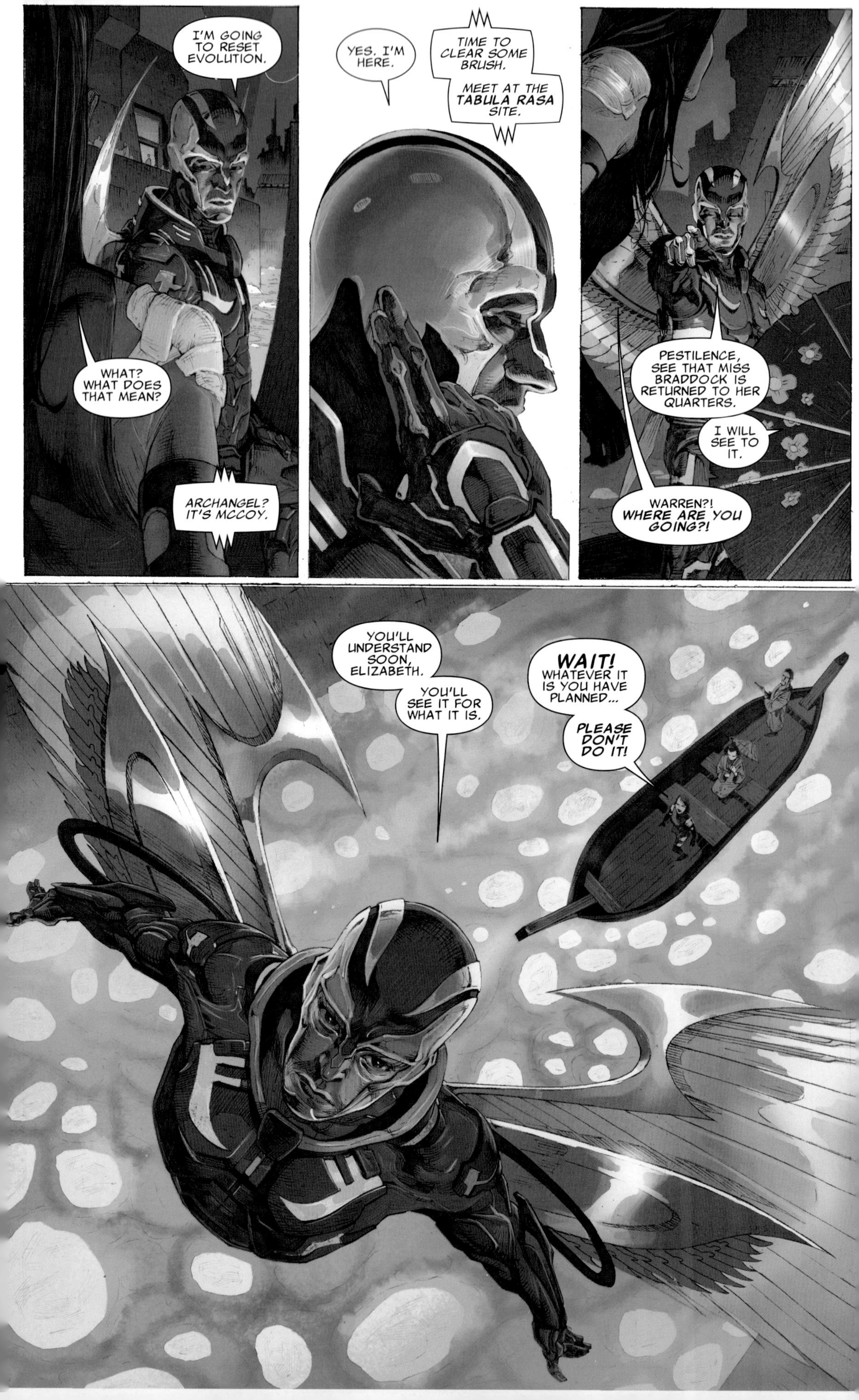
I'M GOING TO RESET EVOLUTION.
WHAT? WHAT DOES THAT MEAN?
ARCHANGEL? IT'S MCCOY.
YES. I'M HERE.
TIME TO CLEAR SOME BRUSH.
MEET AT THE TABULA RASA SITE.
PESTILENCE, SEE THAT MISS BRADDOCK IS RETURNED TO HER QUARTERS.
I WILL SEE TO IT.
WARREN?! WHERE ARE YOU GOING?!
YOU'LL UNDERSTAND SOON, ELIZABETH.
YOU'LL SEE IT FOR WHAT IT IS.
WAIT! WHATEVER IT IS YOU HAVE PLANNED...
PLEASE DON'T DO IT!

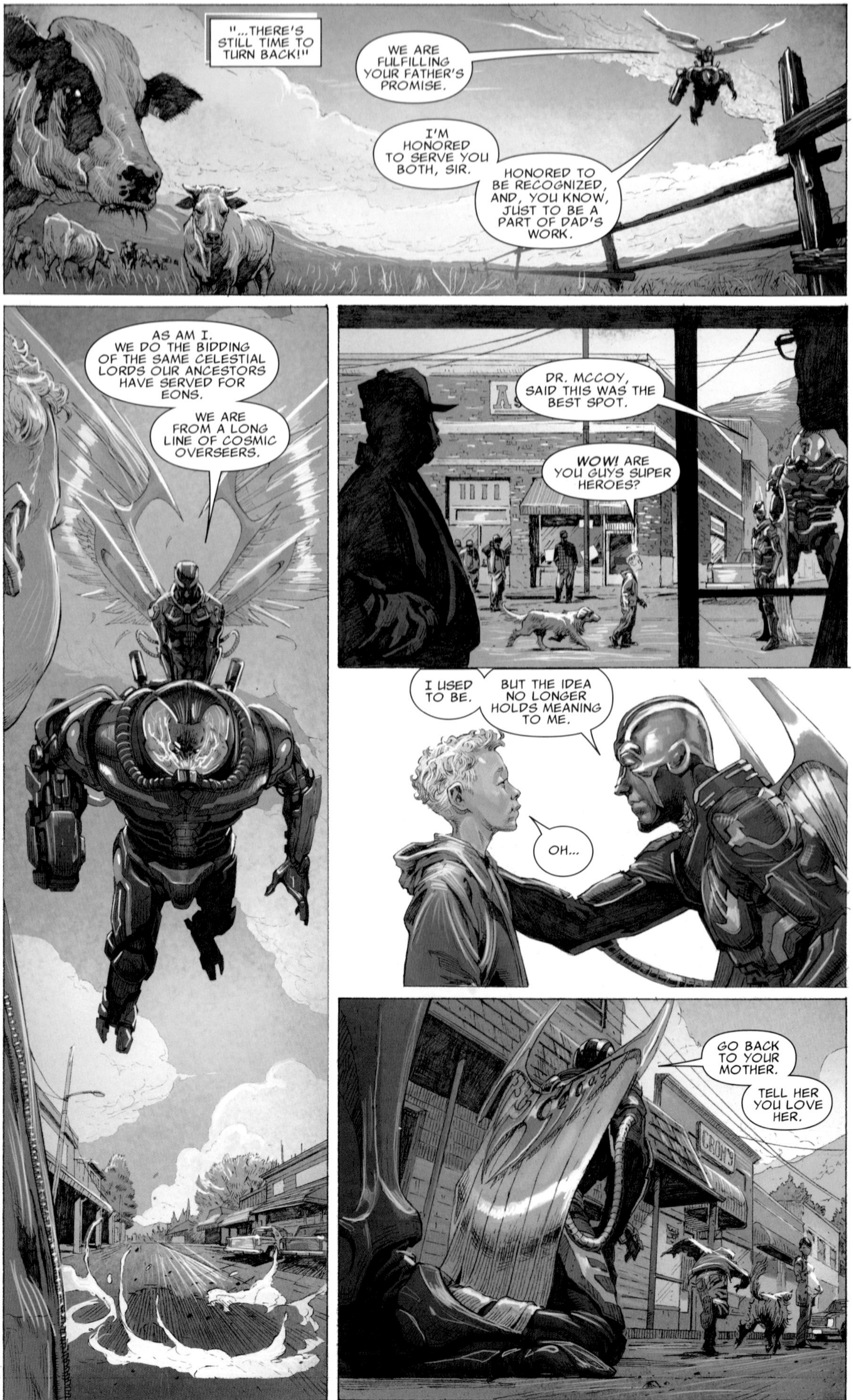
"...THERE'S STILL TIME TO TURN BACK!"
WE ARE FULFILLING YOUR FATHER'S PROMISE.
I'M HONORED TO SERVE YOU BOTH, SIR.
HONORED TO BE RECOGNIZED, AND, YOU KNOW, JUST TO BE A PART OF DAD'S WORK.
AS AM I. WE DO THE BIDDING OF THE SAME CELESTIAL LORDS OUR ANCESTORS HAVE SERVED FOR EONS.
WE ARE FROM A LONG LINE OF COSMIC OVERSEERS.
DR. MCCOY, SAID THIS WAS THE BEST SPOT.
WOW! ARE YOU GUYS SUPER HEROES?
I USED TO BE.
BUT THE IDEA NO LONGER HOLDS MEANING TO ME.
OH...
GO BACK TO YOUR MOTHER.
TELL HER YOU LOVE HER.

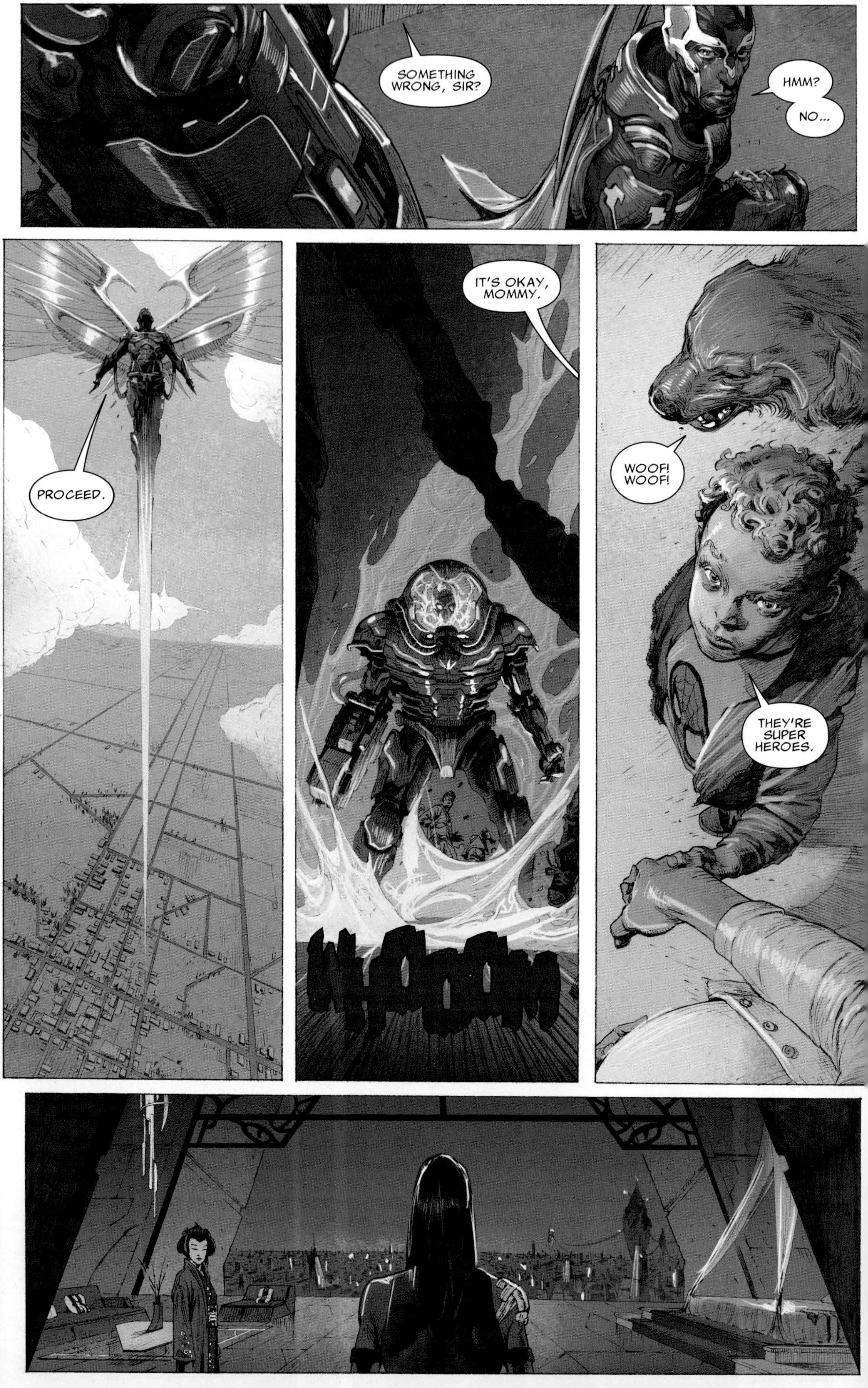
SOMETHING WRONG, SIR?
HMM?
NO...
PROCEED.
IT'S OKAY, MOMMY.
WOOF! WOOF!
THEY'RE SUPER HEROES.

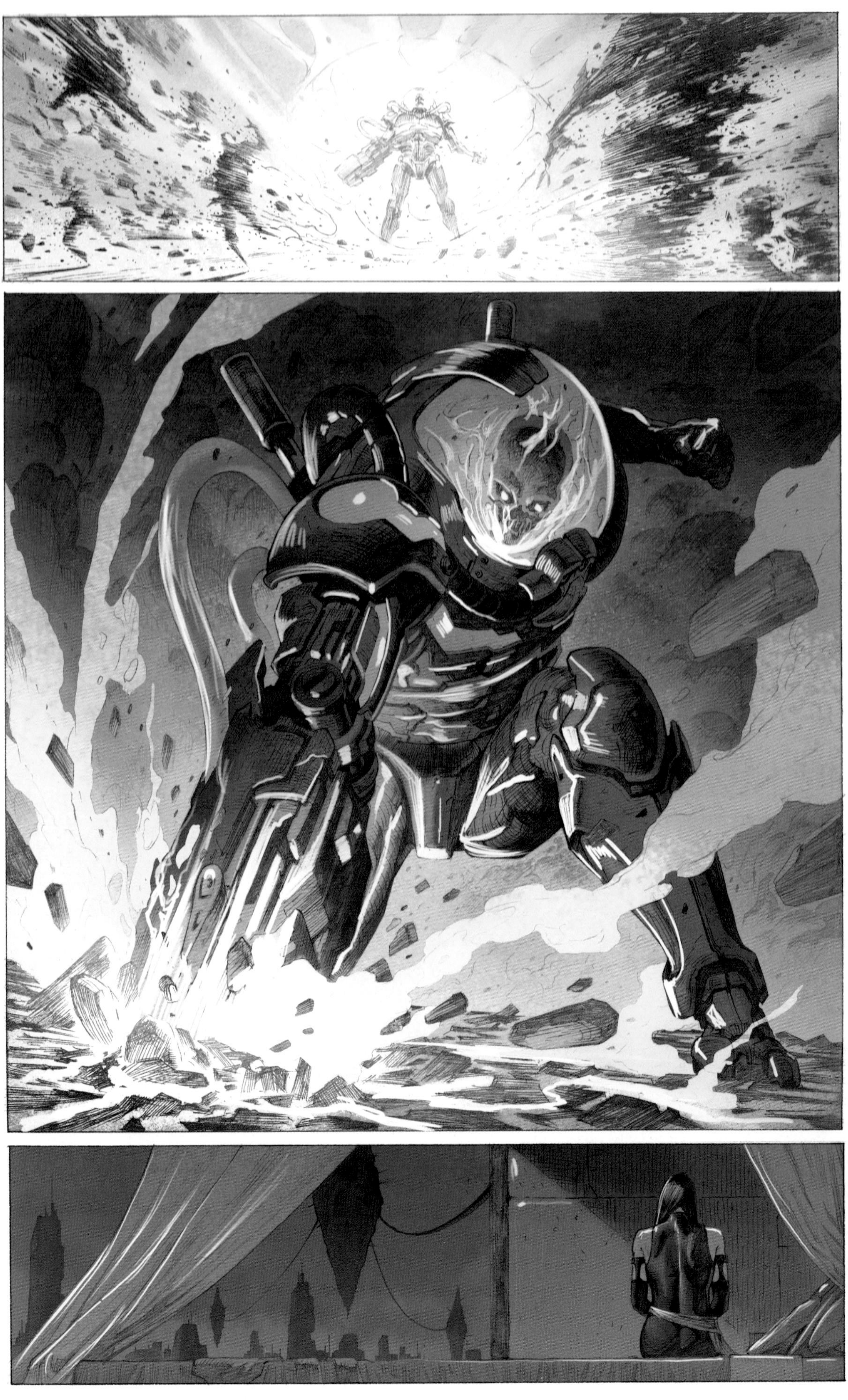

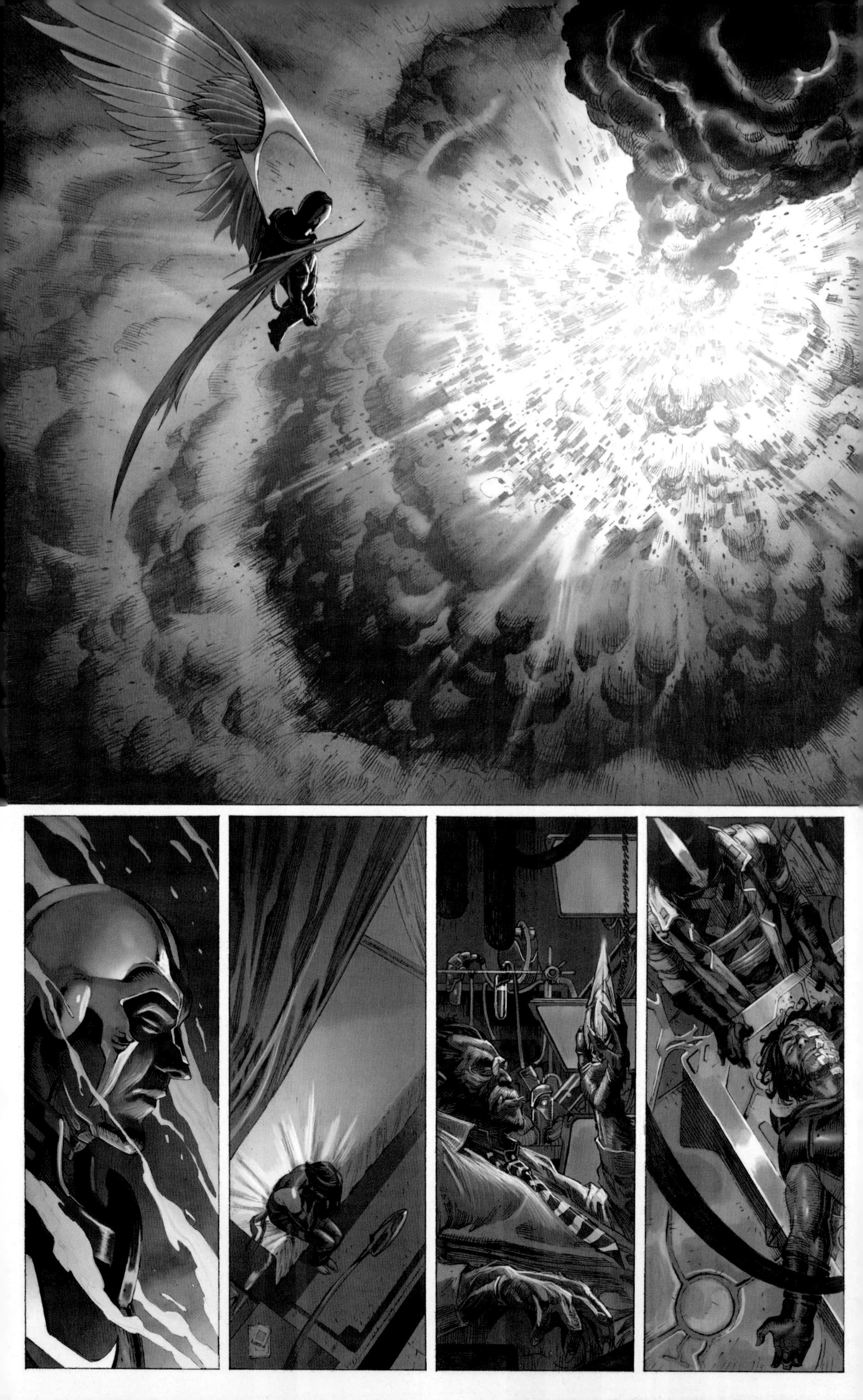

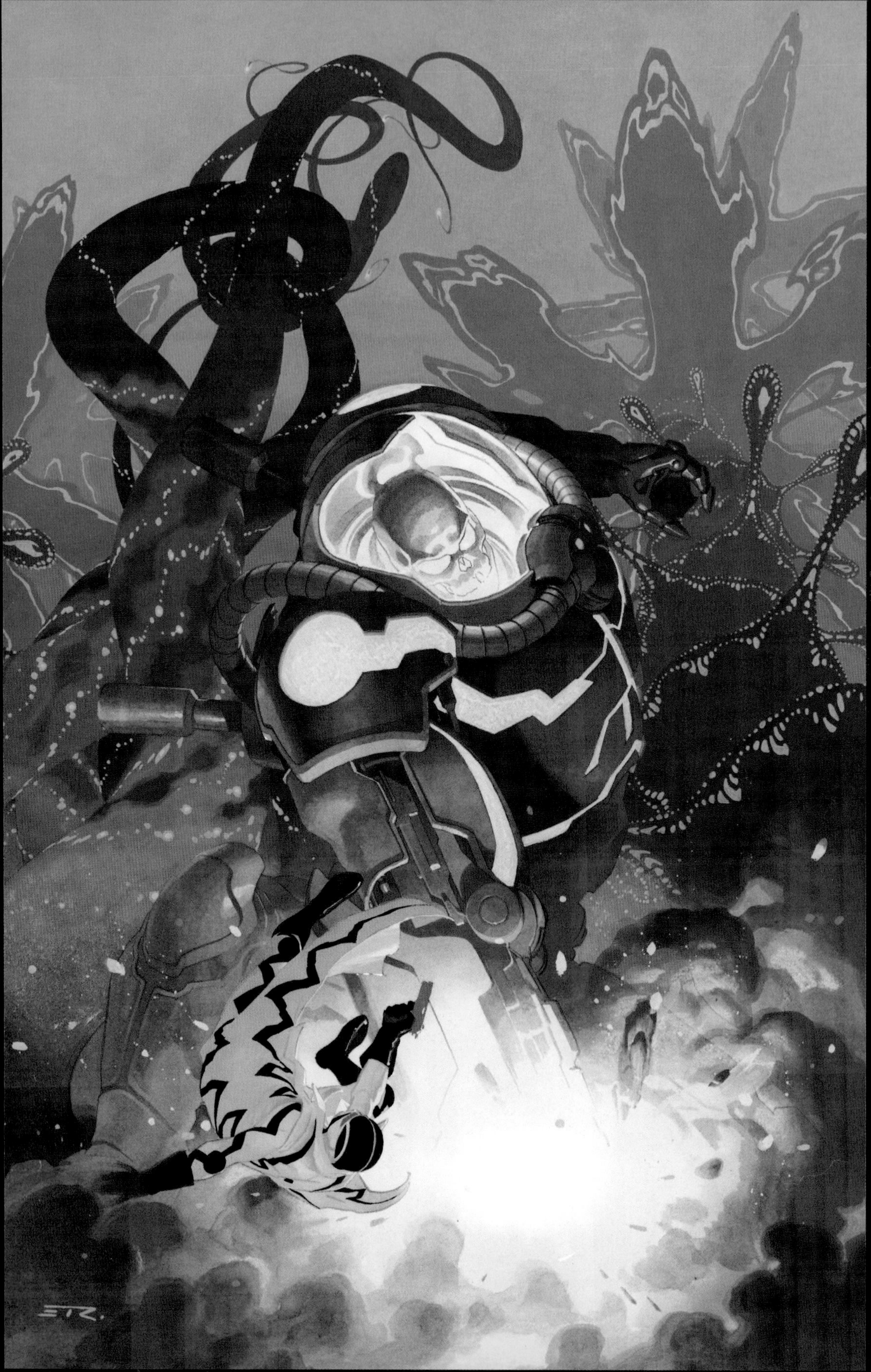
ETR.

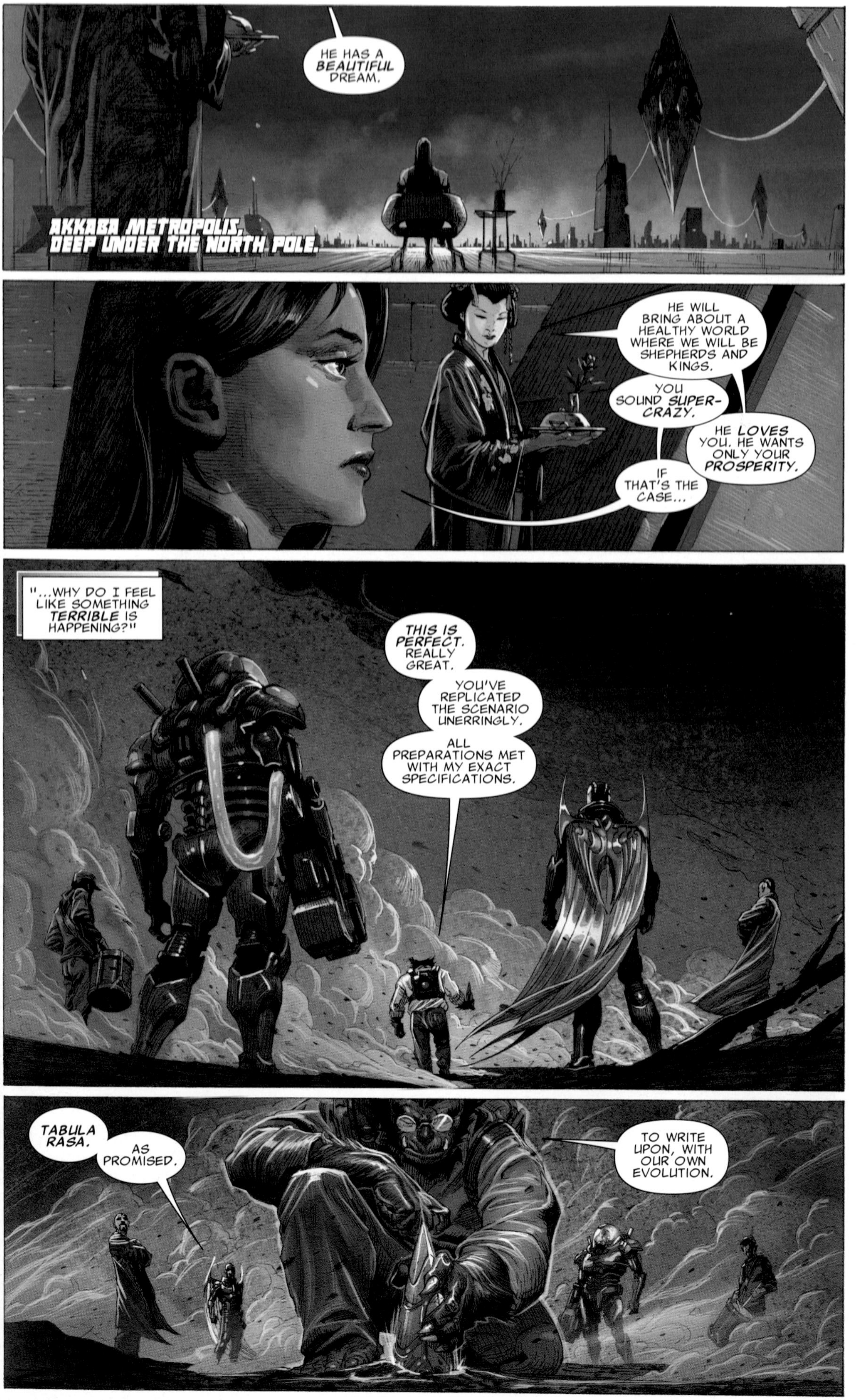
HE HAS A BEAUTIFUL DREAM.
AKKABA METROPOLIS, DEEP UNDER THE NORTH POLE.
HE WILL BRING ABOUT A HEALTHY WORLD WHERE WE WILL BE SHEPHERDS AND KINGS.
YOU SOUND SUPER-CRAZY.
HE LOVES YOU. HE WANTS ONLY YOUR PROSPERITY.
IF THAT'S THE CASE...
"...WHY DO I FEEL LIKE SOMETHING TERRIBLE IS HAPPENING?"
THIS IS PERFECT. REALLY GREAT.
YOU'VE REPLICATED THE SCENARIO UNERRINGLY.
ALL PREPARATIONS MET WITH MY EXACT SPECIFICATIONS.
TABULA RASA.
AS PROMISED.
TO WRITE UPON, WITH OUR OWN EVOLUTION.

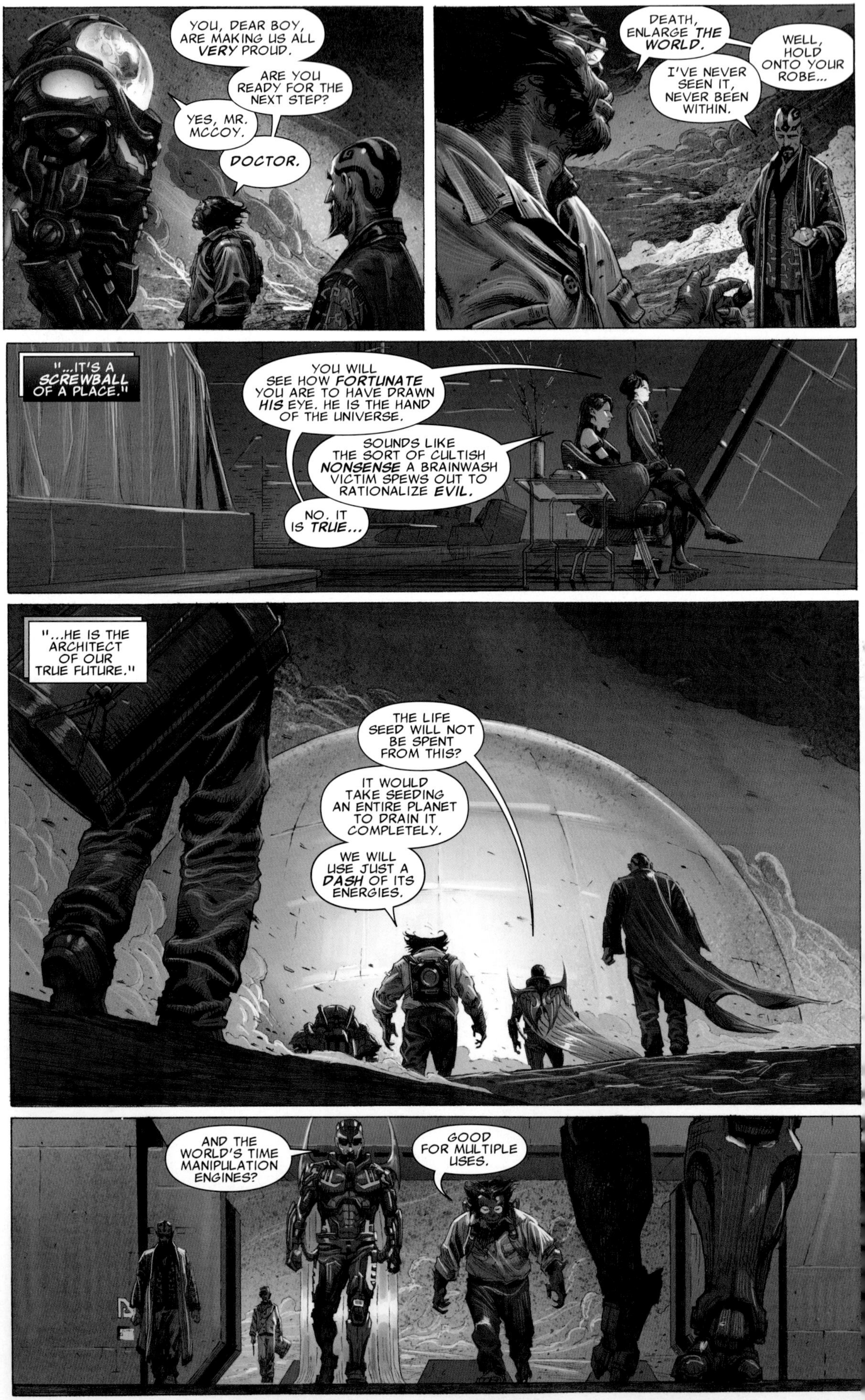
YOU, DEAR BOY, ARE MAKING US ALL VERY PROUD.
ARE YOU READY FOR THE NEXT STEP?
YES, MR. MCCOY.
DOCTOR.
DEATH, ENLARGE THE WORLD.
I'VE NEVER SEEN IT, NEVER BEEN WITHIN.
WELL, HOLD ONTO YOUR ROBE...
"...IT'S A SCREWBALL OF A PLACE."
YOU WILL SEE HOW FORTUNATE YOU ARE TO HAVE DRAWN HIS EYE. HE IS THE HAND OF THE UNIVERSE.
SOUNDS LIKE THE SORT OF CULTISH NONSENSE A BRAINWASH VICTIM SPEWS OUT TO RATIONALIZE EVIL.
NO. IT IS TRUE...
"...HE IS THE ARCHITECT OF OUR TRUE FUTURE."
THE LIFE SEED WILL NOT BE SPENT FROM THIS?
IT WOULD TAKE SEEDING AN ENTIRE PLANET TO DRAIN IT COMPLETELY.
WE WILL USE JUST A DASH OF ITS ENERGIES.
AND THE WORLD'S TIME MANIPULATION ENGINES?
GOOD FOR MULTIPLE USES.

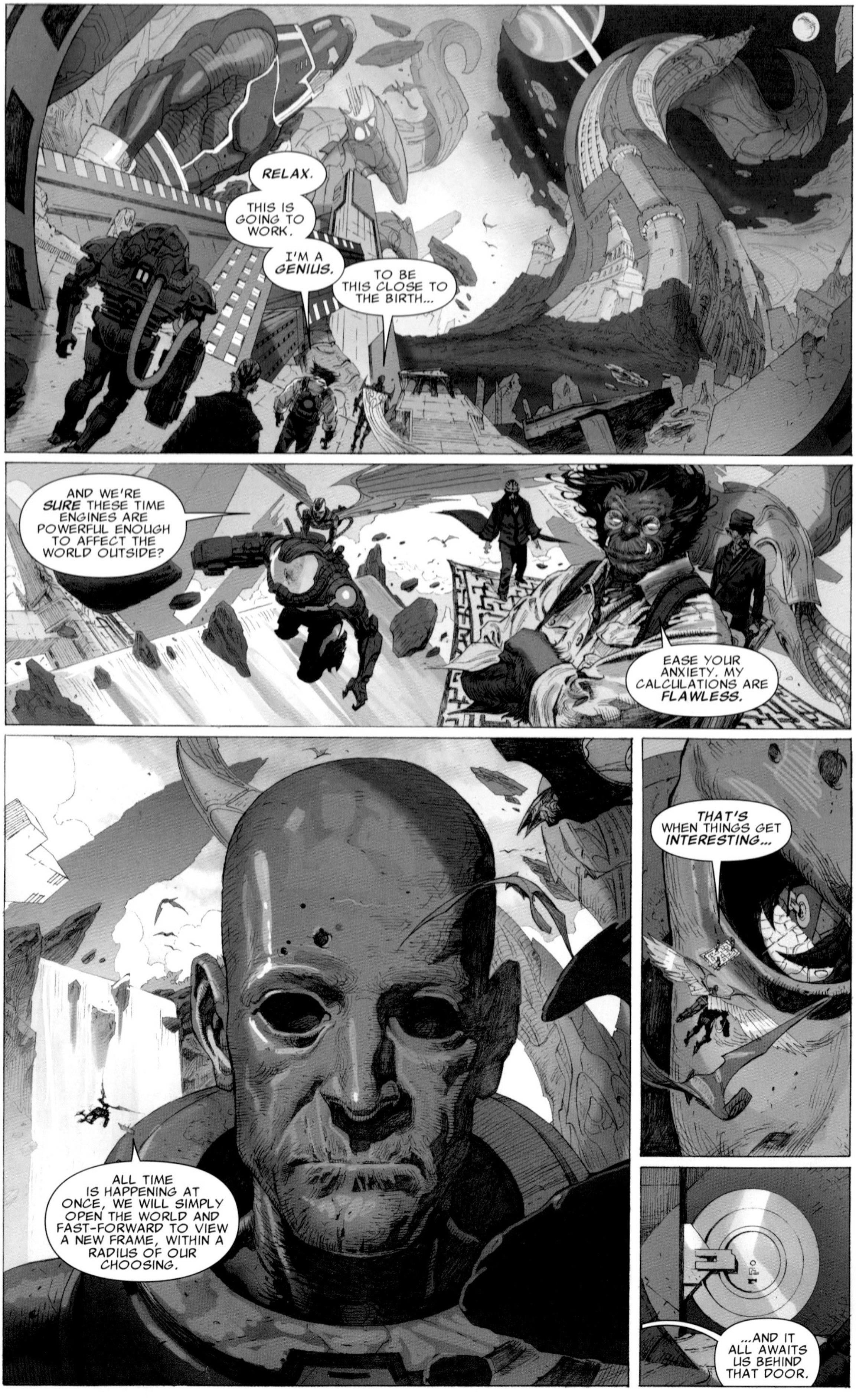
RELAX.
THIS IS GOING TO WORK.
I'M A GENIUS.
TO BE THIS CLOSE TO THE BIRTH...
AND WE'RE SURE THESE TIME ENGINES ARE POWERFUL ENOUGH TO AFFECT THE WORLD OUTSIDE?
EASE YOUR ANXIETY. MY CALCULATIONS ARE FLAWLESS.
ALL TIME IS HAPPENING AT ONCE, WE WILL SIMPLY OPEN THE WORLD AND FAST-FORWARD TO VIEW A NEW FRAME, WITHIN A RADIUS OF OUR CHOOSING.
THAT'S WHEN THINGS GET INTERESTING...
...AND IT ALL AWAITS US BEHIND THAT DOOR.

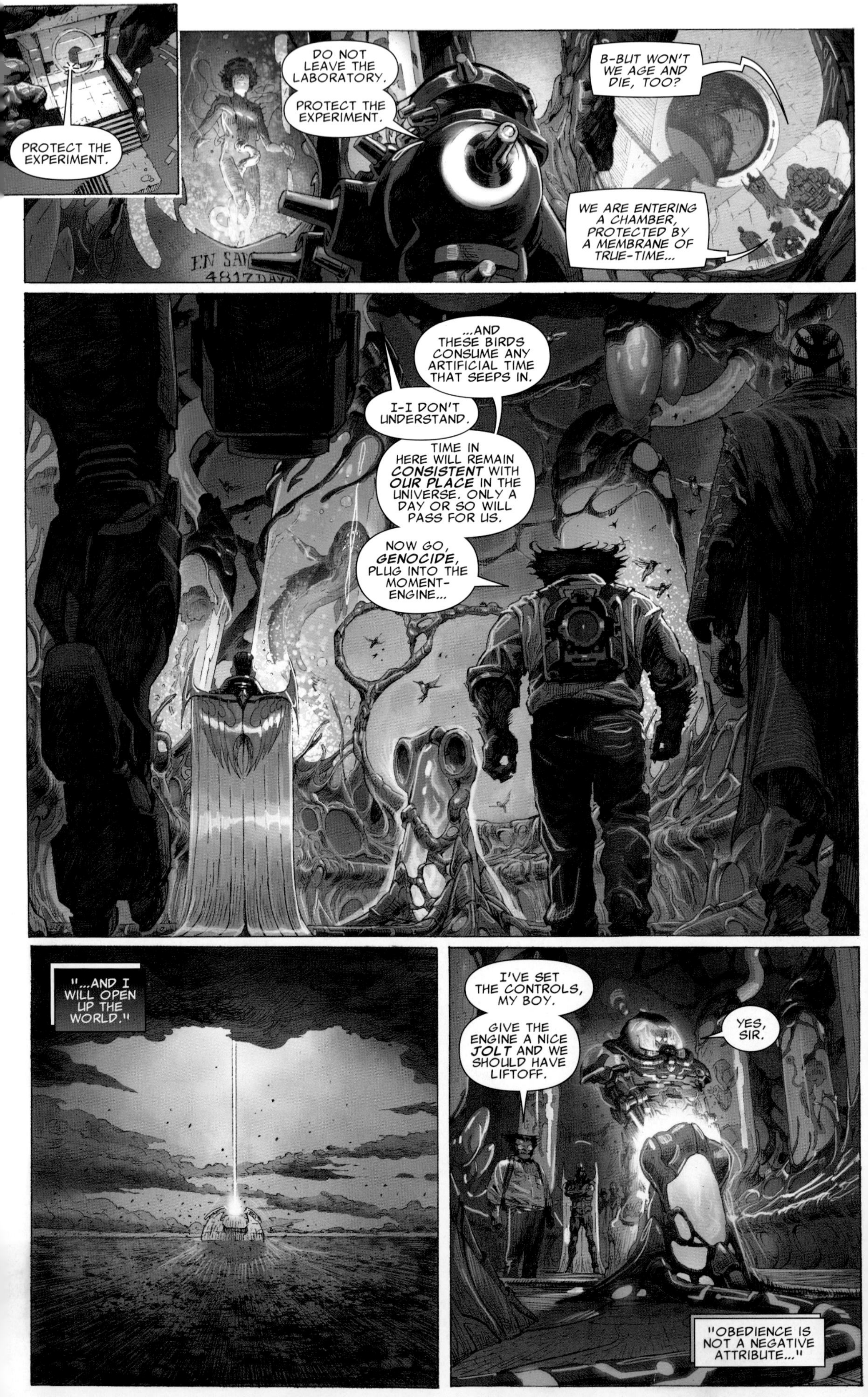
PROTECT THE EXPERIMENT.
DO NOT LEAVE THE LABORATORY.
PROTECT THE EXPERIMENT.
B-BUT WON'T WE AGE AND DIE, TOO?
WE ARE ENTERING A CHAMBER, PROTECTED BY A MEMBRANE OF TRUE-TIME...
...AND THESE BIRDS CONSUME ANY ARTIFICIAL TIME THAT SEEPS IN.
I-I DON'T UNDERSTAND.
TIME IN HERE WILL REMAIN **CONSISTENT** WITH **OUR PLACE** IN THE UNIVERSE. ONLY A DAY OR SO WILL PASS FOR US.
NOW GO, ***GENOCIDE***, PLUG INTO THE MOMENT-ENGINE...
"...AND I WILL OPEN UP THE WORLD."
I'VE SET THE CONTROLS, MY BOY.
GIVE THE ENGINE A NICE ***JOLT*** AND WE SHOULD HAVE LIFTOFF.
YES, SIR.
"OBEDIENCE IS NOT A NEGATIVE ATTRIBUTE..."

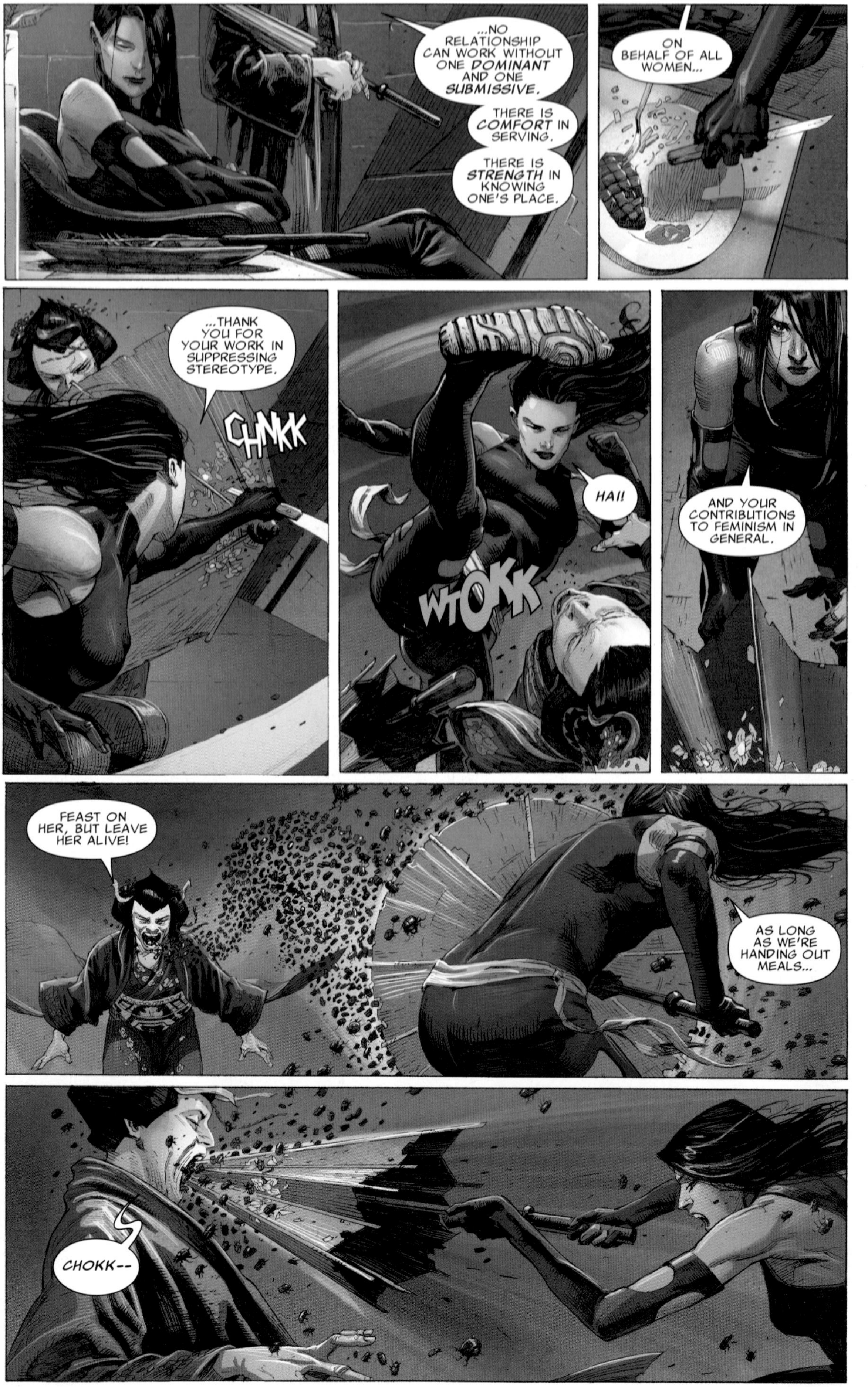
...NO RELATIONSHIP CAN WORK WITHOUT ONE DOMINANT AND ONE SUBMISSIVE.
THERE IS COMFORT IN SERVING.
THERE IS STRENGTH IN KNOWING ONE'S PLACE.
ON BEHALF OF ALL WOMEN...
...THANK YOU FOR YOUR WORK IN SUPPRESSING STEREOTYPE.
CHNKK
HAI!
WTOKK
AND YOUR CONTRIBUTIONS TO FEMINISM IN GENERAL.
FEAST ON HER, BUT LEAVE HER ALIVE!
AS LONG AS WE'RE HANDING OUT MEALS...
CHOKK--

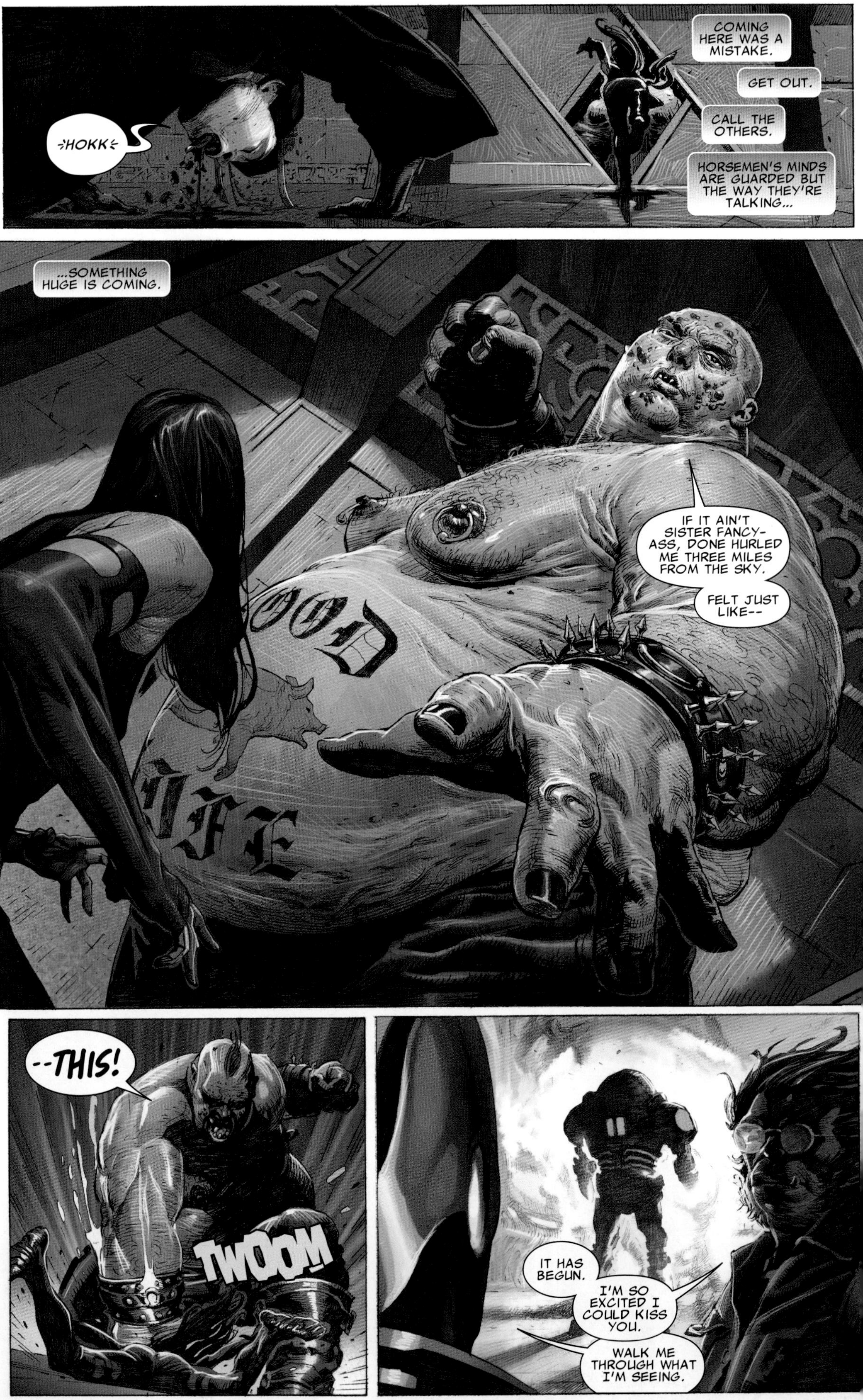
HOKK
COMING HERE WAS A MISTAKE.
GET OUT.
CALL THE OTHERS.
HORSEMEN'S MINDS ARE GUARDED BUT THE WAY THEY'RE TALKING...
...SOMETHING HUGE IS COMING.
IF IT AIN'T SISTER FANCY-ASS, DONE HURLED ME THREE MILES FROM THE SKY.
FELT JUST LIKE--
--THIS!
TWOOM
IT HAS BEGUN.
I'M SO EXCITED I COULD KISS YOU.
WALK ME THROUGH WHAT I'M SEEING.

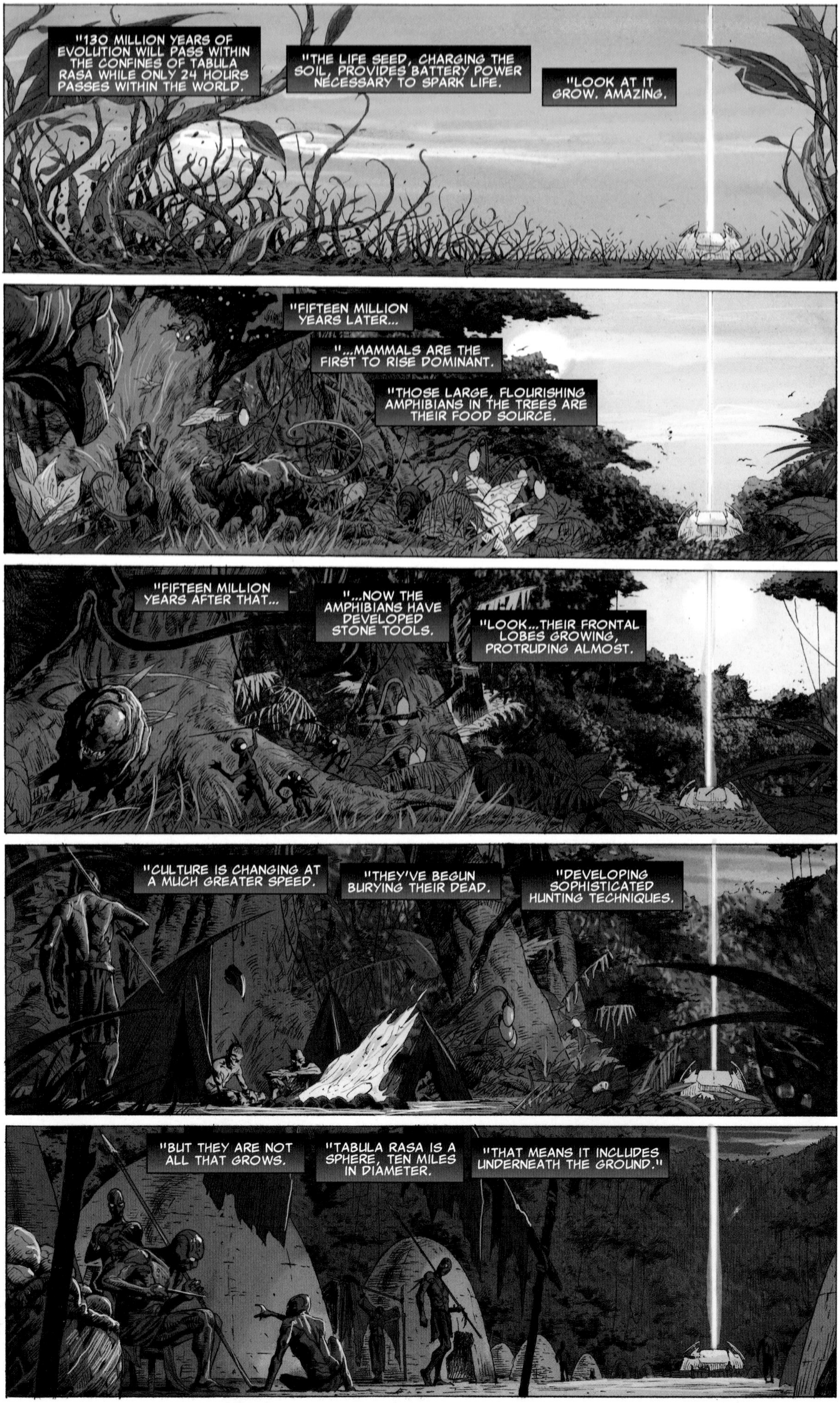
"130 MILLION YEARS OF EVOLUTION WILL PASS WITHIN THE CONFINES OF TABULA RASA WHILE ONLY 24 HOURS PASSES WITHIN THE WORLD.
"THE LIFE SEED, CHARGING THE SOIL, PROVIDES BATTERY POWER NECESSARY TO SPARK LIFE.
"LOOK AT IT GROW. AMAZING.
"FIFTEEN MILLION YEARS LATER...
"...MAMMALS ARE THE FIRST TO RISE DOMINANT.
"THOSE LARGE, FLOURISHING AMPHIBIANS IN THE TREES ARE THEIR FOOD SOURCE.
"FIFTEEN MILLION YEARS AFTER THAT...
"...NOW THE AMPHIBIANS HAVE DEVELOPED STONE TOOLS.
"LOOK...THEIR FRONTAL LOBES GROWING, PROTRUDING ALMOST.
"CULTURE IS CHANGING AT A MUCH GREATER SPEED.
"THEY'VE BEGUN BURYING THEIR DEAD.
"DEVELOPING SOPHISTICATED HUNTING TECHNIQUES.
"BUT THEY ARE NOT ALL THAT GROWS.
"TABULA RASA IS A SPHERE, TEN MILES IN DIAMETER.
"THAT MEANS IT INCLUDES UNDERNEATH THE GROUND."

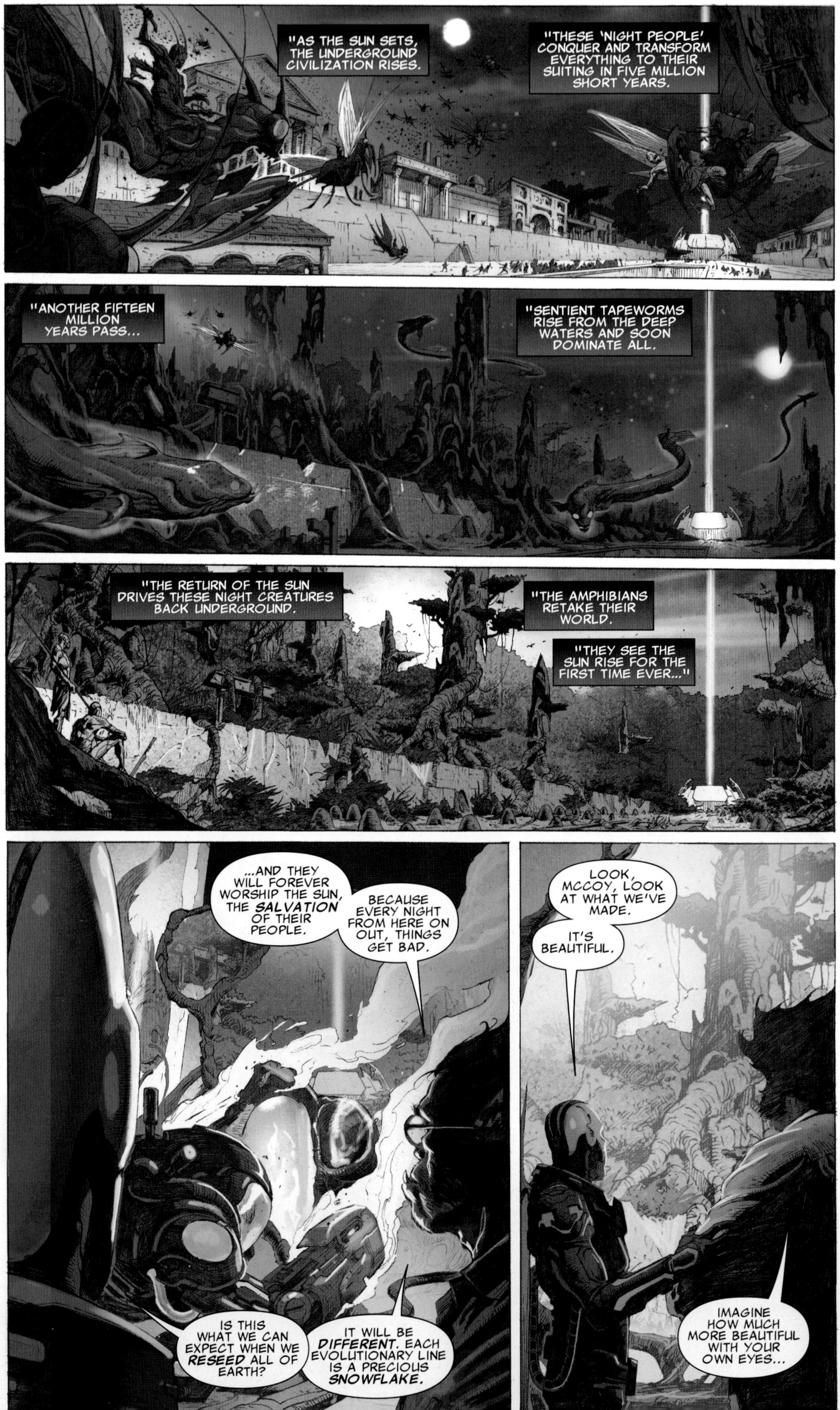
"AS THE SUN SETS, THE UNDERGROUND CIVILIZATION RISES.
"THESE 'NIGHT PEOPLE' CONQUER AND TRANSFORM EVERYTHING TO THEIR SUITING IN FIVE MILLION SHORT YEARS.
"ANOTHER FIFTEEN MILLION YEARS PASS...
"SENTIENT TAPEWORMS RISE FROM THE DEEP WATERS AND SOON DOMINATE ALL.
"THE RETURN OF THE SUN DRIVES THESE NIGHT CREATURES BACK UNDERGROUND.
"THE AMPHIBIANS RETAKE THEIR WORLD.
"THEY SEE THE SUN RISE FOR THE FIRST TIME EVER..."
...AND THEY WILL FOREVER WORSHIP THE SUN, THE SALVATION OF THEIR PEOPLE.
BECAUSE EVERY NIGHT FROM HERE ON OUT, THINGS GET BAD.
IS THIS WHAT WE CAN EXPECT WHEN WE RESEED ALL OF EARTH?
IT WILL BE DIFFERENT. EACH EVOLUTIONARY LINE IS A PRECIOUS SNOWFLAKE.
LOOK, MCCOY, LOOK AT WHAT WE'VE MADE.
IT'S BEAUTIFUL.
IMAGINE HOW MUCH MORE BEAUTIFUL WITH YOUR OWN EYES...

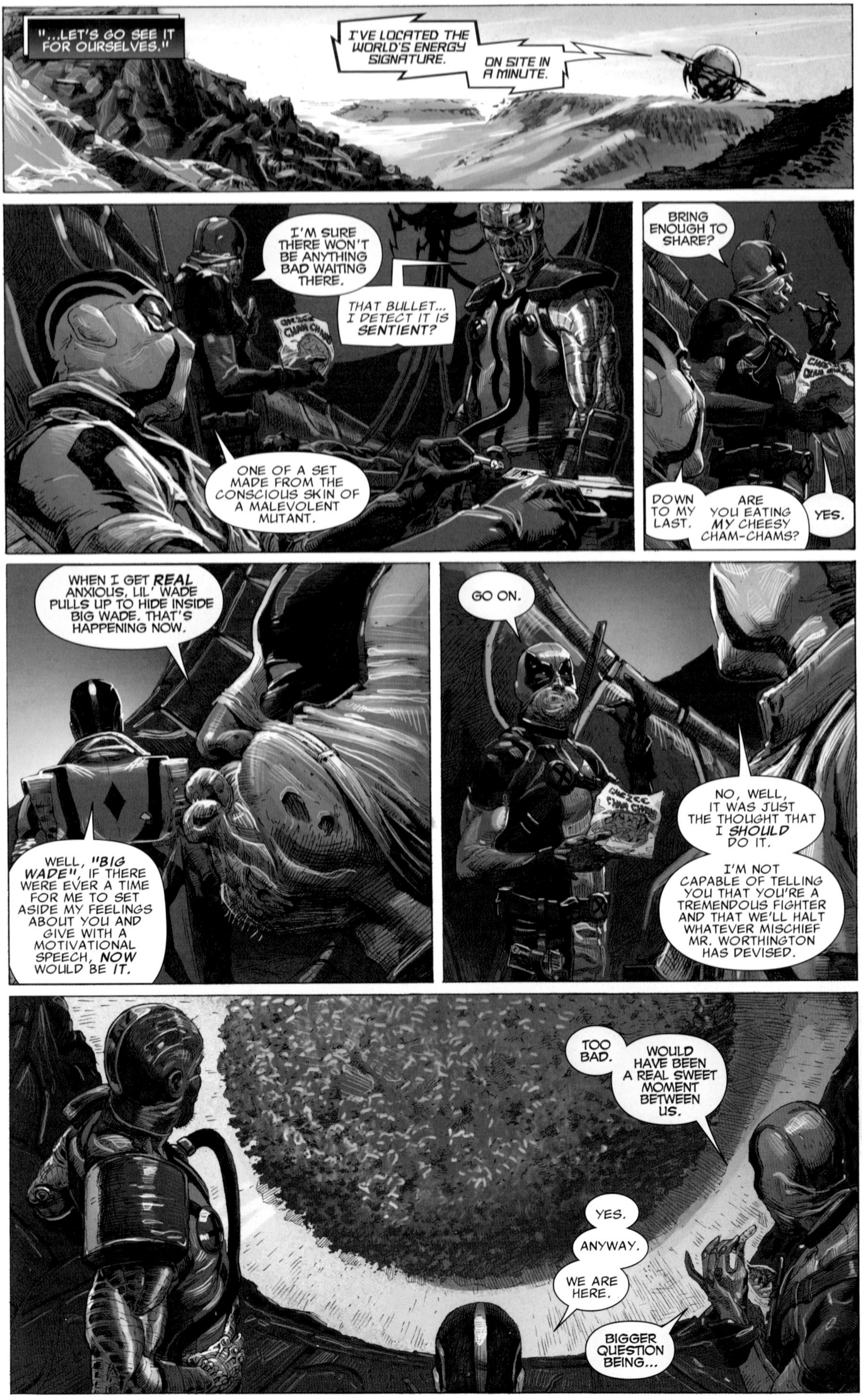
"...LET'S GO SEE IT FOR OURSELVES."
I'VE LOCATED THE WORLD'S ENERGY SIGNATURE.
ON SITE IN A MINUTE.
I'M SURE THERE WON'T BE ANYTHING BAD WAITING THERE.
THAT BULLET... I DETECT IT IS SENTIENT?
ONE OF A SET MADE FROM THE CONSCIOUS SKIN OF A MALEVOLENT MUTANT.
BRING ENOUGH TO SHARE?
DOWN TO MY LAST.
ARE YOU EATING MY CHEESY CHAM-CHAMS?
YES.
WHEN I GET REAL ANXIOUS, LIL' WADE PULLS UP TO HIDE INSIDE BIG WADE. THAT'S HAPPENING NOW.
WELL, "BIG WADE", IF THERE WERE EVER A TIME FOR ME TO SET ASIDE MY FEELINGS ABOUT YOU AND GIVE WITH A MOTIVATIONAL SPEECH, NOW WOULD BE IT.
GO ON.
NO, WELL, IT WAS JUST THE THOUGHT THAT I SHOULD DO IT.
I'M NOT CAPABLE OF TELLING YOU THAT YOU'RE A TREMENDOUS FIGHTER AND THAT WE'LL HALT WHATEVER MISCHIEF MR. WORTHINGTON HAS DEVISED.
TOO BAD.
WOULD HAVE BEEN A REAL SWEET MOMENT BETWEEN US.
YES.
ANYWAY.
WE ARE HERE.
BIGGER QUESTION BEING...

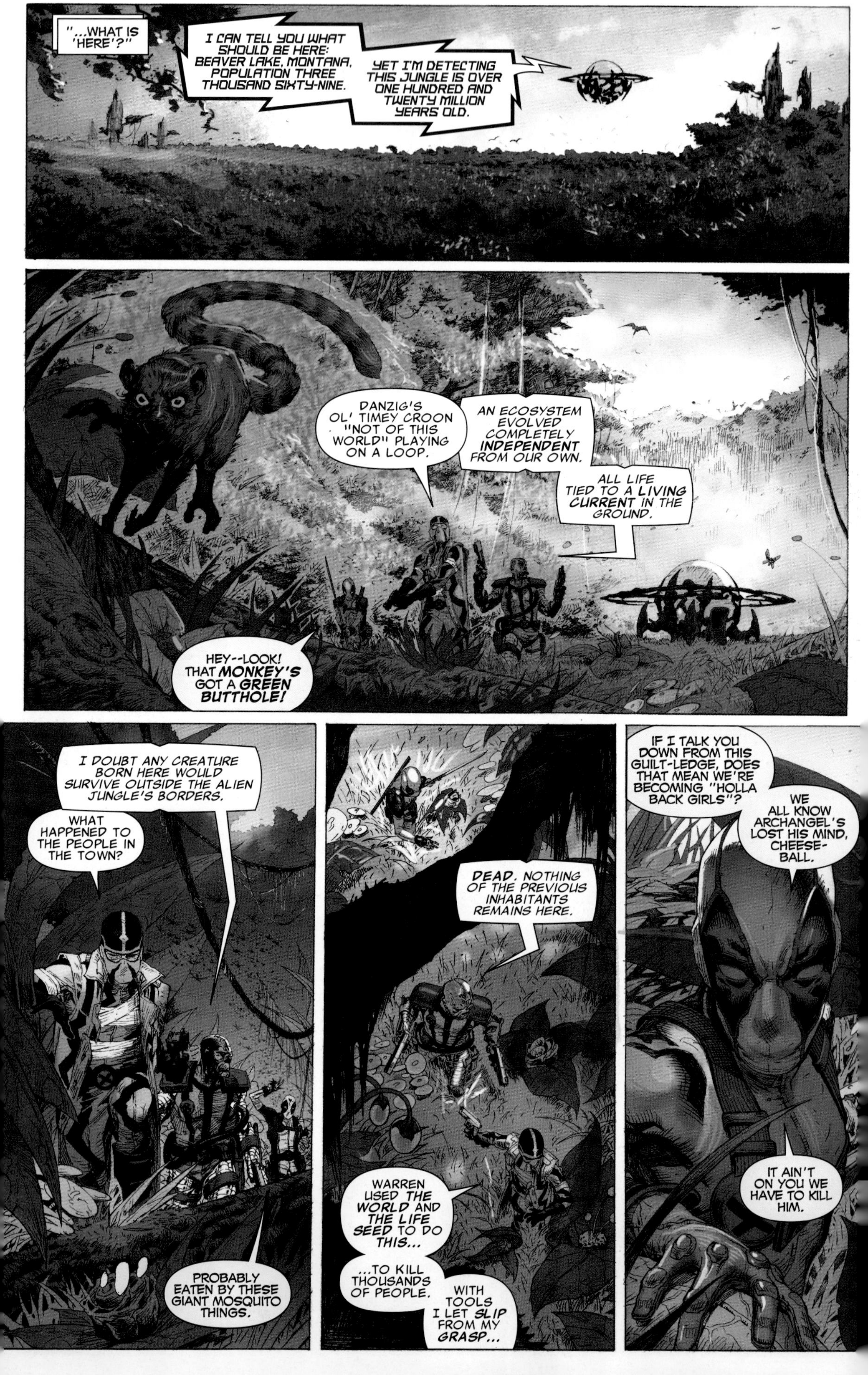
"...WHAT IS 'HERE'?"
I CAN TELL YOU WHAT SHOULD BE HERE: BEAVER LAKE, MONTANA, POPULATION THREE THOUSAND SIXTY-NINE.
YET I'M DETECTING THIS JUNGLE IS OVER ONE HUNDRED AND TWENTY MILLION YEARS OLD.
DANZIG'S OL' TIMEY CROON "NOT OF THIS WORLD" PLAYING ON A LOOP.
AN ECOSYSTEM EVOLVED COMPLETELY INDEPENDENT FROM OUR OWN.
ALL LIFE TIED TO A LIVING CURRENT IN THE GROUND.
HEY--LOOK! THAT MONKEY'S GOT A GREEN BUTTHOLE!
I DOUBT ANY CREATURE BORN HERE WOULD SURVIVE OUTSIDE THE ALIEN JUNGLE'S BORDERS.
WHAT HAPPENED TO THE PEOPLE IN THE TOWN?
PROBABLY EATEN BY THESE GIANT MOSQUITO THINGS.
DEAD. NOTHING OF THE PREVIOUS INHABITANTS REMAINS HERE.
WARREN USED THE WORLD AND THE LIFE SEED TO DO THIS...
...TO KILL THOUSANDS OF PEOPLE.
WITH TOOLS I LET SLIP FROM MY GRASP...
IF I TALK YOU DOWN FROM THIS GUILT-LEDGE, DOES THAT MEAN WE'RE BECOMING "HOLLA BACK GIRLS"?
WE ALL KNOW ARCHANGEL'S LOST HIS MIND, CHEESE-BALL.
IT AIN'T ON YOU WE HAVE TO KILL HIM.

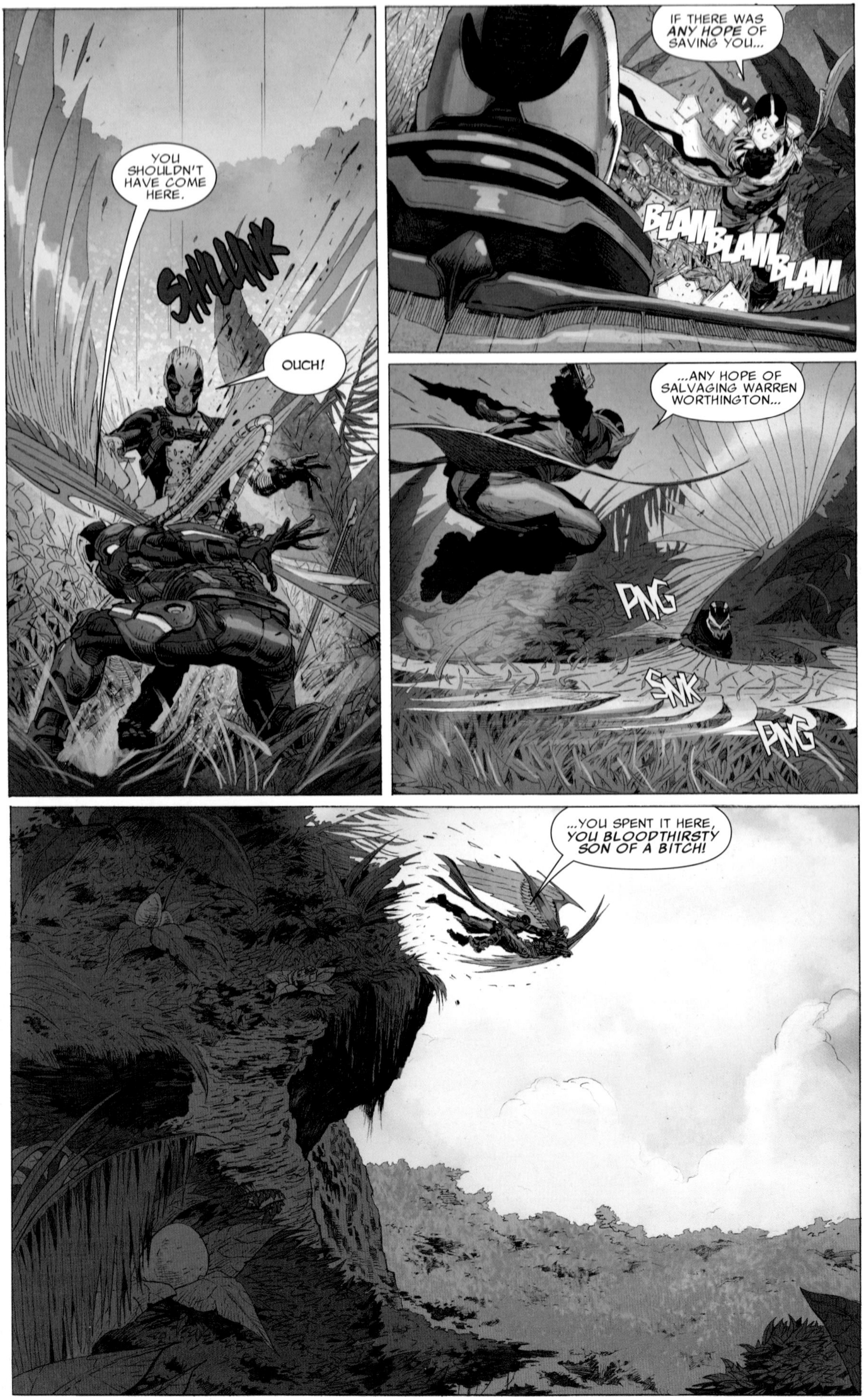
YOU SHOULDN'T HAVE COME HERE.
SHLUNK
OUCH!
IF THERE WAS ANY HOPE OF SAVING YOU...
BLAM BLAM BLAM
...ANY HOPE OF SALVAGING WARREN WORTHINGTON...
PNG
SNK
PNG
...YOU SPENT IT HERE, YOU BLOODTHIRSTY SON OF A BITCH!

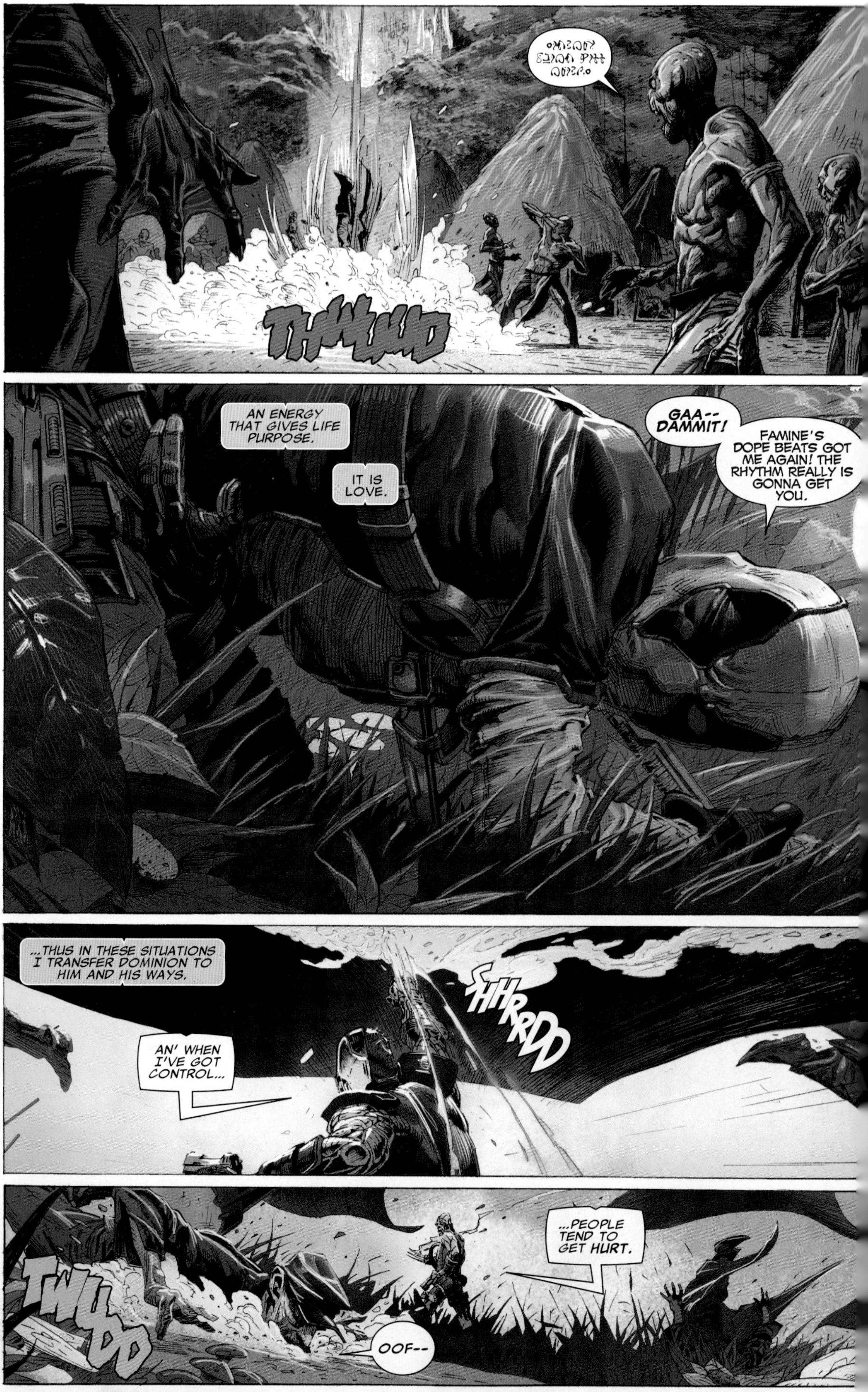
THWUUD
AN ENERGY THAT GIVES LIFE PURPOSE.
IT IS LOVE.
GAA-- DAMMIT!
FAMINE'S DOPE BEATS GOT ME AGAIN! THE RHYTHM REALLY IS GONNA GET YOU.
...THUS IN THESE SITUATIONS I TRANSFER DOMINION TO HIM AND HIS WAYS.
SHHRDD
AN' WHEN I'VE GOT CONTROL...
...PEOPLE TEND TO GET HURT.
TWUDD
OOF--

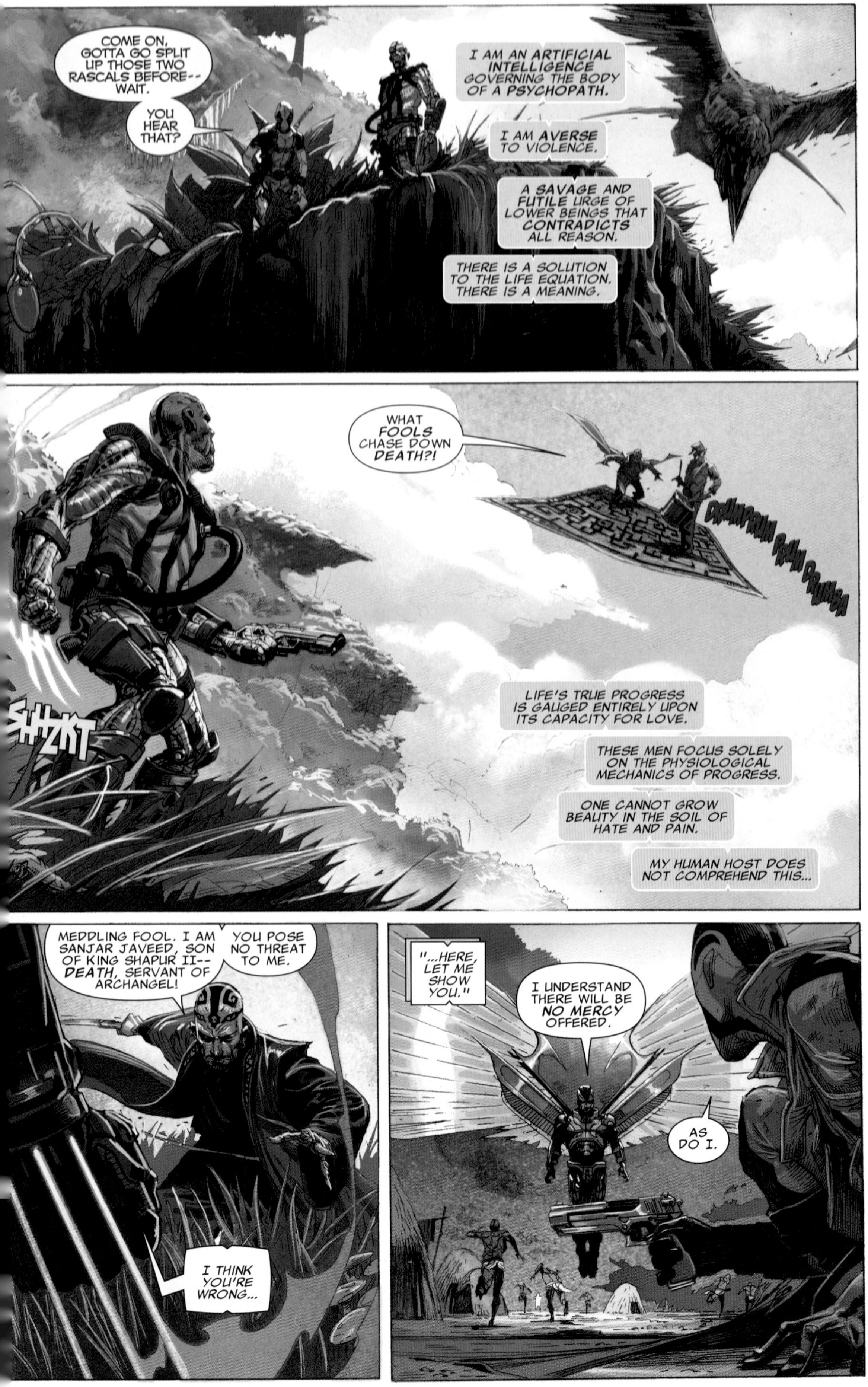
COME ON, GOTTA GO SPLIT UP THOSE TWO RASCALS BEFORE--WAIT.
YOU HEAR THAT?
I AM AN ARTIFICIAL INTELLIGENCE GOVERNING THE BODY OF A PSYCHOPATH.
I AM AVERSE TO VIOLENCE.
A SAVAGE AND FUTILE URGE OF LOWER BEINGS THAT CONTRADICTS ALL REASON.
THERE IS A SOLUTION TO THE LIFE EQUATION. THERE IS A MEANING.
WHAT FOOLS CHASE DOWN DEATH?!
DRUMDRUM DRUM DRUMBA
SHZKT
LIFE'S TRUE PROGRESS IS GAUGED ENTIRELY UPON ITS CAPACITY FOR LOVE.
THESE MEN FOCUS SOLELY ON THE PHYSIOLOGICAL MECHANICS OF PROGRESS.
ONE CANNOT GROW BEAUTY IN THE SOIL OF HATE AND PAIN.
MY HUMAN HOST DOES NOT COMPREHEND THIS...
MEDDLING FOOL. I AM SANJAR JAVEED, SON OF KING SHAPUR II--DEATH, SERVANT OF ARCHANGEL!
YOU POSE NO THREAT TO ME.
I THINK YOU'RE WRONG...
"...HERE, LET ME SHOW YOU."
I UNDERSTAND THERE WILL BE NO MERCY OFFERED.
AS DO I.

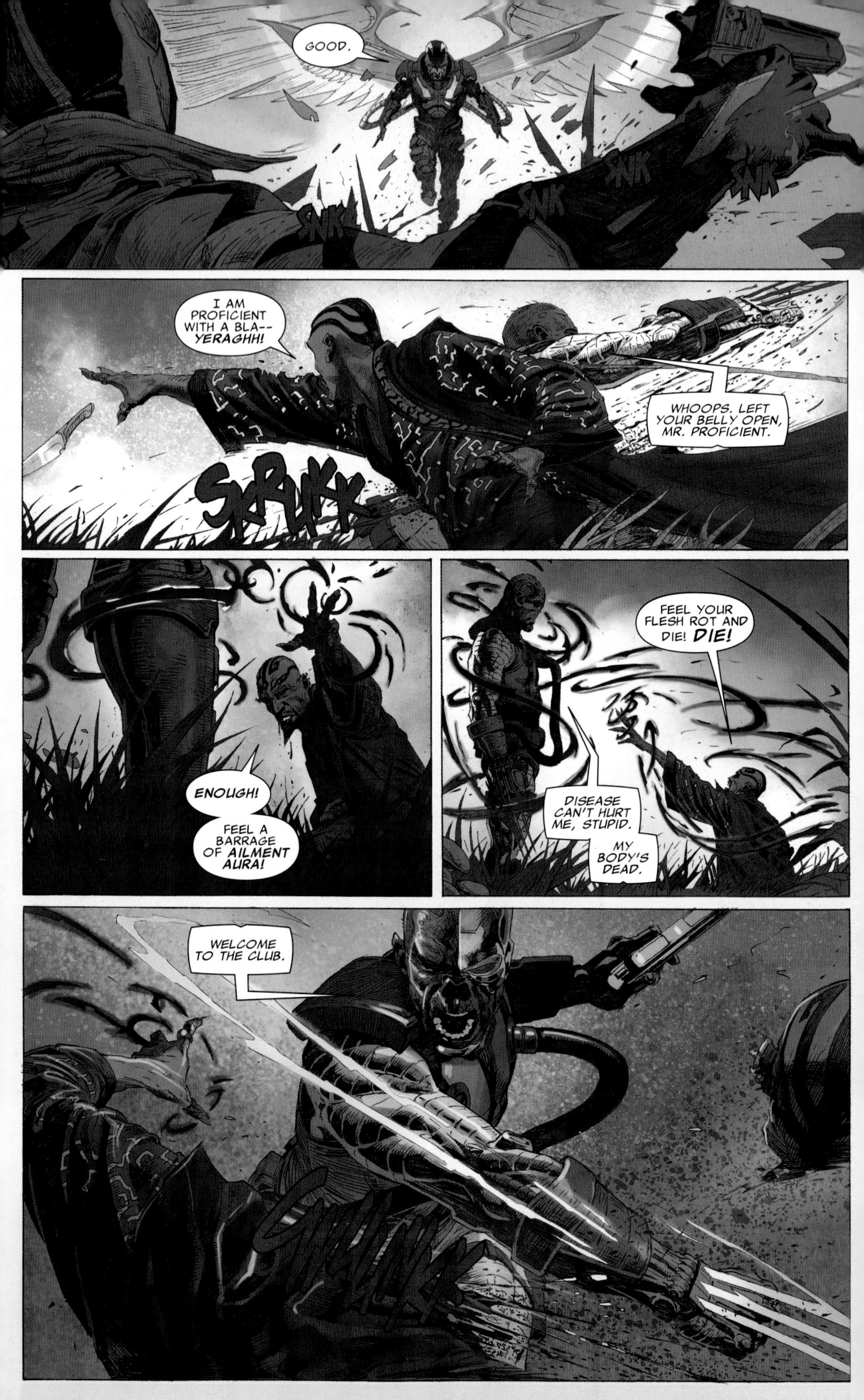
GOOD.
SNK
SNK
SNK
SNK
I AM PROFICIENT WITH A BLA-- YERAGHH!
WHOOPS. LEFT YOUR BELLY OPEN, MR. PROFICIENT.
SKRUKK
ENOUGH!
FEEL A BARRAGE OF AILMENT AURA!
FEEL YOUR FLESH ROT AND DIE! DIE!
DISEASE CAN'T HURT ME, STUPID.
MY BODY'S DEAD.
WELCOME TO THE CLUB.

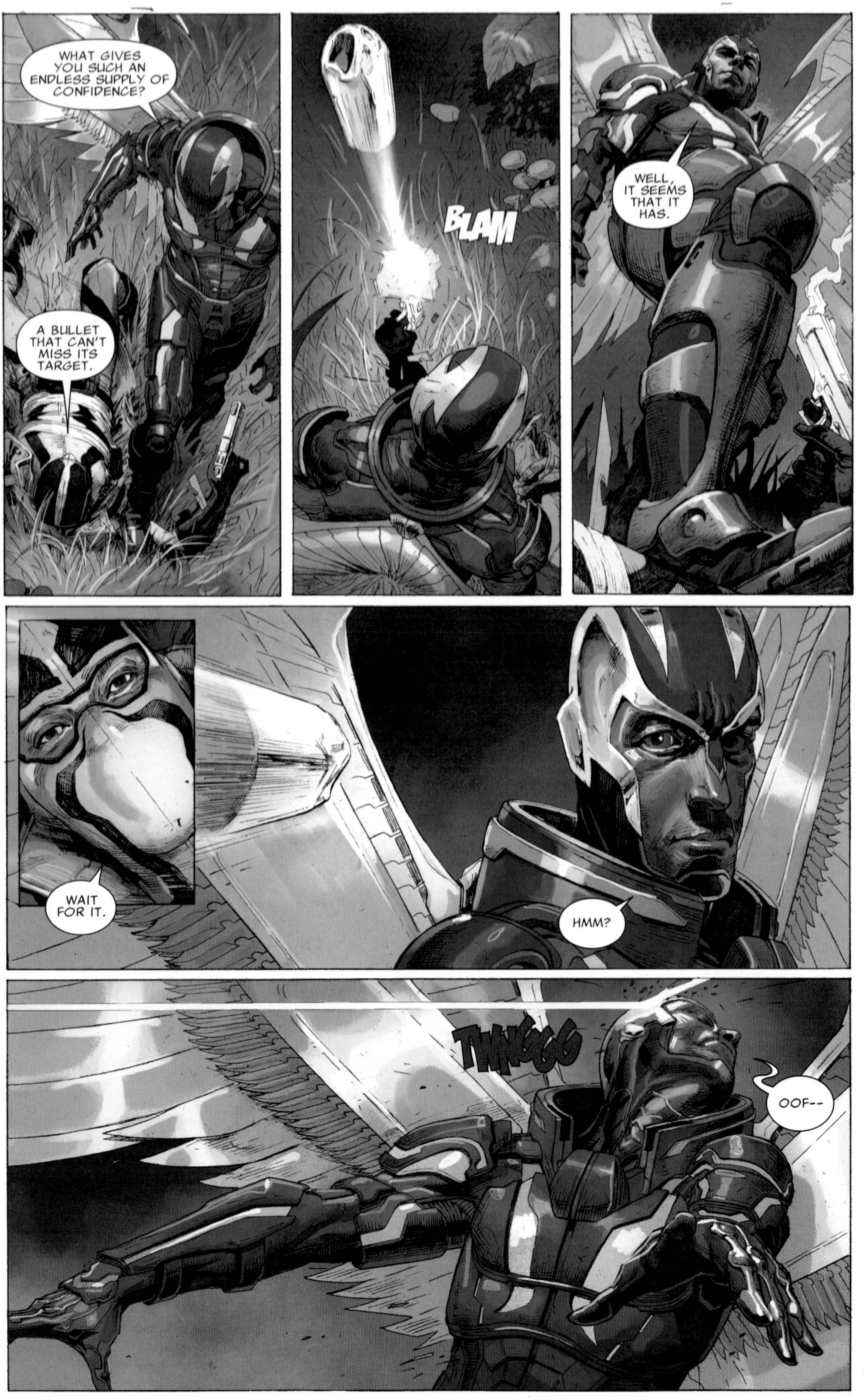
WHAT GIVES YOU SUCH AN ENDLESS SUPPLY OF CONFIDENCE?
A BULLET THAT CAN'T MISS ITS TARGET.
BLAM
WELL, IT SEEMS THAT IT HAS.
WAIT FOR IT.
HMM?
THNGGG
OOF--

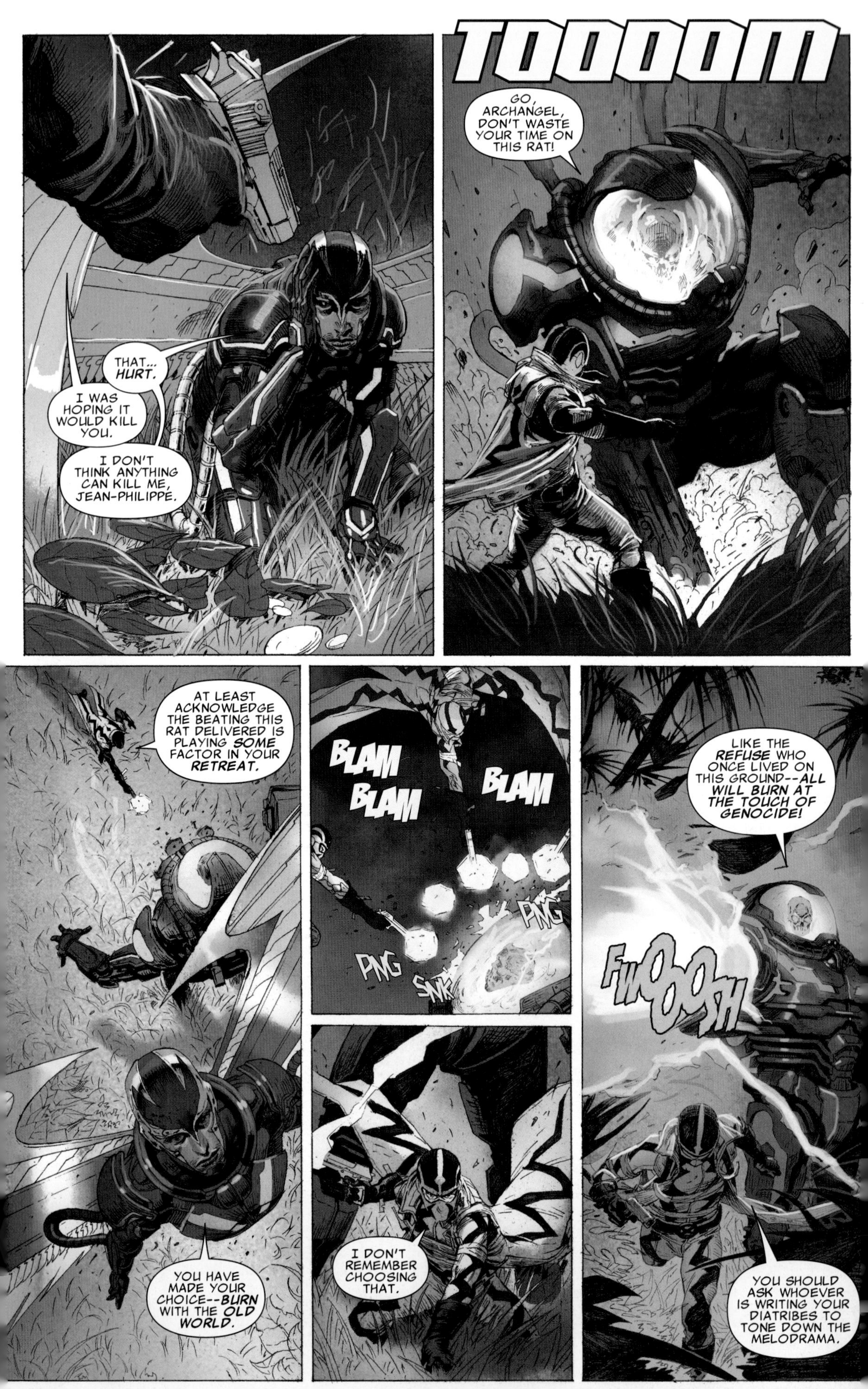
TOOOOM
THAT... HURT.
I WAS HOPING IT WOULD KILL YOU.
I DON'T THINK ANYTHING CAN KILL ME, JEAN-PHILIPPE.
GO, ARCHANGEL, DON'T WASTE YOUR TIME ON THIS RAT!
AT LEAST ACKNOWLEDGE THE BEATING THIS RAT DELIVERED IS PLAYING SOME FACTOR IN YOUR RETREAT.
YOU HAVE MADE YOUR CHOICE--BURN WITH THE OLD WORLD.
BLAM
BLAM
BLAM
PNG
PNG
SNK
I DON'T REMEMBER CHOOSING THAT.
LIKE THE REFUSE WHO ONCE LIVED ON THIS GROUND--ALL WILL BURN AT THE TOUCH OF GENOCIDE!
FWOOOSH
YOU SHOULD ASK WHOEVER IS WRITING YOUR DIATRIBES TO TONE DOWN THE MELODRAMA.

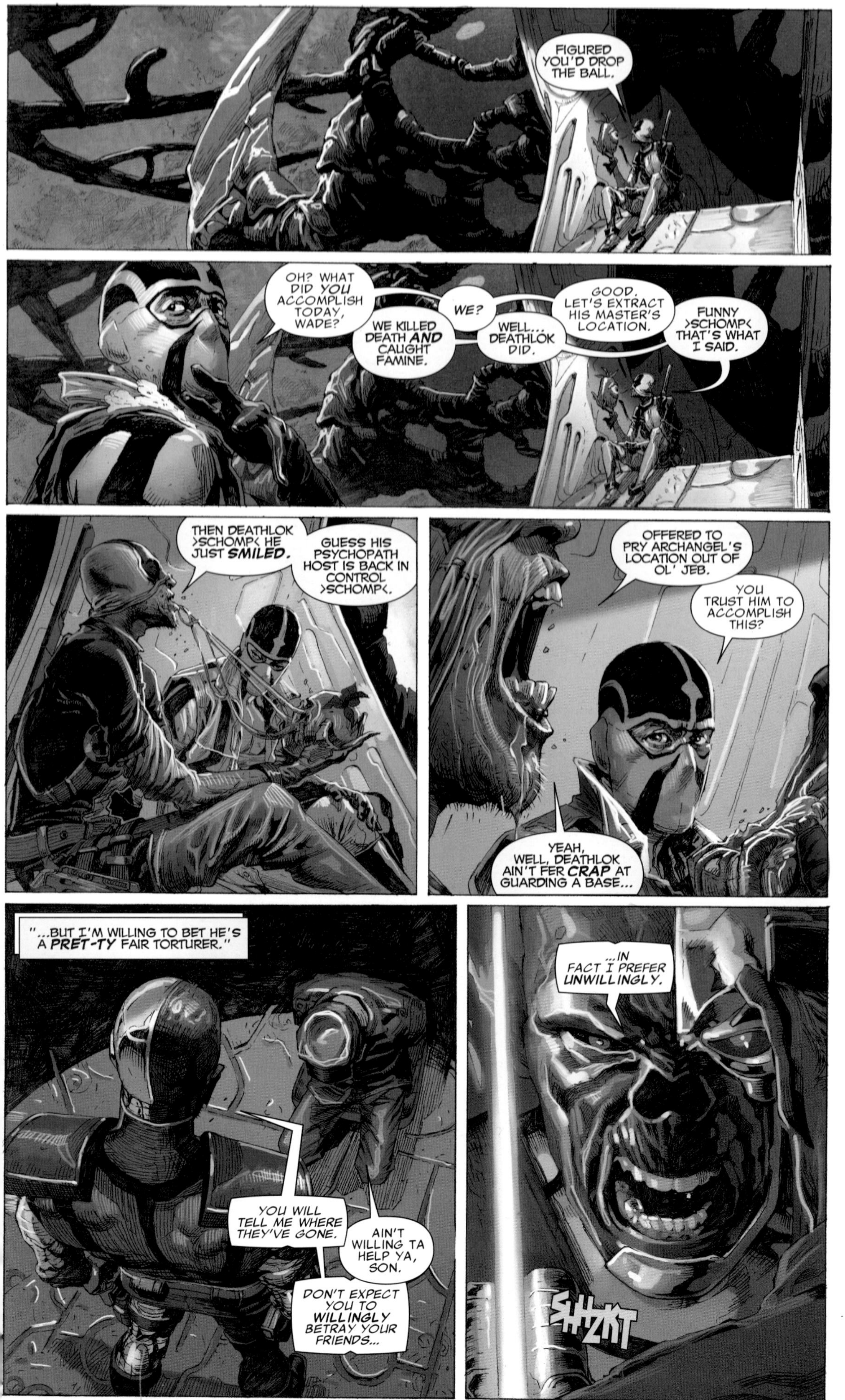
FIGURED YOU'D DROP THE BALL.
OH? WHAT DID YOU ACCOMPLISH TODAY, WADE?'
WE KILLED DEATH AND CAUGHT FAMINE.
WE?
WELL... DEATHLOK DID.
GOOD. LET'S EXTRACT HIS MASTER'S LOCATION.
FUNNY >SCHOMP< THAT'S WHAT I SAID.
THEN DEATHLOK >SCHOMP< HE JUST SMILED.
GUESS HIS PSYCHOPATH HOST IS BACK IN CONTROL >SCHOMP<.
OFFERED TO PRY ARCHANGEL'S LOCATION OUT OF OL' JEB.
YOU TRUST HIM TO ACCOMPLISH THIS?
YEAH, WELL, DEATHLOK AIN'T FER CRAP AT GUARDING A BASE...
"...BUT I'M WILLING TO BET HE'S A PRET-TY FAIR TORTURER."
YOU WILL TELL ME WHERE THEY'VE GONE.
AIN'T WILLING TA HELP YA, SON.
DON'T EXPECT YOU TO WILLINGLY BETRAY YOUR FRIENDS...
...IN FACT I PREFER UNWILLINGLY.
SHZKT

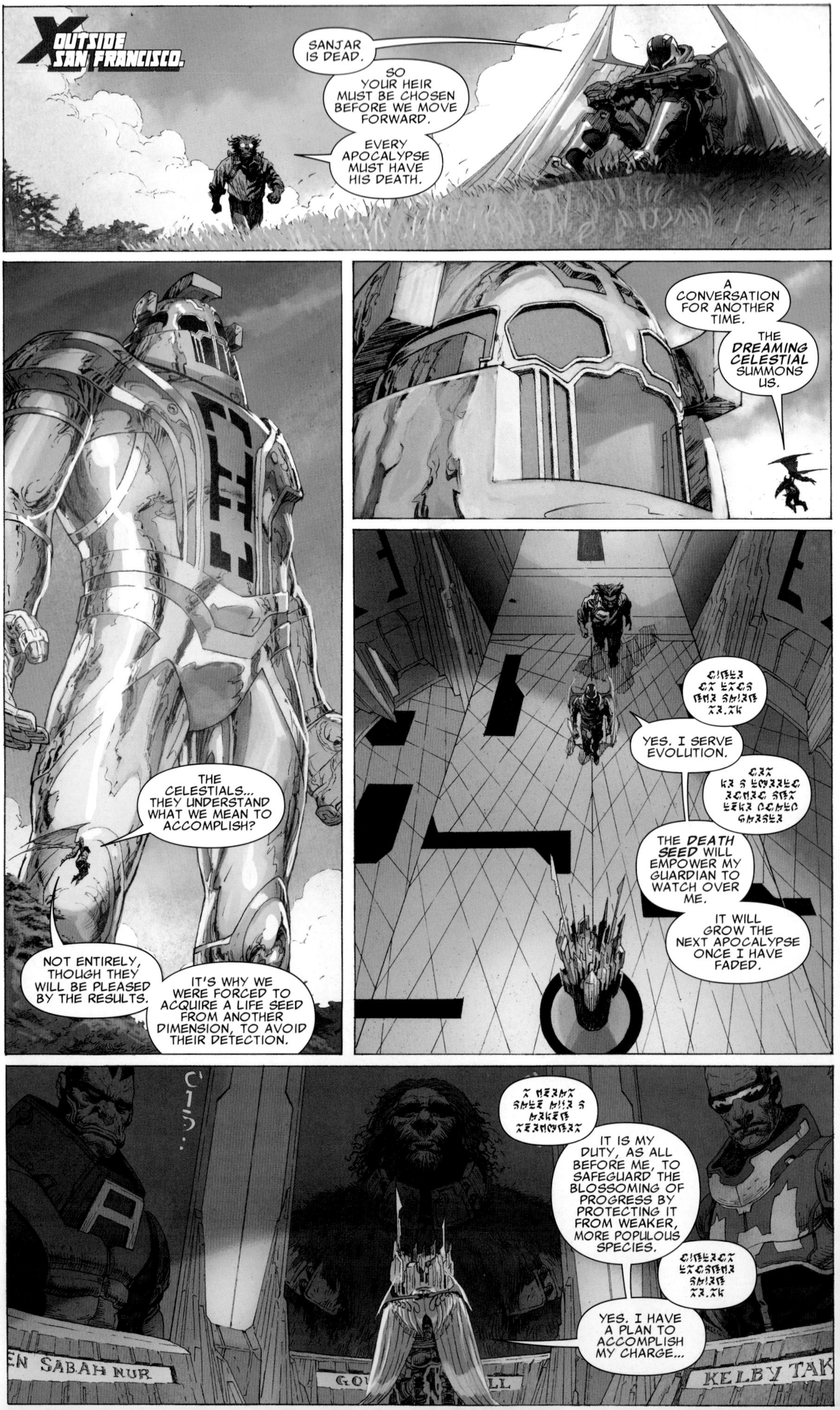
OUTSIDE SAN FRANCISCO.
SANJAR IS DEAD.
SO YOUR HEIR MUST BE CHOSEN BEFORE WE MOVE FORWARD.
EVERY APOCALYPSE MUST HAVE HIS DEATH.
THE CELESTIALS... THEY UNDERSTAND WHAT WE MEAN TO ACCOMPLISH?
NOT ENTIRELY, THOUGH THEY WILL BE PLEASED BY THE RESULTS.
IT'S WHY WE WERE FORCED TO ACQUIRE A LIFE SEED FROM ANOTHER DIMENSION, TO AVOID THEIR DETECTION.
A CONVERSATION FOR ANOTHER TIME.
THE DREAMING CELESTIAL SUMMONS US.
YES. I SERVE EVOLUTION.
THE DEATH SEED WILL EMPOWER MY GUARDIAN TO WATCH OVER ME.
IT WILL GROW THE NEXT APOCALYPSE ONCE I HAVE FADED.
IT IS MY DUTY, AS ALL BEFORE ME, TO SAFEGUARD THE BLOSSOMING OF PROGRESS BY PROTECTING IT FROM WEAKER, MORE POPULOUS SPECIES.
YES. I HAVE A PLAN TO ACCOMPLISH MY CHARGE...
EN SABAH NUR
KELBY TAK

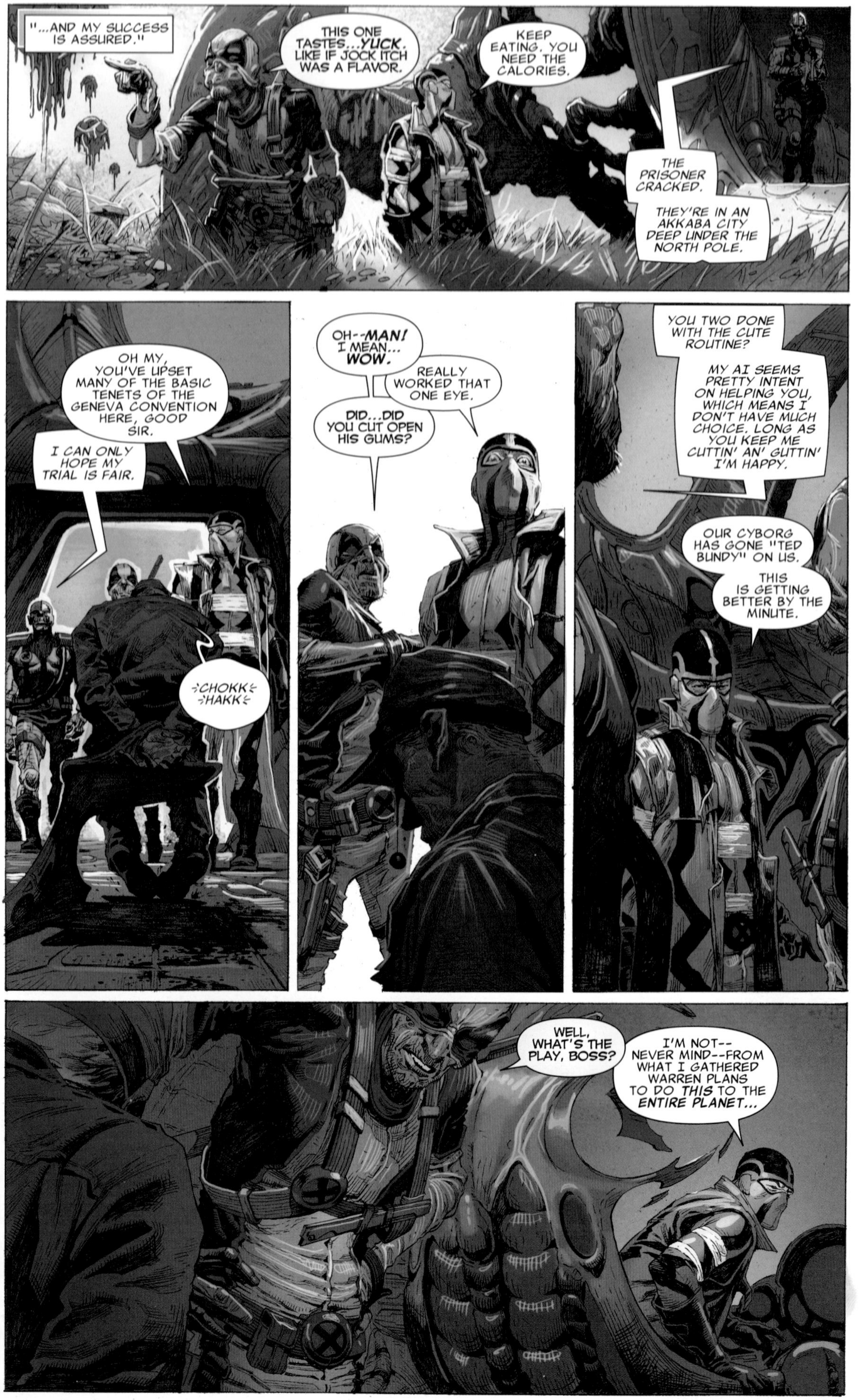
"...AND MY SUCCESS IS ASSURED."
THIS ONE TASTES...YUCK. LIKE IF JOCK ITCH WAS A FLAVOR.
KEEP EATING. YOU NEED THE CALORIES.
THE PRISONER CRACKED.
THEY'RE IN AN AKKABA CITY DEEP UNDER THE NORTH POLE.
OH MY, YOU'VE UPSET MANY OF THE BASIC TENETS OF THE GENEVA CONVENTION HERE, GOOD SIR.
I CAN ONLY HOPE MY TRIAL IS FAIR.
CHOKK HAKK
OH--MAN! I MEAN... WOW.
REALLY WORKED THAT ONE EYE.
DID...DID YOU CUT OPEN HIS GUMS?
YOU TWO DONE WITH THE CUTE ROUTINE?
MY AI SEEMS PRETTY INTENT ON HELPING YOU, WHICH MEANS I DON'T HAVE MUCH CHOICE. LONG AS YOU KEEP ME CUTTIN' AN' GUTTIN' I'M HAPPY.
OUR CYBORG HAS GONE "TED BUNDY" ON US.
THIS IS GETTING BETTER BY THE MINUTE.
WELL, WHAT'S THE PLAY, BOSS?
I'M NOT--NEVER MIND--FROM WHAT I GATHERED WARREN PLANS TO DO THIS TO THE ENTIRE PLANET...

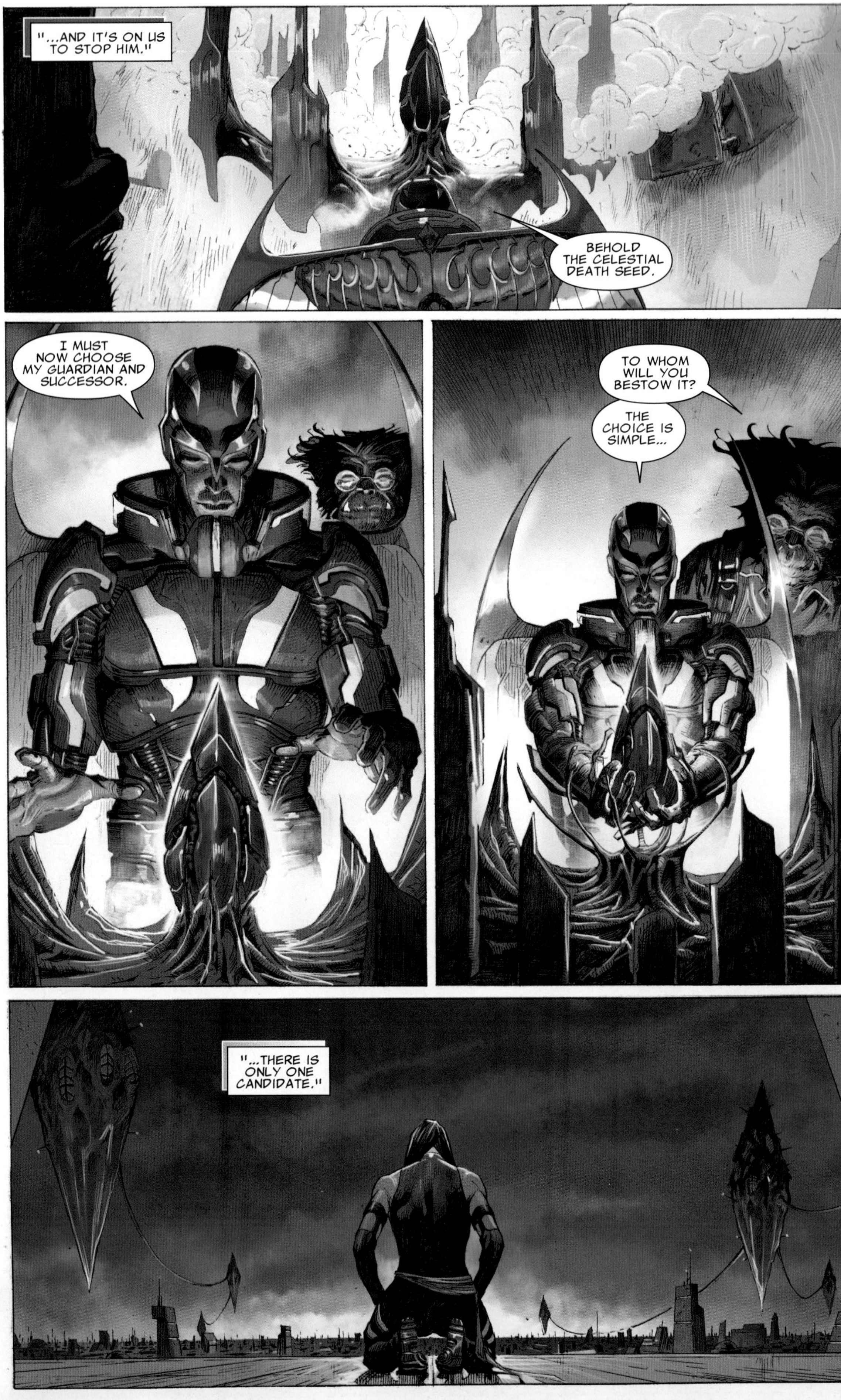
"...AND IT'S ON US TO STOP HIM."
BEHOLD THE CELESTIAL DEATH SEED.
I MUST NOW CHOOSE MY GUARDIAN AND SUCCESSOR.
TO WHOM WILL YOU BESTOW IT?
THE CHOICE IS SIMPLE...
"...THERE IS ONLY ONE CANDIDATE."

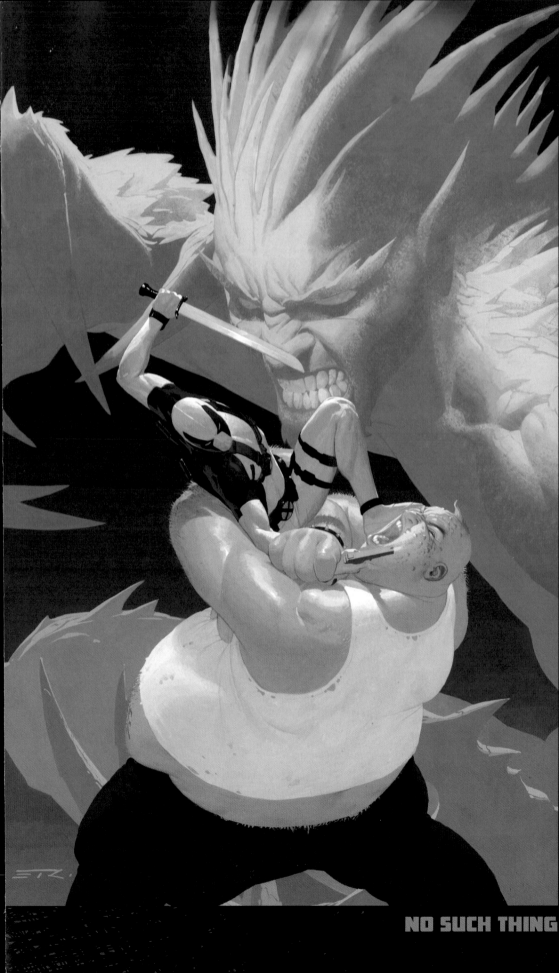

NO SUCH THING

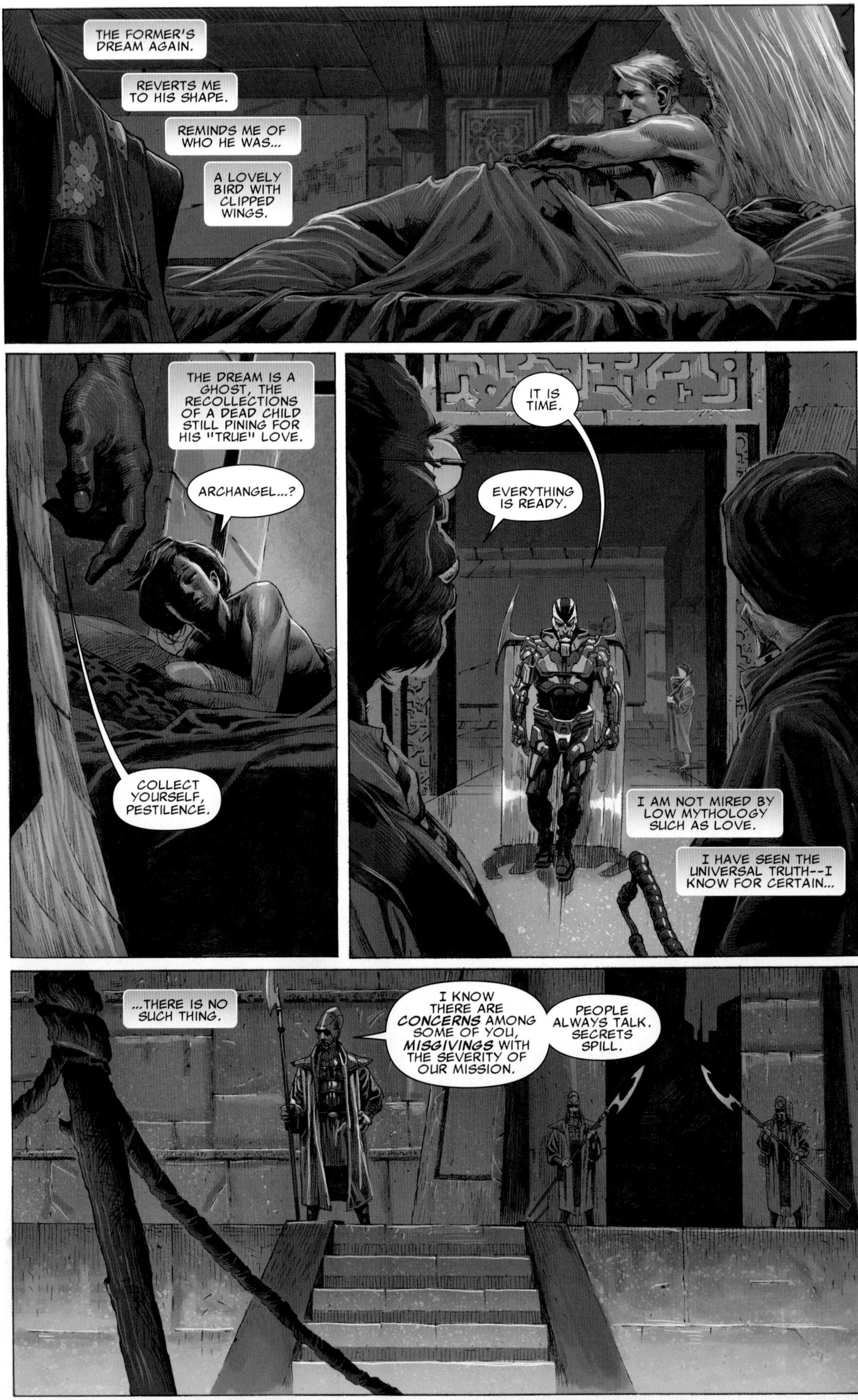
THE FORMER'S DREAM AGAIN.
REVERTS ME TO HIS SHAPE.
REMINDS ME OF WHO HE WAS...
A LOVELY BIRD WITH CLIPPED WINGS.
THE DREAM IS A GHOST, THE RECOLLECTIONS OF A DEAD CHILD STILL PINING FOR HIS "TRUE" LOVE.
ARCHANGEL...?
COLLECT YOURSELF, PESTILENCE.
IT IS TIME.
EVERYTHING IS READY.
I AM NOT MIRED BY LOW MYTHOLOGY SUCH AS LOVE.
I HAVE SEEN THE UNIVERSAL TRUTH--I KNOW FOR CERTAIN...
...THERE IS NO SUCH THING.
I KNOW THERE ARE CONCERNS AMONG SOME OF YOU, MISGIVINGS WITH THE SEVERITY OF OUR MISSION.
PEOPLE ALWAYS TALK. SECRETS SPILL.

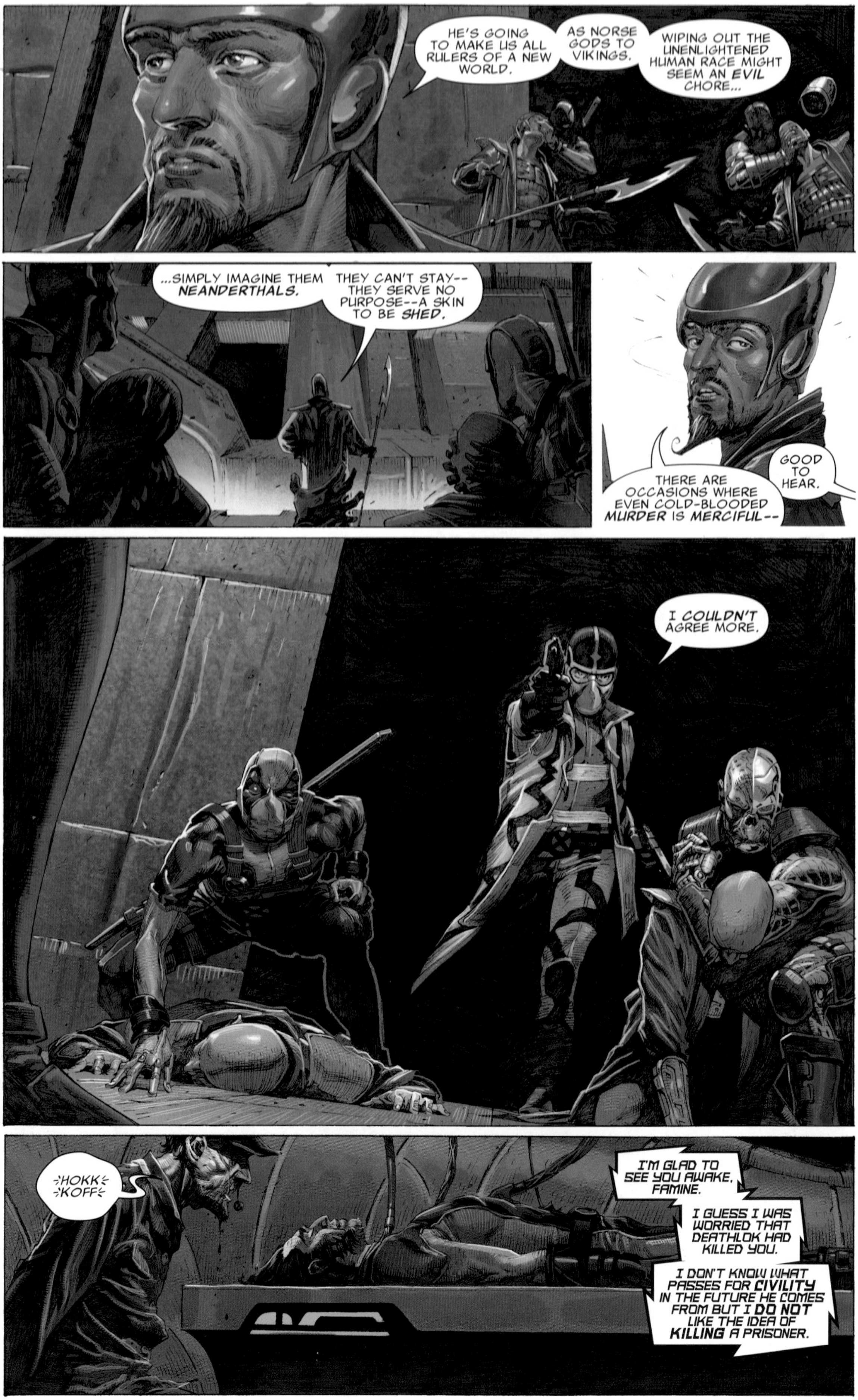
HE'S GOING TO MAKE US ALL RULERS OF A NEW WORLD.
AS NORSE GODS TO VIKINGS.
WIPING OUT THE UNENLIGHTENED HUMAN RACE MIGHT SEEM AN EVIL CHORE...
...SIMPLY IMAGINE THEM NEANDERTHALS.
THEY CAN'T STAY--THEY SERVE NO PURPOSE--A SKIN TO BE SHED.
THERE ARE OCCASIONS WHERE EVEN COLD-BLOODED MURDER IS MERCIFUL--
GOOD TO HEAR.
I COULDN'T AGREE MORE.
HOKK KOFF
I'M GLAD TO SEE YOU AWAKE, FAMINE.
I GUESS I WAS WORRIED THAT DEATHLOK HAD KILLED YOU.
I DON'T KNOW WHAT PASSES FOR CIVILITY IN THE FUTURE HE COMES FROM BUT I DO NOT LIKE THE IDEA OF KILLING A PRISONER.

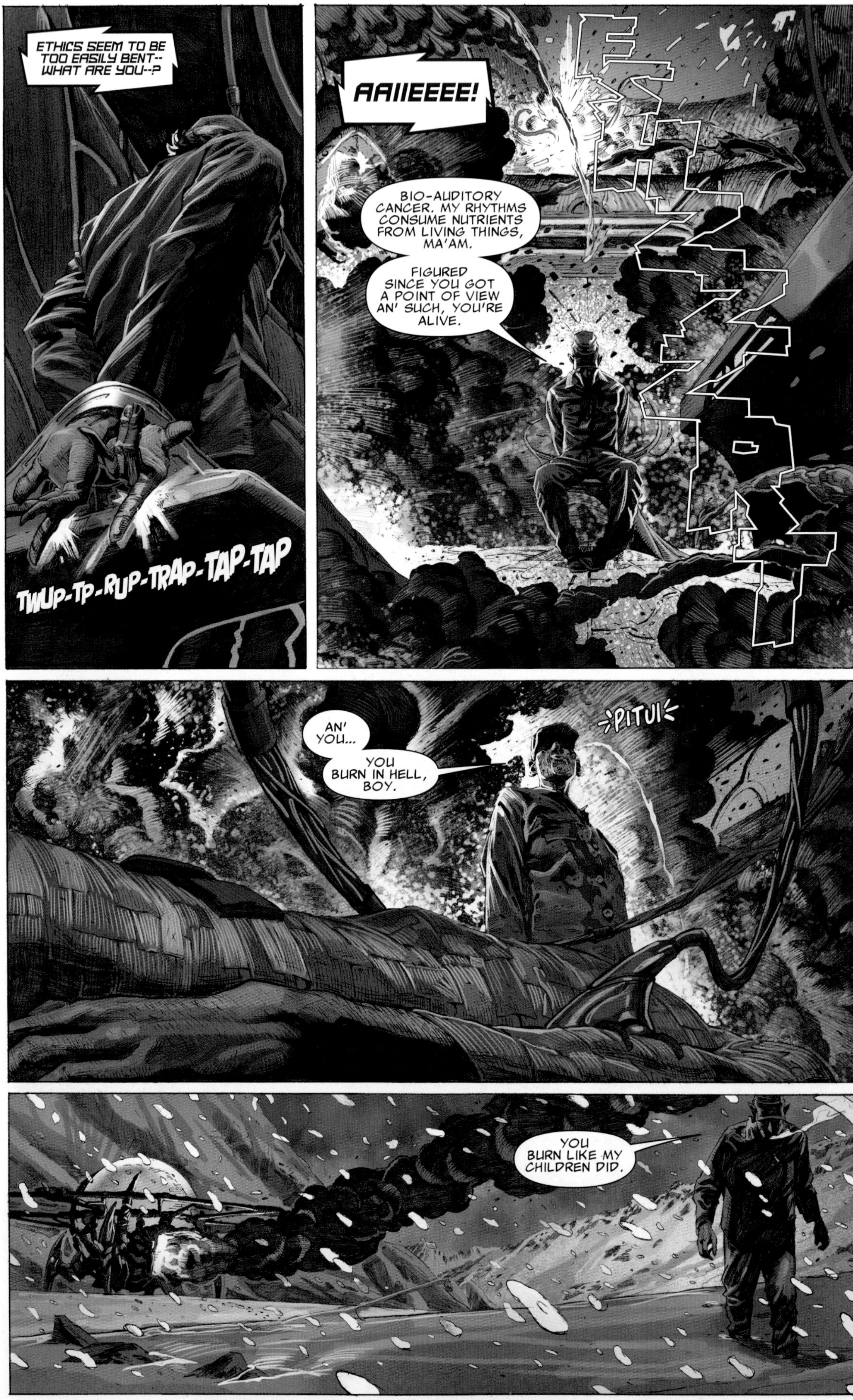
ETHICS SEEM TO BE TOO EASILY BENT-- WHAT ARE YOU--?
TWUP-TP-RUP-TRAP-TAP-TAP
AAIIEEEE!
BIO-AUDITORY CANCER. MY RHYTHMS CONSUME NUTRIENTS FROM LIVING THINGS, MA'AM.
FIGURED SINCE YOU GOT A POINT OF VIEW AN' SUCH, YOU'RE ALIVE.
AN' YOU...
YOU BURN IN HELL, BOY.
PITUI
YOU BURN LIKE MY CHILDREN DID.

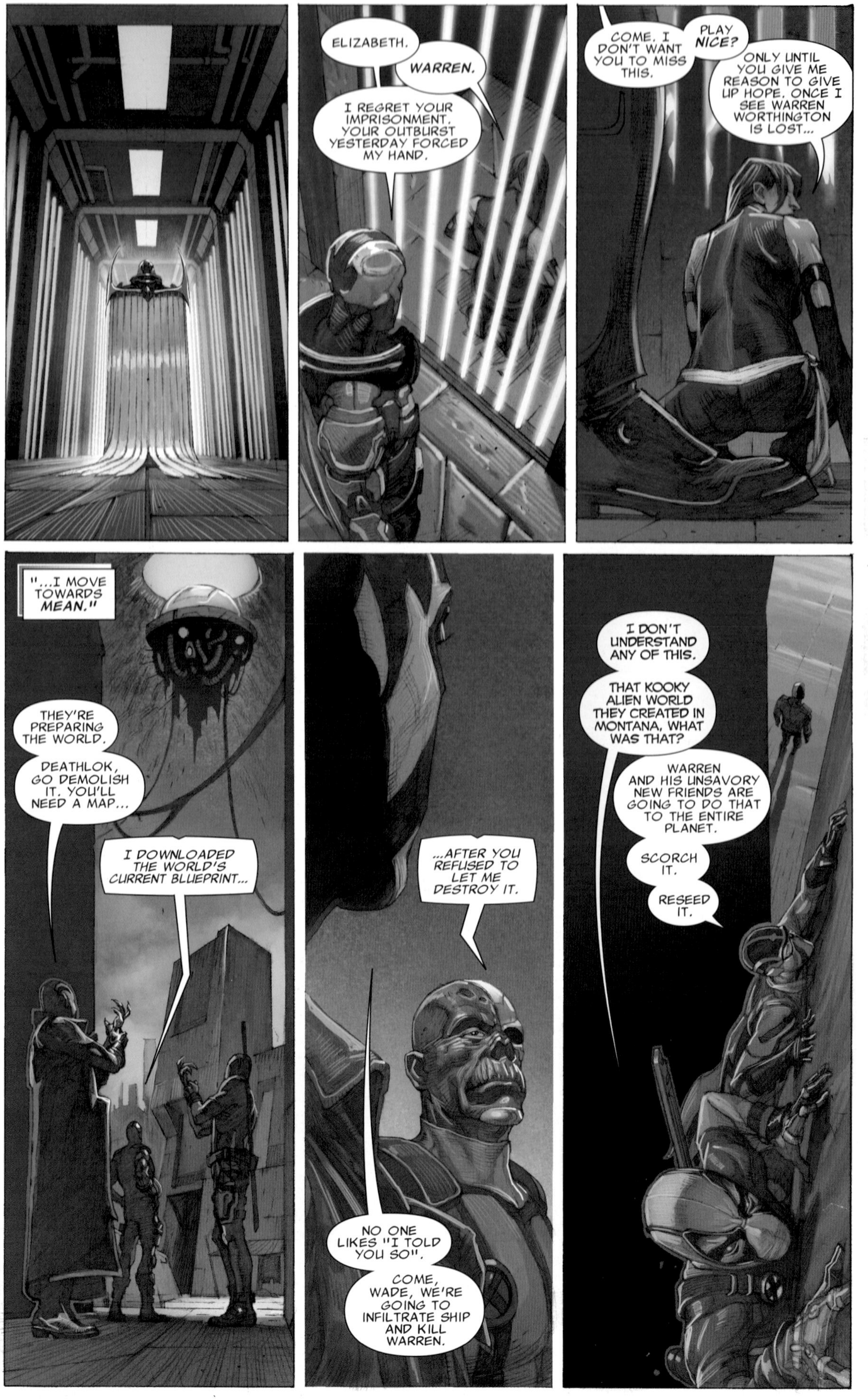
ELIZABETH.
WARREN.
I REGRET YOUR IMPRISONMENT. YOUR OUTBURST YESTERDAY FORCED MY HAND.
COME. I DON'T WANT YOU TO MISS THIS.
PLAY NICE?
ONLY UNTIL YOU GIVE ME REASON TO GIVE UP HOPE. ONCE I SEE WARREN WORTHINGTON IS LOST...
"...I MOVE TOWARDS MEAN."
THEY'RE PREPARING THE WORLD.
DEATHLOK, GO DEMOLISH IT. YOU'LL NEED A MAP...
I DOWNLOADED THE WORLD'S CURRENT BLUEPRINT...
...AFTER YOU REFUSED TO LET ME DESTROY IT.
NO ONE LIKES "I TOLD YOU SO".
COME, WADE, WE'RE GOING TO INFILTRATE SHIP AND KILL WARREN.
I DON'T UNDERSTAND ANY OF THIS.
THAT KOOKY ALIEN WORLD THEY CREATED IN MONTANA, WHAT WAS THAT?
WARREN AND HIS UNSAVORY NEW FRIENDS ARE GOING TO DO THAT TO THE ENTIRE PLANET.
SCORCH IT.
RESEED IT.

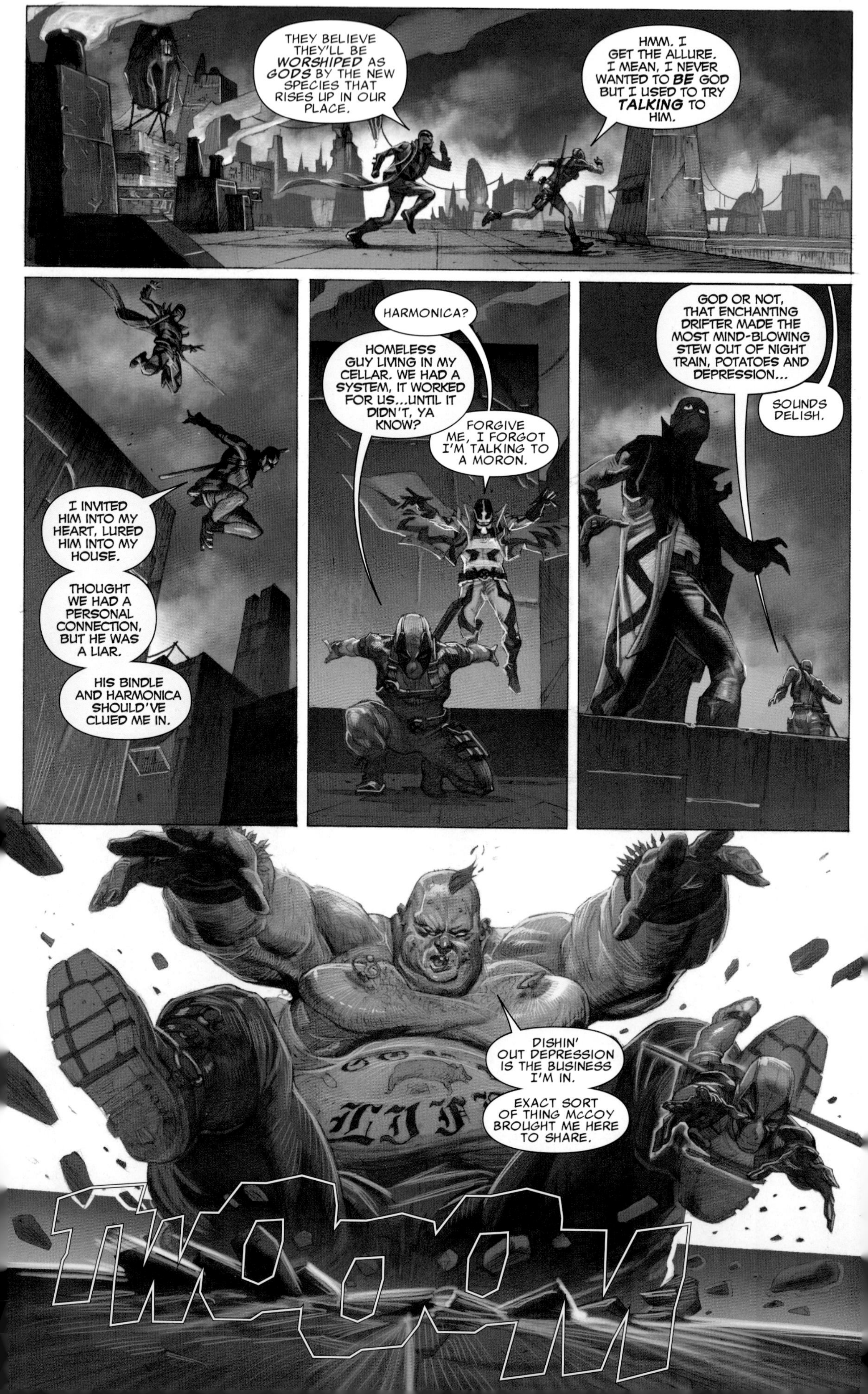
THEY BELIEVE THEY'LL BE WORSHIPED AS GODS BY THE NEW SPECIES THAT RISES UP IN OUR PLACE.
HMM. I GET THE ALLURE. I MEAN, I NEVER WANTED TO BE GOD BUT I USED TO TRY TALKING TO HIM.
I INVITED HIM INTO MY HEART, LURED HIM INTO MY HOUSE.
THOUGHT WE HAD A PERSONAL CONNECTION, BUT HE WAS A LIAR.
HIS BINDLE AND HARMONICA SHOULD'VE CLUED ME IN.
HARMONICA?
HOMELESS GUY LIVING IN MY CELLAR. WE HAD A SYSTEM, IT WORKED FOR US...UNTIL IT DIDN'T, YA KNOW?
FORGIVE ME, I FORGOT I'M TALKING TO A MORON.
GOD OR NOT, THAT ENCHANTING DRIFTER MADE THE MOST MIND-BLOWING STEW OUT OF NIGHT TRAIN, POTATOES AND DEPRESSION...
SOUNDS DELISH.
DISHIN' OUT DEPRESSION IS THE BUSINESS I'M IN.
EXACT SORT OF THING McCOY BROUGHT ME HERE TO SHARE.
TKOOOM

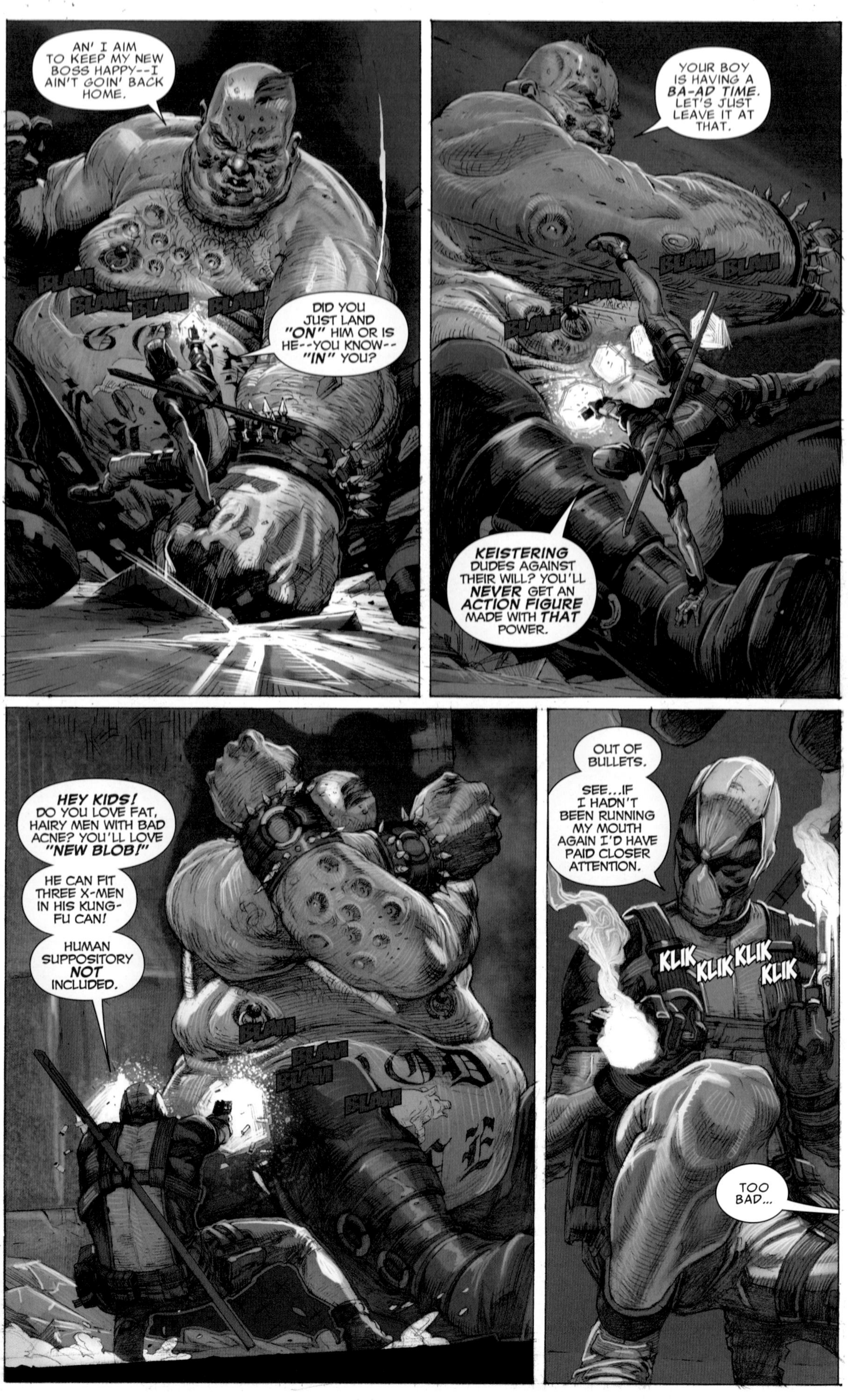
AN' I AIM TO KEEP MY NEW BOSS HAPPY--I AIN'T GOIN' BACK HOME.
BLAM BLAM BLAM BLAM
DID YOU JUST LAND "ON" HIM OR IS HE--YOU KNOW--"IN" YOU?
YOUR BOY IS HAVING A BA-AD TIME. LET'S JUST LEAVE IT AT THAT.
BLAM BLAM BLAM BLAM
KEISTERING DUDES AGAINST THEIR WILL? YOU'LL NEVER GET AN ACTION FIGURE MADE WITH THAT POWER.
HEY KIDS! DO YOU LOVE FAT, HAIRY MEN WITH BAD ACNE? YOU'LL LOVE "NEW BLOB!"
HE CAN FIT THREE X-MEN IN HIS KUNG-FU CAN!
HUMAN SUPPOSITORY NOT INCLUDED.
BLAM BLAM BLAM BLAM
OUT OF BULLETS.
SEE...IF I HADN'T BEEN RUNNING MY MOUTH AGAIN I'D HAVE PAID CLOSER ATTENTION.
KLIK KLIK KLIK KLIK
TOO BAD...

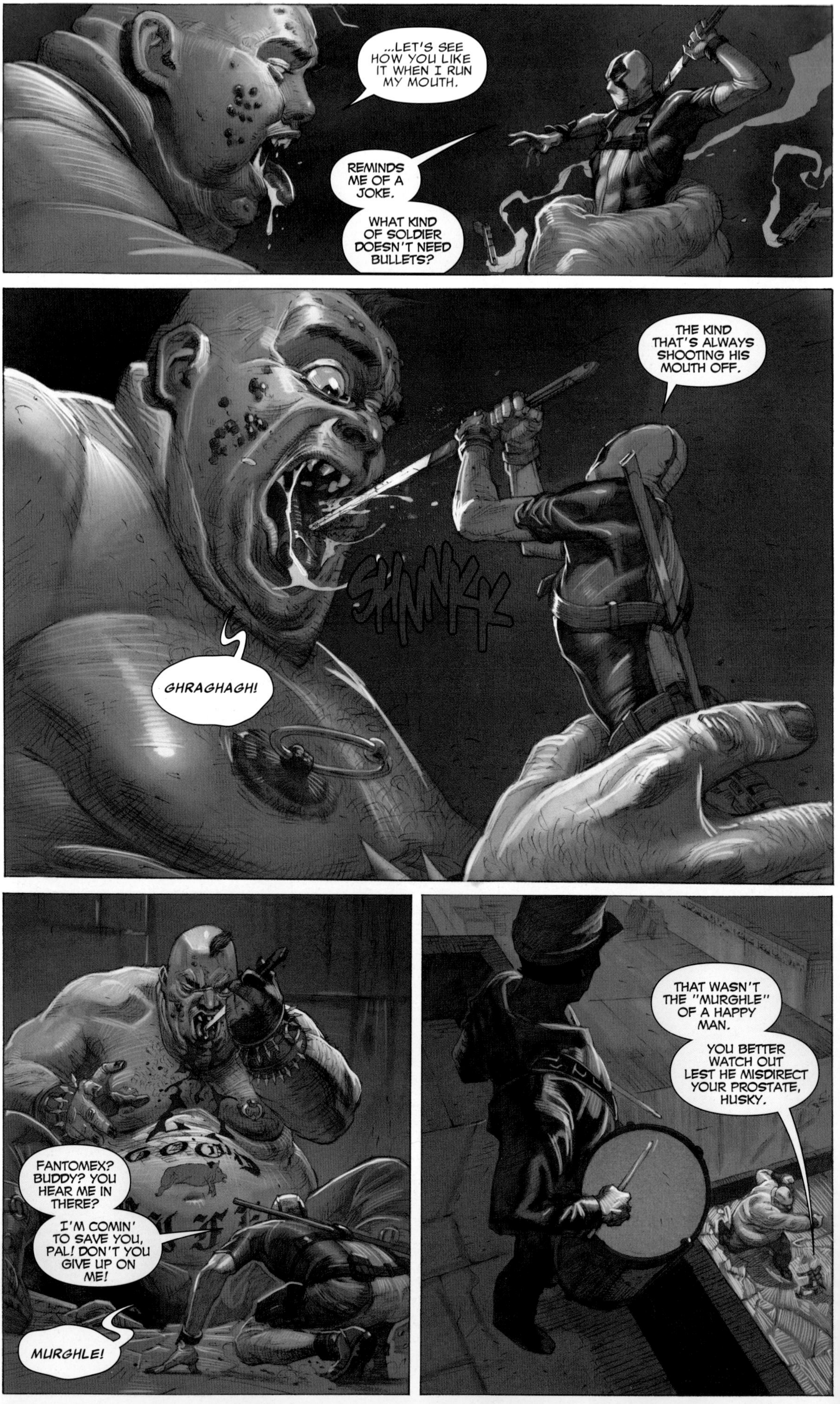
...LET'S SEE HOW YOU LIKE IT WHEN I RUN MY MOUTH.
REMINDS ME OF A JOKE.
WHAT KIND OF SOLDIER DOESN'T NEED BULLETS?
THE KIND THAT'S ALWAYS SHOOTING HIS MOUTH OFF.
SHNNKK
GHRAGHAGH!
FANTOMEX? BUDDY? YOU HEAR ME IN THERE?
I'M COMIN' TO SAVE YOU, PAL! DON'T YOU GIVE UP ON ME!
MURGHLE!
THAT WASN'T THE "MURGHLE" OF A HAPPY MAN.
YOU BETTER WATCH OUT LEST HE MISDIRECT YOUR PROSTATE, HUSKY.

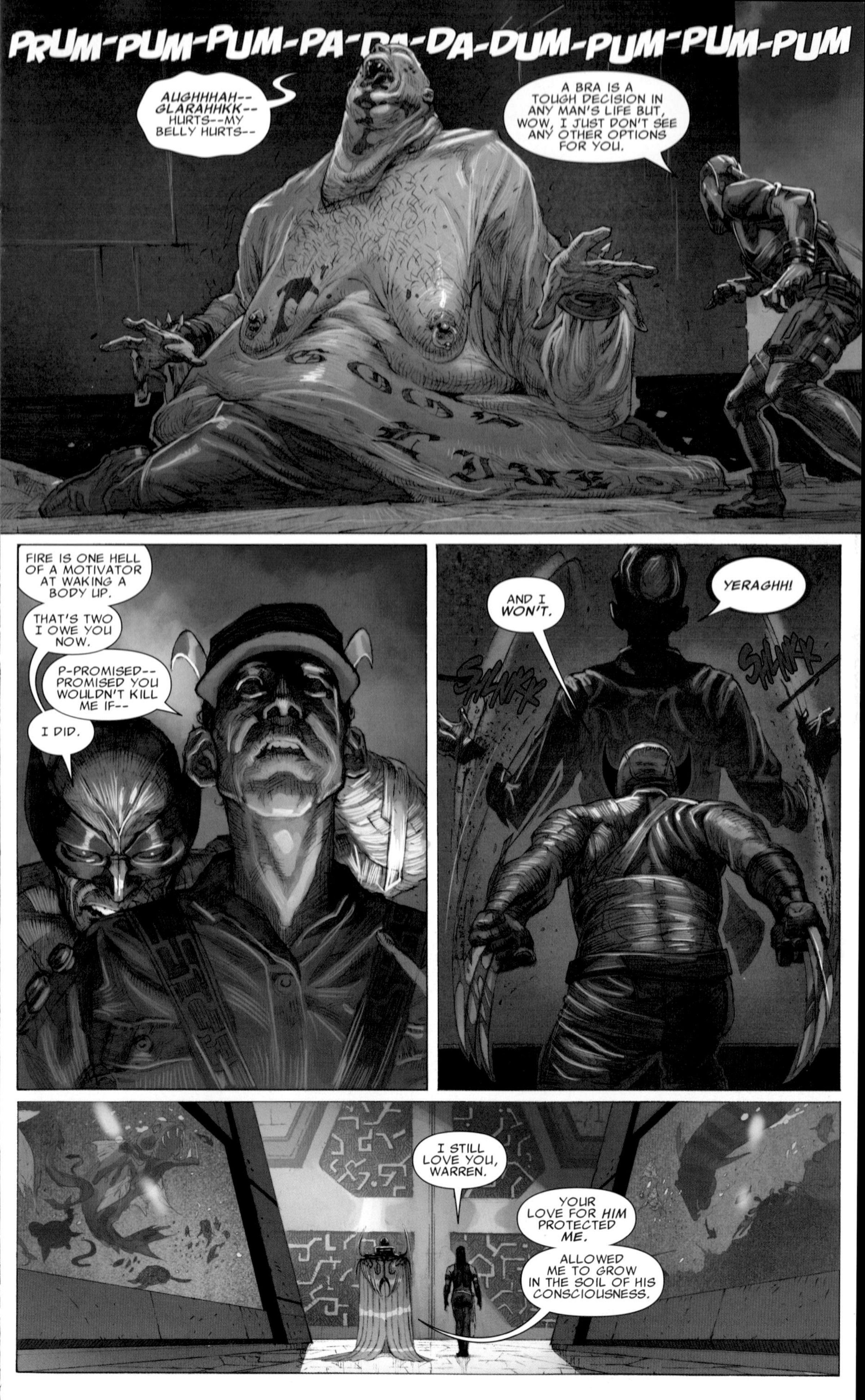
PRUM-PUM-PUM-PA-DA-DA-DUM-PUM-PUM-PUM
AUGHHHAH-- GLARAHHKK-- HURTS--MY BELLY HURTS--
A BRA IS A TOUGH DECISION IN ANY MAN'S LIFE BUT, WOW, I JUST DON'T SEE ANY OTHER OPTIONS FOR YOU.
FIRE IS ONE HELL OF A MOTIVATOR AT WAKING A BODY UP.
THAT'S TWO I OWE YOU NOW.
P-PROMISED-- PROMISED YOU WOULDN'T KILL ME IF--
I DID.
AND I WON'T.
YERAGHH!
SNIKT
SNIKT
I STILL LOVE YOU, WARREN.
YOUR LOVE FOR HIM PROTECTED ME.
ALLOWED ME TO GROW IN THE SOIL OF HIS CONSCIOUSNESS.

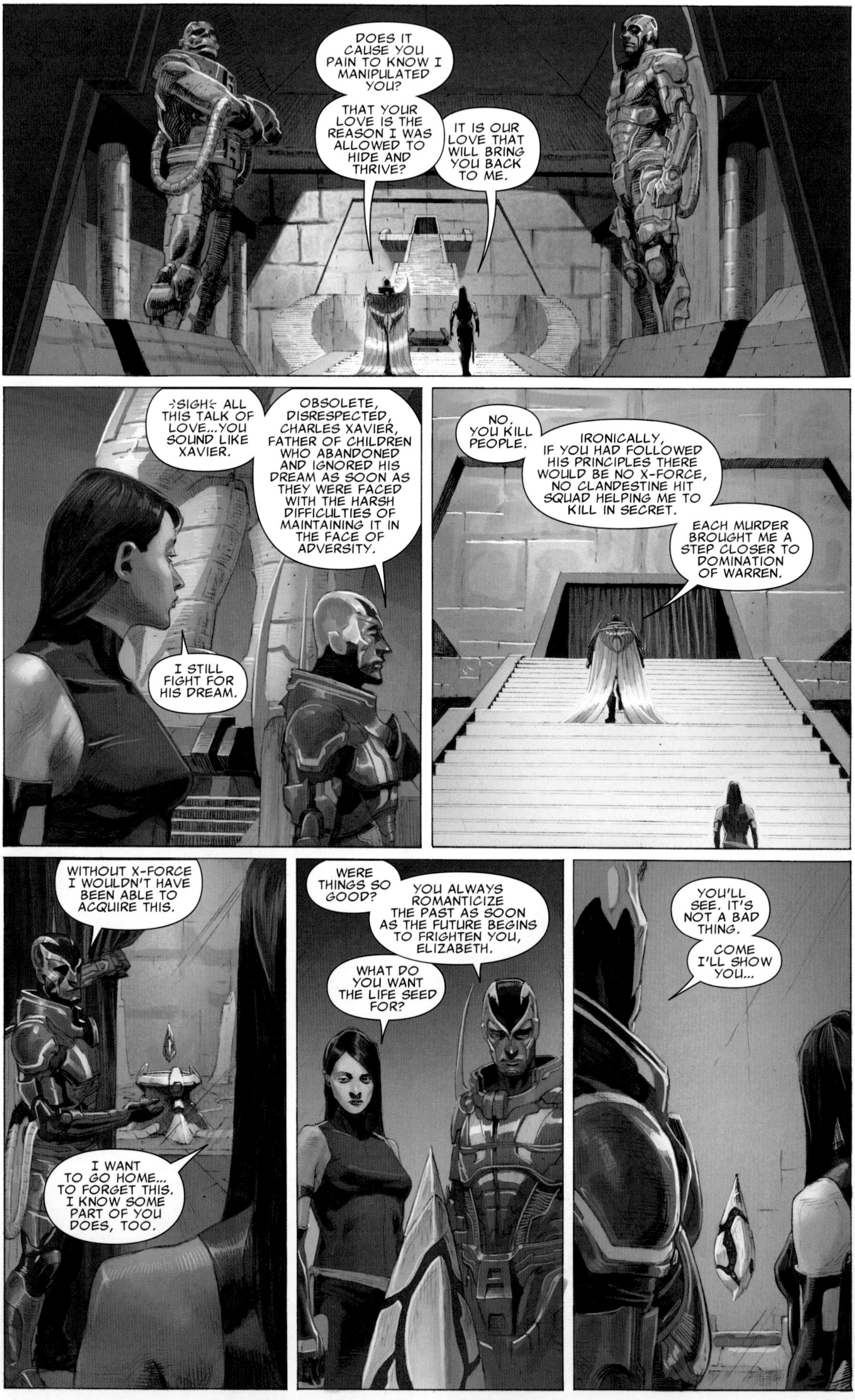
DOES IT CAUSE YOU PAIN TO KNOW I MANIPULATED YOU?
THAT YOUR LOVE IS THE REASON I WAS ALLOWED TO HIDE AND THRIVE?
IT IS OUR LOVE THAT WILL BRING YOU BACK TO ME.
SIGH ALL THIS TALK OF LOVE...YOU SOUND LIKE XAVIER.
OBSOLETE, DISRESPECTED, CHARLES XAVIER, FATHER OF CHILDREN WHO ABANDONED AND IGNORED HIS DREAM AS SOON AS THEY WERE FACED WITH THE HARSH DIFFICULTIES OF MAINTAINING IT IN THE FACE OF ADVERSITY.
I STILL FIGHT FOR HIS DREAM.
NO. YOU KILL PEOPLE.
IRONICALLY, IF YOU HAD FOLLOWED HIS PRINCIPLES THERE WOULD BE NO X-FORCE, NO CLANDESTINE HIT SQUAD HELPING ME TO KILL IN SECRET.
EACH MURDER BROUGHT ME A STEP CLOSER TO DOMINATION OF WARREN.
WITHOUT X-FORCE I WOULDN'T HAVE BEEN ABLE TO ACQUIRE THIS.
I WANT TO GO HOME... TO FORGET THIS. I KNOW SOME PART OF YOU DOES, TOO.
WERE THINGS SO GOOD?
YOU ALWAYS ROMANTICIZE THE PAST AS SOON AS THE FUTURE BEGINS TO FRIGHTEN YOU, ELIZABETH.
WHAT DO YOU WANT THE LIFE SEED FOR?
YOU'LL SEE. IT'S NOT A BAD THING.
COME I'LL SHOW YOU...

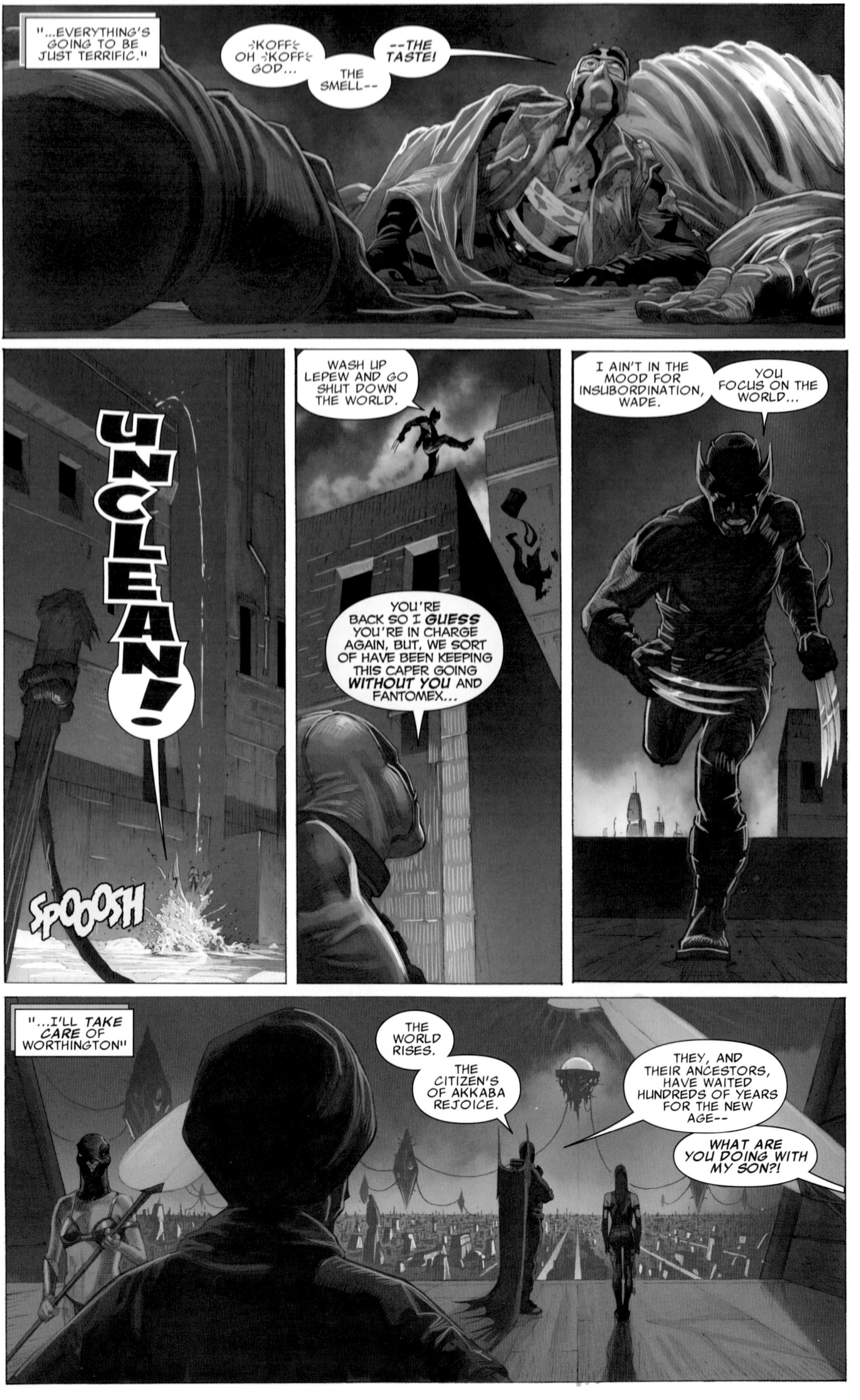

"...EVERYTHING'S GOING TO BE JUST TERRIFIC."
KOFF OH *KOFF* GOD...
THE SMELL--
--THE TASTE!
UNCLEAN!
SPOOOSH
WASH UP LEPEW AND GO SHUT DOWN THE WORLD.
YOU'RE BACK SO I GUESS YOU'RE IN CHARGE AGAIN, BUT, WE SORT OF HAVE BEEN KEEPING THIS CAPER GOING WITHOUT YOU AND FANTOMEX...
I AIN'T IN THE MOOD FOR INSUBORDINATION, WADE.
YOU FOCUS ON THE WORLD...
"...I'LL TAKE CARE OF WORTHINGTON"
THE WORLD RISES.
THE CITIZEN'S OF AKKABA REJOICE.
THEY, AND THEIR ANCESTORS, HAVE WAITED HUNDREDS OF YEARS FOR THE NEW AGE--
WHAT ARE YOU DOING WITH MY SON?!

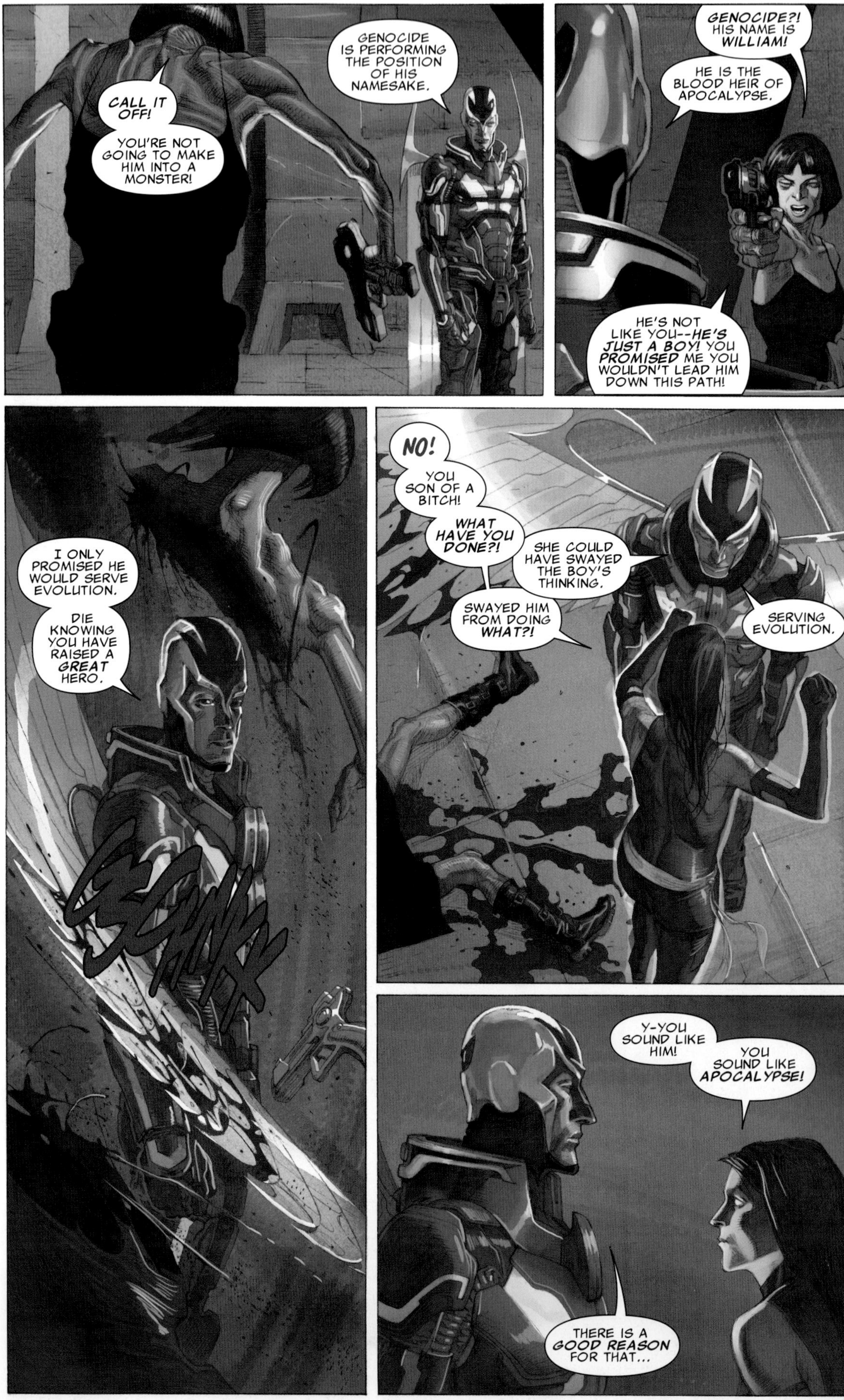
CALL IT OFF!
YOU'RE NOT GOING TO MAKE HIM INTO A MONSTER!
GENOCIDE IS PERFORMING THE POSITION OF HIS NAMESAKE.
GENOCIDE?! HIS NAME IS WILLIAM!
HE IS THE BLOOD HEIR OF APOCALYPSE.
HE'S NOT LIKE YOU--HE'S JUST A BOY! YOU PROMISED ME YOU WOULDN'T LEAD HIM DOWN THIS PATH!
I ONLY PROMISED HE WOULD SERVE EVOLUTION.
DIE KNOWING YOU HAVE RAISED A GREAT HERO.
NO!
YOU SON OF A BITCH!
WHAT HAVE YOU DONE?!
SHE COULD HAVE SWAYED THE BOY'S THINKING.
SWAYED HIM FROM DOING WHAT?!
SERVING EVOLUTION.
Y-YOU SOUND LIKE HIM!
YOU SOUND LIKE APOCALYPSE!
THERE IS A GOOD REASON FOR THAT...

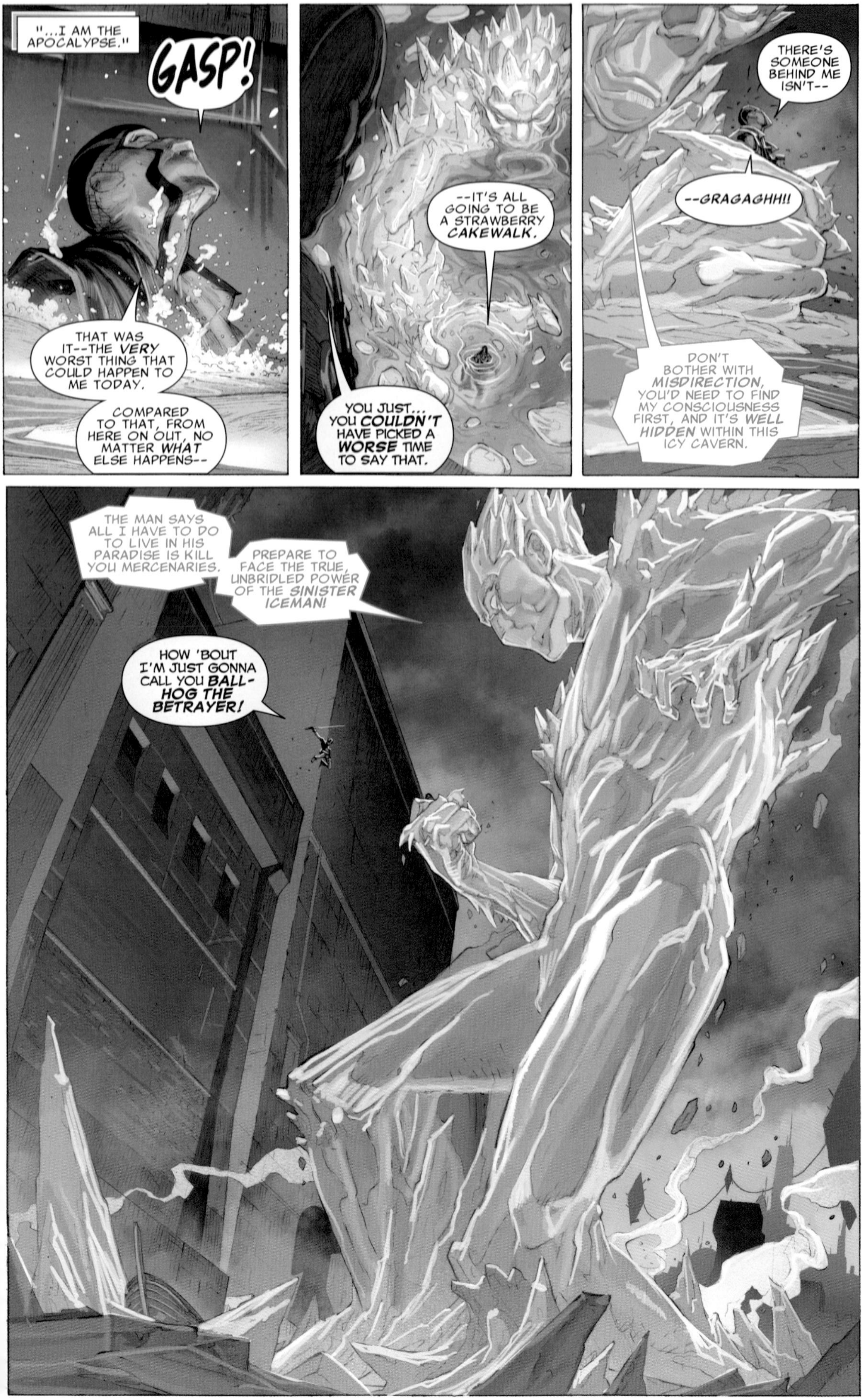
"...I AM THE APOCALYPSE."
GASP!
THAT WAS IT--THE VERY WORST THING THAT COULD HAPPEN TO ME TODAY.
COMPARED TO THAT, FROM HERE ON OUT, NO MATTER WHAT ELSE HAPPENS--
--IT'S ALL GOING TO BE A STRAWBERRY CAKEWALK.
YOU JUST... YOU COULDN'T HAVE PICKED A WORSE TIME TO SAY THAT.
THERE'S SOMEONE BEHIND ME ISN'T--
--GRAGAGHH!!
DON'T BOTHER WITH MISDIRECTION, YOU'D NEED TO FIND MY CONSCIOUSNESS FIRST, AND IT'S WELL HIDDEN WITHIN THIS ICY CAVERN.
THE MAN SAYS ALL I HAVE TO DO TO LIVE IN HIS PARADISE IS KILL YOU MERCENARIES.
PREPARE TO FACE THE TRUE, UNBRIDLED POWER OF THE SINISTER ICEMAN!
HOW 'BOUT I'M JUST GONNA CALL YOU BALL-HOG THE BETRAYER!

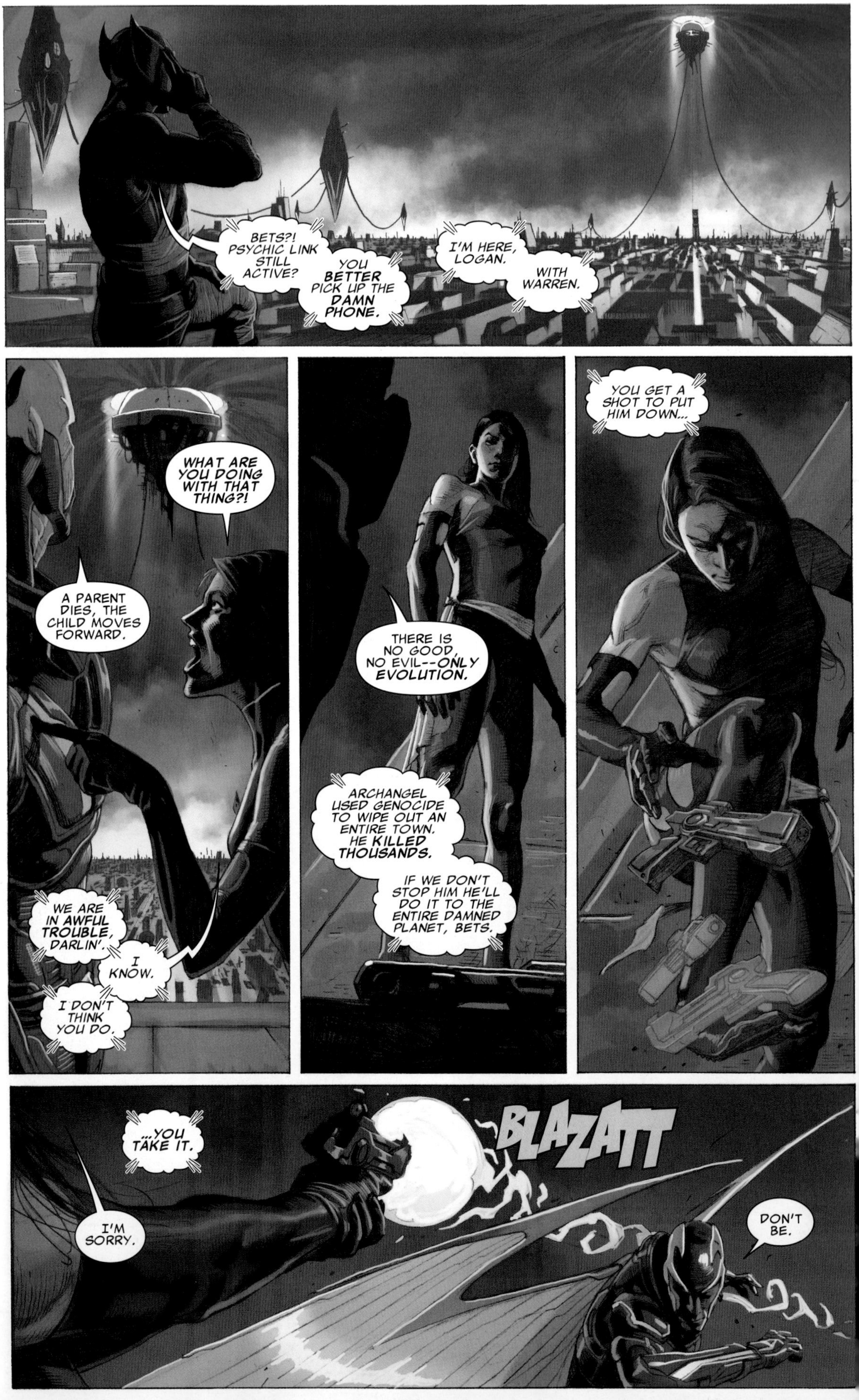
BETS?! PSYCHIC LINK STILL ACTIVE?
YOU BETTER PICK UP THE DAMN PHONE.
I'M HERE, LOGAN.
WITH WARREN.
WHAT ARE YOU DOING WITH THAT THING?!
A PARENT DIES, THE CHILD MOVES FORWARD.
WE ARE IN AWFUL TROUBLE, DARLIN'.
I KNOW.
I DON'T THINK YOU DO.
THERE IS NO GOOD, NO EVIL--ONLY EVOLUTION.
ARCHANGEL USED GENOCIDE TO WIPE OUT AN ENTIRE TOWN. HE KILLED THOUSANDS.
IF WE DON'T STOP HIM HE'LL DO IT TO THE ENTIRE DAMNED PLANET, BETS.
YOU GET A SHOT TO PUT HIM DOWN...
...YOU TAKE IT.
I'M SORRY.
BLAZATT
DON'T BE.

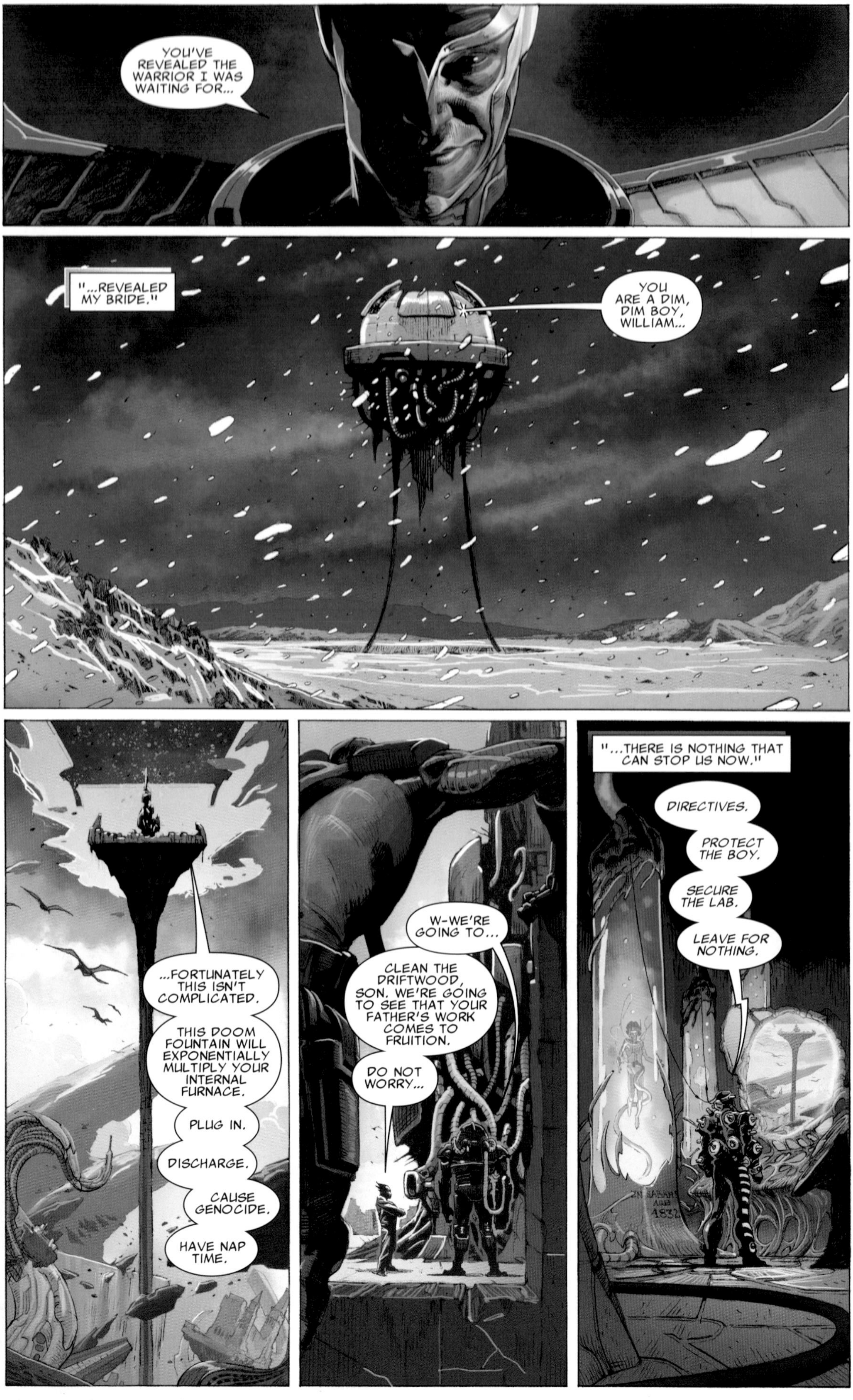
YOU'VE REVEALED THE WARRIOR I WAS WAITING FOR...
"...REVEALED MY BRIDE."
YOU ARE A DIM, DIM BOY, WILLIAM...
...FORTUNATELY THIS ISN'T COMPLICATED.
THIS DOOM FOUNTAIN WILL EXPONENTIALLY MULTIPLY YOUR INTERNAL FURNACE.
PLUG IN.
DISCHARGE.
CAUSE GENOCIDE.
HAVE NAP TIME.
W-WE'RE GOING TO...
CLEAN THE DRIFTWOOD, SON. WE'RE GOING TO SEE THAT YOUR FATHER'S WORK COMES TO FRUITION.
DO NOT WORRY...
"...THERE IS NOTHING THAT CAN STOP US NOW."
DIRECTIVES.
PROTECT THE BOY.
SECURE THE LAB.
LEAVE FOR NOTHING.

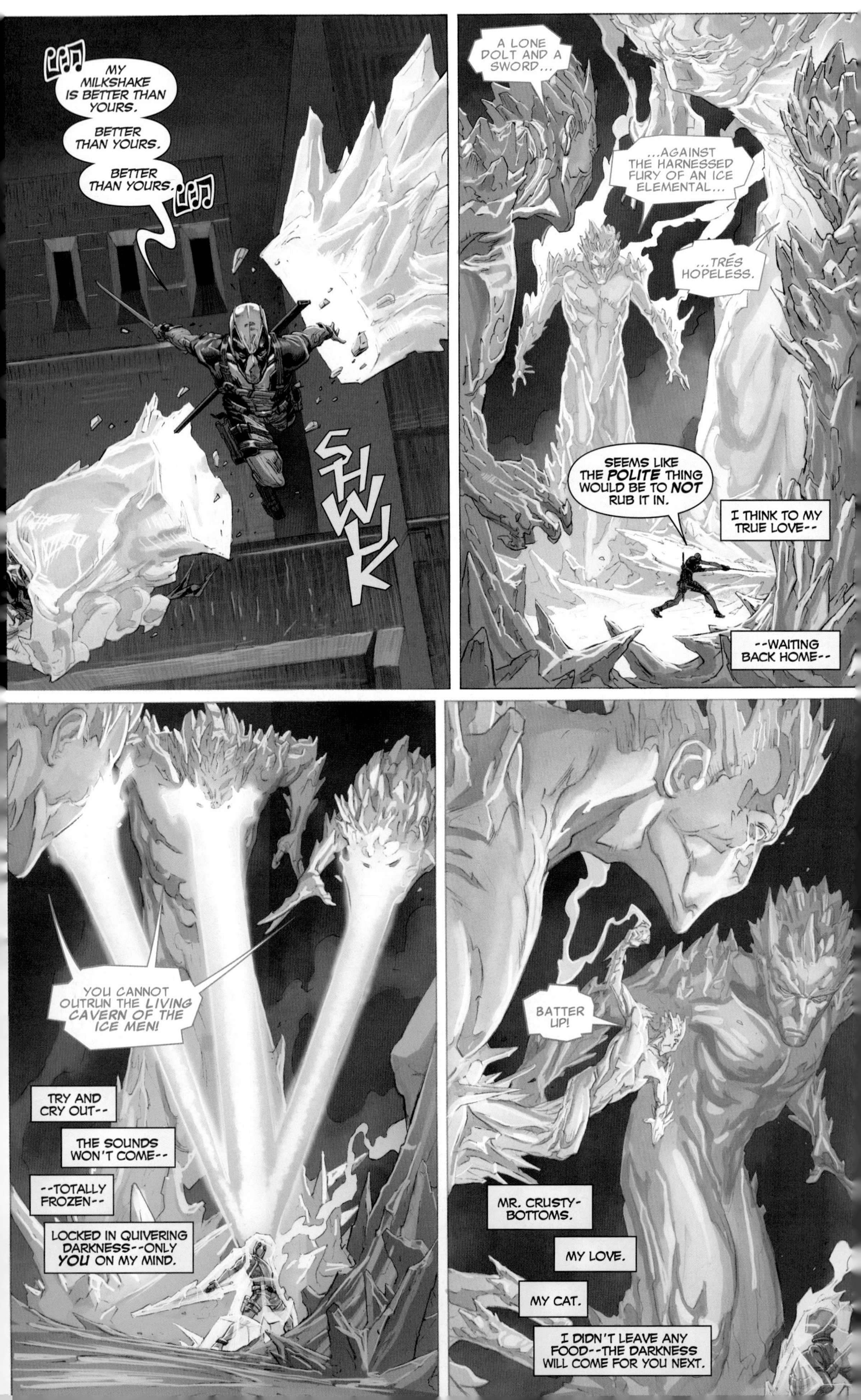
MY MILKSHAKE IS BETTER THAN YOURS.
BETTER THAN YOURS.
BETTER THAN YOURS.
SHWUK
A LONE DOLT AND A SWORD...
...AGAINST THE HARNESSED FURY OF AN ICE ELEMENTAL...
...TRÉS HOPELESS.
SEEMS LIKE THE POLITE THING WOULD BE TO NOT RUB IT IN.
I THINK TO MY TRUE LOVE--
--WAITING BACK HOME--
YOU CANNOT OUTRUN THE LIVING CAVERN OF THE ICE MEN!
TRY AND CRY OUT--
THE SOUNDS WON'T COME--
--TOTALLY FROZEN--
LOCKED IN QUIVERING DARKNESS--ONLY YOU ON MY MIND.
BATTER UP!
MR. CRUSTY-BOTTOMS.
MY LOVE.
MY CAT.
I DIDN'T LEAVE ANY FOOD--THE DARKNESS WILL COME FOR YOU NEXT.

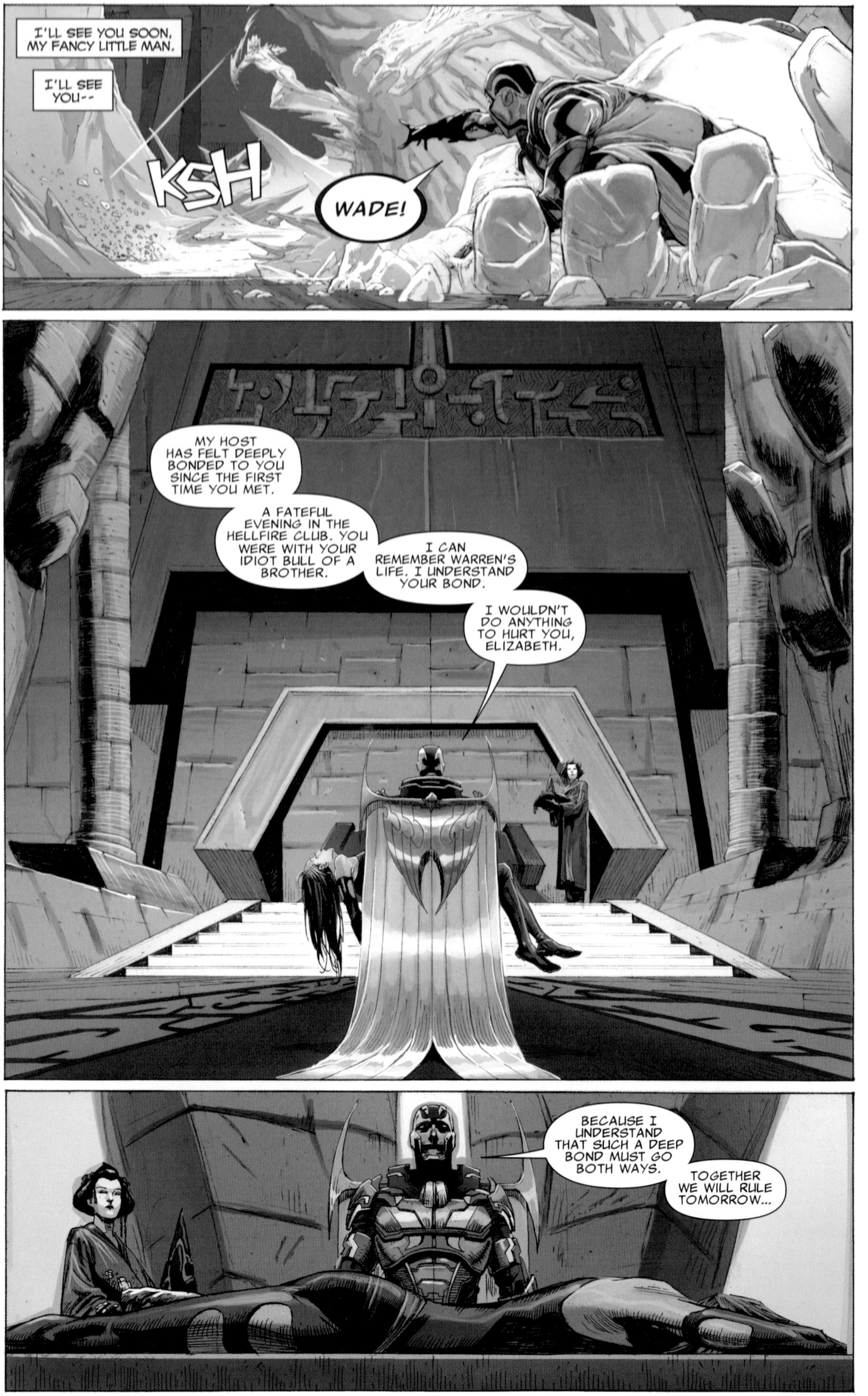
I'LL SEE YOU SOON, MY FANCY LITTLE MAN.
I'LL SEE YOU--
KSH
WADE!
MY HOST HAS FELT DEEPLY BONDED TO YOU SINCE THE FIRST TIME YOU MET.
A FATEFUL EVENING IN THE HELLFIRE CLUB. YOU WERE WITH YOUR IDIOT BULL OF A BROTHER.
I CAN REMEMBER WARREN'S LIFE. I UNDERSTAND YOUR BOND.
I WOULDN'T DO ANYTHING TO HURT YOU, ELIZABETH.
BECAUSE I UNDERSTAND THAT SUCH A DEEP BOND MUST GO BOTH WAYS.
TOGETHER WE WILL RULE TOMORROW...

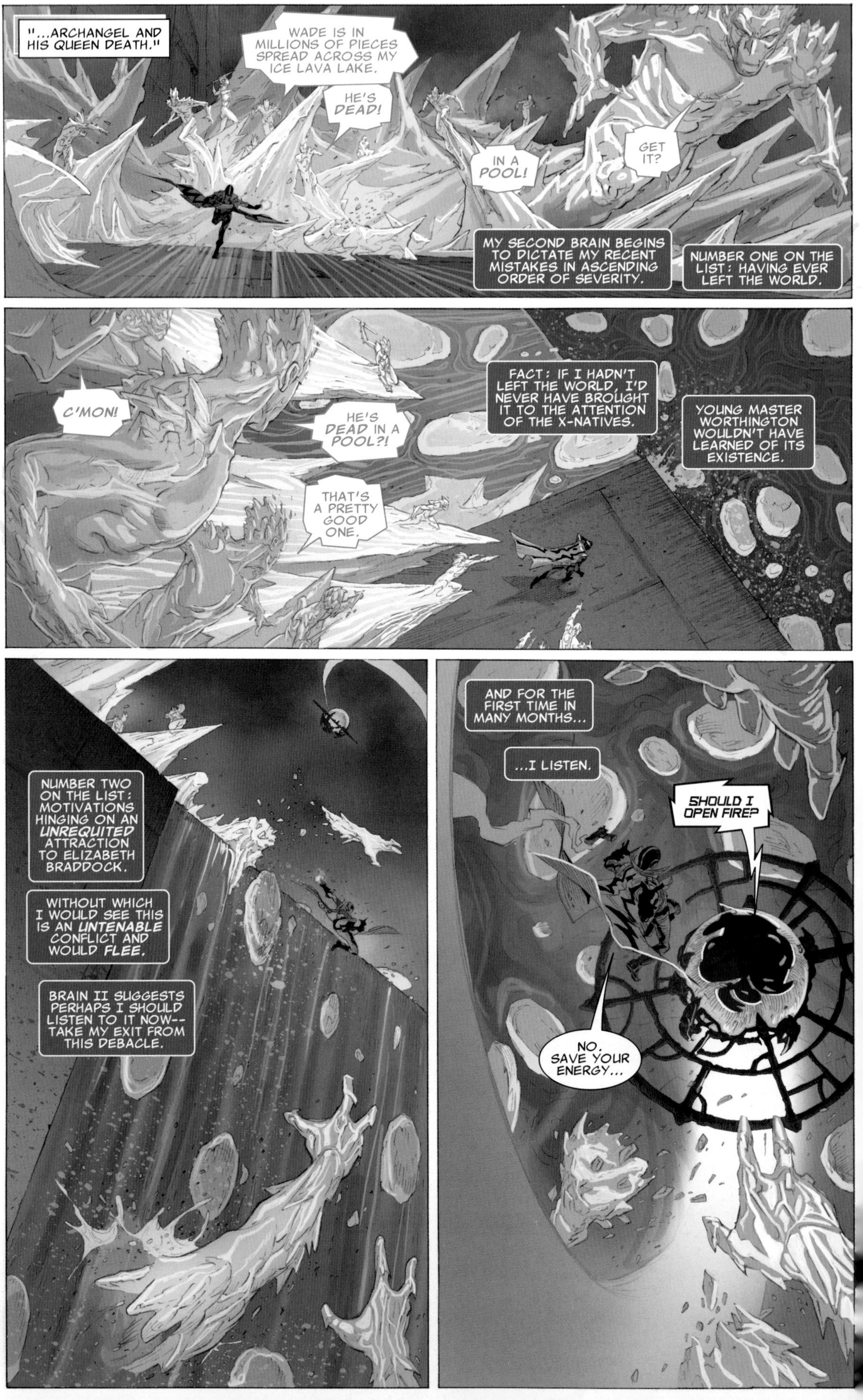
"...ARCHANGEL AND HIS QUEEN DEATH."
WADE IS IN MILLIONS OF PIECES SPREAD ACROSS MY ICE LAVA LAKE.
HE'S DEAD!
IN A POOL!
GET IT?
MY SECOND BRAIN BEGINS TO DICTATE MY RECENT MISTAKES IN ASCENDING ORDER OF SEVERITY.
NUMBER ONE ON THE LIST: HAVING EVER LEFT THE WORLD.
C'MON!
HE'S DEAD IN A POOL?!
THAT'S A PRETTY GOOD ONE.
FACT: IF I HADN'T LEFT THE WORLD, I'D NEVER HAVE BROUGHT IT TO THE ATTENTION OF THE X-NATIVES.
YOUNG MASTER WORTHINGTON WOULDN'T HAVE LEARNED OF ITS EXISTENCE.
NUMBER TWO ON THE LIST: MOTIVATIONS HINGING ON AN UNREQUITED ATTRACTION TO ELIZABETH BRADDOCK.
WITHOUT WHICH I WOULD SEE THIS IS AN UNTENABLE CONFLICT AND WOULD FLEE.
BRAIN II SUGGESTS PERHAPS I SHOULD LISTEN TO IT NOW--TAKE MY EXIT FROM THIS DEBACLE.
AND FOR THE FIRST TIME IN MANY MONTHS...
...I LISTEN.
SHOULD I OPEN FIRE?
NO. SAVE YOUR ENERGY...

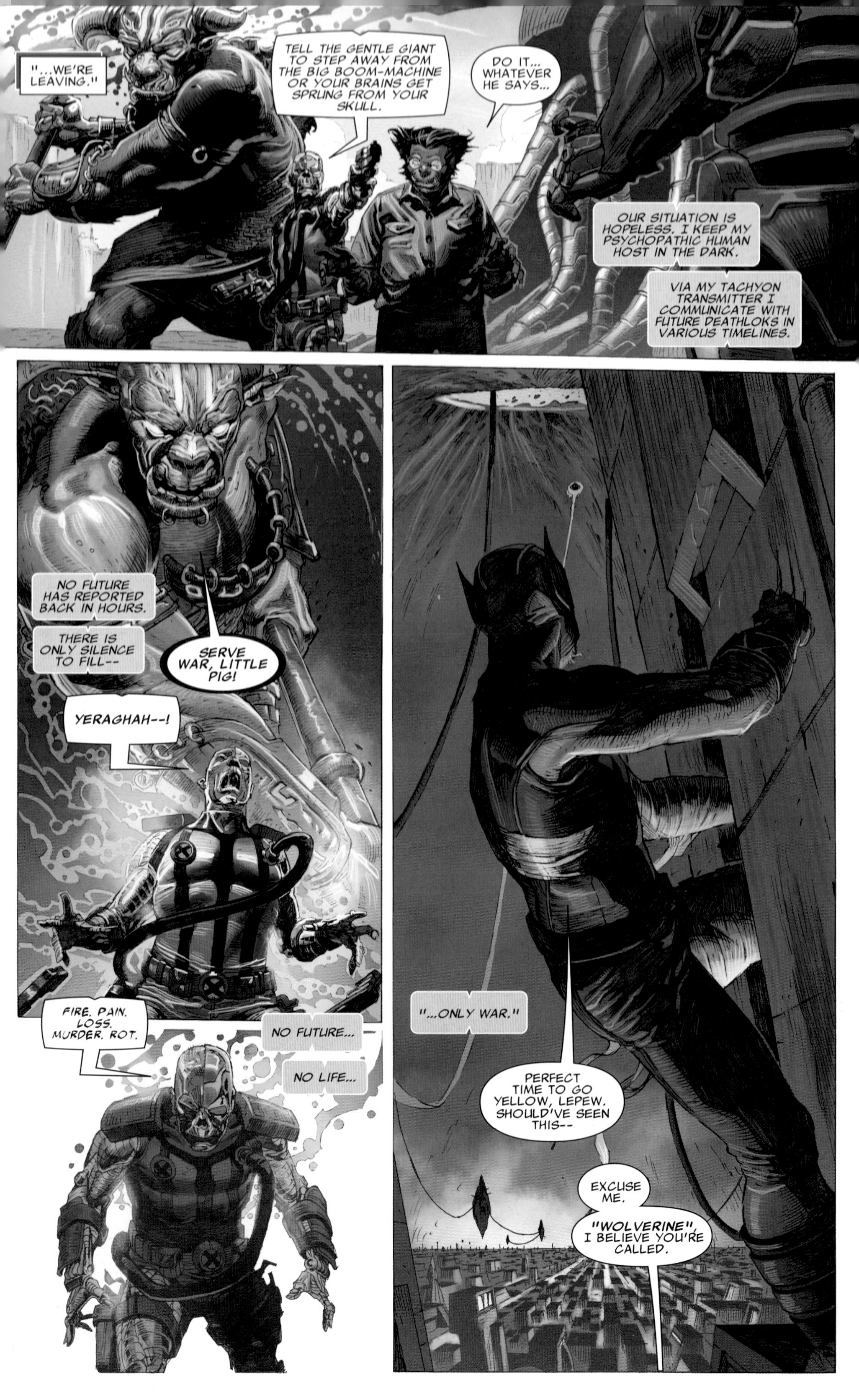
"...WE'RE LEAVING."
TELL THE GENTLE GIANT TO STEP AWAY FROM THE BIG BOOM-MACHINE OR YOUR BRAINS GET SPRUNG FROM YOUR SKULL.
DO IT... WHATEVER HE SAYS...
OUR SITUATION IS HOPELESS. I KEEP MY PSYCHOPATHIC HUMAN HOST IN THE DARK.
VIA MY TACHYON TRANSMITTER I COMMUNICATE WITH FUTURE DEATHLOKS IN VARIOUS TIMELINES.
NO FUTURE HAS REPORTED BACK IN HOURS.
THERE IS ONLY SILENCE TO FILL--
SERVE WAR, LITTLE PIG!
YERAGHAH--!
FIRE. PAIN. LOSS. MURDER. ROT.
NO FUTURE...
NO LIFE...
"...ONLY WAR."
PERFECT TIME TO GO YELLOW, LEPEW. SHOULD'VE SEEN THIS--
EXCUSE ME.
"WOLVERINE", I BELIEVE YOU'RE CALLED.

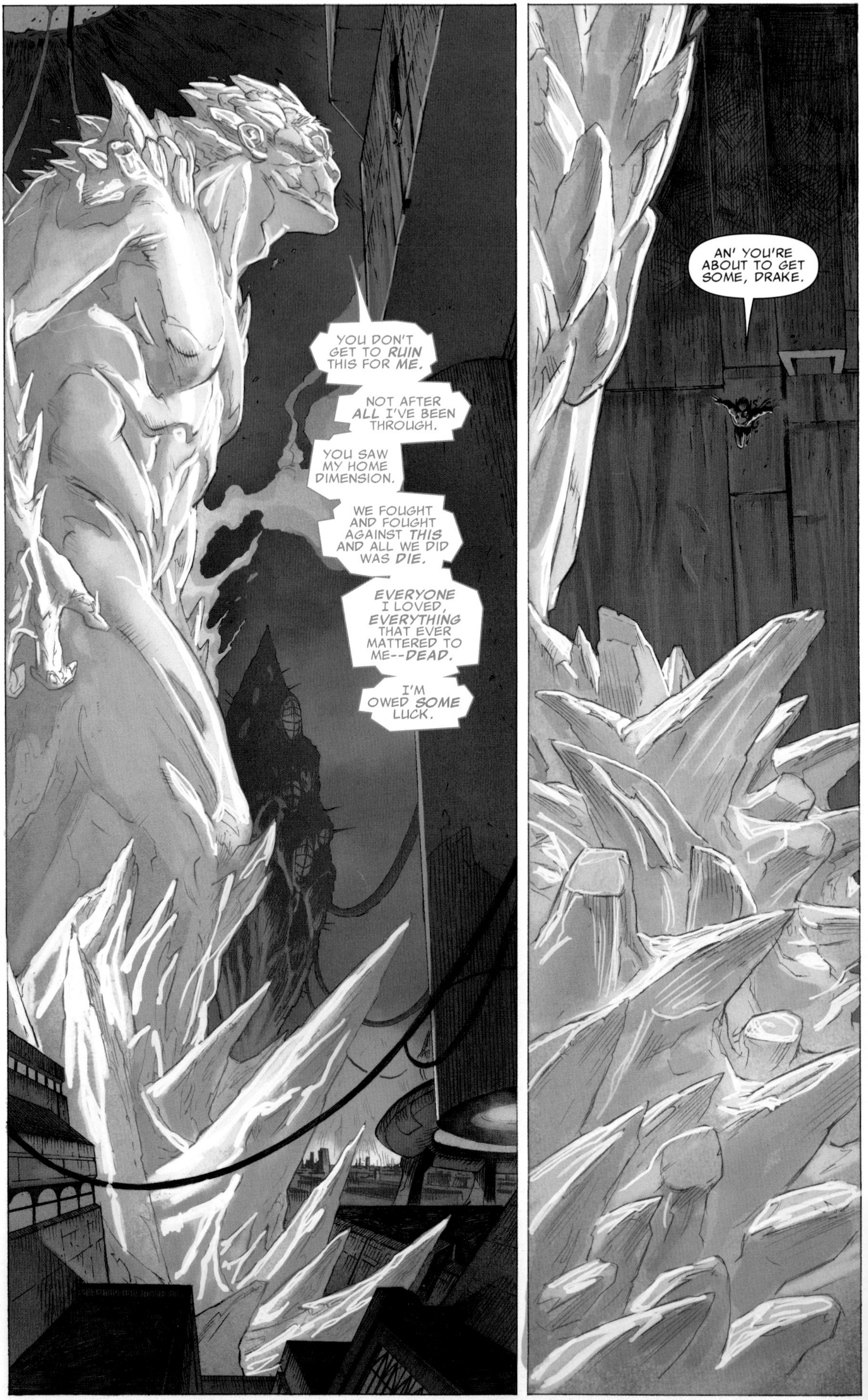
YOU DON'T GET TO RUIN THIS FOR ME.
NOT AFTER ALL I'VE BEEN THROUGH.
YOU SAW MY HOME DIMENSION.
WE FOUGHT AND FOUGHT AGAINST THIS AND ALL WE DID WAS DIE.
EVERYONE I LOVED, EVERYTHING THAT EVER MATTERED TO ME--DEAD.
I'M OWED SOME LUCK.
AN' YOU'RE ABOUT TO GET SOME, DRAKE.

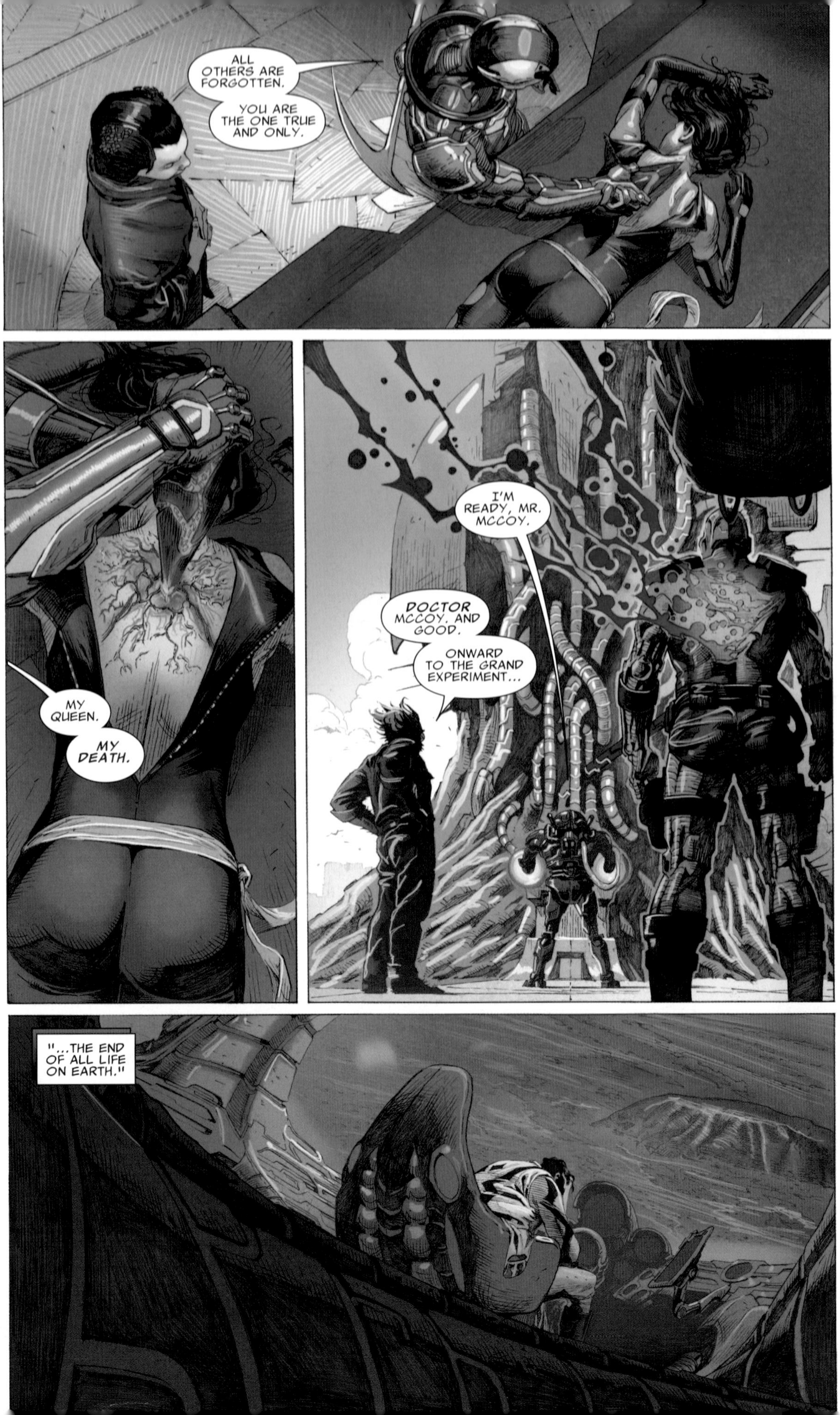
ALL OTHERS ARE FORGOTTEN.
YOU ARE THE ONE TRUE AND ONLY.
MY QUEEN.
MY DEATH.
I'M READY, MR. MCCOY.
DOCTOR MCCOY. AND GOOD.
ONWARD TO THE GRAND EXPERIMENT...
"...THE END OF ALL LIFE ON EARTH."

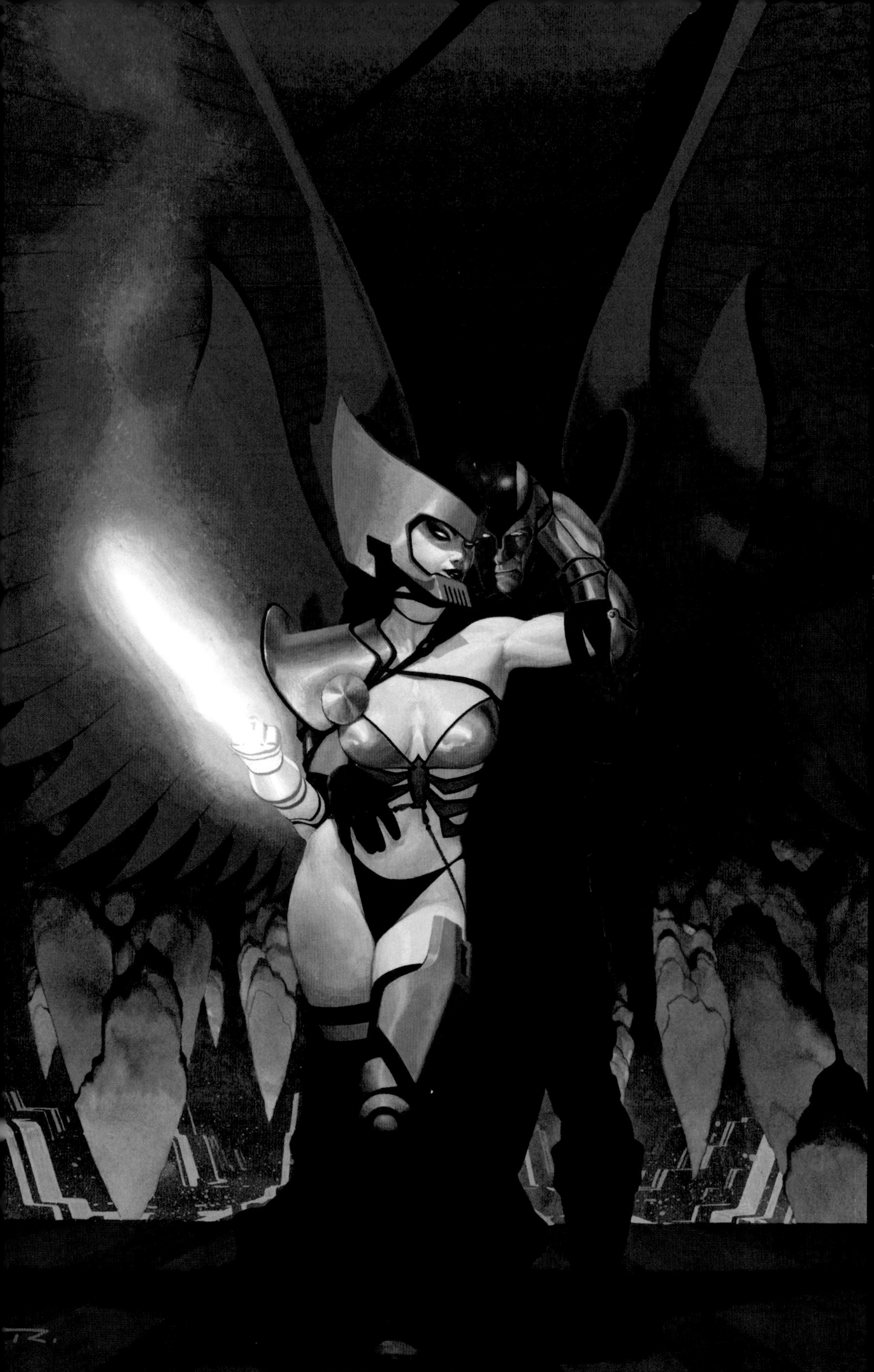

OPENS A WINDOW

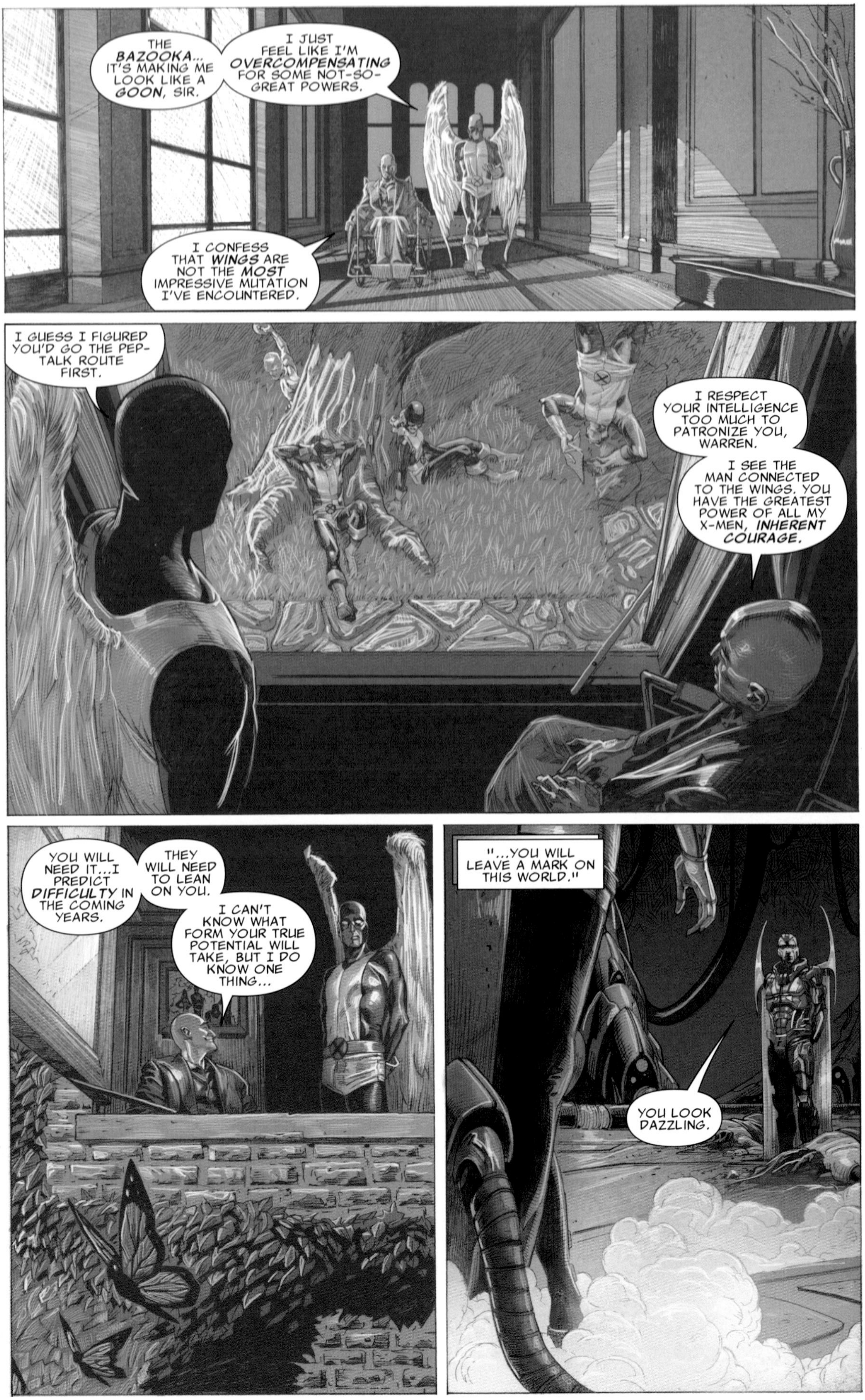
THE BAZOOKA... IT'S MAKING ME LOOK LIKE A GOON, SIR.
I JUST FEEL LIKE I'M OVERCOMPENSATING FOR SOME NOT-SO-GREAT POWERS.
I CONFESS THAT WINGS ARE NOT THE MOST IMPRESSIVE MUTATION I'VE ENCOUNTERED.
I GUESS I FIGURED YOU'D GO THE PEP-TALK ROUTE FIRST.
I RESPECT YOUR INTELLIGENCE TOO MUCH TO PATRONIZE YOU, WARREN.
I SEE THE MAN CONNECTED TO THE WINGS. YOU HAVE THE GREATEST POWER OF ALL MY X-MEN, INHERENT COURAGE.
YOU WILL NEED IT...I PREDICT DIFFICULTY IN THE COMING YEARS.
THEY WILL NEED TO LEAN ON YOU.
I CAN'T KNOW WHAT FORM YOUR TRUE POTENTIAL WILL TAKE, BUT I DO KNOW ONE THING...
"...YOU WILL LEAVE A MARK ON THIS WORLD."
YOU LOOK DAZZLING.

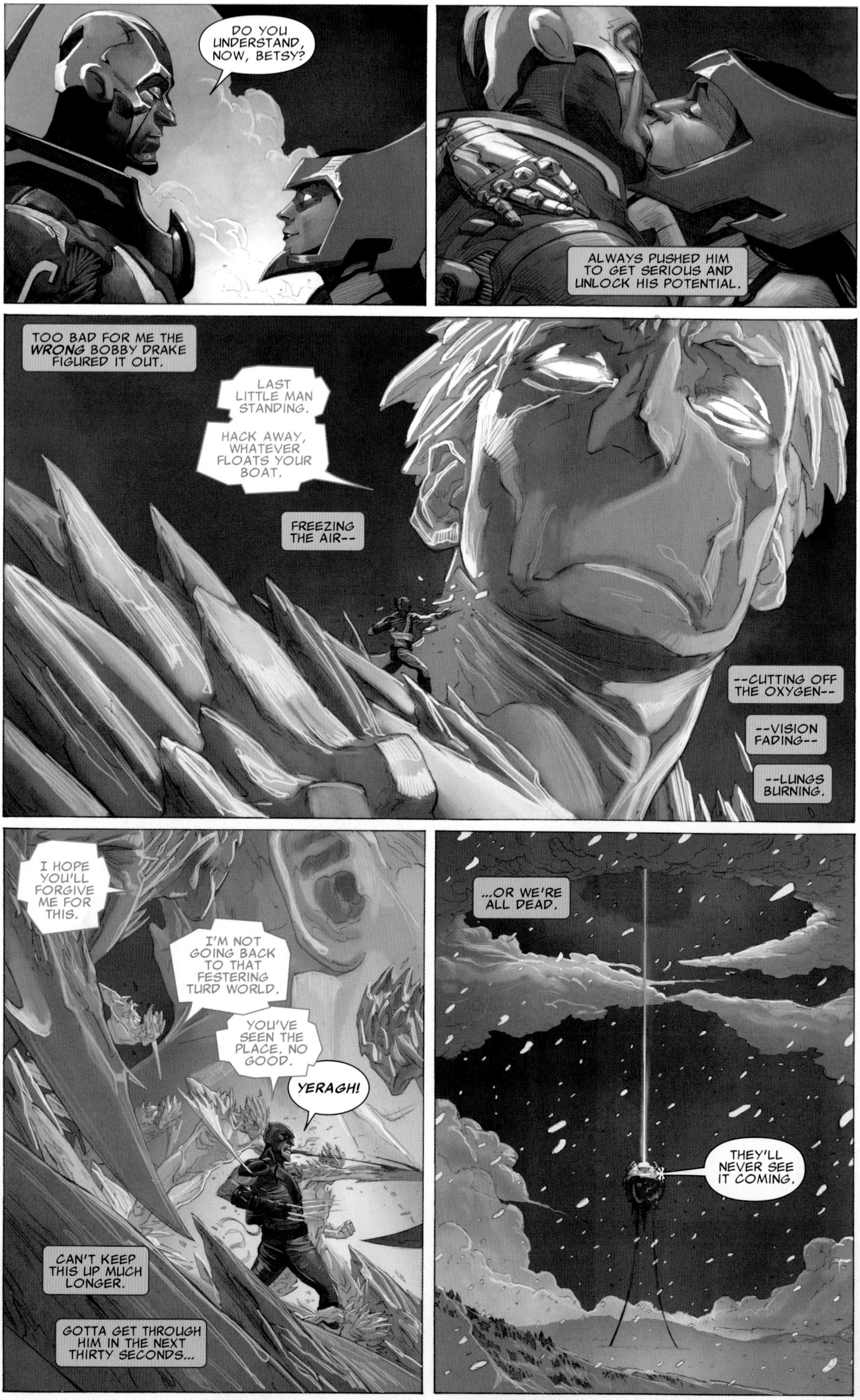
DO YOU UNDERSTAND, NOW, BETSY?
ALWAYS PUSHED HIM TO GET SERIOUS AND UNLOCK HIS POTENTIAL.
TOO BAD FOR ME THE *WRONG* BOBBY DRAKE FIGURED IT OUT.
LAST LITTLE MAN STANDING.
HACK AWAY, WHATEVER FLOATS YOUR BOAT.
FREEZING THE AIR--
--CUTTING OFF THE OXYGEN--
--VISION FADING--
--LUNGS BURNING.
I HOPE YOU'LL FORGIVE ME FOR THIS.
I'M NOT GOING BACK TO THAT FESTERING TURD WORLD.
YOU'VE SEEN THE PLACE. NO GOOD.
YERAGH!
CAN'T KEEP THIS UP MUCH LONGER.
GOTTA GET THROUGH HIM IN THE NEXT THIRTY SECONDS...
...OR WE'RE ALL DEAD.
THEY'LL NEVER SEE IT COMING.

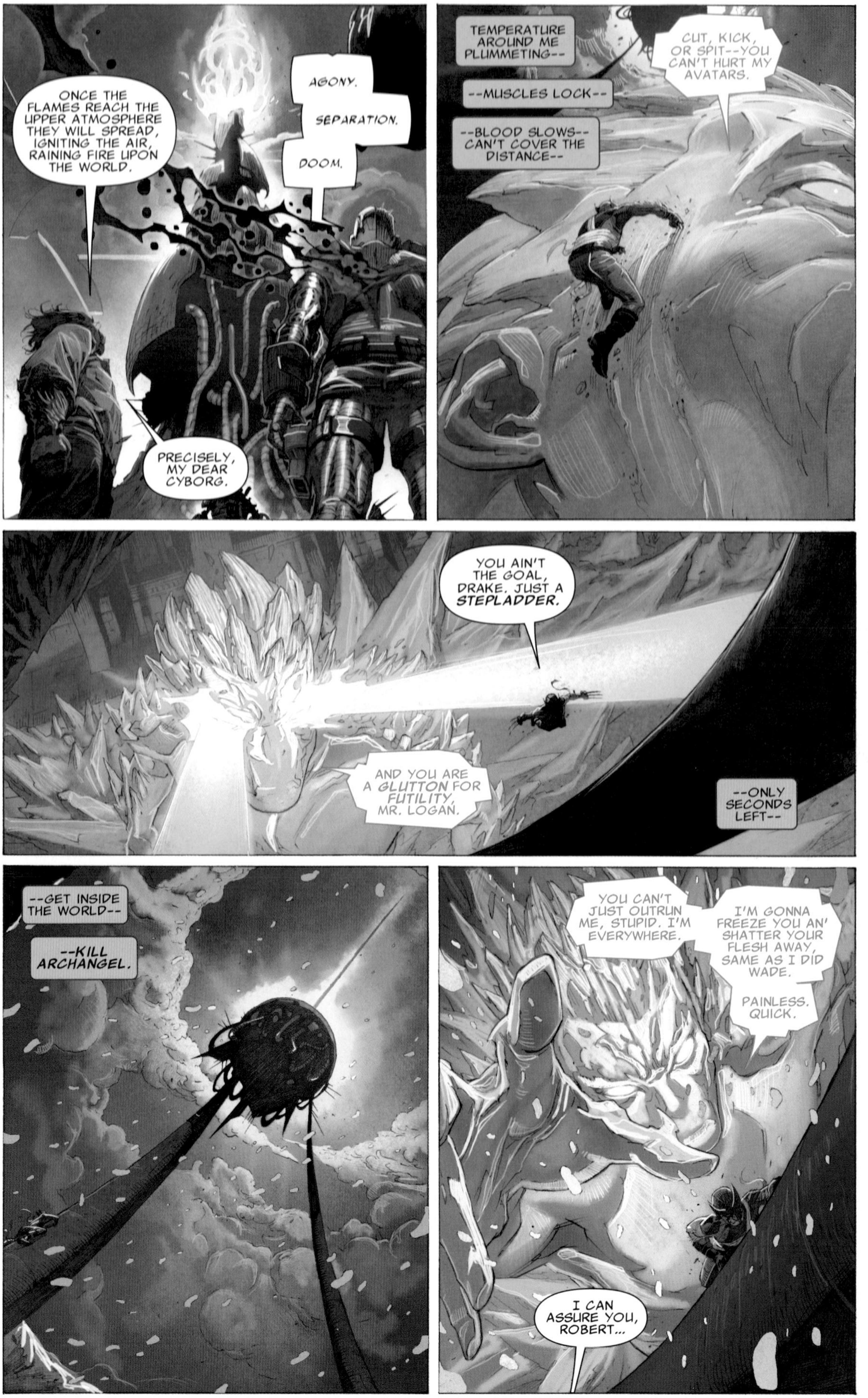
ONCE THE FLAMES REACH THE UPPER ATMOSPHERE THEY WILL SPREAD, IGNITING THE AIR, RAINING FIRE UPON THE WORLD.
AGONY.
SEPARATION.
DOOM.
PRECISELY, MY DEAR CYBORG.
TEMPERATURE AROUND ME PLUMMETING--
--MUSCLES LOCK--
--BLOOD SLOWS-- CAN'T COVER THE DISTANCE--
CUT, KICK, OR SPIT--YOU CAN'T HURT MY AVATARS.
YOU AIN'T THE GOAL, DRAKE. JUST A STEPLADDER.
AND YOU ARE A GLUTTON FOR FUTILITY, MR. LOGAN.
--ONLY SECONDS LEFT--
--GET INSIDE THE WORLD--
--KILL ARCHANGEL.
YOU CAN'T JUST OUTRUN ME, STUPID. I'M EVERYWHERE.
I'M GONNA FREEZE YOU AN' SHATTER YOUR FLESH AWAY, SAME AS I DID WADE.
PAINLESS. QUICK.
I CAN ASSURE YOU, ROBERT...

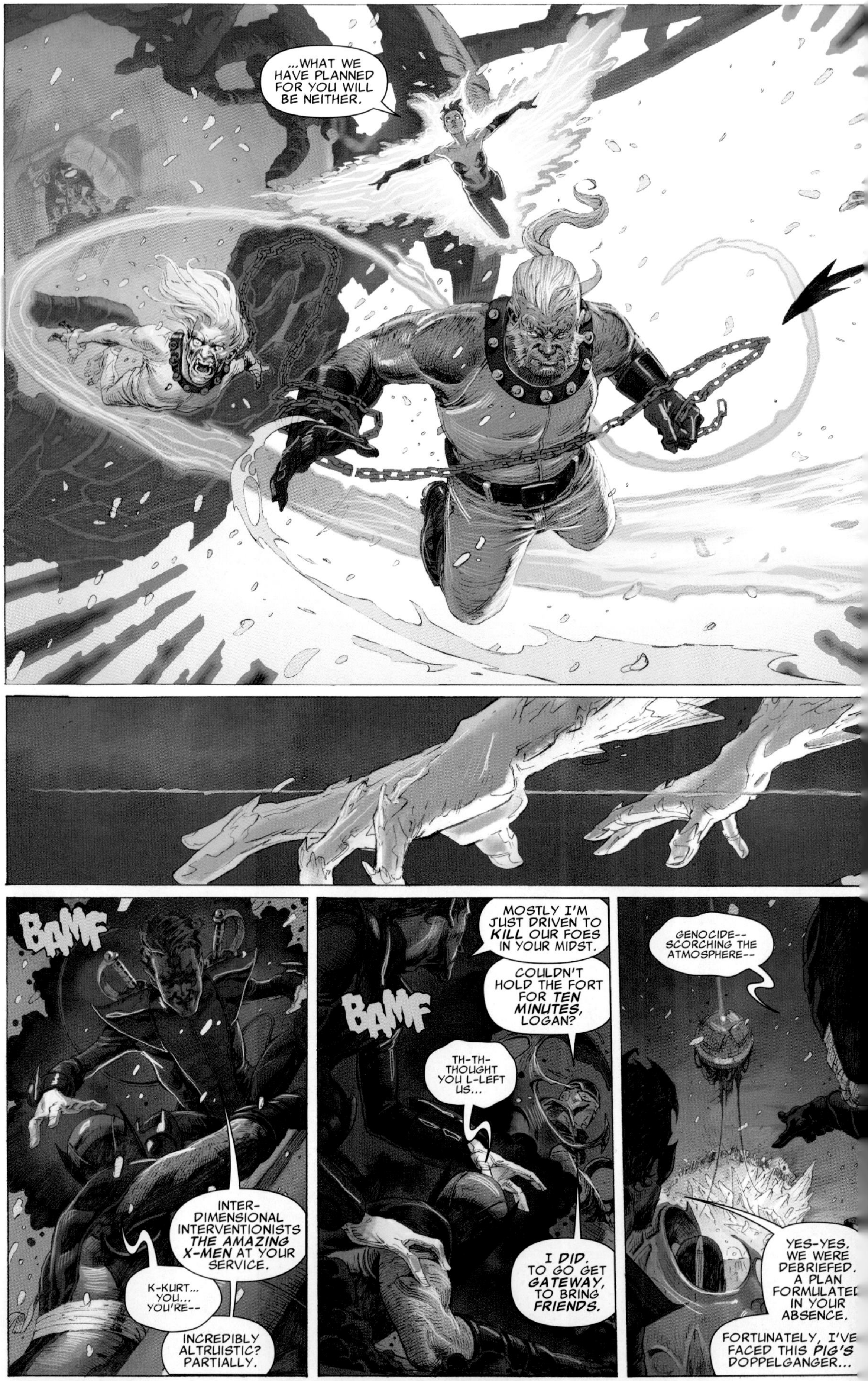
...WHAT WE HAVE PLANNED FOR YOU WILL BE NEITHER.
BAMF
INTER-DIMENSIONAL INTERVENTIONISTS THE AMAZING X-MEN AT YOUR SERVICE.
K-KURT... YOU... YOU'RE--
INCREDIBLY ALTRUISTIC? PARTIALLY.
MOSTLY I'M JUST DRIVEN TO KILL OUR FOES IN YOUR MIDST.
COULDN'T HOLD THE FORT FOR TEN MINUTES, LOGAN?
BAMF
TH-TH-THOUGHT YOU L-LEFT US...
I DID. TO GO GET GATEWAY, TO BRING FRIENDS.
GENOCIDE--SCORCHING THE ATMOSPHERE--
YES-YES. WE WERE DEBRIEFED. A PLAN FORMULATED IN YOUR ABSENCE.
FORTUNATELY, I'VE FACED THIS PIG'S DOPPELGANGER...

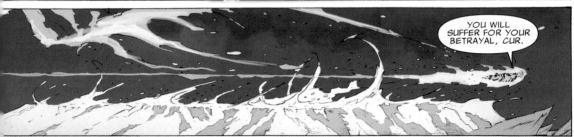

YOU WILL SUFFER FOR YOUR BETRAYAL, CUR.

BAMF

...AND I KNOW JUST THE THING.

DARKHOLME!?

NEED TO BORROW YOUR FRIEND.

BACK FOR YOU IN A BIT, MCCOY.

BAMF

GUTEN TAG.

MAKE PEACE WITH WHATEVER DEVILS YOU WORSHIP.

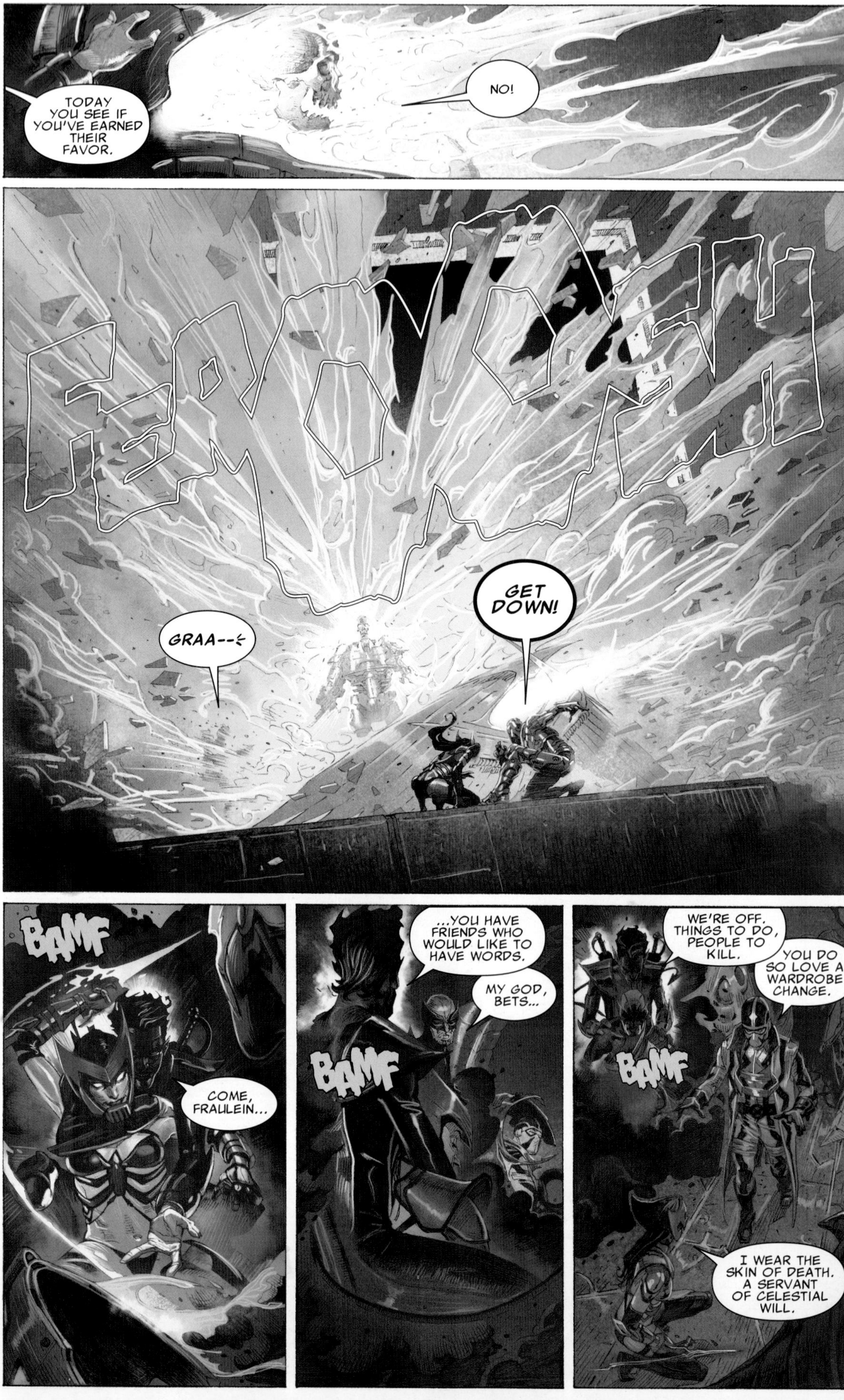
TODAY YOU SEE IF YOU'VE EARNED THEIR FAVOR.
NO!
GRAA--!
GET DOWN!
BAMF
COME, FRAULEIN...
...YOU HAVE FRIENDS WHO WOULD LIKE TO HAVE WORDS.
MY GOD, BETS...
BAMF
WE'RE OFF. THINGS TO DO, PEOPLE TO KILL.
YOU DO SO LOVE A WARDROBE CHANGE.
BAMF
I WEAR THE SKIN OF DEATH. A SERVANT OF CELESTIAL WILL.

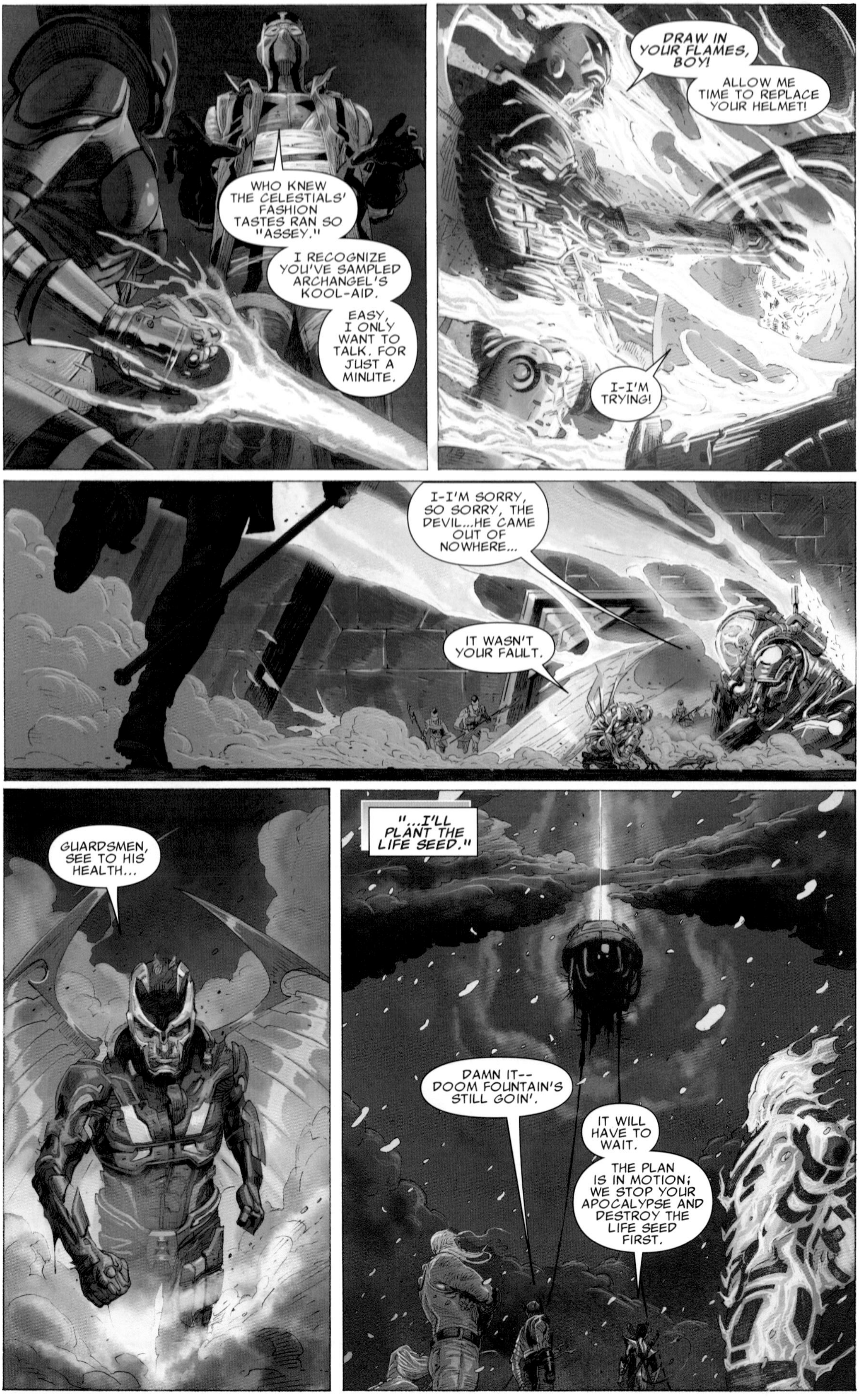
WHO KNEW THE CELESTIALS' FASHION TASTES RAN SO "ASSEY."
I RECOGNIZE YOU'VE SAMPLED ARCHANGEL'S KOOL-AID.
EASY, I ONLY WANT TO TALK. FOR JUST A MINUTE.
DRAW IN YOUR FLAMES, BOY!
ALLOW ME TIME TO REPLACE YOUR HELMET!
I-I'M TRYING!
I-I'M SORRY, SO SORRY, THE DEVIL...HE CAME OUT OF NOWHERE...
IT WASN'T YOUR FAULT.
GUARDSMEN, SEE TO HIS HEALTH...
"...I'LL PLANT THE LIFE SEED."
DAMN IT-- DOOM FOUNTAIN'S STILL GOIN'.
IT WILL HAVE TO WAIT.
THE PLAN IS IN MOTION; WE STOP YOUR APOCALYPSE AND DESTROY THE LIFE SEED FIRST.

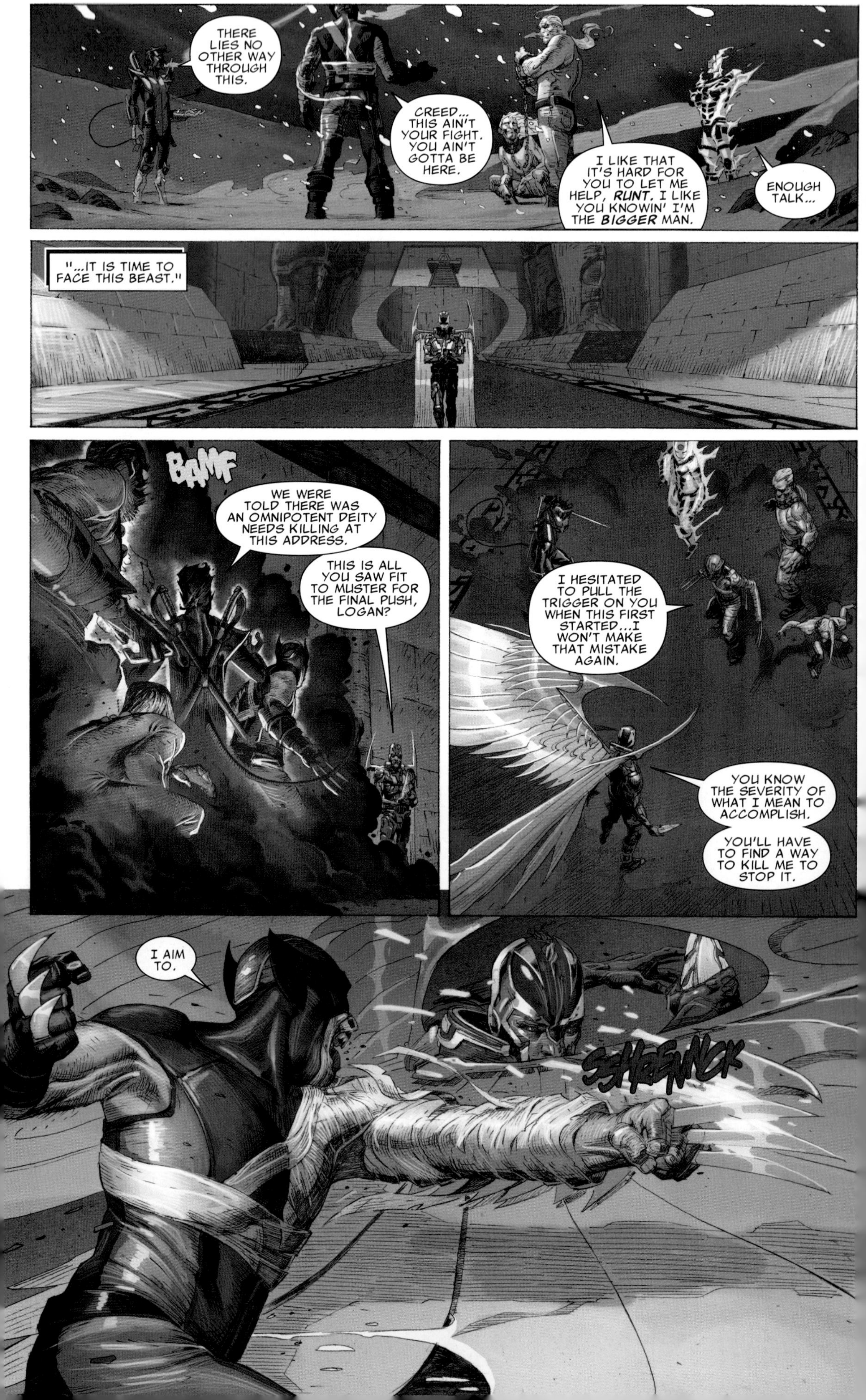
THERE LIES NO OTHER WAY THROUGH THIS.
CREED... THIS AIN'T YOUR FIGHT. YOU AIN'T GOTTA BE HERE.
I LIKE THAT IT'S HARD FOR YOU TO LET ME HELP, RUNT. I LIKE YOU KNOWIN' I'M THE BIGGER MAN.
ENOUGH TALK...
"...IT IS TIME TO FACE THIS BEAST."
BAMF
WE WERE TOLD THERE WAS AN OMNIPOTENT DEITY NEEDS KILLING AT THIS ADDRESS.
THIS IS ALL YOU SAW FIT TO MUSTER FOR THE FINAL PUSH, LOGAN?
I HESITATED TO PULL THE TRIGGER ON YOU WHEN THIS FIRST STARTED...I WON'T MAKE THAT MISTAKE AGAIN.
YOU KNOW THE SEVERITY OF WHAT I MEAN TO ACCOMPLISH.
YOU'LL HAVE TO FIND A WAY TO KILL ME TO STOP IT.
I AIM TO.
SSHREWNCK

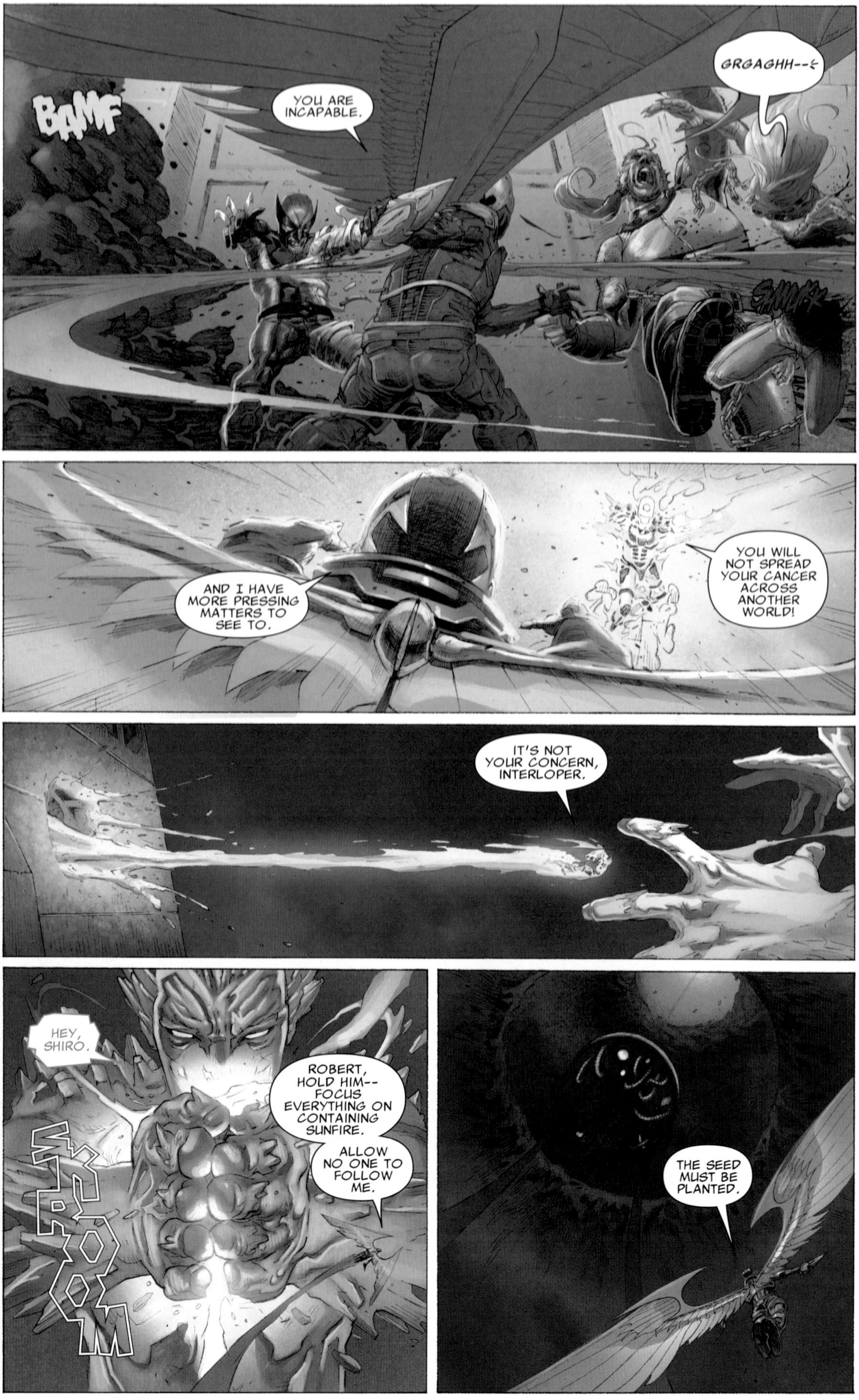
BAMF
YOU ARE INCAPABLE.
GRGAGHH--!
AND I HAVE MORE PRESSING MATTERS TO SEE TO.
YOU WILL NOT SPREAD YOUR CANCER ACROSS ANOTHER WORLD!
IT'S NOT YOUR CONCERN, INTERLOPER.
HEY, SHIRO.
ROBERT, HOLD HIM--FOCUS EVERYTHING ON CONTAINING SUNFIRE.
ALLOW NO ONE TO FOLLOW ME.
THE SEED MUST BE PLANTED.

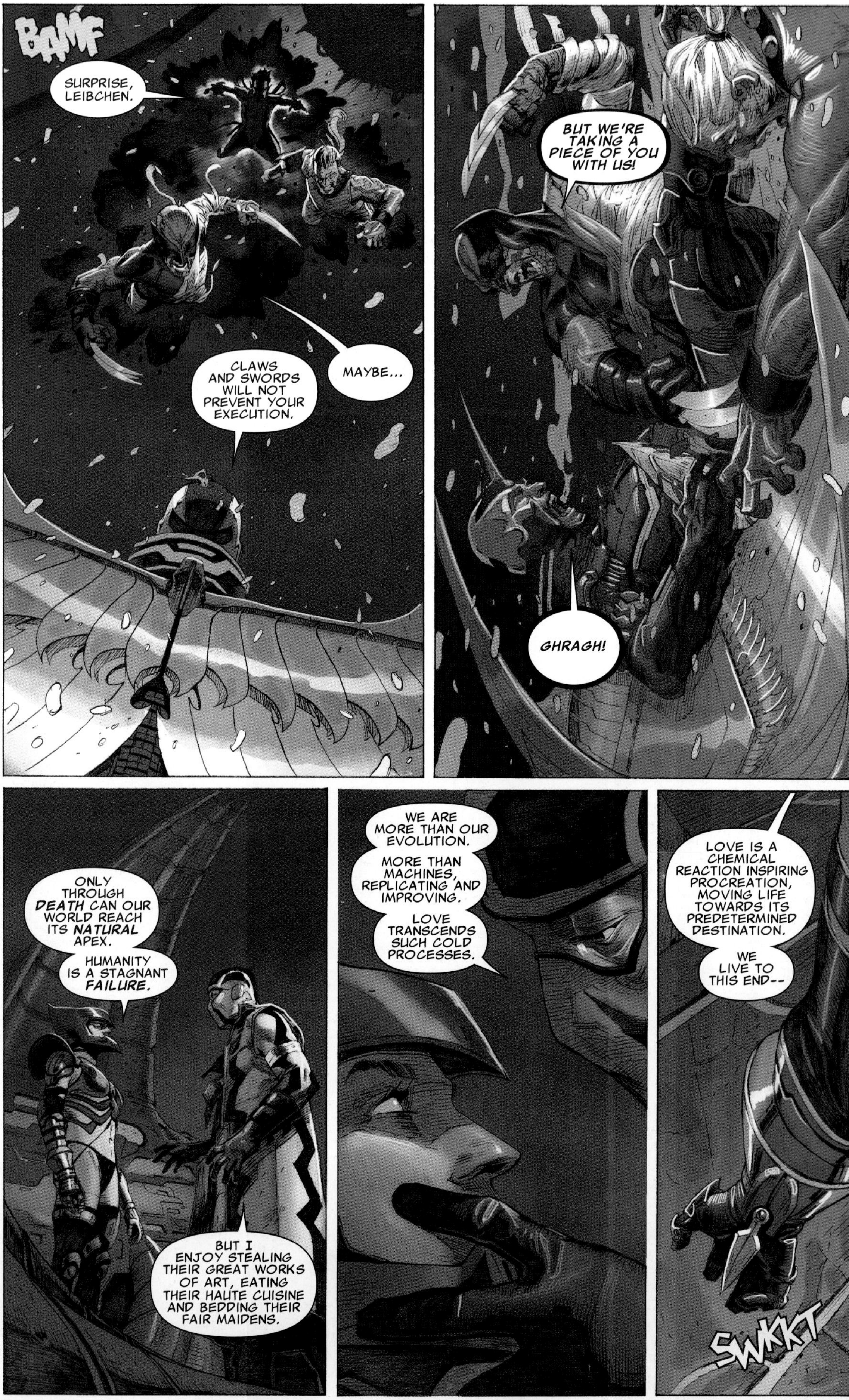
BAMF
SURPRISE, LEIBCHEN.
MAYBE...
CLAWS AND SWORDS WILL NOT PREVENT YOUR EXECUTION.
BUT WE'RE TAKING A PIECE OF YOU WITH US!
GHRAGH!
ONLY THROUGH DEATH CAN OUR WORLD REACH ITS NATURAL APEX.
HUMANITY IS A STAGNANT FAILURE.
BUT I ENJOY STEALING THEIR GREAT WORKS OF ART, EATING THEIR HAUTE CUISINE AND BEDDING THEIR FAIR MAIDENS.
WE ARE MORE THAN OUR EVOLUTION.
MORE THAN MACHINES, REPLICATING AND IMPROVING.
LOVE TRANSCENDS SUCH COLD PROCESSES.
LOVE IS A CHEMICAL REACTION INSPIRING PROCREATION, MOVING LIFE TOWARDS ITS PREDETERMINED DESTINATION.
WE LIVE TO THIS END--
SWKKT

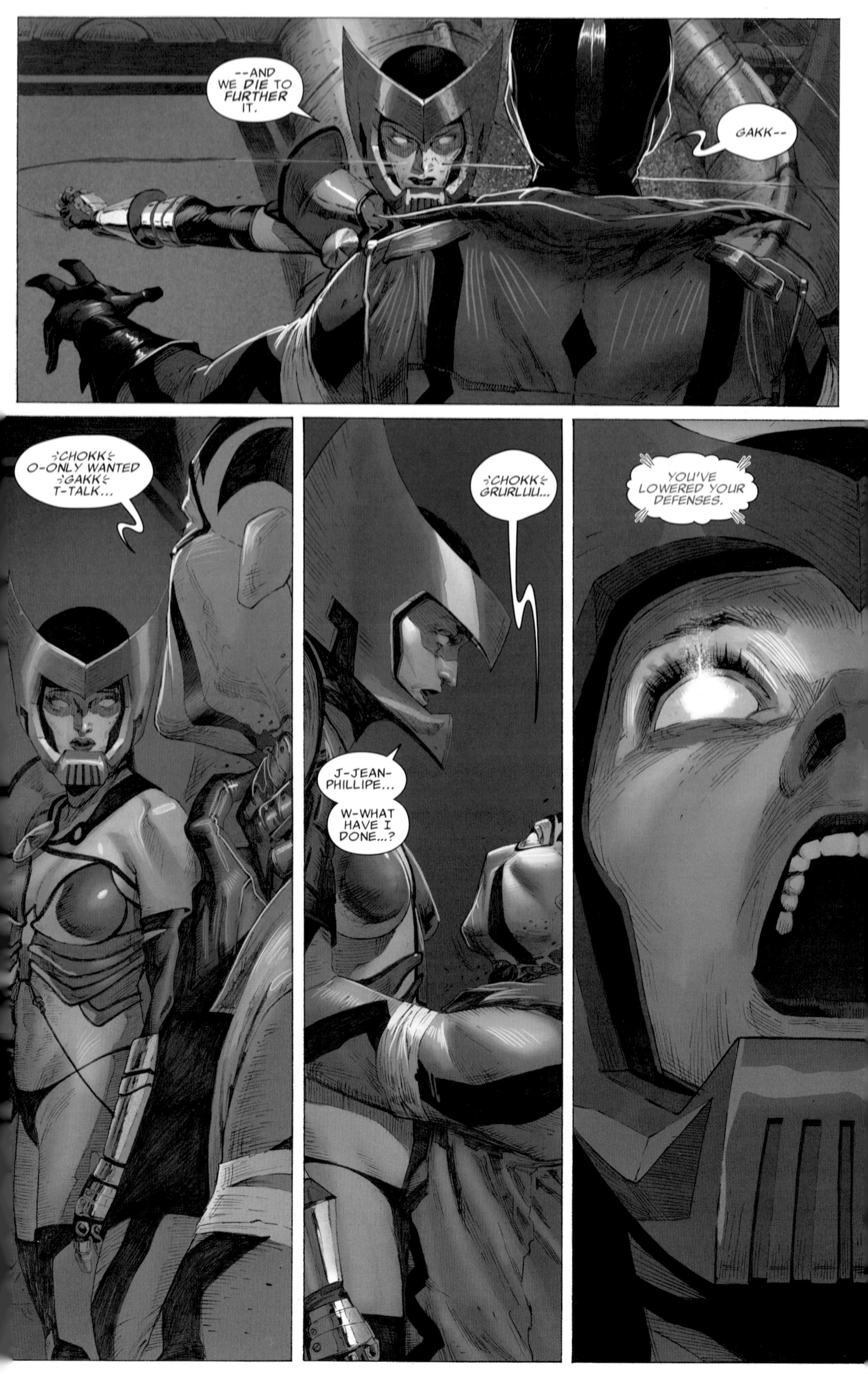
--AND WE DIE TO FURTHER IT.
GAKK--
-CHOKK- O-ONLY WANTED -GAKK- T-TALK...
-CHOKK- GRURLUU...
J-JEAN-PHILLIPE...
W-WHAT HAVE I DONE...?
YOU'VE LOWERED YOUR DEFENSES.

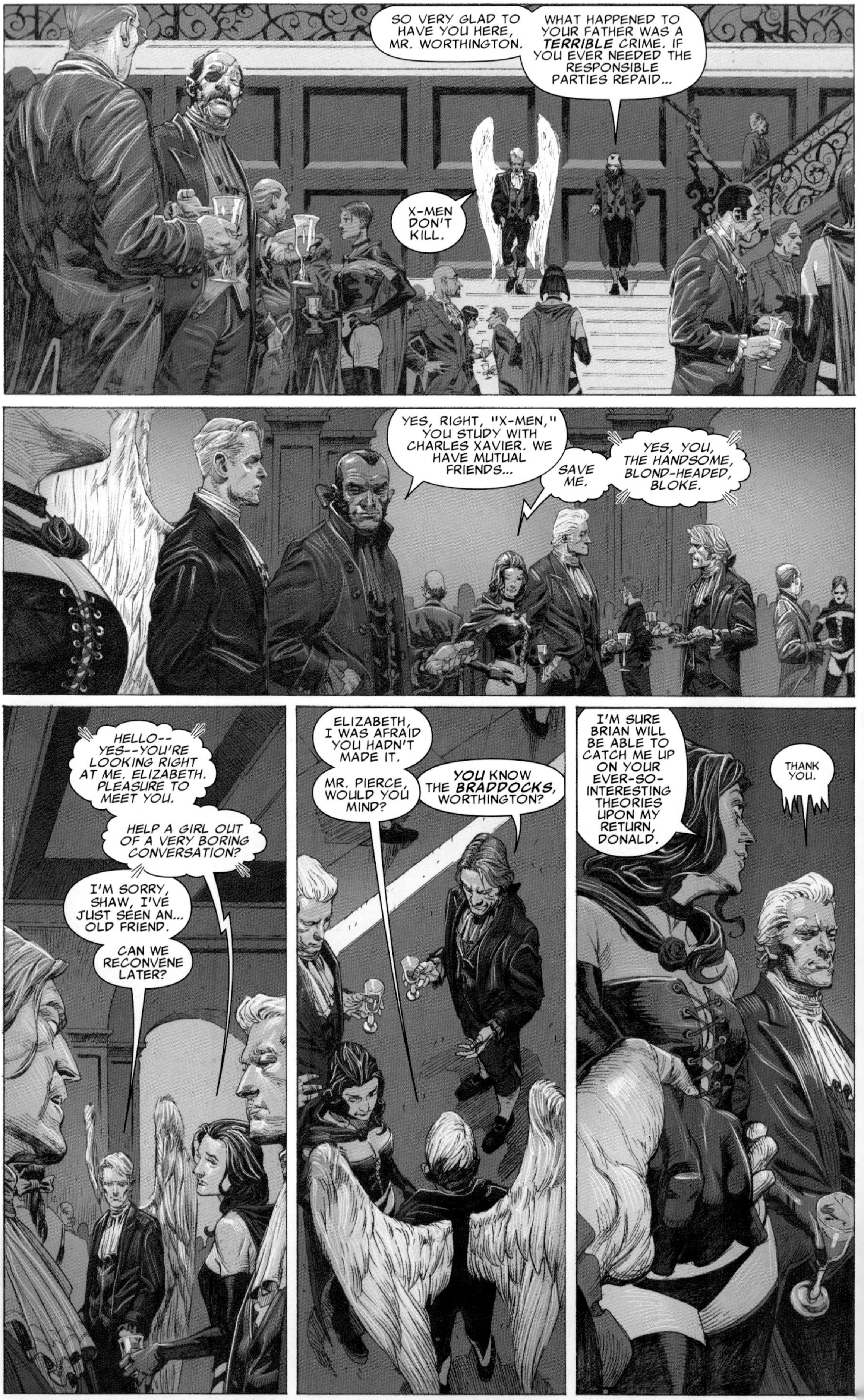
SO VERY GLAD TO HAVE YOU HERE, MR. WORTHINGTON.
WHAT HAPPENED TO YOUR FATHER WAS A TERRIBLE CRIME. IF YOU EVER NEEDED THE RESPONSIBLE PARTIES REPAID...
X-MEN DON'T KILL.
YES, RIGHT, "X-MEN," YOU STUDY WITH CHARLES XAVIER. WE HAVE MUTUAL FRIENDS...
SAVE ME.
YES, YOU, THE HANDSOME, BLOND-HEADED, BLOKE.
HELLO-- YES--YOU'RE LOOKING RIGHT AT ME. ELIZABETH. PLEASURE TO MEET YOU.
HELP A GIRL OUT OF A VERY BORING CONVERSATION?
I'M SORRY, SHAW, I'VE JUST SEEN AN... OLD FRIEND.
CAN WE RECONVENE LATER?
ELIZABETH, I WAS AFRAID YOU HADN'T MADE IT.
MR. PIERCE, WOULD YOU MIND?
YOU KNOW THE BRADDOCKS, WORTHINGTON?
I'M SURE BRIAN WILL BE ABLE TO CATCH ME UP ON YOUR EVER-SO-INTERESTING THEORIES UPON MY RETURN, DONALD.
THANK YOU.

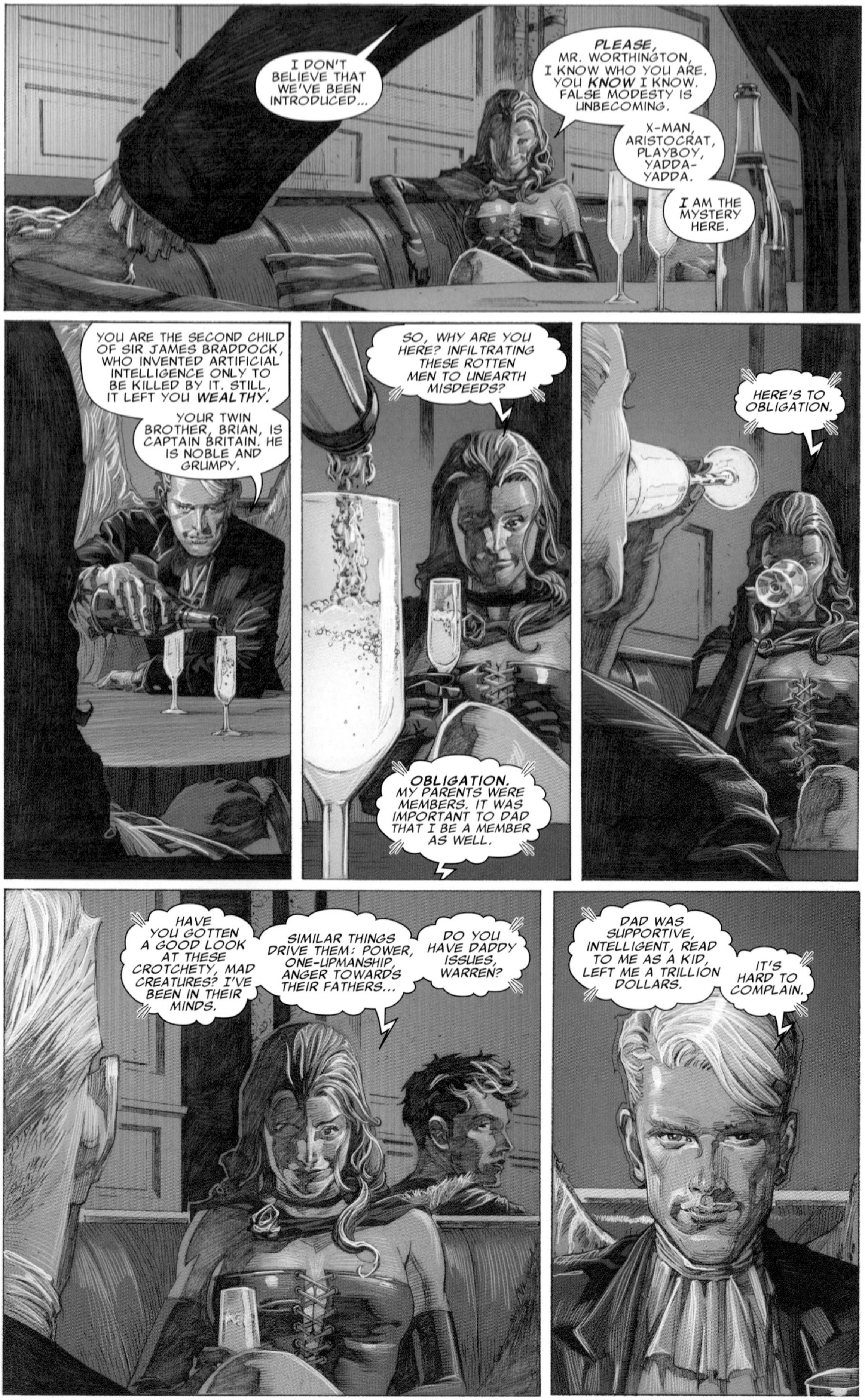
I DON'T BELIEVE THAT WE'VE BEEN INTRODUCED...
PLEASE, MR. WORTHINGTON, I KNOW WHO YOU ARE. YOU KNOW I KNOW. FALSE MODESTY IS UNBECOMING.
X-MAN, ARISTOCRAT, PLAYBOY, YADDA-YADDA.
I AM THE MYSTERY HERE.
YOU ARE THE SECOND CHILD OF SIR JAMES BRADDOCK, WHO INVENTED ARTIFICIAL INTELLIGENCE ONLY TO BE KILLED BY IT. STILL, IT LEFT YOU WEALTHY.
YOUR TWIN BROTHER, BRIAN, IS CAPTAIN BRITAIN. HE IS NOBLE AND GRUMPY.
SO, WHY ARE YOU HERE? INFILTRATING THESE ROTTEN MEN TO UNEARTH MISDEEDS?
OBLIGATION. MY PARENTS WERE MEMBERS. IT WAS IMPORTANT TO DAD THAT I BE A MEMBER AS WELL.
HERE'S TO OBLIGATION.
HAVE YOU GOTTEN A GOOD LOOK AT THESE CROTCHETY, MAD CREATURES? I'VE BEEN IN THEIR MINDS.
SIMILAR THINGS DRIVE THEM: POWER, ONE-UPMANSHIP, ANGER TOWARDS THEIR FATHERS...
DO YOU HAVE DADDY ISSUES, WARREN?
DAD WAS SUPPORTIVE, INTELLIGENT, READ TO ME AS A KID, LEFT ME A TRILLION DOLLARS.
IT'S HARD TO COMPLAIN.

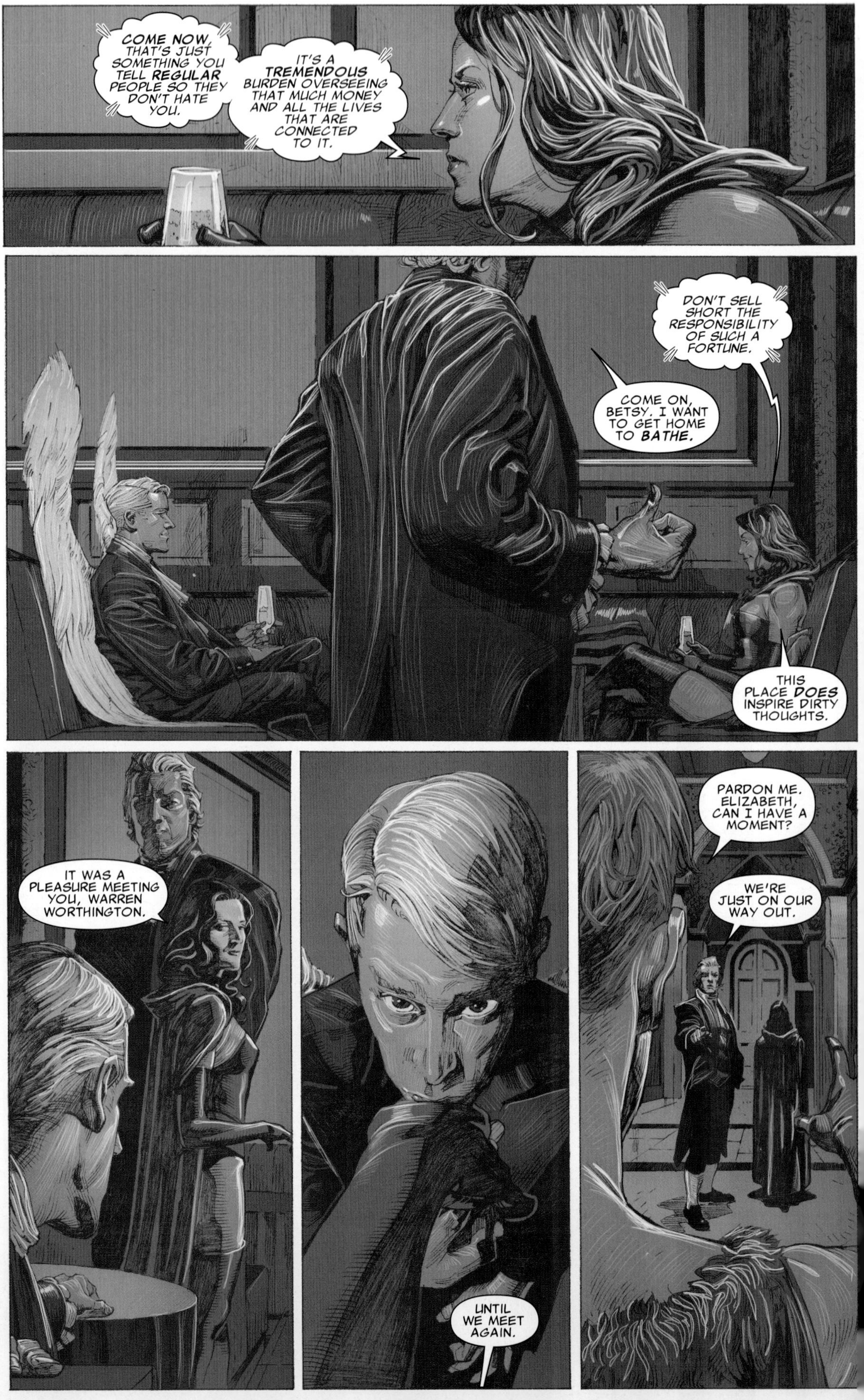
COME NOW, THAT'S JUST SOMETHING YOU TELL REGULAR PEOPLE SO THEY DON'T HATE YOU.
IT'S A TREMENDOUS BURDEN OVERSEEING THAT MUCH MONEY AND ALL THE LIVES THAT ARE CONNECTED TO IT.
DON'T SELL SHORT THE RESPONSIBILITY OF SUCH A FORTUNE.
COME ON, BETSY. I WANT TO GET HOME TO BATHE.
THIS PLACE DOES INSPIRE DIRTY THOUGHTS.
IT WAS A PLEASURE MEETING YOU, WARREN WORTHINGTON.
UNTIL WE MEET AGAIN.
PARDON ME. ELIZABETH, CAN I HAVE A MOMENT?
WE'RE JUST ON OUR WAY OUT.

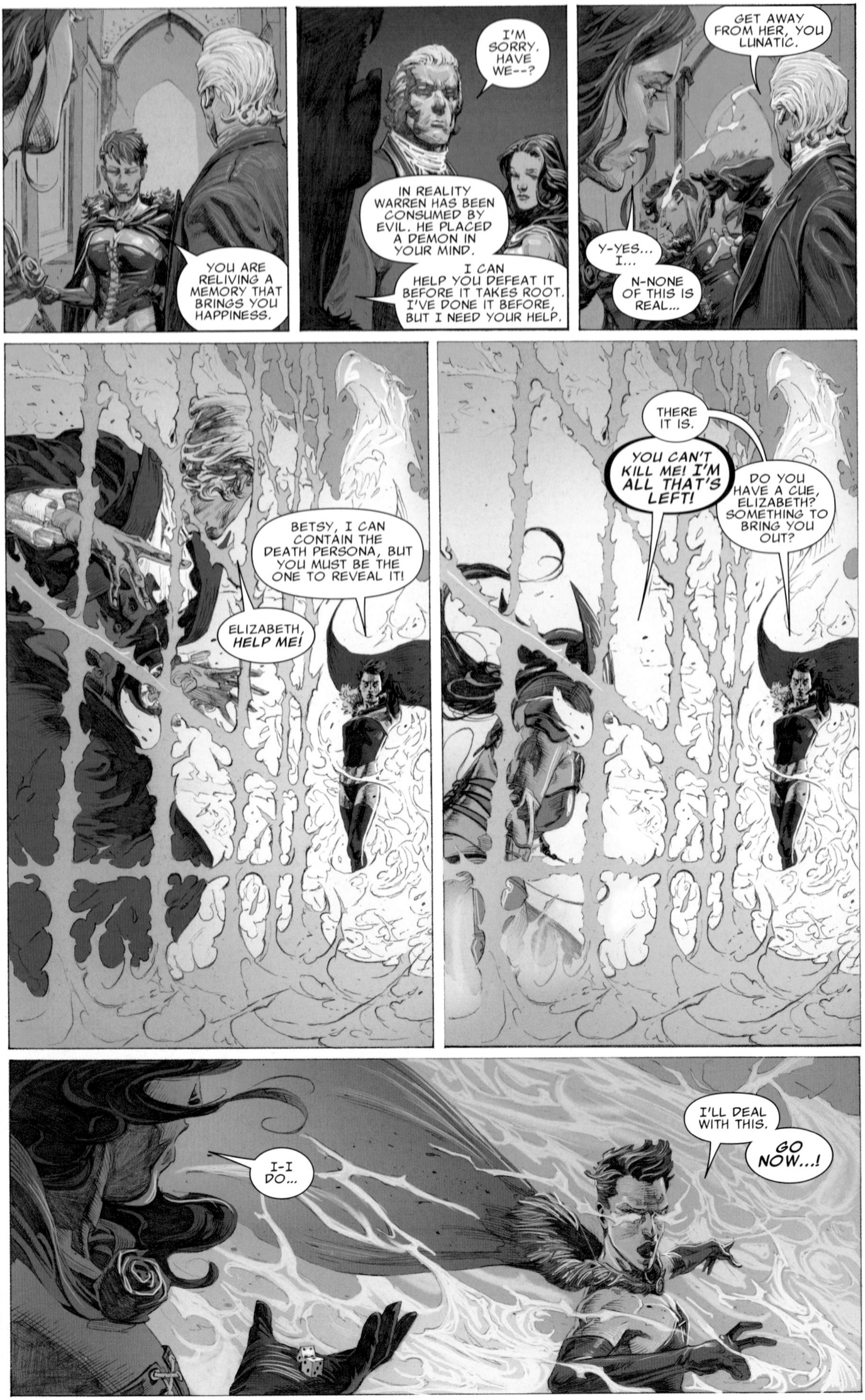
YOU ARE RELIVING A MEMORY THAT BRINGS YOU HAPPINESS.
I'M SORRY. HAVE WE--?
IN REALITY WARREN HAS BEEN CONSUMED BY EVIL. HE PLACED A DEMON IN YOUR MIND.
I CAN HELP YOU DEFEAT IT BEFORE IT TAKES ROOT. I'VE DONE IT BEFORE, BUT I NEED YOUR HELP.
GET AWAY FROM HER, YOU LUNATIC.
Y-YES... I...
N-NONE OF THIS IS REAL...
BETSY, I CAN CONTAIN THE DEATH PERSONA, BUT YOU MUST BE THE ONE TO REVEAL IT!
ELIZABETH, HELP ME!
THERE IT IS.
YOU CAN'T KILL ME! I'M ALL THAT'S LEFT!
DO YOU HAVE A CUE, ELIZABETH? SOMETHING TO BRING YOU OUT?
I-I DO...
I'LL DEAL WITH THIS.
GO NOW...!

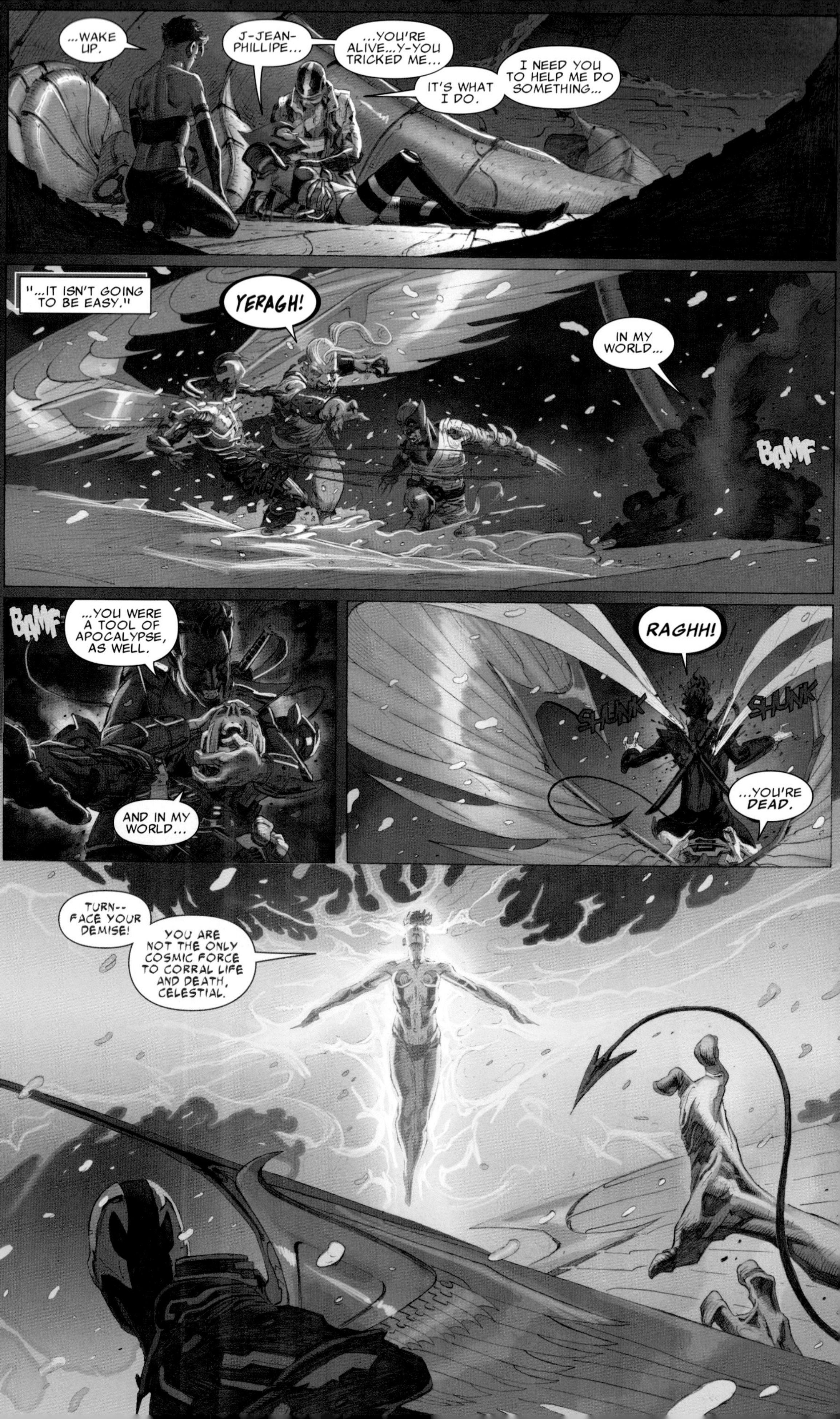
...WAKE UP.
J-JEAN-PHILLIPE...
...YOU'RE ALIVE...Y-YOU TRICKED ME...
IT'S WHAT I DO.
I NEED YOU TO HELP ME DO SOMETHING...
"...IT ISN'T GOING TO BE EASY."
YERAGH!
IN MY WORLD...
BAMF
BAMF
...YOU WERE A TOOL OF APOCALYPSE, AS WELL.
AND IN MY WORLD...
RAGHH!
SHUNK
SHUNK
...YOU'RE DEAD.
TURN--FACE YOUR DEMISE!
YOU ARE NOT THE ONLY COSMIC FORCE TO CORRAL LIFE AND DEATH, CELESTIAL.

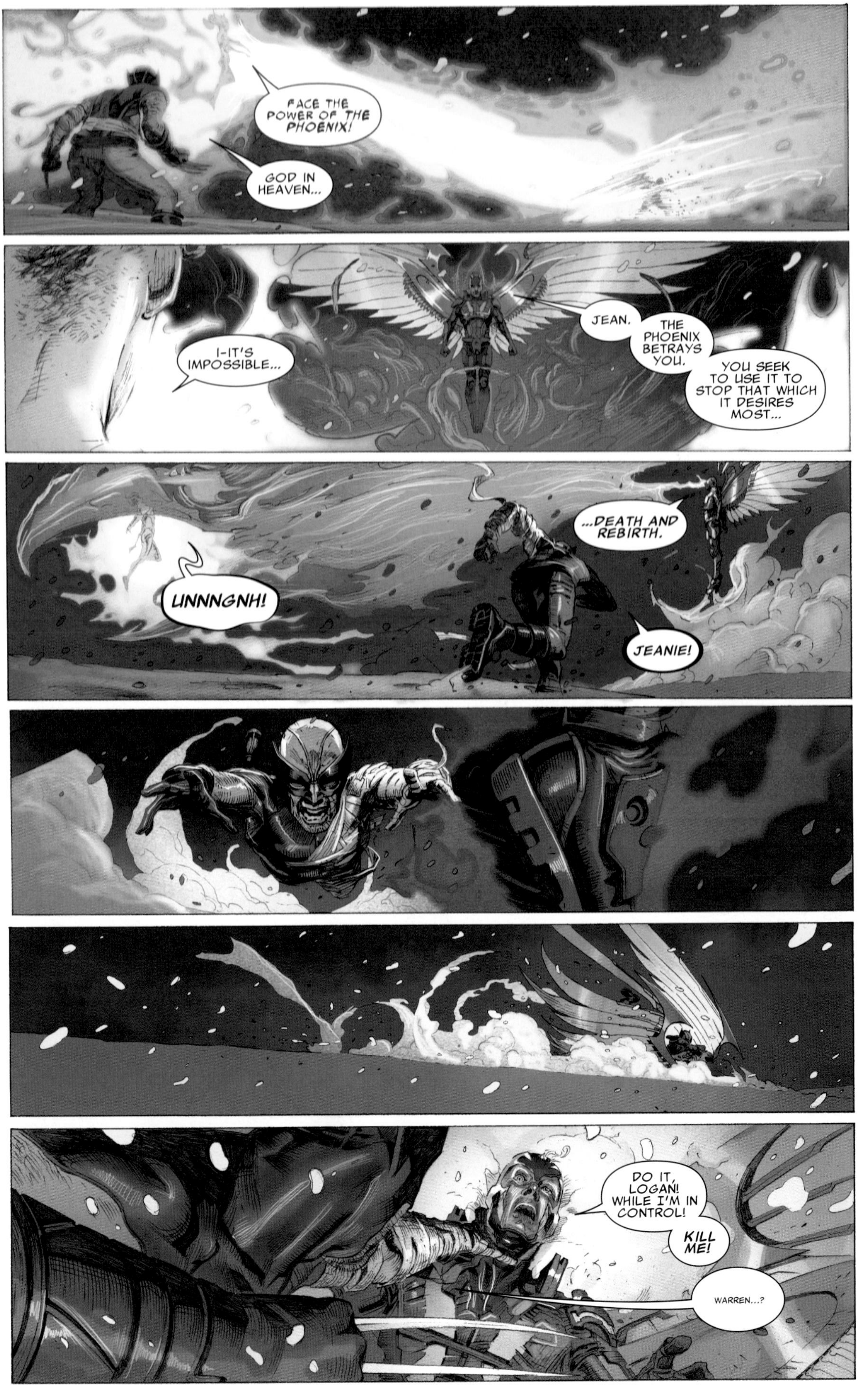
FACE THE POWER OF THE PHOENIX!
GOD IN HEAVEN...
I-IT'S IMPOSSIBLE...
JEAN.
THE PHOENIX BETRAYS YOU.
YOU SEEK TO USE IT TO STOP THAT WHICH IT DESIRES MOST...
...DEATH AND REBIRTH.
UNNNGNH!
JEANIE!
DO IT, LOGAN! WHILE I'M IN CONTROL!
KILL ME!
WARREN...?

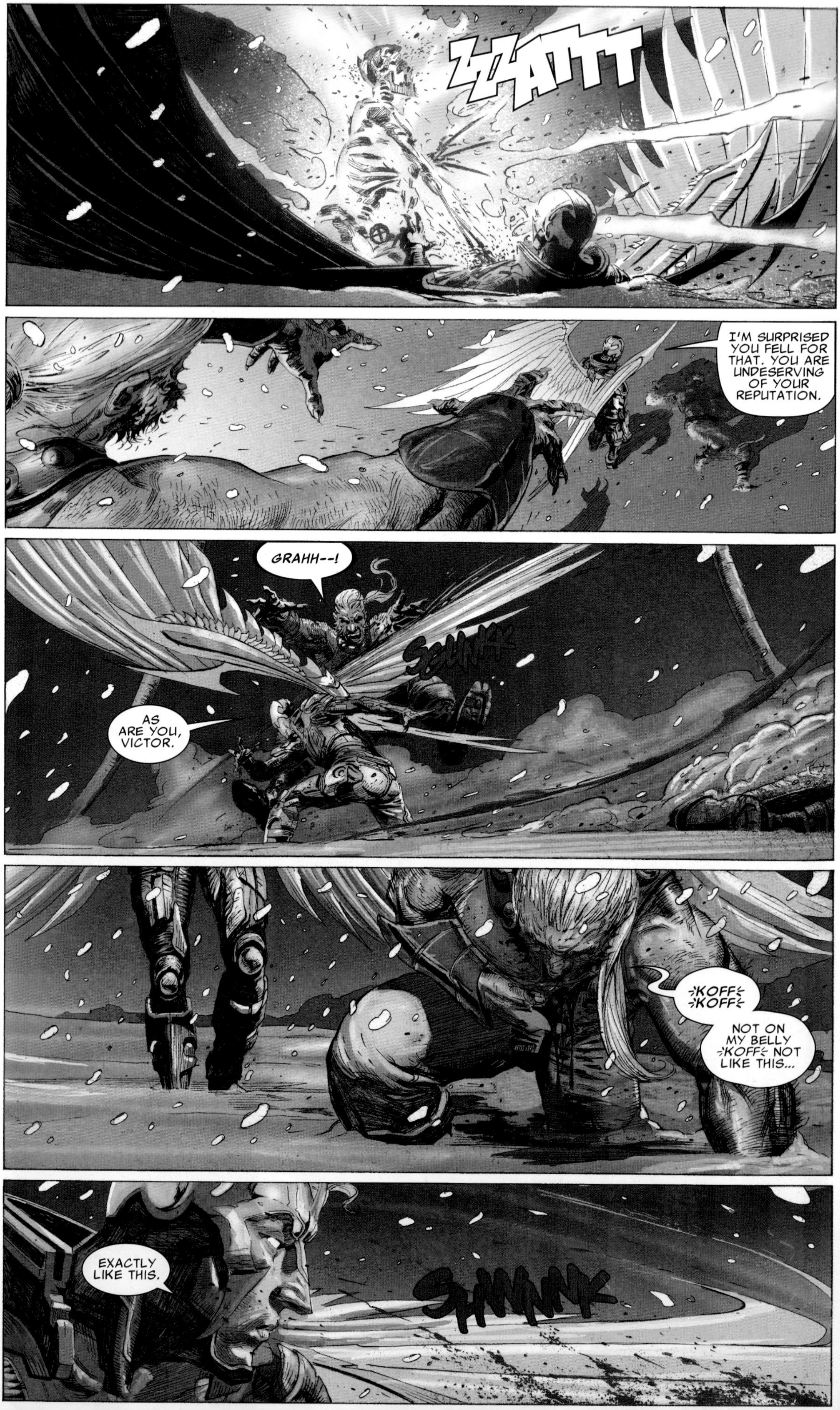
ZZZATTT
I'M SURPRISED YOU FELL FOR THAT. YOU ARE UNDESERVING OF YOUR REPUTATION.
GRAHH--!
AS ARE YOU, VICTOR.
KOFF *KOFF*
NOT ON MY BELLY *KOFF* NOT LIKE THIS...
EXACTLY LIKE THIS.
SHNNNK

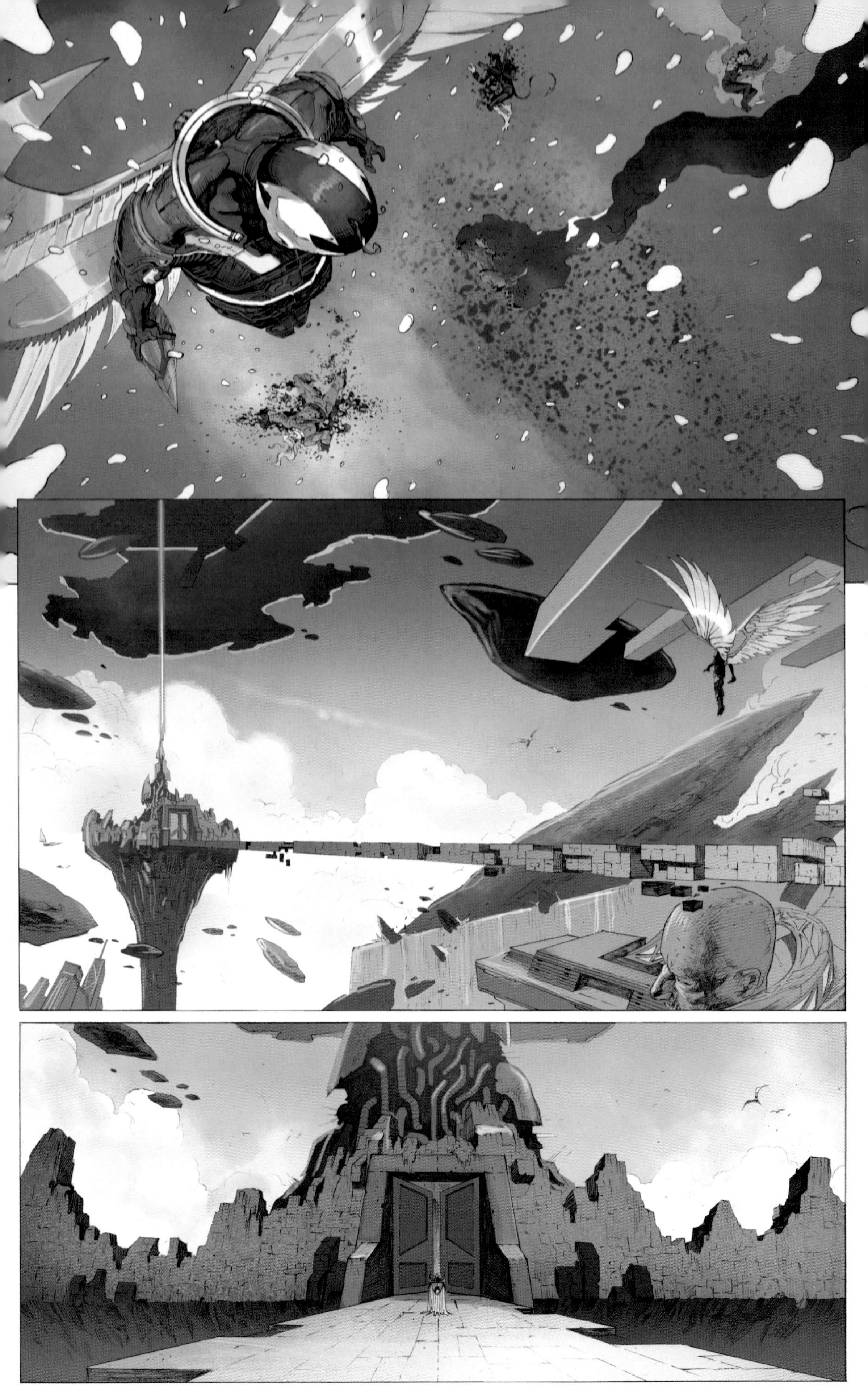

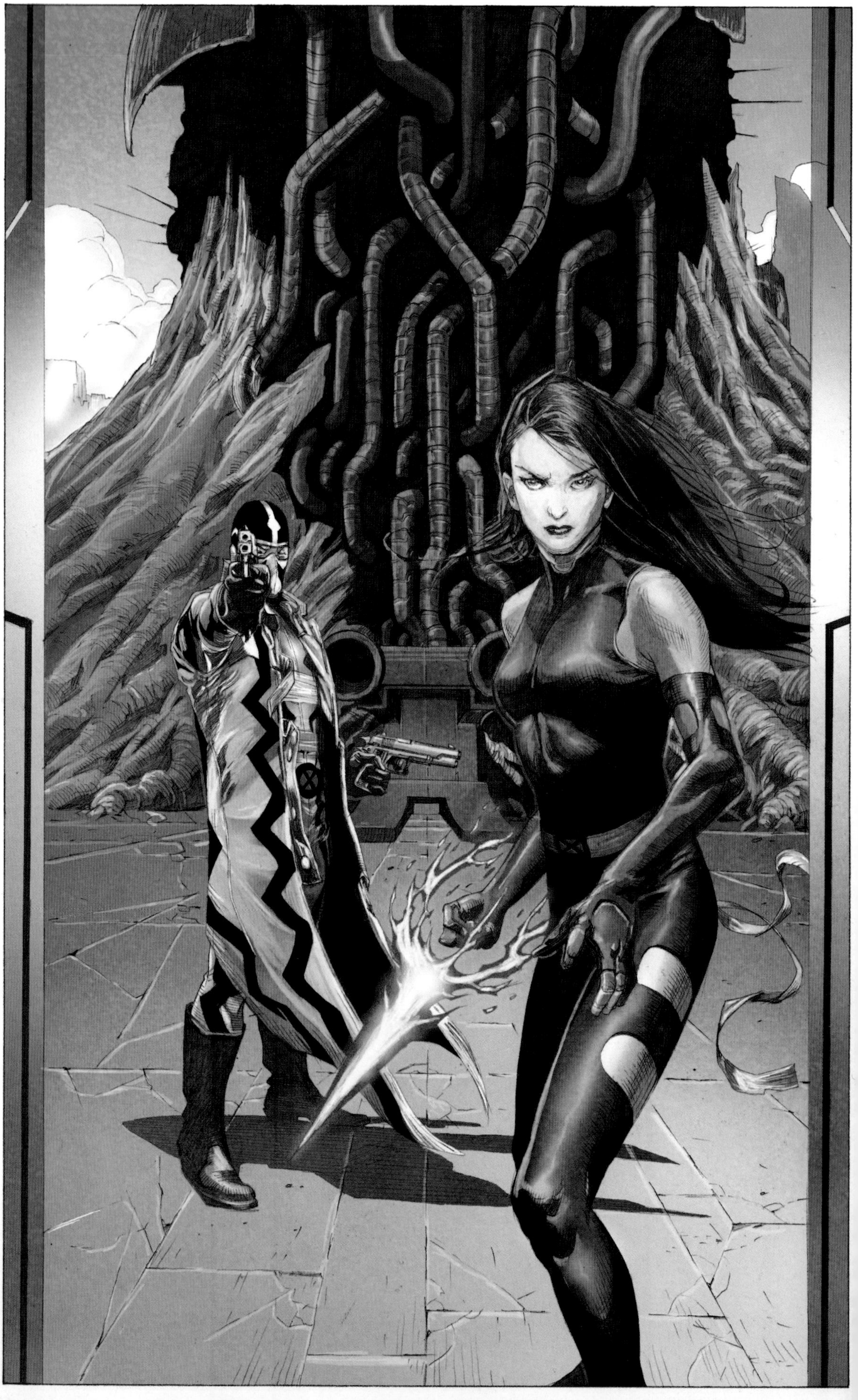

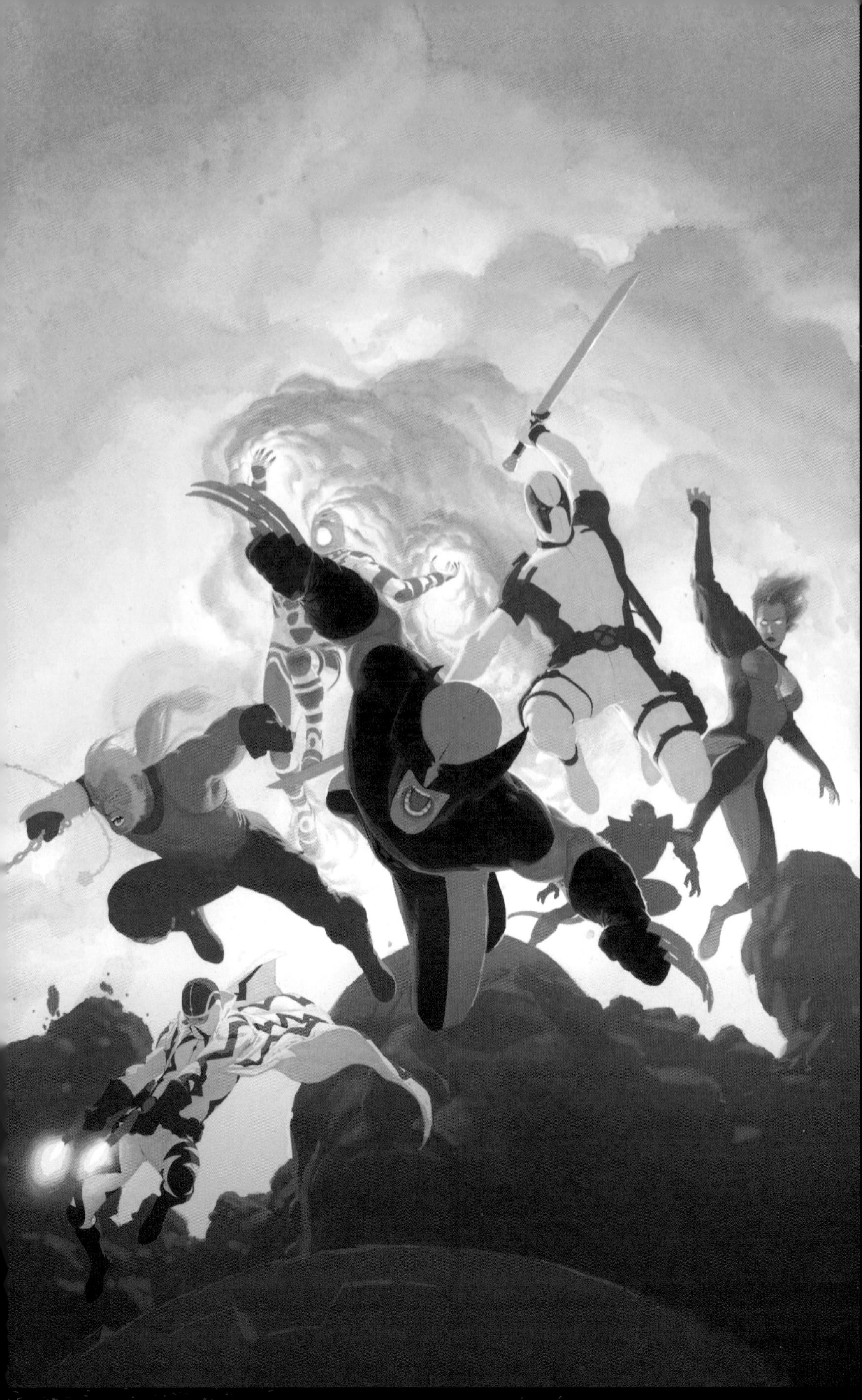

RED SKY BLUE

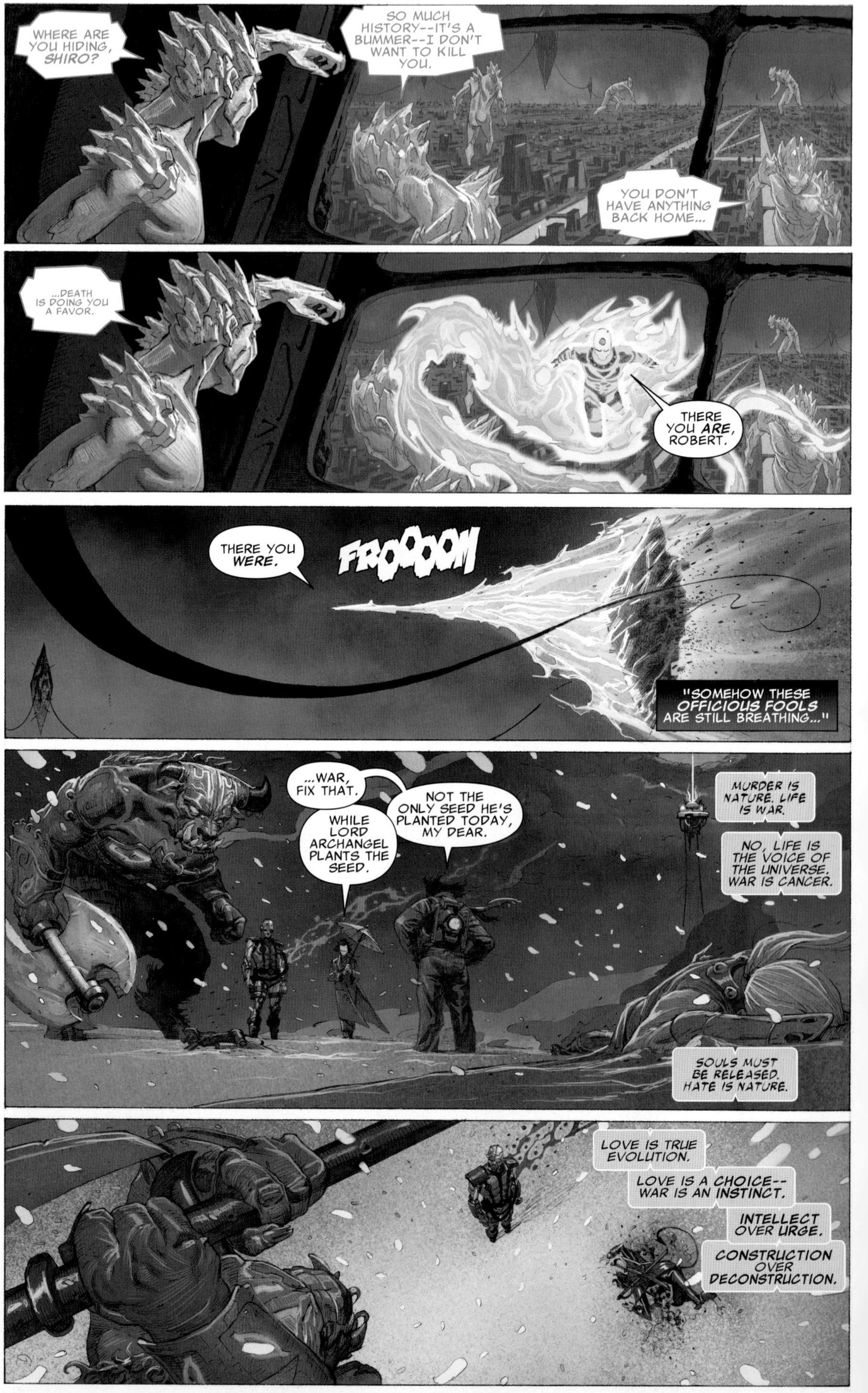
WHERE ARE YOU HIDING, SHIRO?
SO MUCH HISTORY--IT'S A BUMMER--I DON'T WANT TO KILL YOU.
YOU DON'T HAVE ANYTHING BACK HOME...
...DEATH IS DOING YOU A FAVOR.
THERE YOU ARE, ROBERT.
THERE YOU WERE.
FROOOOM
"SOMEHOW THESE OFFICIOUS FOOLS ARE STILL BREATHING..."
...WAR, FIX THAT.
WHILE LORD ARCHANGEL PLANTS THE SEED.
NOT THE ONLY SEED HE'S PLANTED TODAY, MY DEAR.
MURDER IS NATURE. LIFE IS WAR.
NO, LIFE IS THE VOICE OF THE UNIVERSE. WAR IS CANCER.
SOULS MUST BE RELEASED. HATE IS NATURE.
LOVE IS TRUE EVOLUTION.
LOVE IS A CHOICE-- WAR IS AN INSTINCT.
INTELLECT OVER URGE.
CONSTRUCTION OVER DECONSTRUCTION.

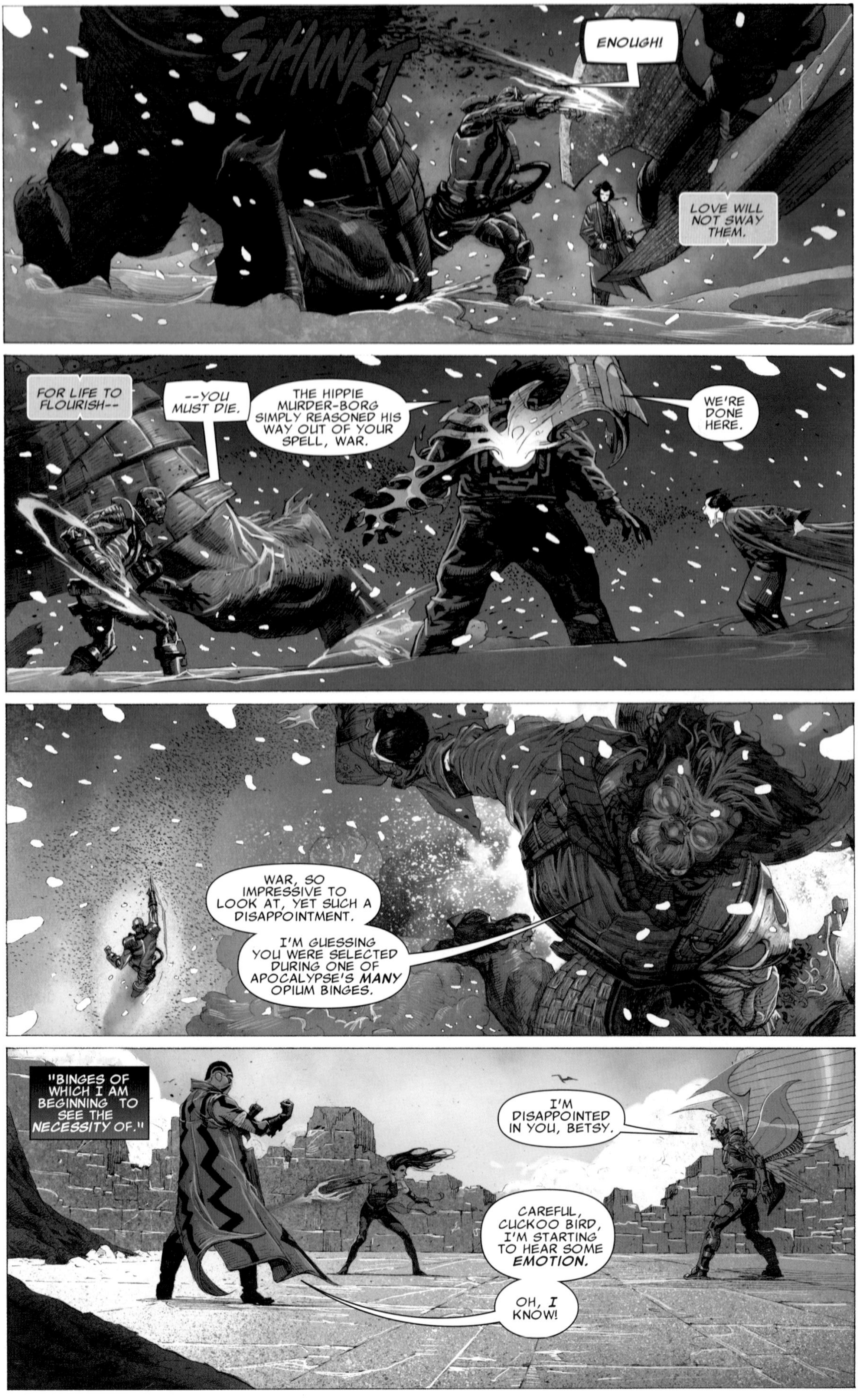
SHHNNK!
ENOUGH!
LOVE WILL NOT SWAY THEM.
FOR LIFE TO FLOURISH--
--YOU MUST DIE.
THE HIPPIE MURDER-BORG SIMPLY REASONED HIS WAY OUT OF YOUR SPELL, WAR.
WE'RE DONE HERE.
WAR, SO IMPRESSIVE TO LOOK AT, YET SUCH A DISAPPOINTMENT.
I'M GUESSING YOU WERE SELECTED DURING ONE OF APOCALYPSE'S MANY OPIUM BINGES.
"BINGES OF WHICH I AM BEGINNING TO SEE THE NECESSITY OF."
I'M DISAPPOINTED IN YOU, BETSY.
CAREFUL, CUCKOO BIRD, I'M STARTING TO HEAR SOME EMOTION.
OH, I KNOW!

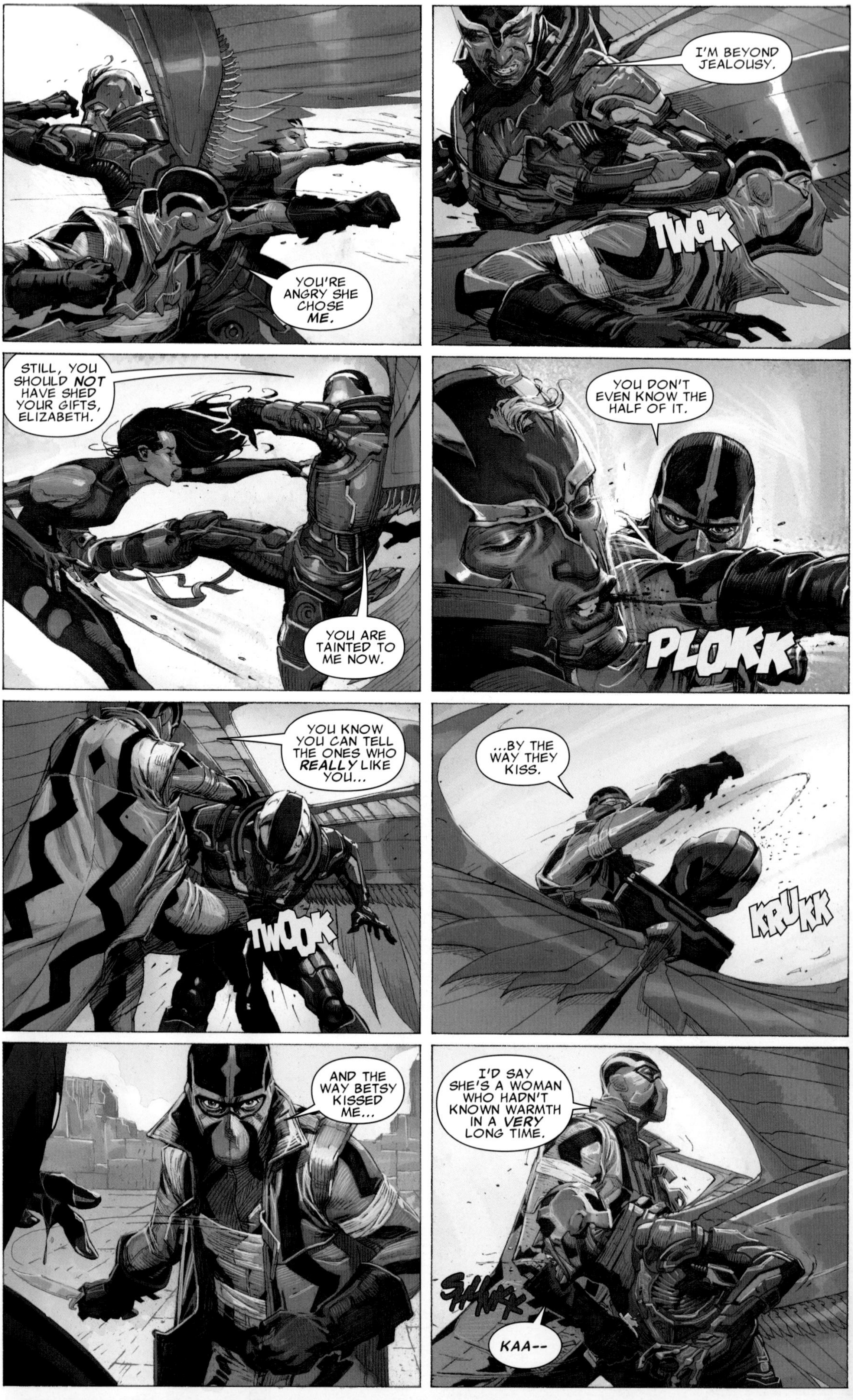
YOU'RE ANGRY SHE CHOSE *ME.*
I'M BEYOND JEALOUSY.
TWOK
STILL, YOU SHOULD *NOT* HAVE SHED YOUR GIFTS, ELIZABETH.
YOU ARE TAINTED TO ME NOW.
YOU DON'T EVEN KNOW THE HALF OF IT.
PLOKK
YOU KNOW YOU CAN TELL THE ONES WHO *REALLY* LIKE YOU...
TWOOK
...BY THE WAY THEY KISS.
KRUKK
AND THE WAY BETSY KISSED ME...
I'D SAY SHE'S A WOMAN WHO HADN'T KNOWN WARMTH IN A *VERY* LONG TIME.
KAA--

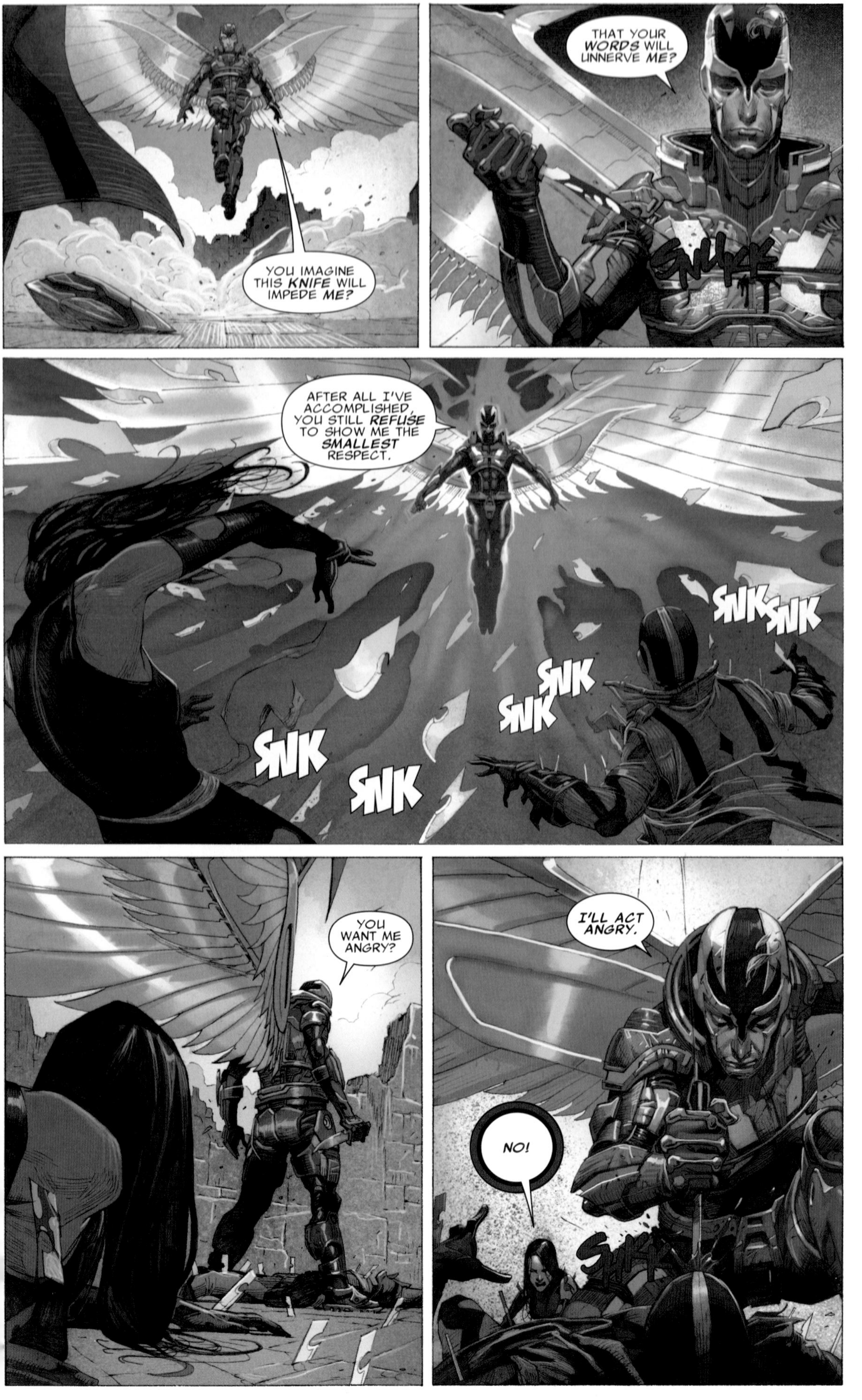
YOU IMAGINE THIS KNIFE WILL IMPEDE ME?
THAT YOUR WORDS WILL UNNERVE ME?
AFTER ALL I'VE ACCOMPLISHED, YOU STILL REFUSE TO SHOW ME THE SMALLEST RESPECT.
SNK
SNK
SNK
SNK
SNK
SNK
YOU WANT ME ANGRY?
I'LL ACT ANGRY.
NO!

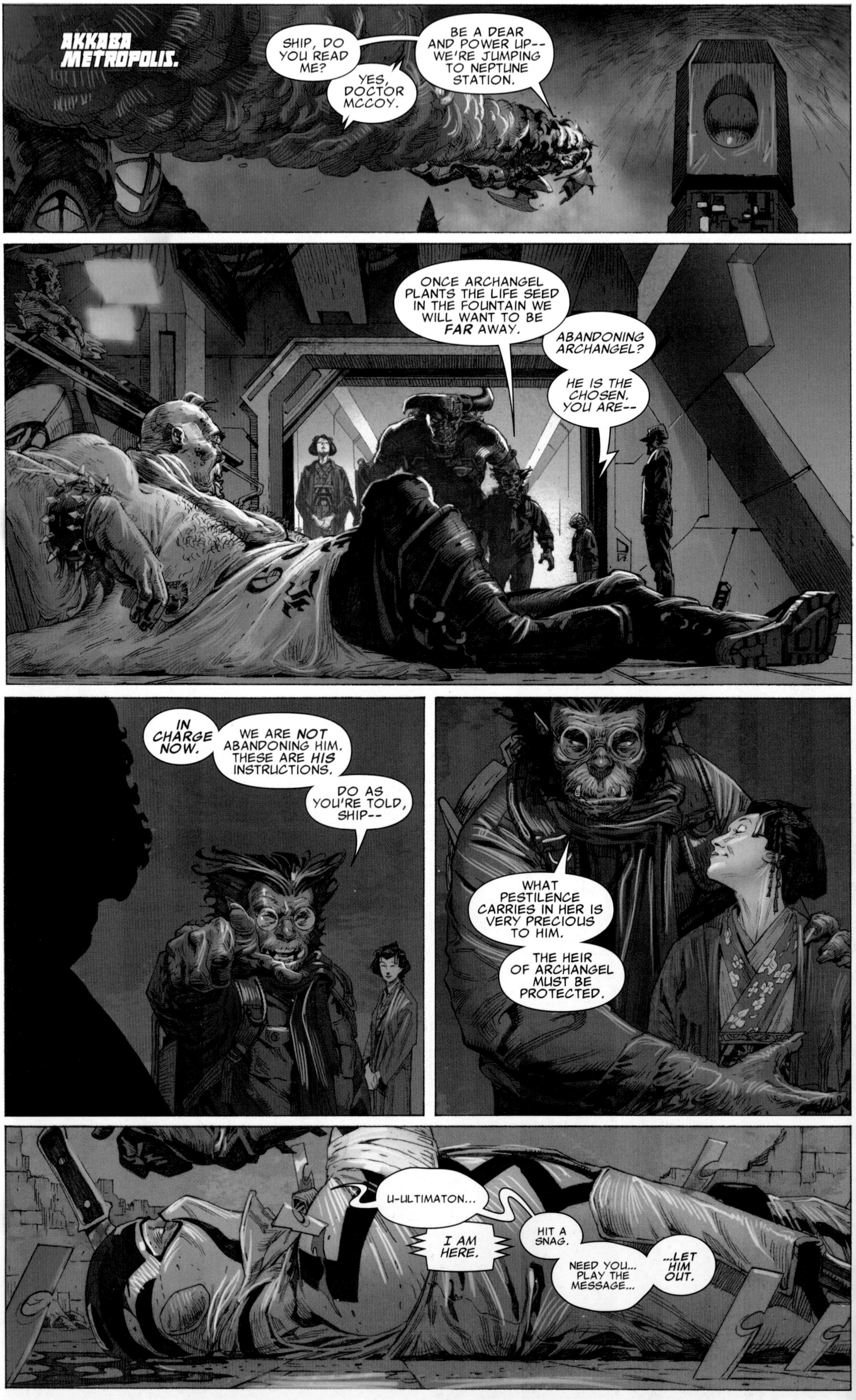
AKKABA METROPOLIS.
SHIP, DO YOU READ ME?
YES, DOCTOR MCCOY.
BE A DEAR AND POWER UP--WE'RE JUMPING TO NEPTUNE STATION.
ONCE ARCHANGEL PLANTS THE LIFE SEED IN THE FOUNTAIN WE WILL WANT TO BE FAR AWAY.
ABANDONING ARCHANGEL?
HE IS THE CHOSEN. YOU ARE--
IN CHARGE NOW.
WE ARE NOT ABANDONING HIM. THESE ARE HIS INSTRUCTIONS.
DO AS YOU'RE TOLD, SHIP--
WHAT PESTILENCE CARRIES IN HER IS VERY PRECIOUS TO HIM.
THE HEIR OF ARCHANGEL MUST BE PROTECTED.
U-ULTIMATON...
I AM HERE.
HIT A SNAG.
NEED YOU... PLAY THE MESSAGE...
...LET HIM OUT.

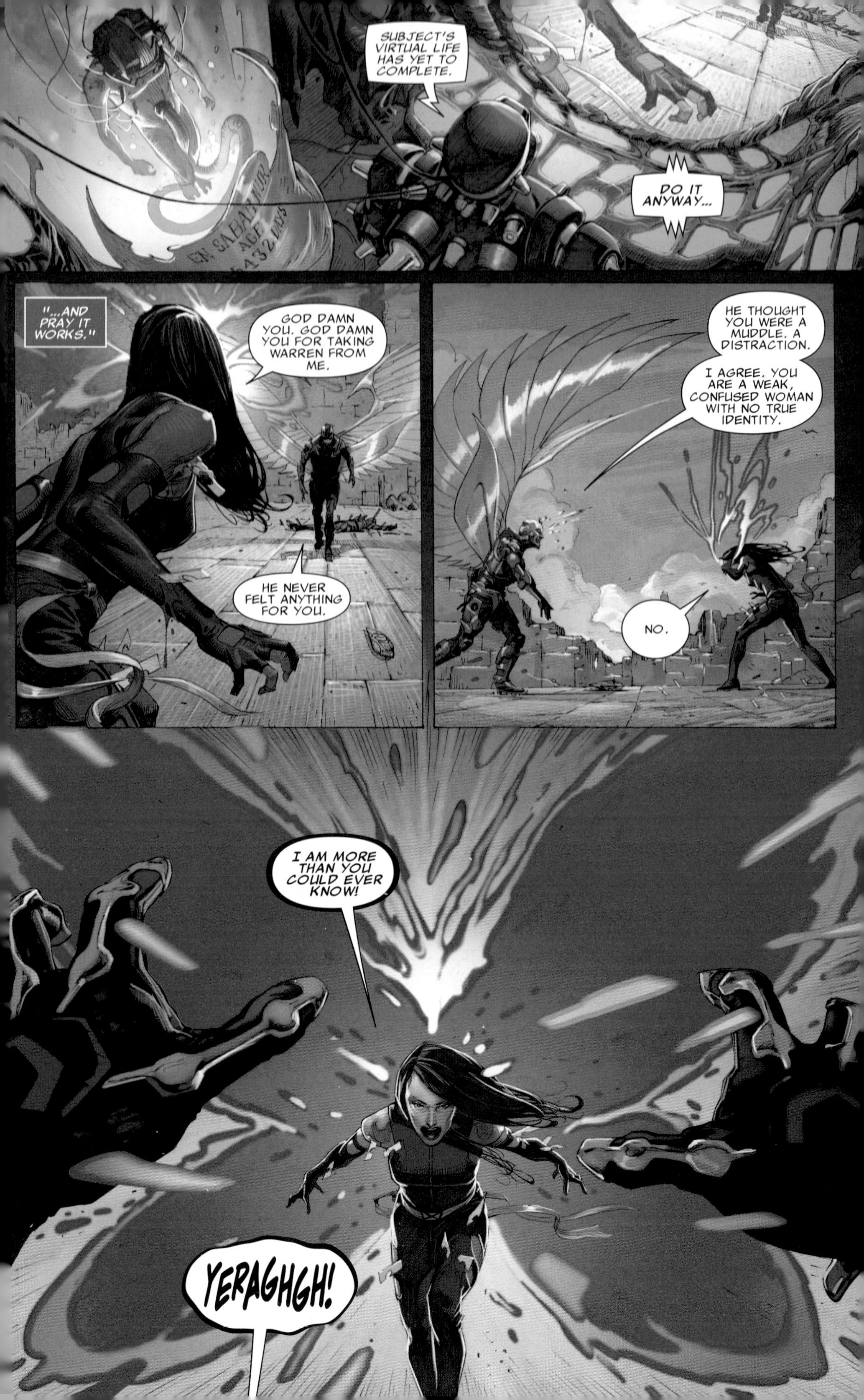
SUBJECT'S VIRTUAL LIFE HAS YET TO COMPLETE.
DO IT ANYWAY...
"...AND PRAY IT WORKS."
GOD DAMN YOU. GOD DAMN YOU FOR TAKING WARREN FROM ME.
HE NEVER FELT ANYTHING FOR YOU.
HE THOUGHT YOU WERE A MUDDLE, A DISTRACTION.
I AGREE. YOU ARE A WEAK, CONFUSED WOMAN WITH NO TRUE IDENTITY.
NO.
I AM MORE THAN YOU COULD EVER KNOW!
YERAGHGH!

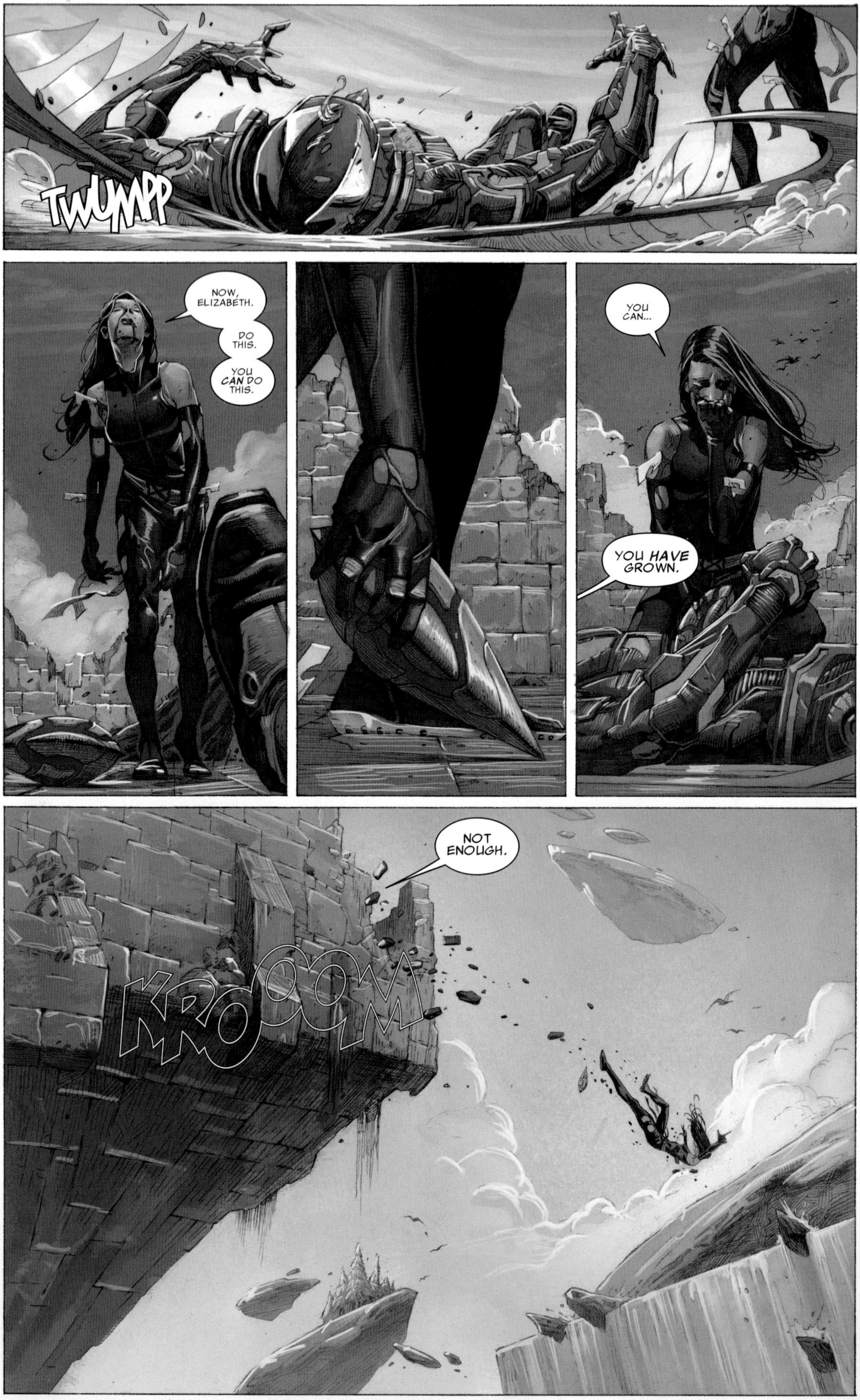
TWUMPP
NOW, ELIZABETH.
DO THIS.
YOU CAN DO THIS.
YOU CAN...
YOU HAVE GROWN.
NOT ENOUGH.
KROOOOM

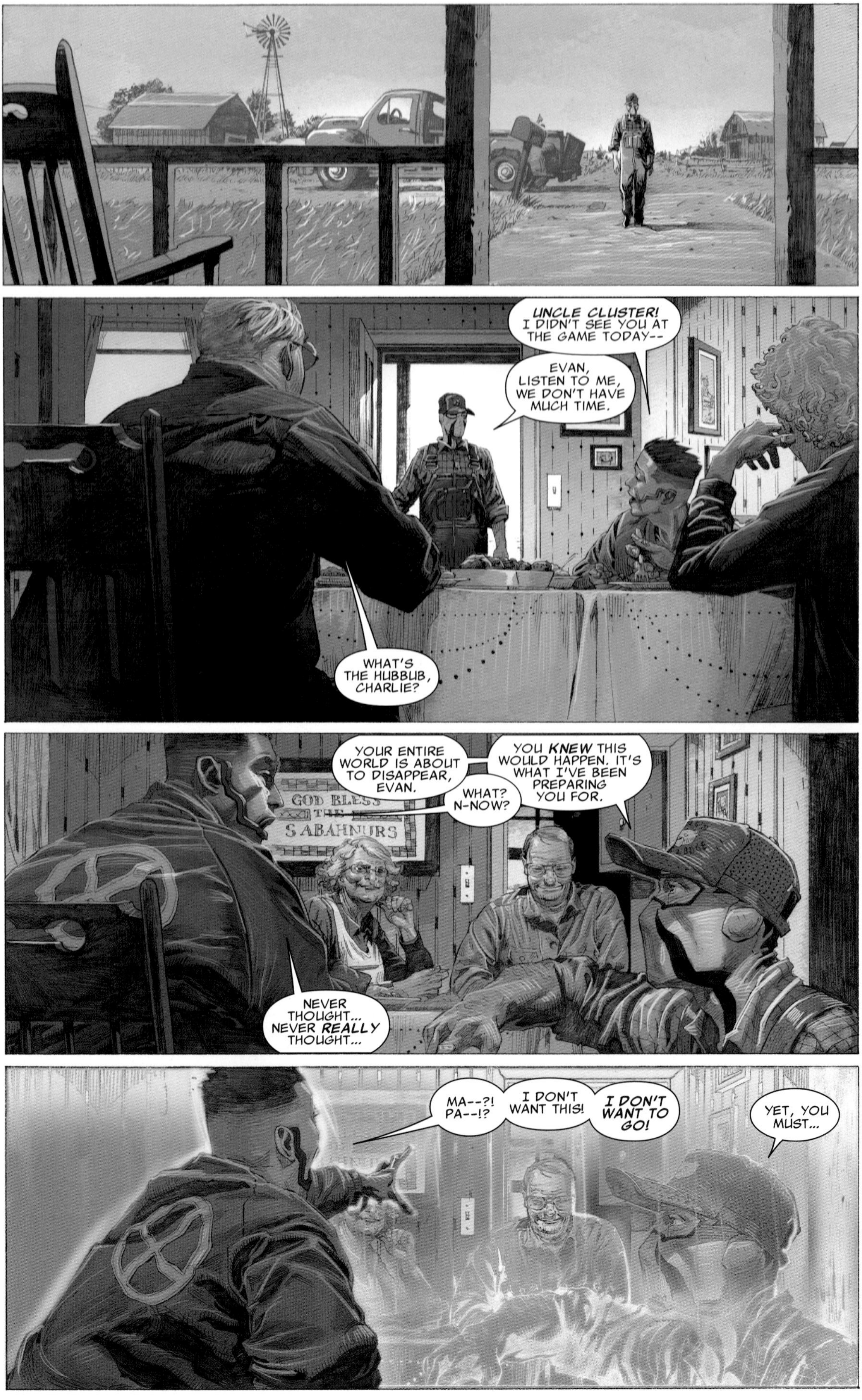
UNCLE CLUSTER! I DIDN'T SEE YOU AT THE GAME TODAY--
EVAN, LISTEN TO ME, WE DON'T HAVE MUCH TIME.
WHAT'S THE HUBBUB, CHARLIE?
YOUR ENTIRE WORLD IS ABOUT TO DISAPPEAR, EVAN.
GOD BLESS THE SABAHNURS
WHAT? N-NOW?
YOU **KNEW** THIS WOULD HAPPEN. IT'S WHAT I'VE BEEN PREPARING YOU FOR.
NEVER THOUGHT... NEVER **REALLY** THOUGHT...
MA--?! PA--!?
I DON'T WANT THIS!
I DON'T WANT TO GO!
YET, YOU MUST...

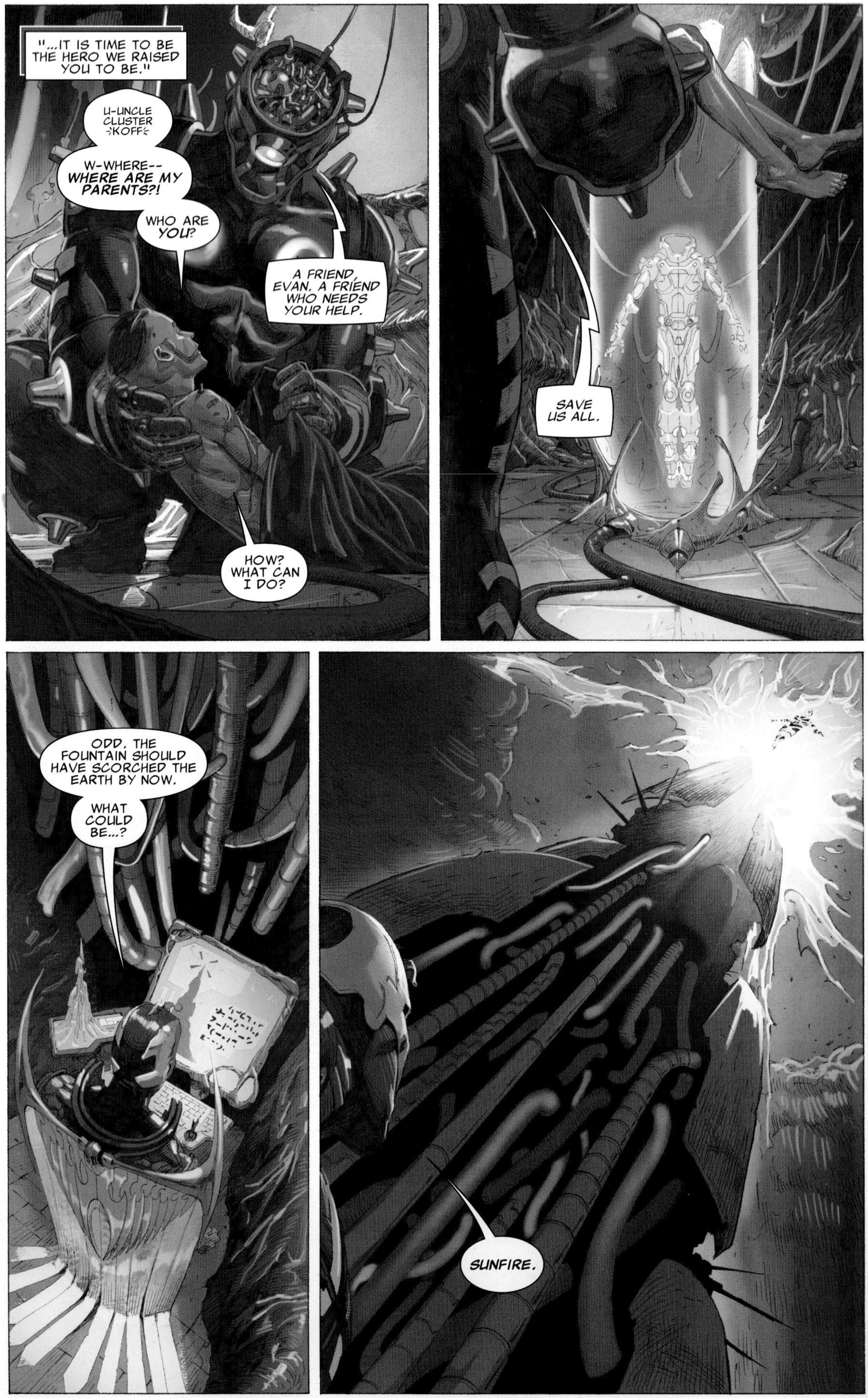
"...IT IS TIME TO BE THE HERO WE RAISED YOU TO BE."
U-UNCLE CLUSTER -KOFF-
W-WHERE-- WHERE ARE MY PARENTS?!
WHO ARE YOU?
A FRIEND, EVAN. A FRIEND WHO NEEDS YOUR HELP.
HOW? WHAT CAN I DO?
SAVE US ALL.
ODD. THE FOUNTAIN SHOULD HAVE SCORCHED THE EARTH BY NOW.
WHAT COULD BE...?
SUNFIRE.

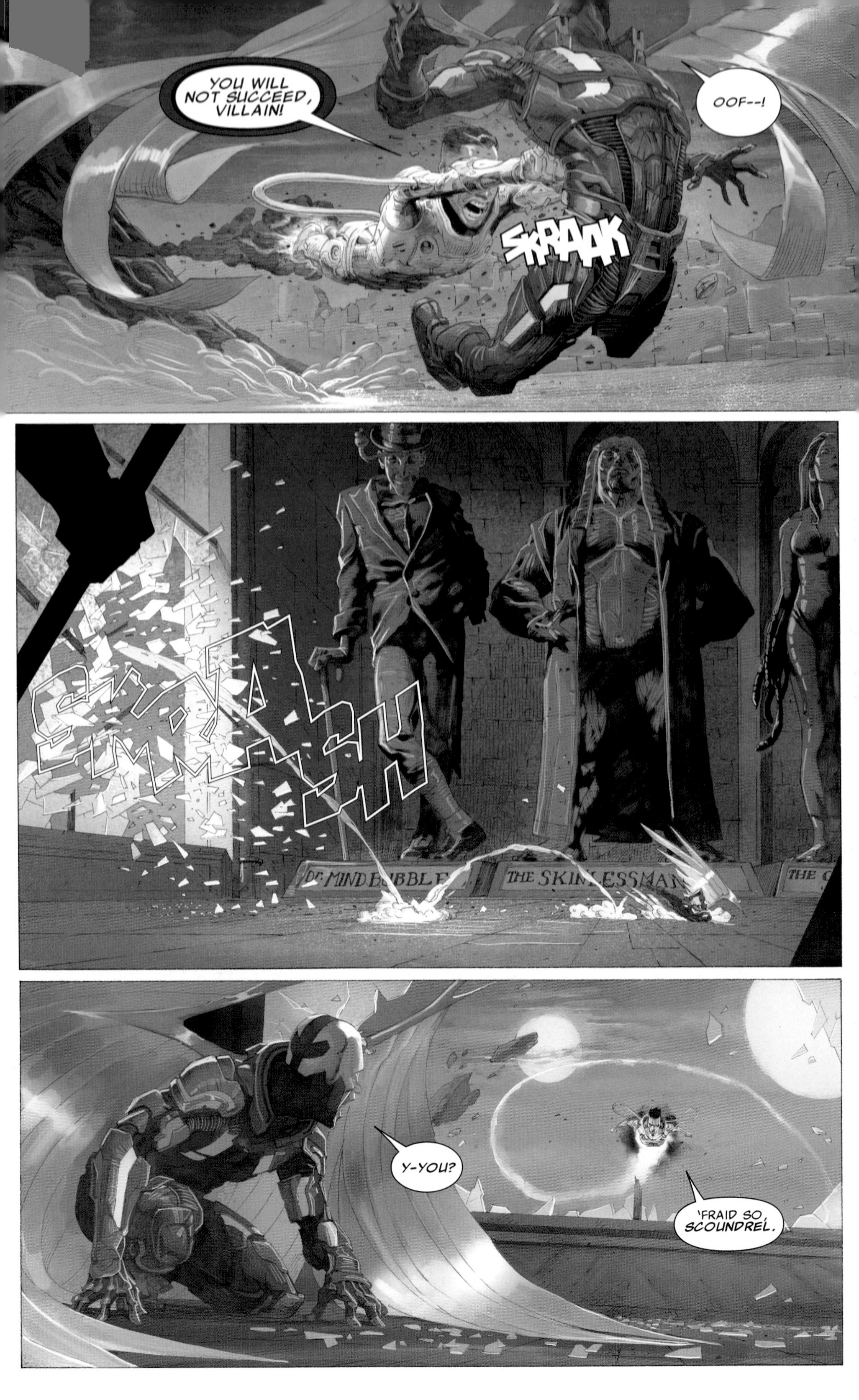
YOU WILL NOT SUCCEED, VILLAIN!
OOF--!
SKRAAK
Y-YOU?
'FRAID SO, SCOUNDREL.

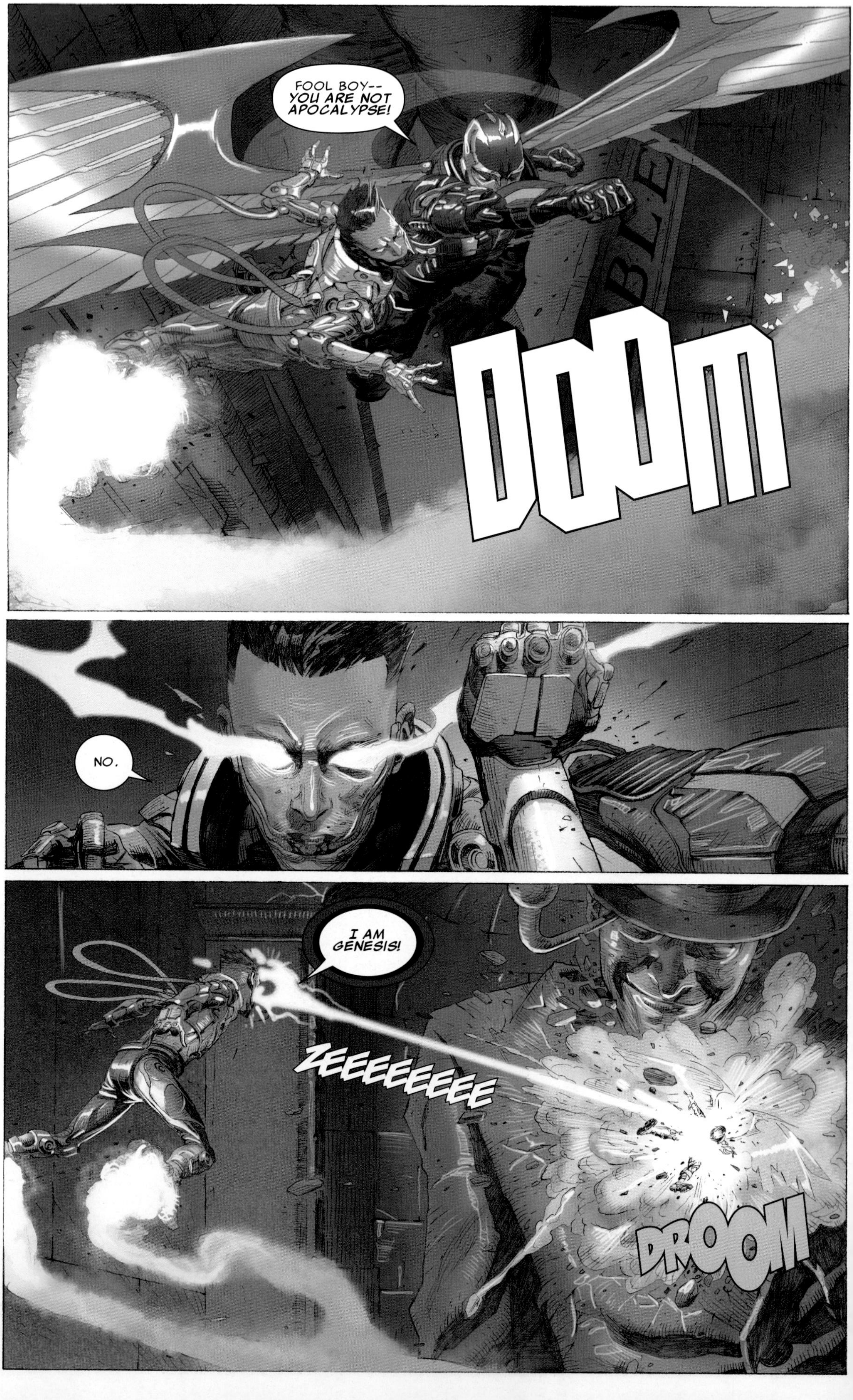
FOOL BOY--
YOU ARE NOT APOCALYPSE!
DOOM
NO.
I AM GENESIS!
ZEEEEEEEE
DROOM

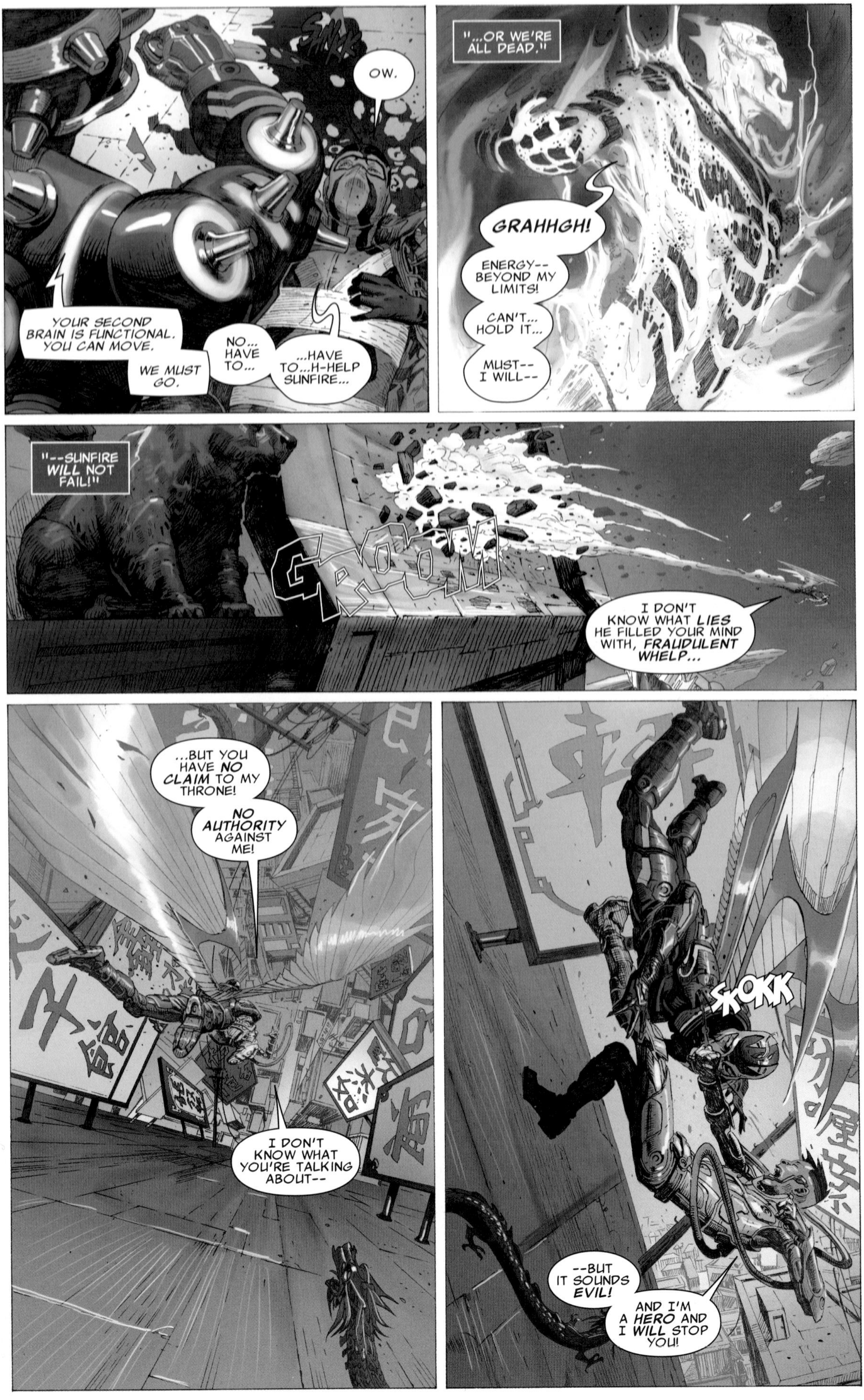
SNKK
OW.
YOUR SECOND BRAIN IS FUNCTIONAL. YOU CAN MOVE.
WE MUST GO.
NO... HAVE TO...
...HAVE TO...H-HELP SUNFIRE...
"...OR WE'RE ALL DEAD."
GRAHHGH!
ENERGY-- BEYOND MY LIMITS!
CAN'T... HOLD IT...
MUST-- I WILL--
"--SUNFIRE WILL NOT FAIL!"
GROOOM
I DON'T KNOW WHAT LIES HE FILLED YOUR MIND WITH, FRAUDULENT WHELP...
...BUT YOU HAVE NO CLAIM TO MY THRONE!
NO AUTHORITY AGAINST ME!
I DON'T KNOW WHAT YOU'RE TALKING ABOUT--
SKOKK
--BUT IT SOUNDS EVIL!
AND I'M A HERO AND I WILL STOP YOU!

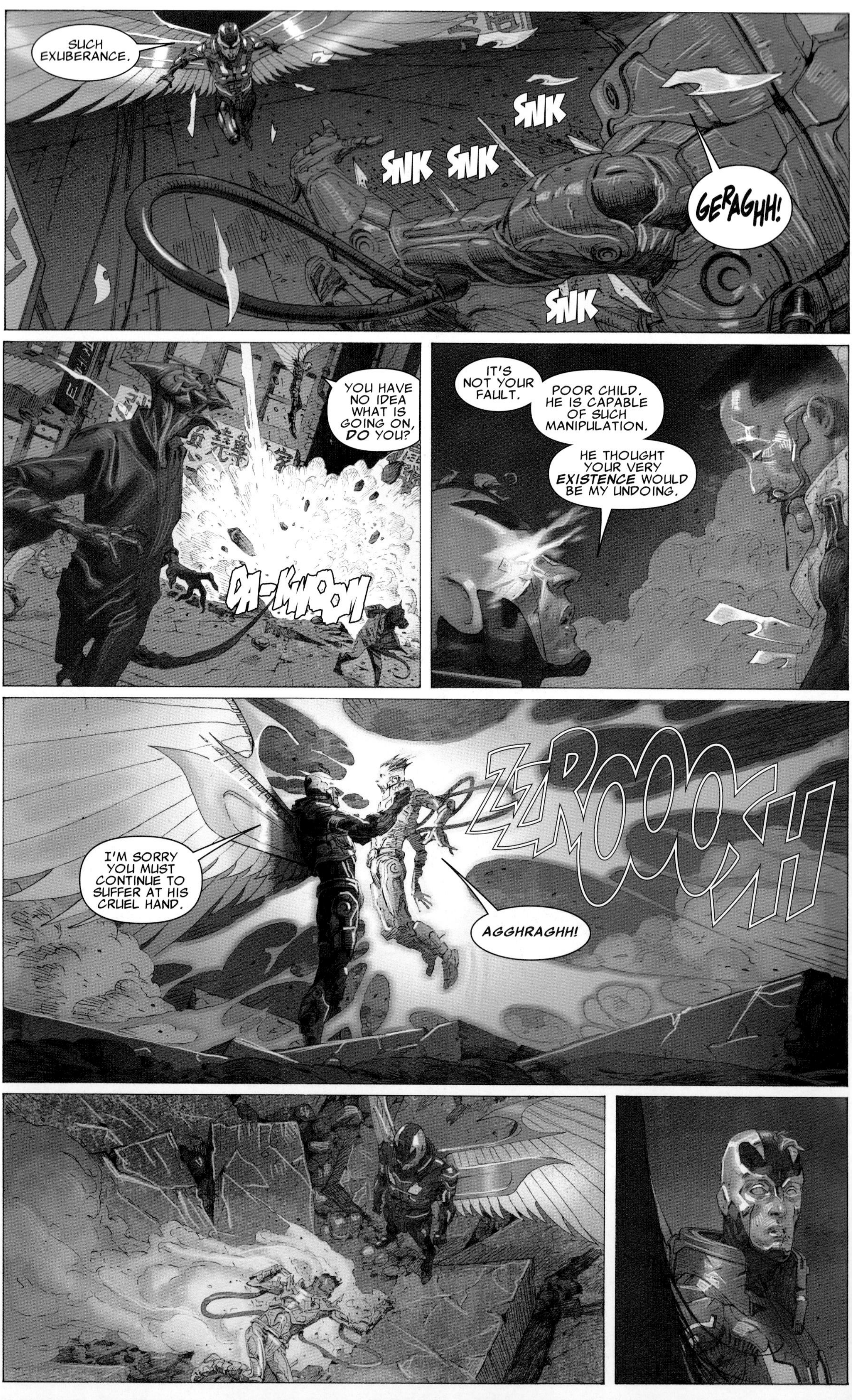
SUCH EXUBERANCE.
SNK
SNK SNK
GERAGHH!
SNK
YOU HAVE NO IDEA WHAT IS GOING ON, DO YOU?
DA-KOOM
IT'S NOT YOUR FAULT.
POOR CHILD. HE IS CAPABLE OF SUCH MANIPULATION.
HE THOUGHT YOUR VERY EXISTENCE WOULD BE MY UNDOING.
ZZROOOOOOOOOOOOOOOOOCH
I'M SORRY YOU MUST CONTINUE TO SUFFER AT HIS CRUEL HAND.
AGGHRAGHH!

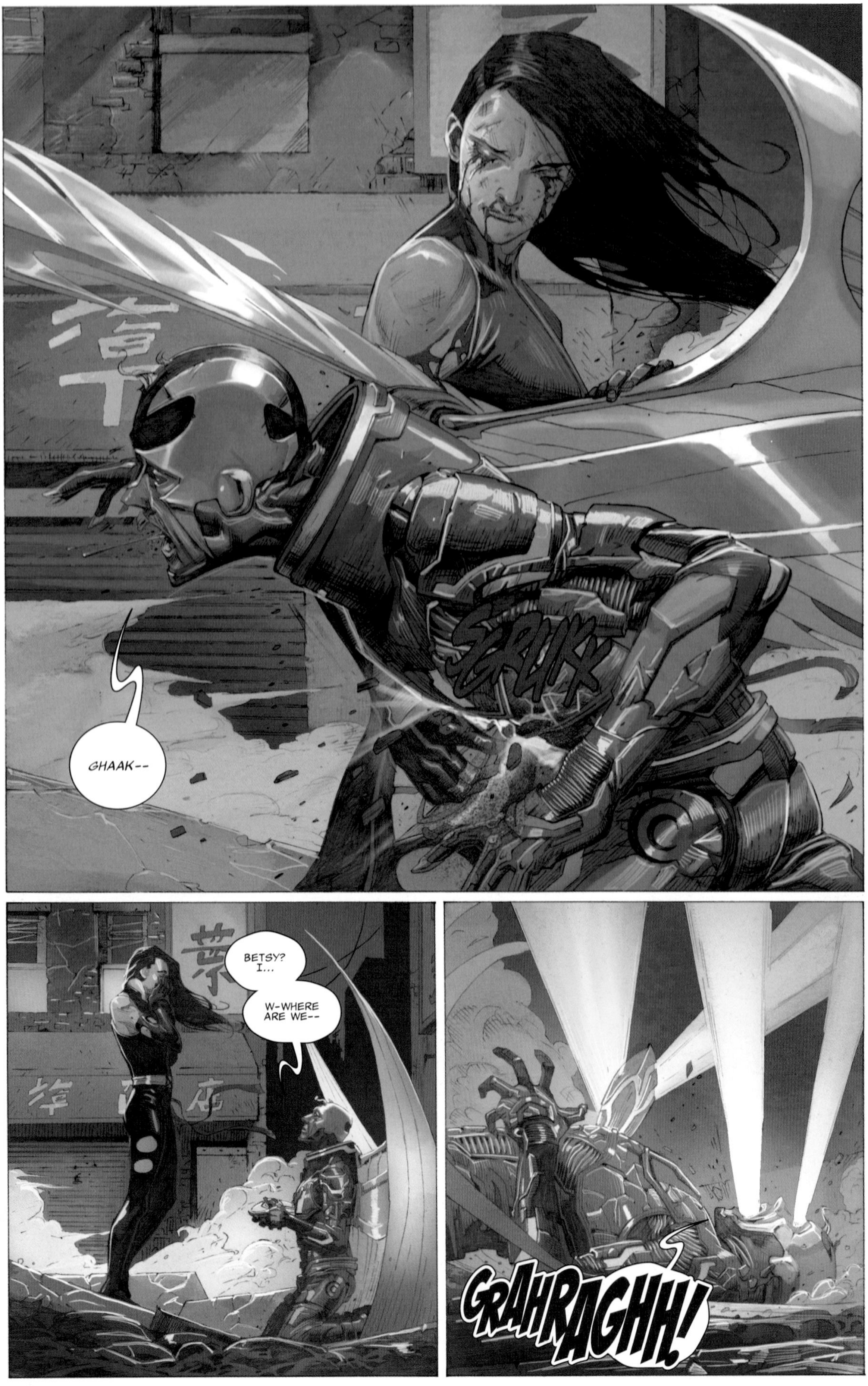
SCRUKK
GHAAK--
BETSY? I...
W-WHERE ARE WE--
GRAHRAGHH!

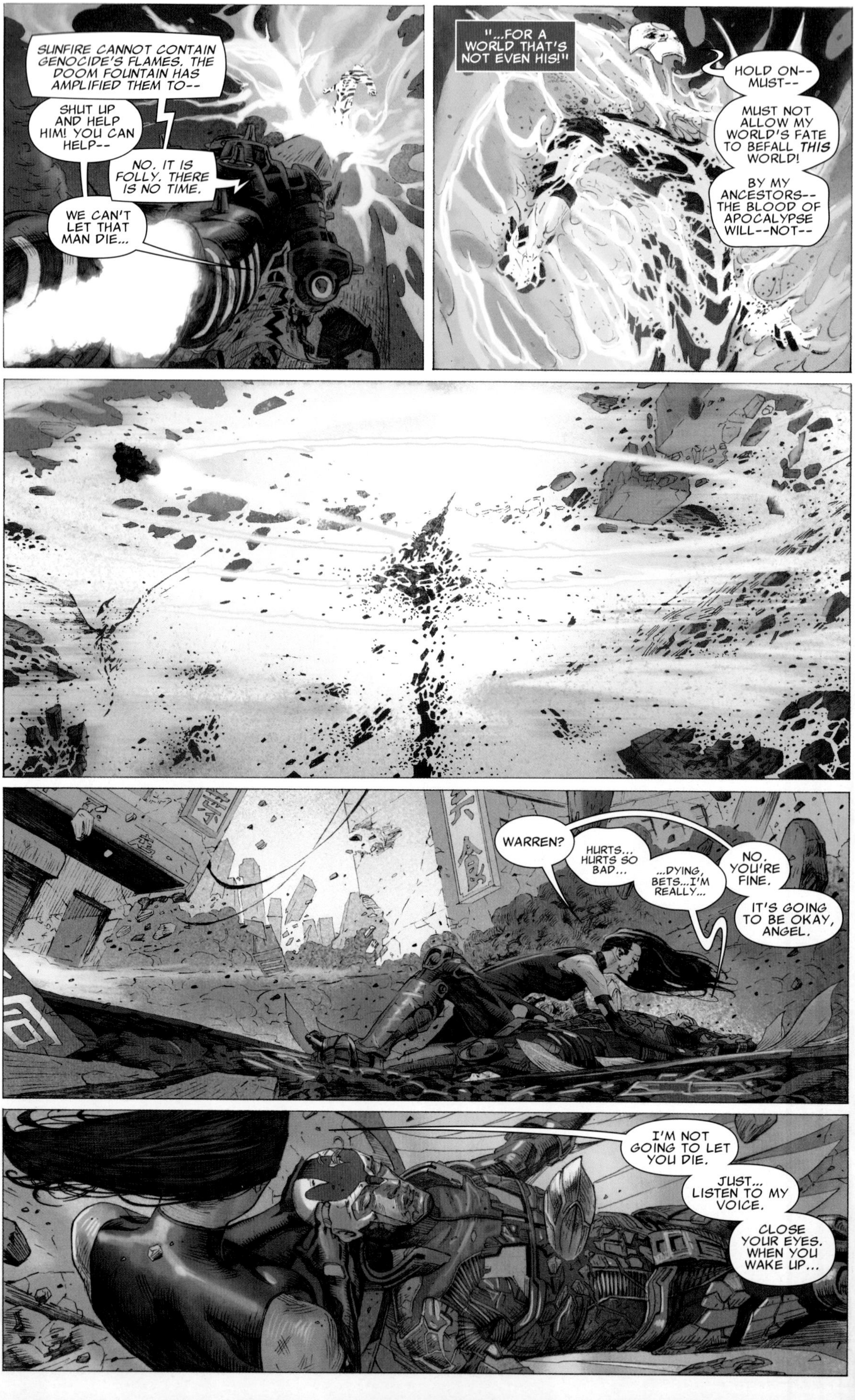
SUNFIRE CANNOT CONTAIN GENOCIDE'S FLAMES. THE DOOM FOUNTAIN HAS AMPLIFIED THEM TO--
SHUT UP AND HELP HIM! YOU CAN HELP--
NO. IT IS FOLLY. THERE IS NO TIME.
WE CAN'T LET THAT MAN DIE...
"...FOR A WORLD THAT'S NOT EVEN HIS!"
HOLD ON-- MUST--
MUST NOT ALLOW MY WORLD'S FATE TO BEFALL THIS WORLD!
BY MY ANCESTORS-- THE BLOOD OF APOCALYPSE WILL--NOT--
WARREN?
HURTS... HURTS SO BAD...
...DYING, BETS...I'M REALLY...
NO. YOU'RE FINE.
IT'S GOING TO BE OKAY, ANGEL.
I'M NOT GOING TO LET YOU DIE.
JUST... LISTEN TO MY VOICE.
CLOSE YOUR EYES. WHEN YOU WAKE UP...

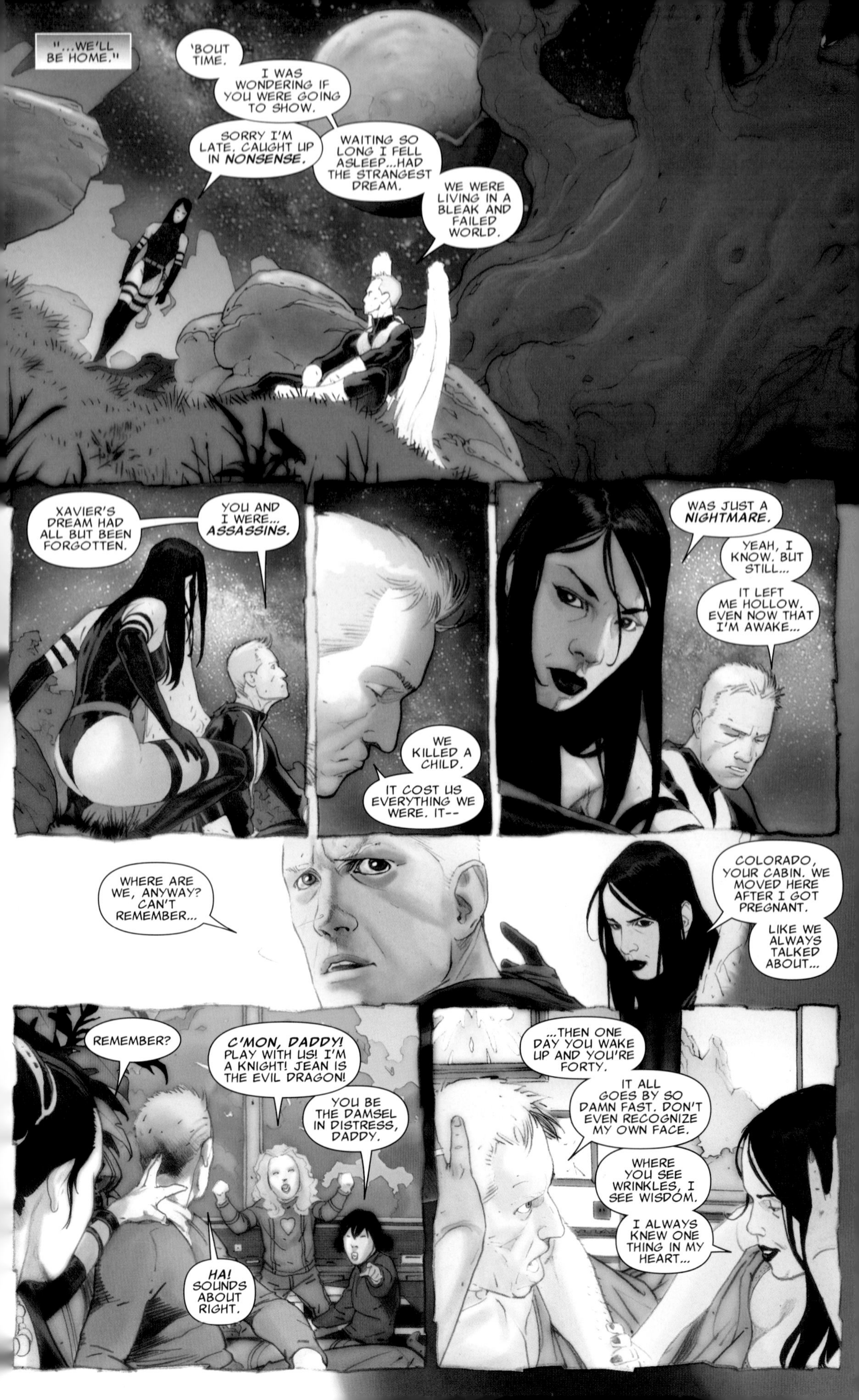
"...WE'LL BE HOME."
'BOUT TIME.
I WAS WONDERING IF YOU WERE GOING TO SHOW.
SORRY I'M LATE. CAUGHT UP IN *NONSENSE.*
WAITING SO LONG I FELL ASLEEP...HAD THE STRANGEST DREAM.
WE WERE LIVING IN A BLEAK AND FAILED WORLD.
XAVIER'S DREAM HAD ALL BUT BEEN FORGOTTEN.
YOU AND I WERE... *ASSASSINS.*
WE KILLED A CHILD.
IT COST US EVERYTHING WE WERE. IT--
WAS JUST A *NIGHTMARE.*
YEAH, I KNOW. BUT STILL...
IT LEFT ME HOLLOW. EVEN NOW THAT I'M AWAKE...
WHERE ARE WE, ANYWAY? CAN'T REMEMBER...
COLORADO, YOUR CABIN. WE MOVED HERE AFTER I GOT PREGNANT.
LIKE WE ALWAYS TALKED ABOUT...
REMEMBER?
C'MON, DADDY! PLAY WITH US! I'M A KNIGHT! JEAN IS THE EVIL DRAGON!
YOU BE THE DAMSEL IN DISTRESS, DADDY.
HA! SOUNDS ABOUT RIGHT.
...THEN ONE DAY YOU WAKE UP AND YOU'RE FORTY.
IT ALL GOES BY SO DAMN FAST. DON'T EVEN RECOGNIZE MY OWN FACE.
WHERE YOU SEE WRINKLES, I SEE WISDOM.
I ALWAYS KNEW ONE THING IN MY HEART...

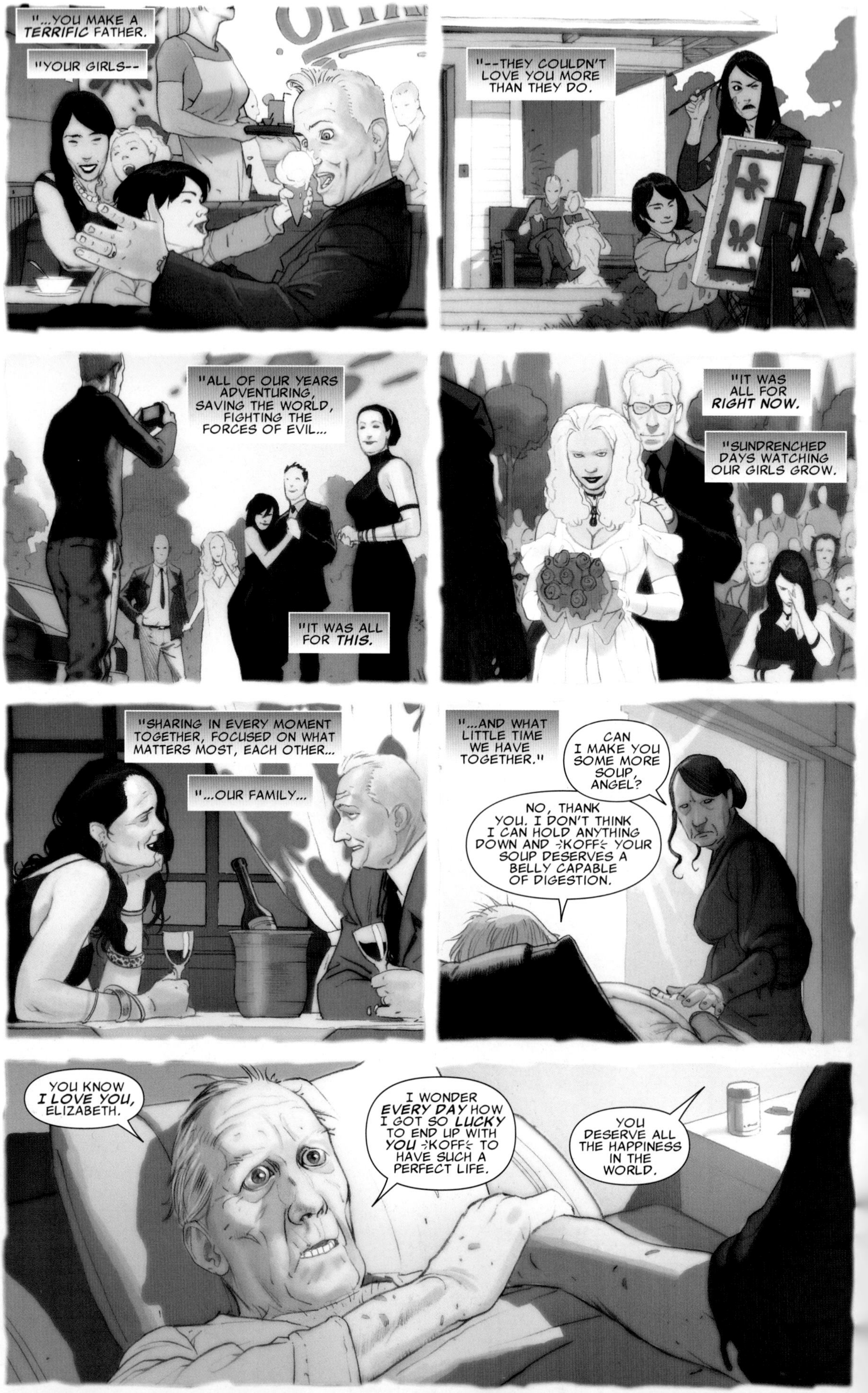
"...YOU MAKE A TERRIFIC FATHER.
"YOUR GIRLS--
"--THEY COULDN'T LOVE YOU MORE THAN THEY DO.
"ALL OF OUR YEARS ADVENTURING, SAVING THE WORLD, FIGHTING THE FORCES OF EVIL...
"IT WAS ALL FOR THIS.
"IT WAS ALL FOR RIGHT NOW.
"SUNDRENCHED DAYS WATCHING OUR GIRLS GROW.
"SHARING IN EVERY MOMENT TOGETHER, FOCUSED ON WHAT MATTERS MOST, EACH OTHER...
"...OUR FAMILY...
"...AND WHAT LITTLE TIME WE HAVE TOGETHER."
CAN I MAKE YOU SOME MORE SOUP, ANGEL?
NO, THANK YOU. I DON'T THINK I CAN HOLD ANYTHING DOWN AND *KOFF* YOUR SOUP DESERVES A BELLY CAPABLE OF DIGESTION.
YOU KNOW I LOVE YOU, ELIZABETH.
I WONDER EVERY DAY HOW I GOT SO LUCKY TO END UP WITH YOU *KOFF* TO HAVE SUCH A PERFECT LIFE.
YOU DESERVE ALL THE HAPPINESS IN THE WORLD.

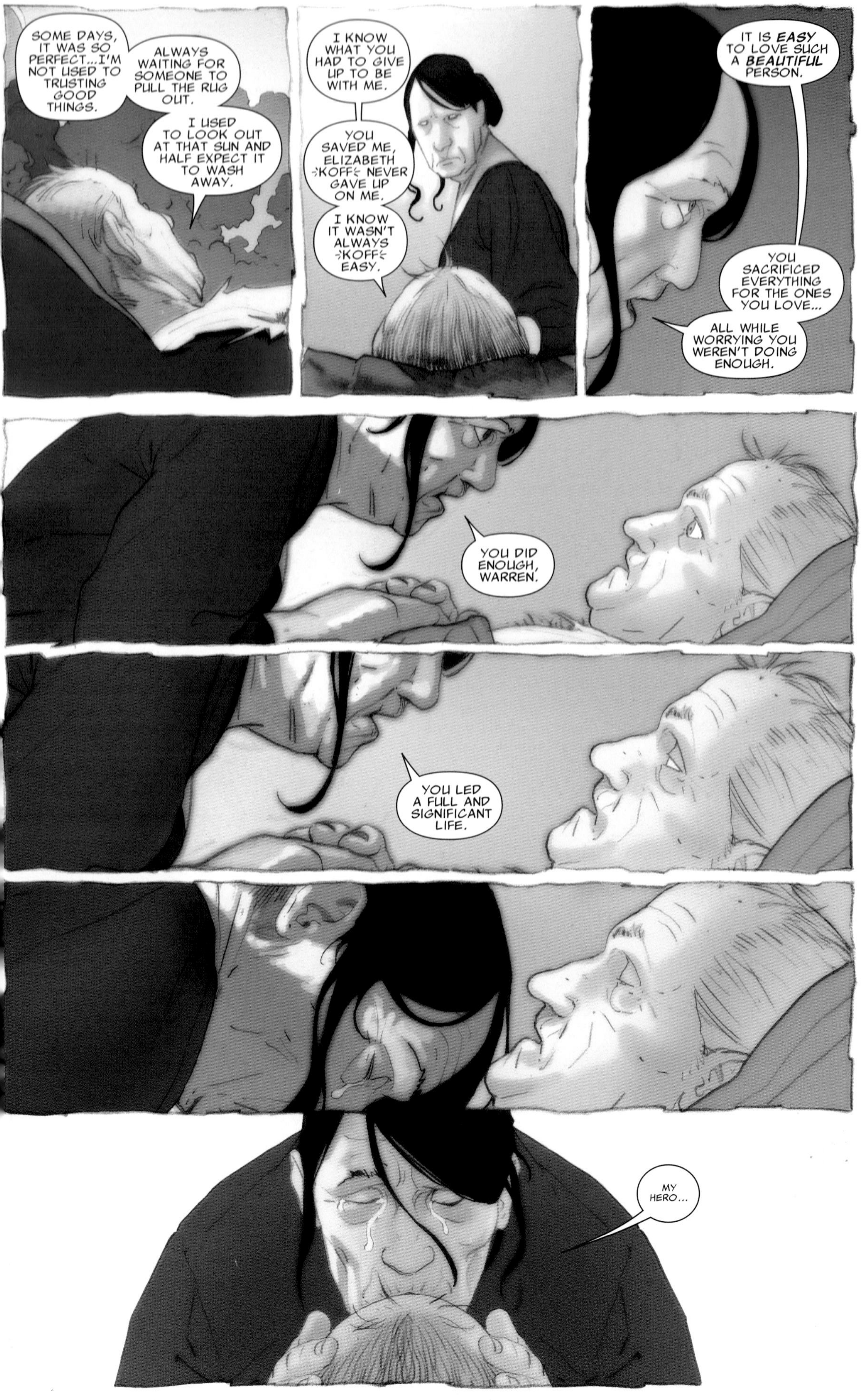
SOME DAYS, IT WAS SO PERFECT...I'M NOT USED TO TRUSTING GOOD THINGS.
ALWAYS WAITING FOR SOMEONE TO PULL THE RUG OUT.
I USED TO LOOK OUT AT THAT SUN AND HALF EXPECT IT TO WASH AWAY.
I KNOW WHAT YOU HAD TO GIVE UP TO BE WITH ME.
YOU SAVED ME, ELIZABETH *KOFF* NEVER GAVE UP ON ME.
I KNOW IT WASN'T ALWAYS *KOFF* EASY.
IT IS EASY TO LOVE SUCH A BEAUTIFUL PERSON.
YOU SACRIFICED EVERYTHING FOR THE ONES YOU LOVE...
ALL WHILE WORRYING YOU WEREN'T DOING ENOUGH.
YOU DID ENOUGH, WARREN.
YOU LED A FULL AND SIGNIFICANT LIFE.
MY HERO...

WAKE UP!

BRADDOCK! THIS PLACE IS COMING DOWN--

WE HAVE TO GO!

NO...

LEAVE ME-- LEAVE ME WITH HIM!

I WILL NOT.

IS THE KID SECURE?

YES.

GOOD...

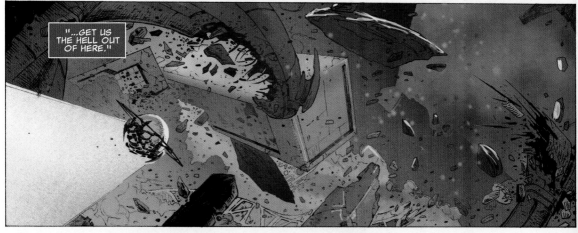

"...GET US THE HELL OUT OF HERE."

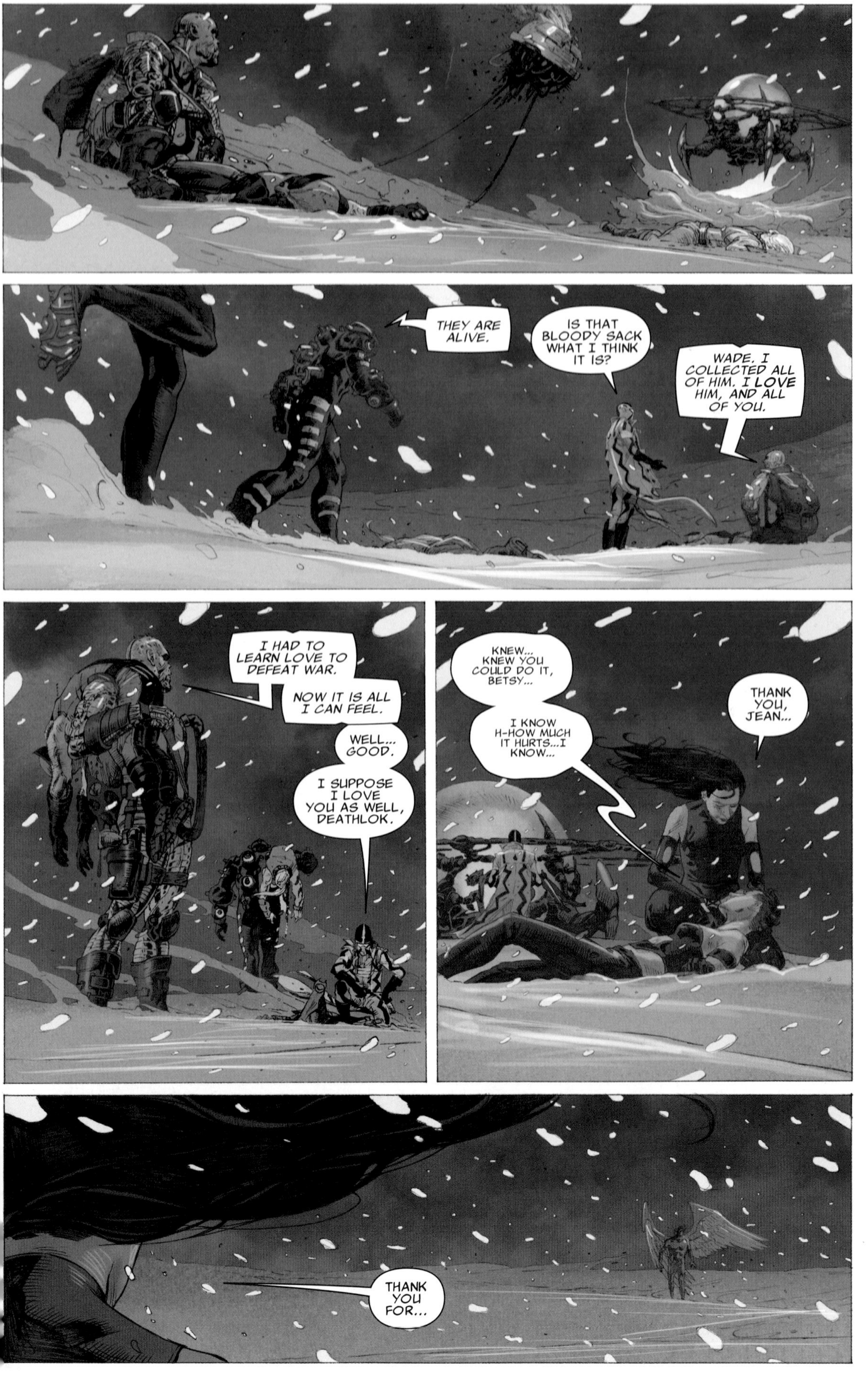
THEY ARE ALIVE.
IS THAT BLOODY SACK WHAT I THINK IT IS?
WADE. I COLLECTED ALL OF HIM. I LOVE HIM, AND ALL OF YOU.
I HAD TO LEARN LOVE TO DEFEAT WAR.
NOW IT IS ALL I CAN FEEL.
WELL... GOOD.
I SUPPOSE I LOVE YOU AS WELL, DEATHLOK.
KNEW... KNEW YOU COULD DO IT, BETSY...
I KNOW H-HOW MUCH IT HURTS...I KNOW...
THANK YOU, JEAN...
THANK YOU FOR...

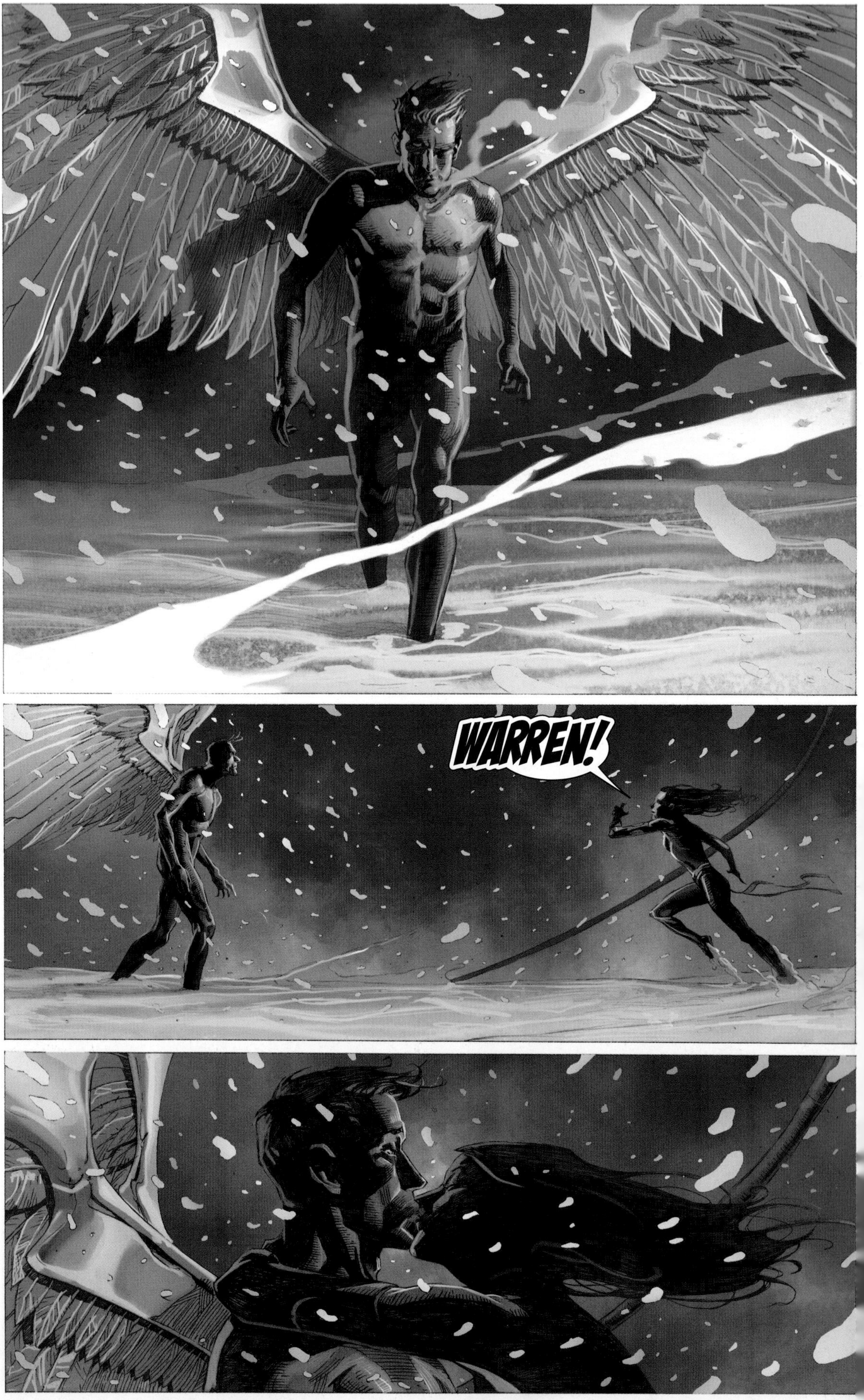
WARREN!

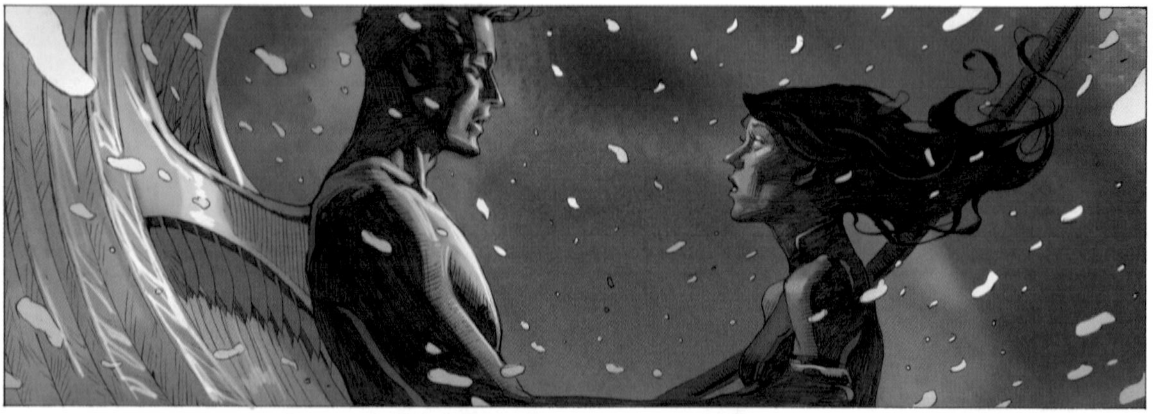

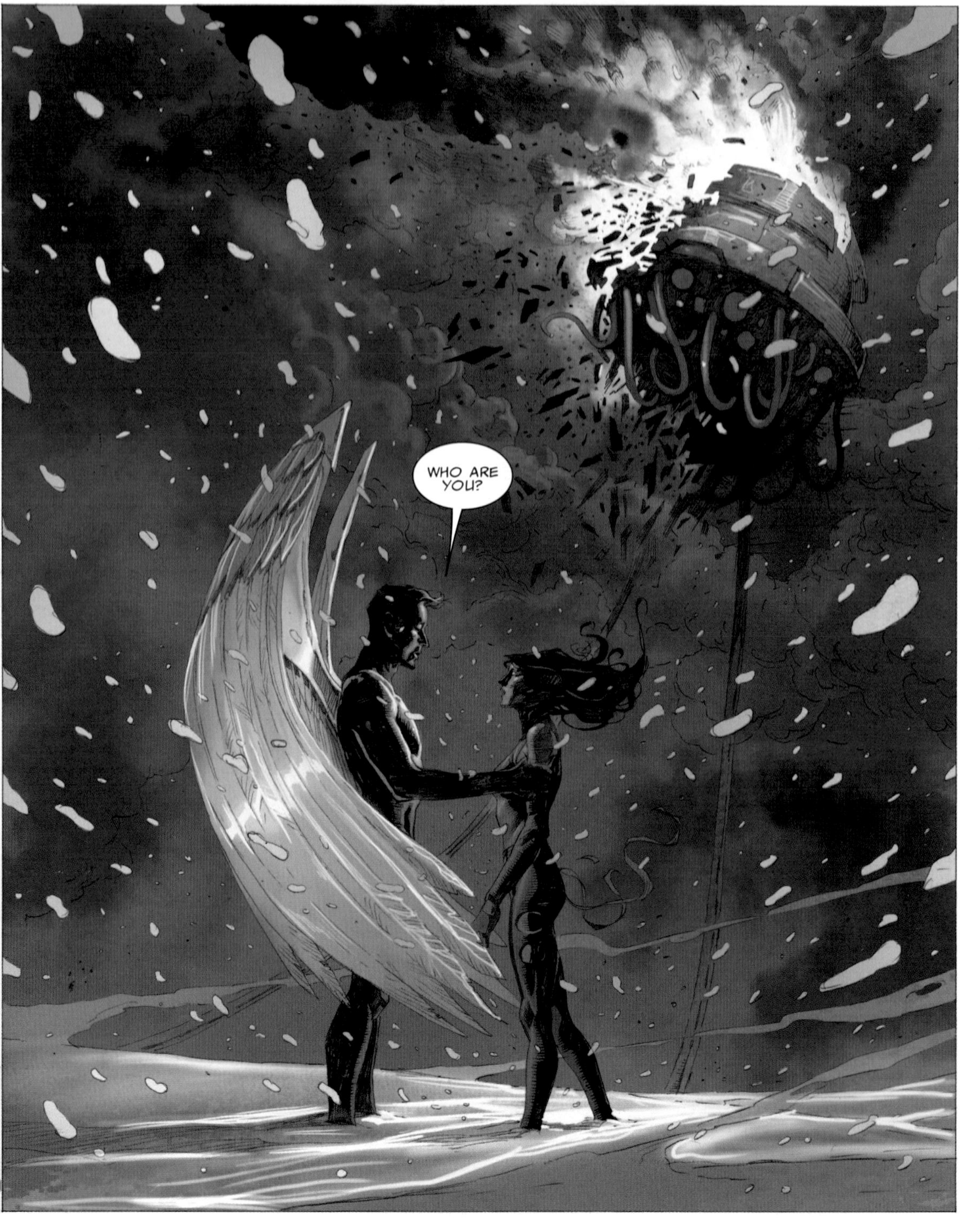
WHO ARE YOU?

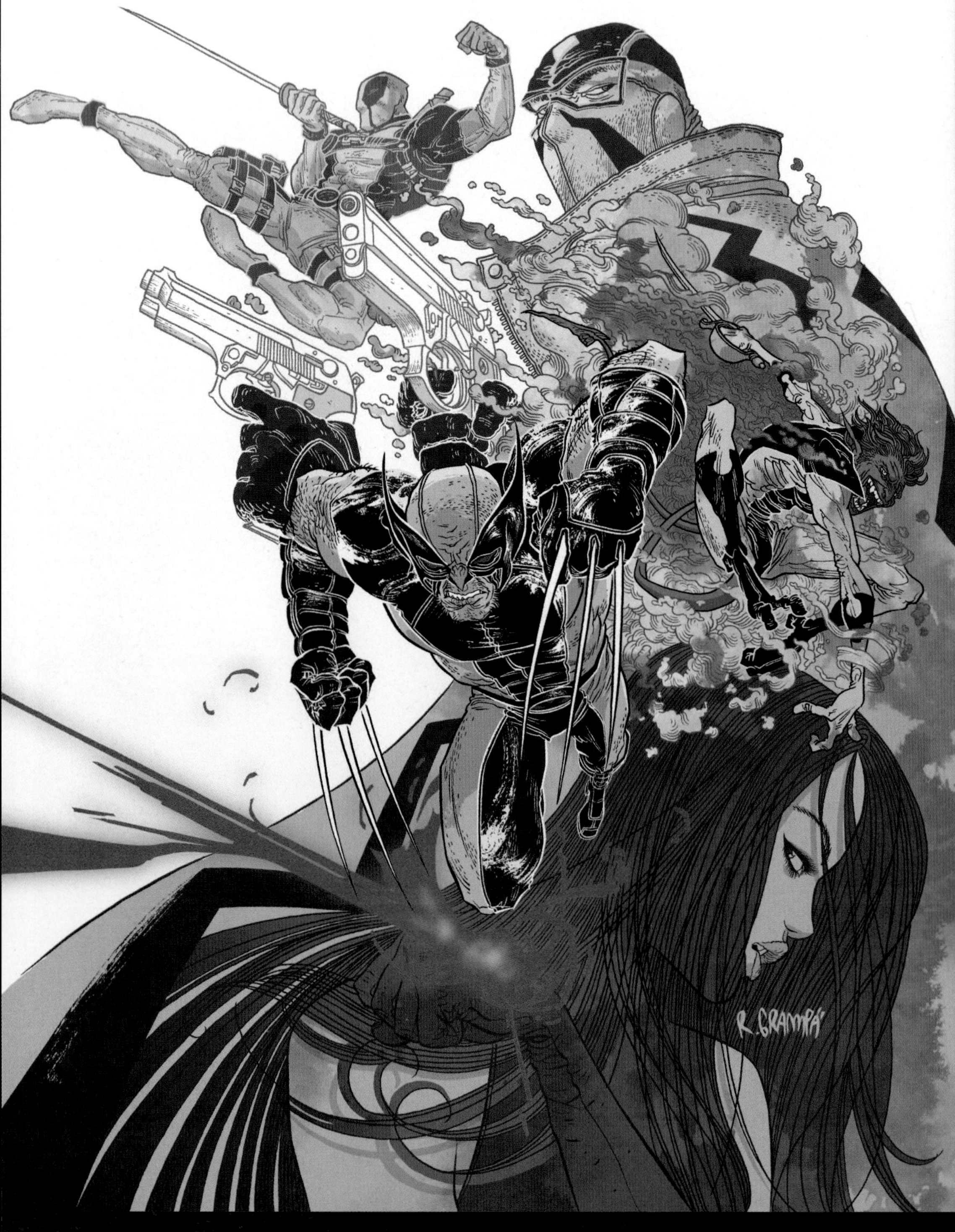
R. GRAMPA

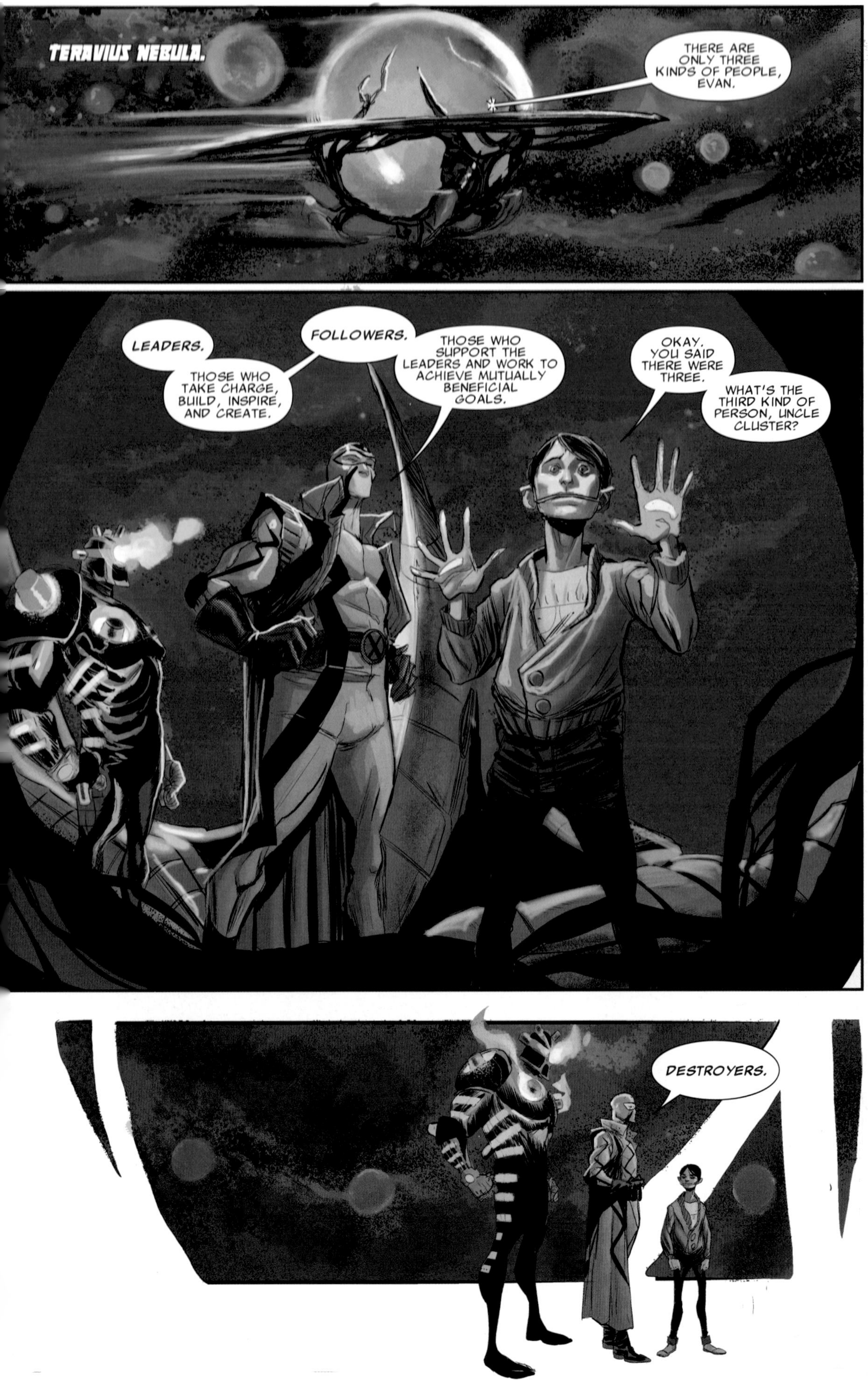
TERAVIUS NEBULA.
THERE ARE ONLY THREE KINDS OF PEOPLE, EVAN.
LEADERS.
THOSE WHO TAKE CHARGE, BUILD, INSPIRE, AND CREATE.
FOLLOWERS.
THOSE WHO SUPPORT THE LEADERS AND WORK TO ACHIEVE MUTUALLY BENEFICIAL GOALS.
OKAY. YOU SAID THERE WERE THREE.
WHAT'S THE THIRD KIND OF PERSON, UNCLE CLUSTER?
DESTROYERS.

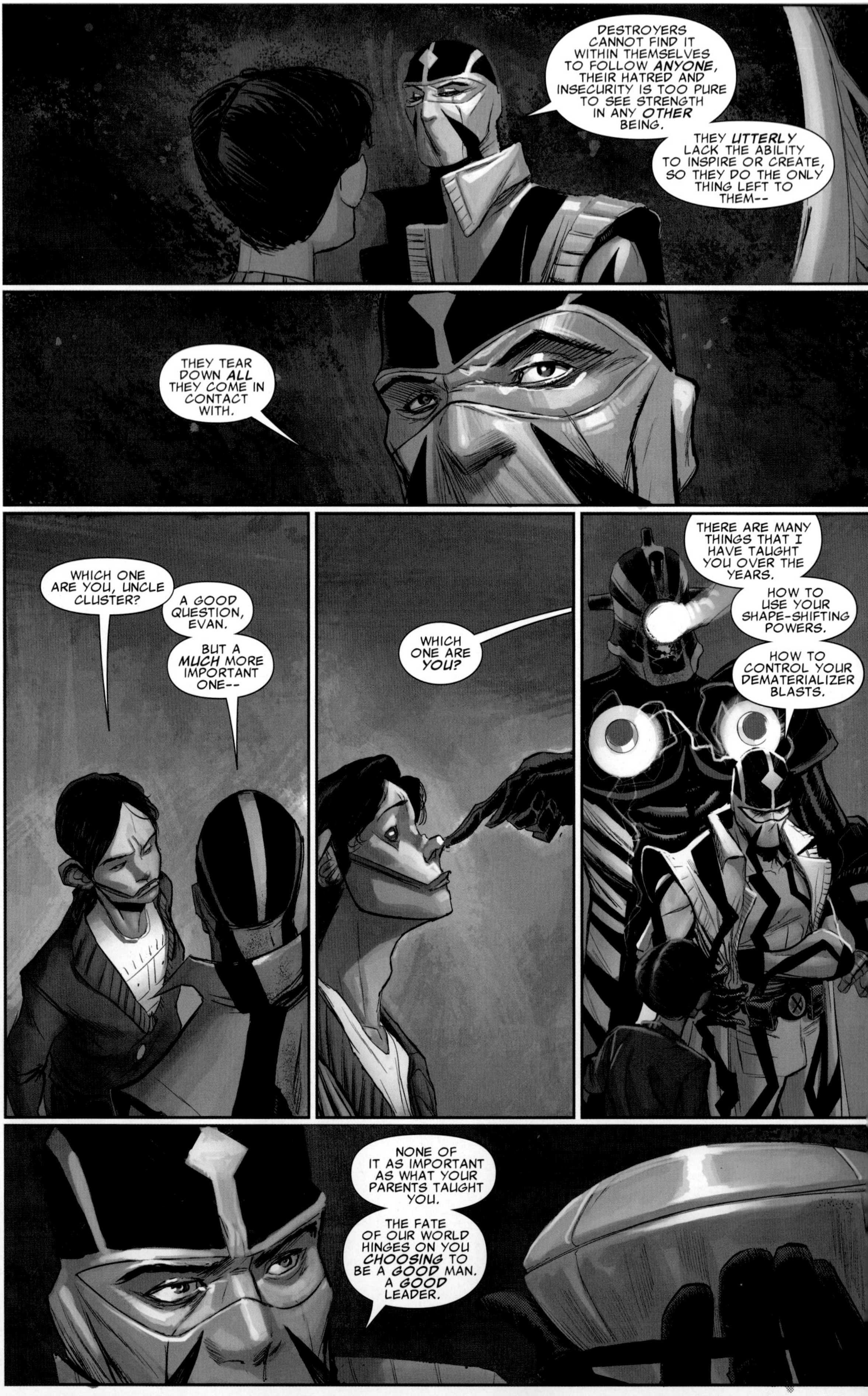
DESTROYERS CANNOT FIND IT WITHIN THEMSELVES TO FOLLOW ANYONE, THEIR HATRED AND INSECURITY IS TOO PURE TO SEE STRENGTH IN ANY OTHER BEING.
THEY UTTERLY LACK THE ABILITY TO INSPIRE OR CREATE, SO THEY DO THE ONLY THING LEFT TO THEM--
THEY TEAR DOWN ALL THEY COME IN CONTACT WITH.
WHICH ONE ARE YOU, UNCLE CLUSTER?
A GOOD QUESTION, EVAN.
BUT A MUCH MORE IMPORTANT ONE--
WHICH ONE ARE YOU?
THERE ARE MANY THINGS THAT I HAVE TAUGHT YOU OVER THE YEARS.
HOW TO USE YOUR SHAPE-SHIFTING POWERS.
HOW TO CONTROL YOUR DEMATERIALIZER BLASTS.
NONE OF IT AS IMPORTANT AS WHAT YOUR PARENTS TAUGHT YOU.
THE FATE OF OUR WORLD HINGES ON YOU CHOOSING TO BE A GOOD MAN. A GOOD LEADER.

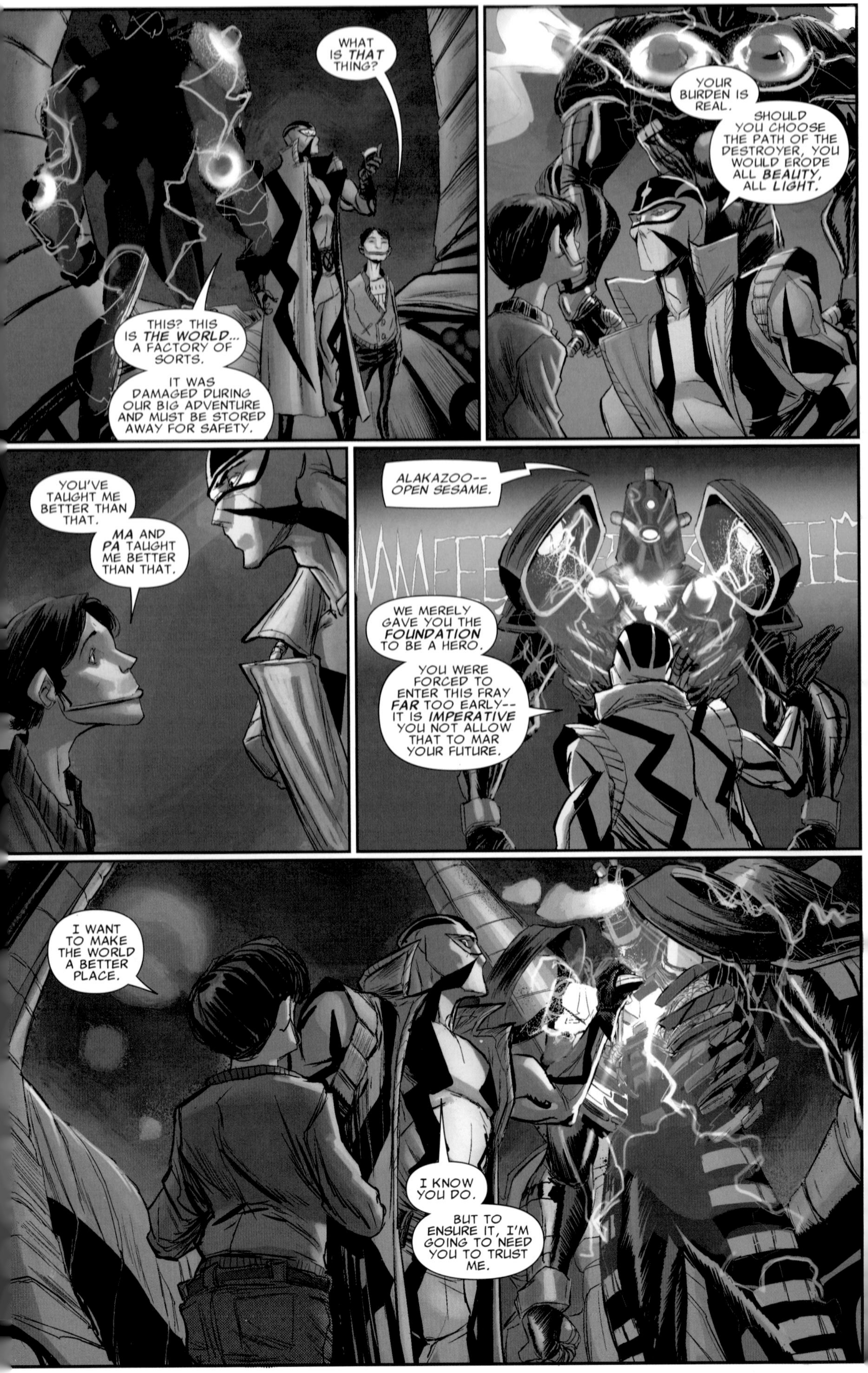
WHAT IS THAT THING?
THIS? THIS IS THE WORLD... A FACTORY OF SORTS.
IT WAS DAMAGED DURING OUR BIG ADVENTURE AND MUST BE STORED AWAY FOR SAFETY.
YOUR BURDEN IS REAL.
SHOULD YOU CHOOSE THE PATH OF THE DESTROYER, YOU WOULD ERODE ALL BEAUTY, ALL LIGHT.
YOU'VE TAUGHT ME BETTER THAN THAT.
MA AND PA TAUGHT ME BETTER THAN THAT.
ALAKAZOO-- OPEN SESAME.
WE MERELY GAVE YOU THE FOUNDATION TO BE A HERO.
YOU WERE FORCED TO ENTER THIS FRAY FAR TOO EARLY-- IT IS IMPERATIVE YOU NOT ALLOW THAT TO MAR YOUR FUTURE.
I WANT TO MAKE THE WORLD A BETTER PLACE.
I KNOW YOU DO.
BUT TO ENSURE IT, I'M GOING TO NEED YOU TO TRUST ME.

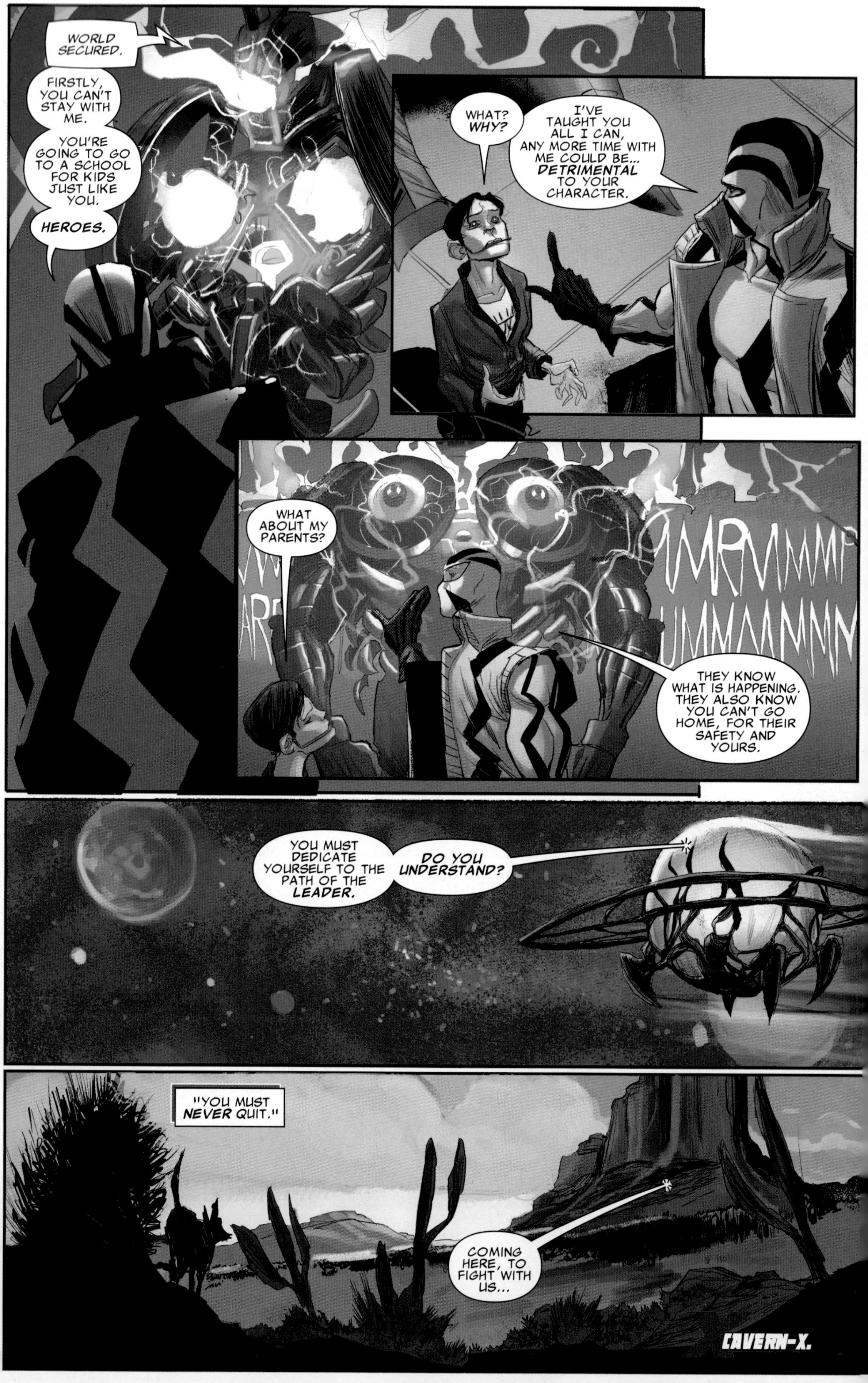
WORLD SECURED.
FIRSTLY, YOU CAN'T STAY WITH ME.
YOU'RE GOING TO GO TO A SCHOOL FOR KIDS JUST LIKE YOU.
HEROES.
WHAT? WHY?
I'VE TAUGHT YOU ALL I CAN, ANY MORE TIME WITH ME COULD BE... DETRIMENTAL TO YOUR CHARACTER.
WHAT ABOUT MY PARENTS?
MRVMMM
UMMAAMNN
THEY KNOW WHAT IS HAPPENING. THEY ALSO KNOW YOU CAN'T GO HOME, FOR THEIR SAFETY AND YOURS.
YOU MUST DEDICATE YOURSELF TO THE PATH OF THE LEADER.
DO YOU UNDERSTAND?
"YOU MUST NEVER QUIT."
COMING HERE, TO FIGHT WITH US...
CAVERN-X.

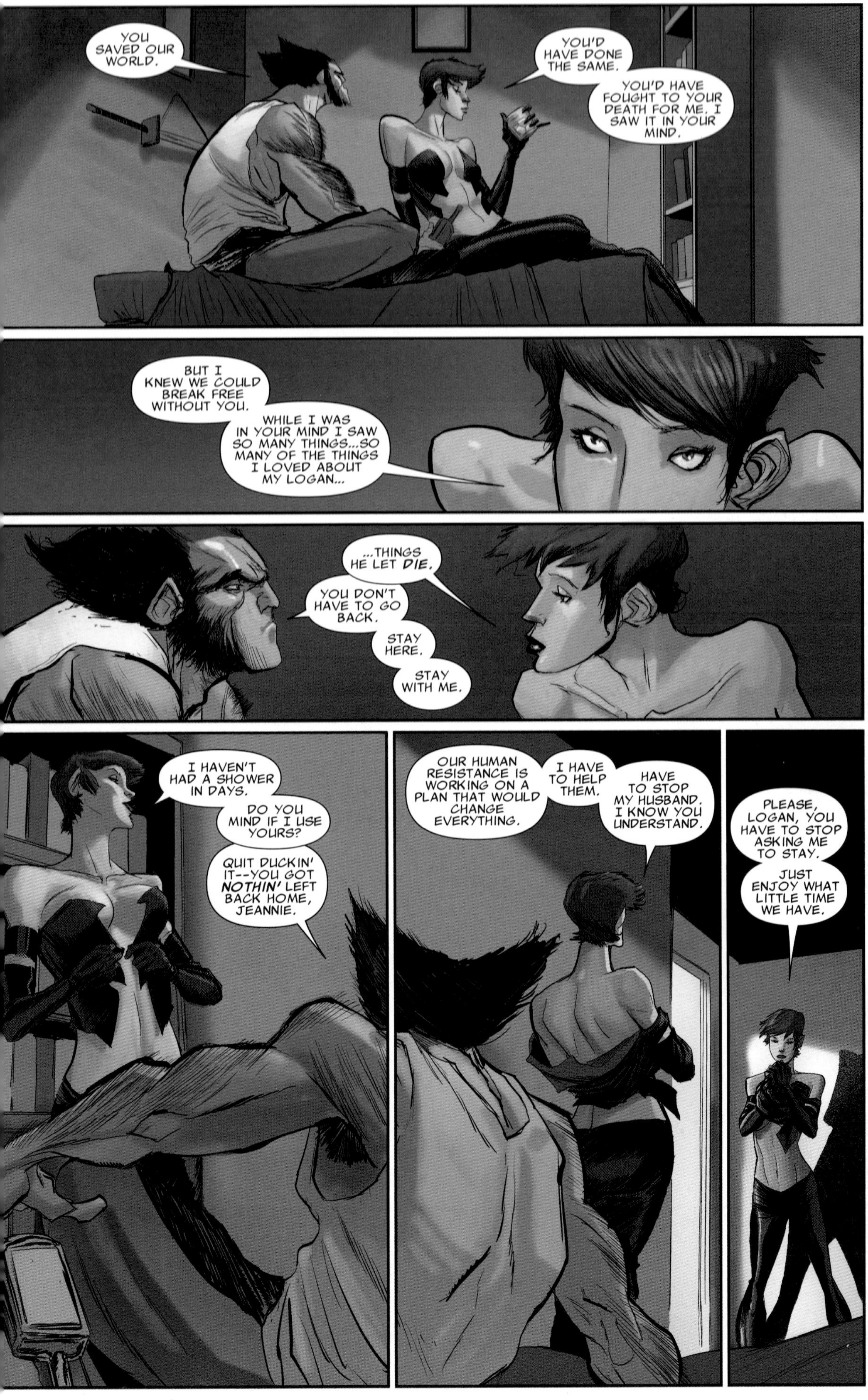
YOU SAVED OUR WORLD.
YOU'D HAVE DONE THE SAME.
YOU'D HAVE FOUGHT TO YOUR DEATH FOR ME. I SAW IT IN YOUR MIND.
BUT I KNEW WE COULD BREAK FREE WITHOUT YOU.
WHILE I WAS IN YOUR MIND I SAW SO MANY THINGS...SO MANY OF THE THINGS I LOVED ABOUT MY LOGAN...
...THINGS HE LET *DIE*.
YOU DON'T HAVE TO GO BACK.
STAY HERE.
STAY WITH ME.
I HAVEN'T HAD A SHOWER IN DAYS.
DO YOU MIND IF I USE YOURS?
QUIT DUCKIN' IT--YOU GOT ***NOTHIN'*** LEFT BACK HOME, JEANNIE.
OUR HUMAN RESISTANCE IS WORKING ON A PLAN THAT WOULD CHANGE EVERYTHING.
I HAVE TO HELP THEM.
HAVE TO STOP MY HUSBAND. I KNOW YOU UNDERSTAND.
PLEASE, LOGAN, YOU HAVE TO STOP ASKING ME TO STAY.
JUST ENJOY WHAT LITTLE TIME WE HAVE.

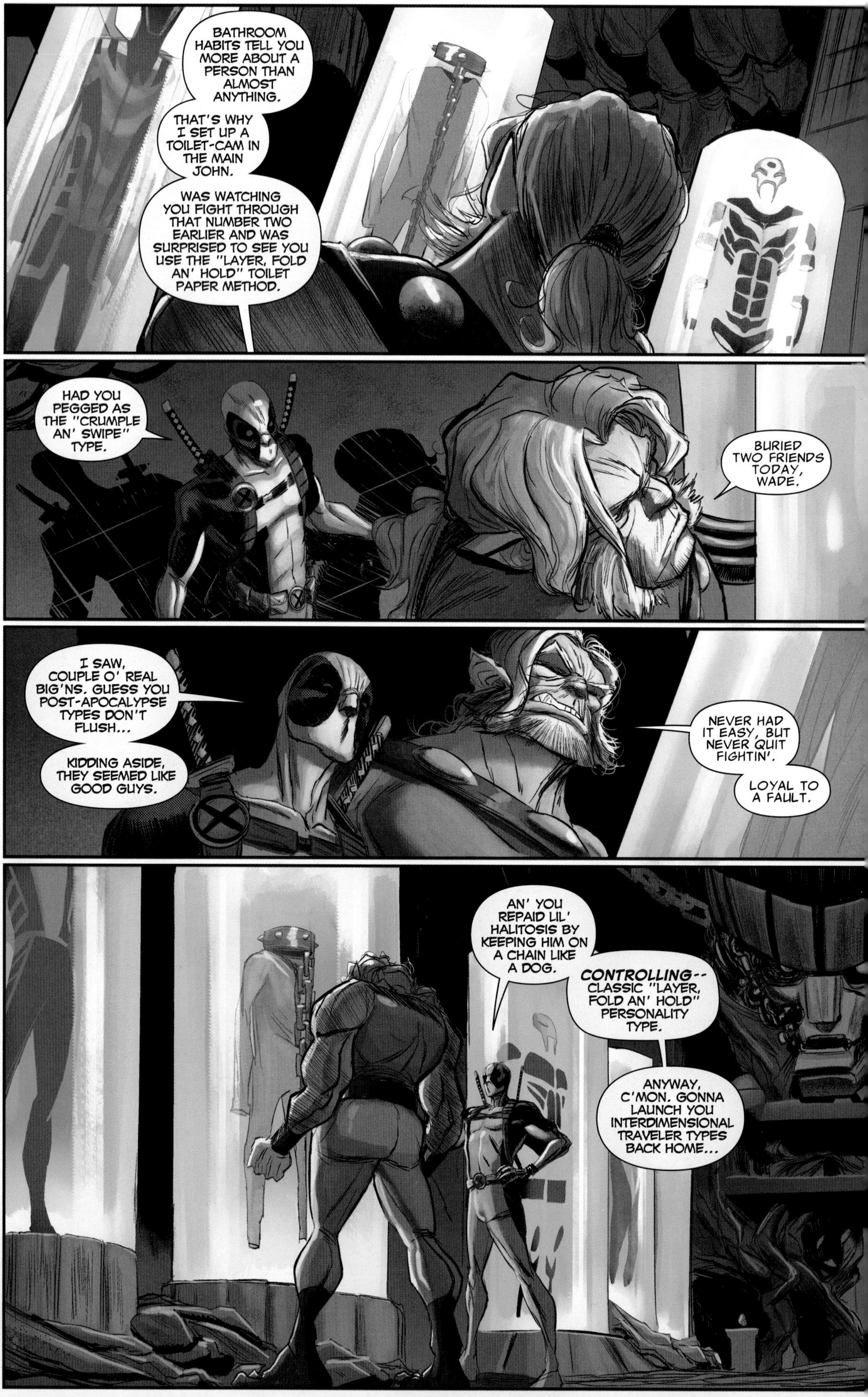
BATHROOM HABITS TELL YOU MORE ABOUT A PERSON THAN ALMOST ANYTHING.
THAT'S WHY I SET UP A TOILET-CAM IN THE MAIN JOHN.
WAS WATCHING YOU FIGHT THROUGH THAT NUMBER TWO EARLIER AND WAS SURPRISED TO SEE YOU USE THE "LAYER, FOLD AN' HOLD" TOILET PAPER METHOD.
HAD YOU PEGGED AS THE "CRUMPLE AN' SWIPE" TYPE.
BURIED TWO FRIENDS TODAY, WADE.
I SAW, COUPLE O' REAL BIG'NS. GUESS YOU POST-APOCALYPSE TYPES DON'T FLUSH...
KIDDING ASIDE, THEY SEEMED LIKE GOOD GUYS.
NEVER HAD IT EASY, BUT NEVER QUIT FIGHTIN'.
LOYAL TO A FAULT.
AN' YOU REPAID LIL' HALITOSIS BY KEEPING HIM ON A CHAIN LIKE A DOG.
CONTROLLING--CLASSIC "LAYER, FOLD AN' HOLD" PERSONALITY TYPE.
ANYWAY, C'MON. GONNA LAUNCH YOU INTERDIMENSIONAL TRAVELER TYPES BACK HOME...

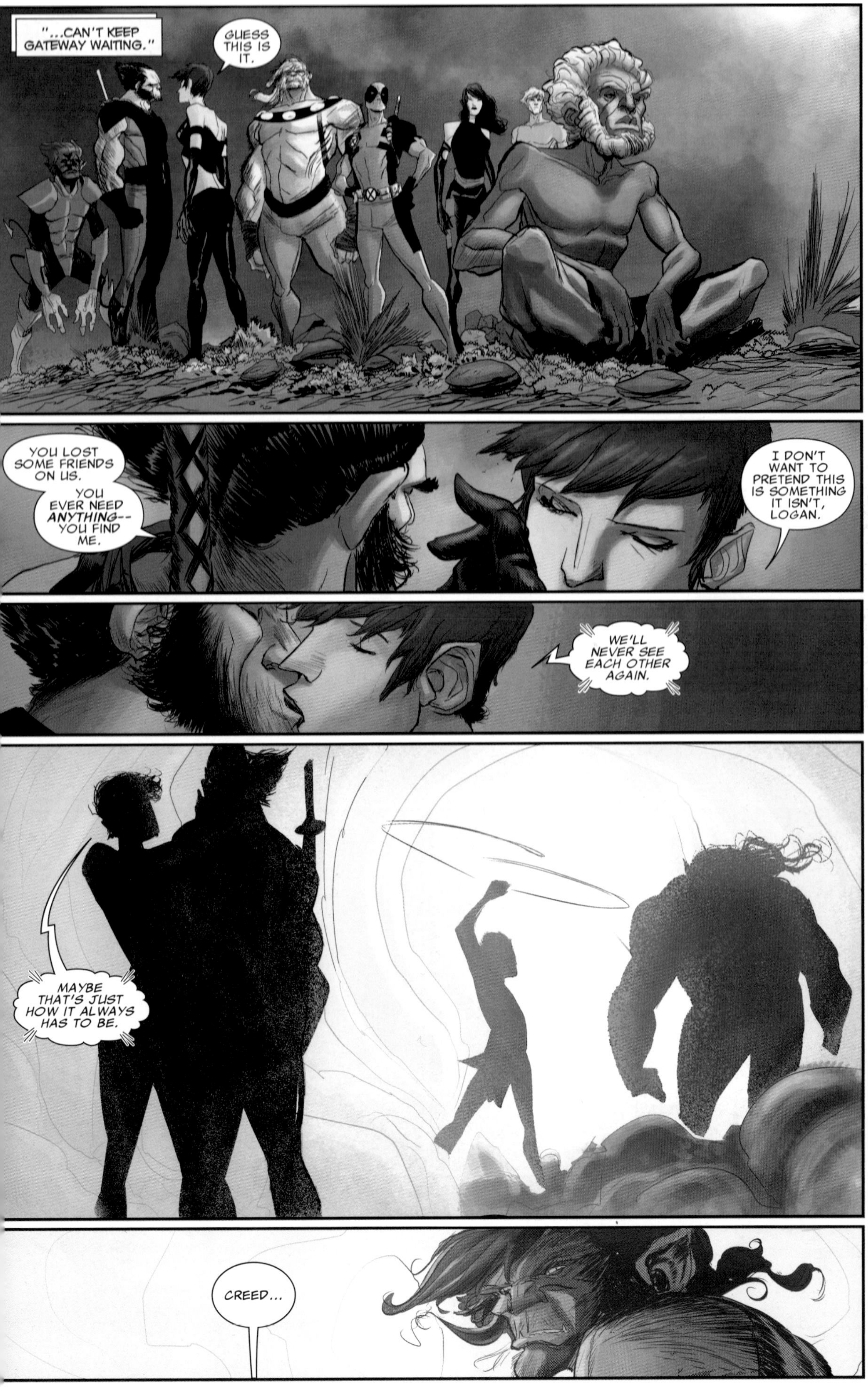
"...CAN'T KEEP GATEWAY WAITING."
GUESS THIS IS IT.
YOU LOST SOME FRIENDS ON US.
YOU EVER NEED *ANYTHING*-- YOU FIND ME.
I DON'T WANT TO PRETEND THIS IS SOMETHING IT ISN'T, LOGAN.
WE'LL NEVER SEE EACH OTHER AGAIN.
MAYBE THAT'S JUST HOW IT ALWAYS HAS TO BE.
CREED...

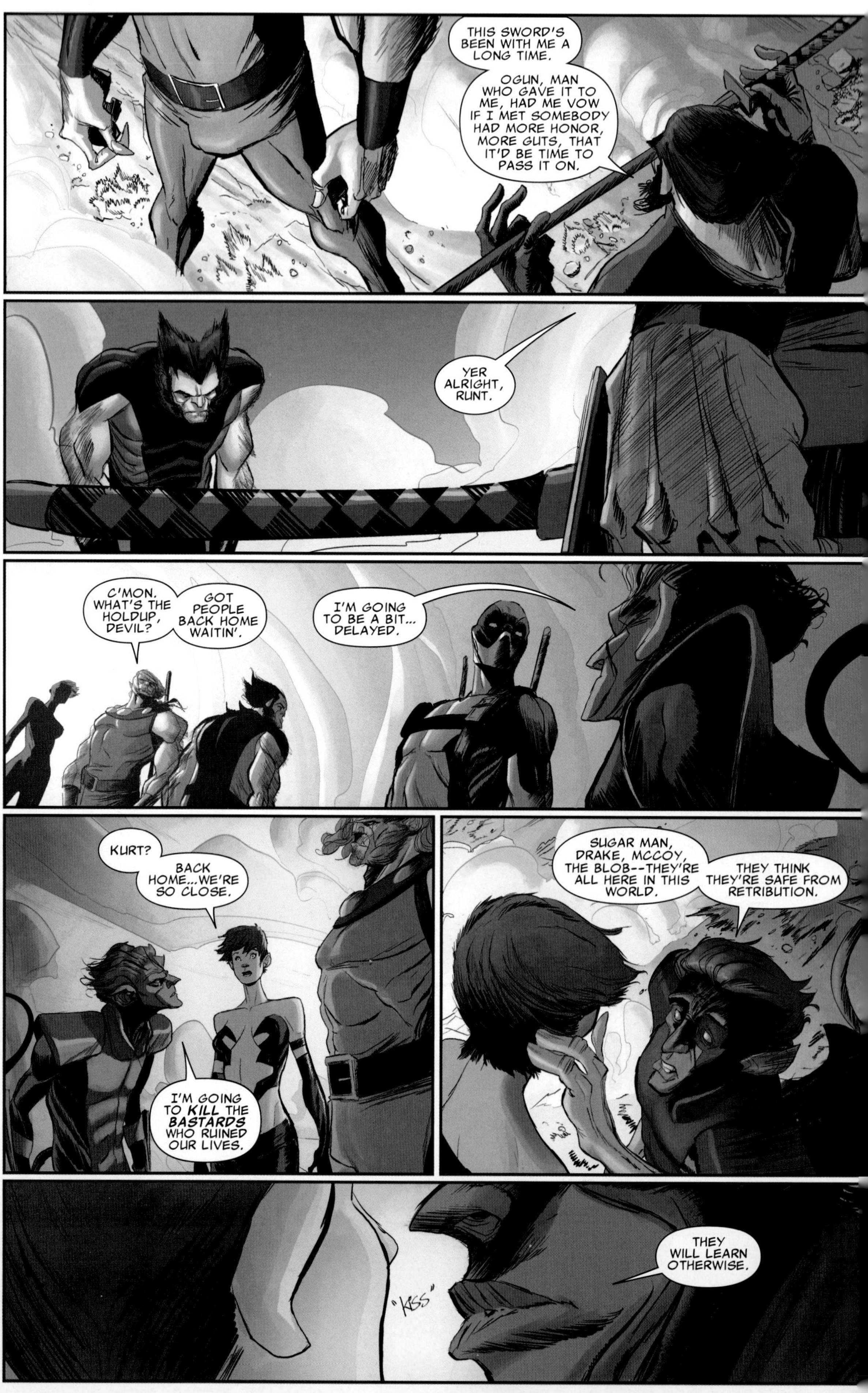

THIS SWORD'S BEEN WITH ME A LONG TIME.
OGUN, MAN WHO GAVE IT TO ME, HAD ME VOW IF I MET SOMEBODY HAD MORE HONOR, MORE GUTS, THAT IT'D BE TIME TO PASS IT ON.
YER ALRIGHT, RUNT.
C'MON. WHAT'S THE HOLDUP, DEVIL?
GOT PEOPLE BACK HOME WAITIN'.
I'M GOING TO BE A BIT... DELAYED.
KURT?
BACK HOME...WE'RE SO CLOSE.
I'M GOING TO KILL THE BASTARDS WHO RUINED OUR LIVES.
SUGAR MAN, DRAKE, MCCOY, THE BLOB--THEY'RE ALL HERE IN THIS WORLD.
THEY THINK THEY'RE SAFE FROM RETRIBUTION.
THEY WILL LEARN OTHERWISE.
"KISS"

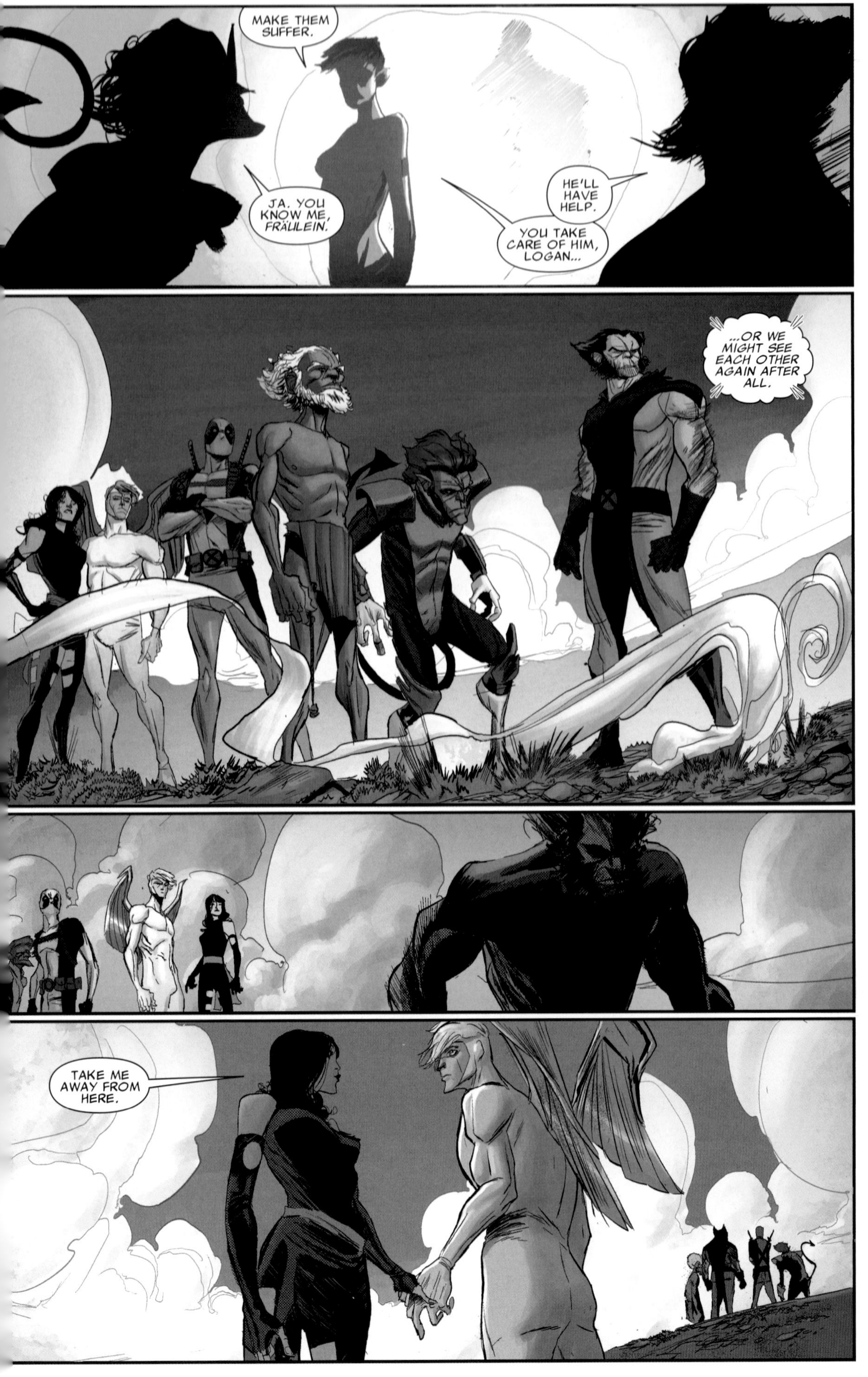
MAKE THEM SUFFER.
JA. YOU KNOW ME, FRÄULEIN.
HE'LL HAVE HELP.
YOU TAKE CARE OF HIM, LOGAN...
...OR WE MIGHT SEE EACH OTHER AGAIN AFTER ALL.
TAKE ME AWAY FROM HERE.

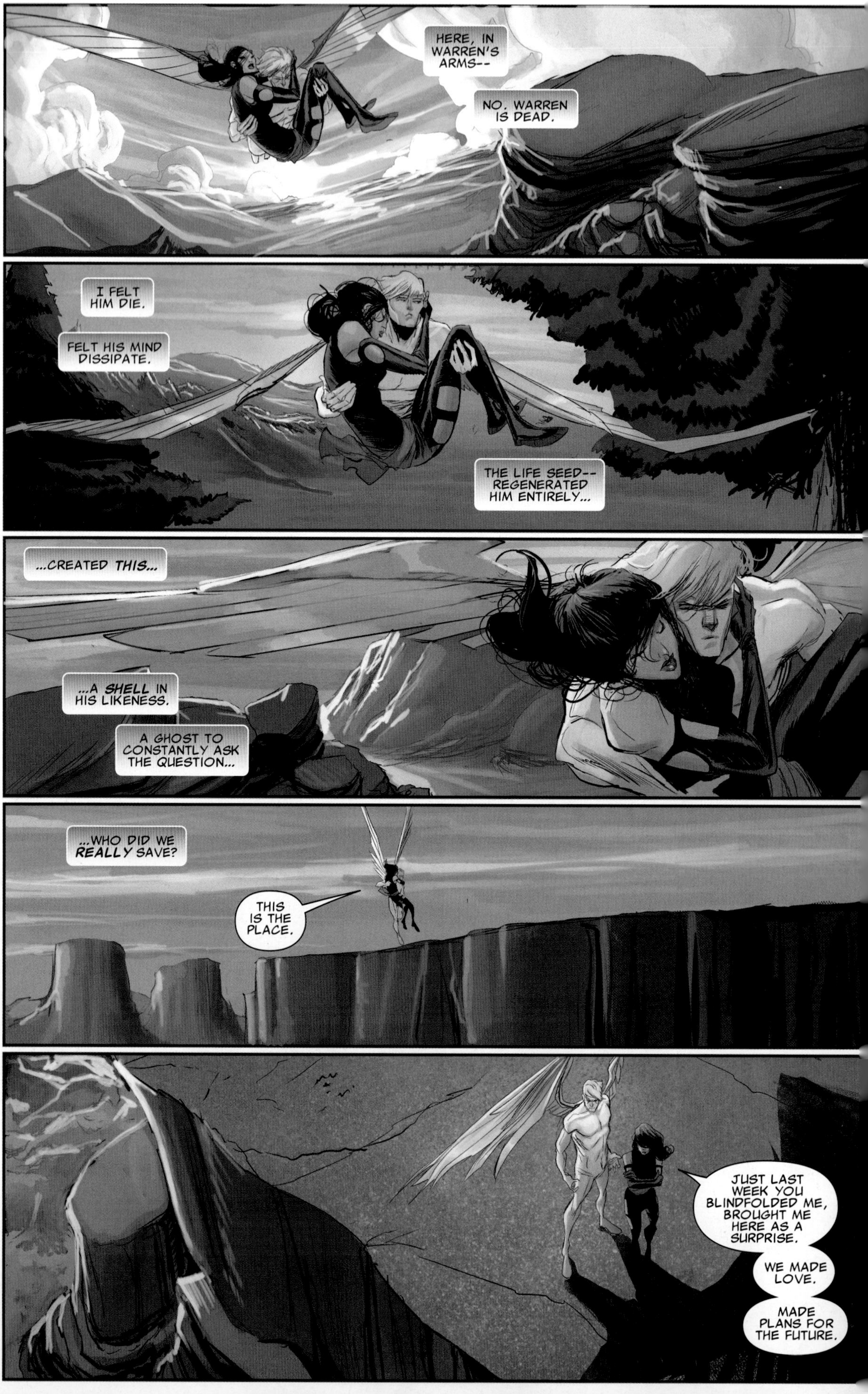
HERE, IN WARREN'S ARMS--
NO. WARREN IS DEAD.
I FELT HIM DIE.
FELT HIS MIND DISSIPATE.
THE LIFE SEED--REGENERATED HIM ENTIRELY...
...CREATED THIS...
...A SHELL IN HIS LIKENESS.
A GHOST TO CONSTANTLY ASK THE QUESTION...
...WHO DID WE REALLY SAVE?
THIS IS THE PLACE.
JUST LAST WEEK YOU BLINDFOLDED ME, BROUGHT ME HERE AS A SURPRISE.
WE MADE LOVE.
MADE PLANS FOR THE FUTURE.

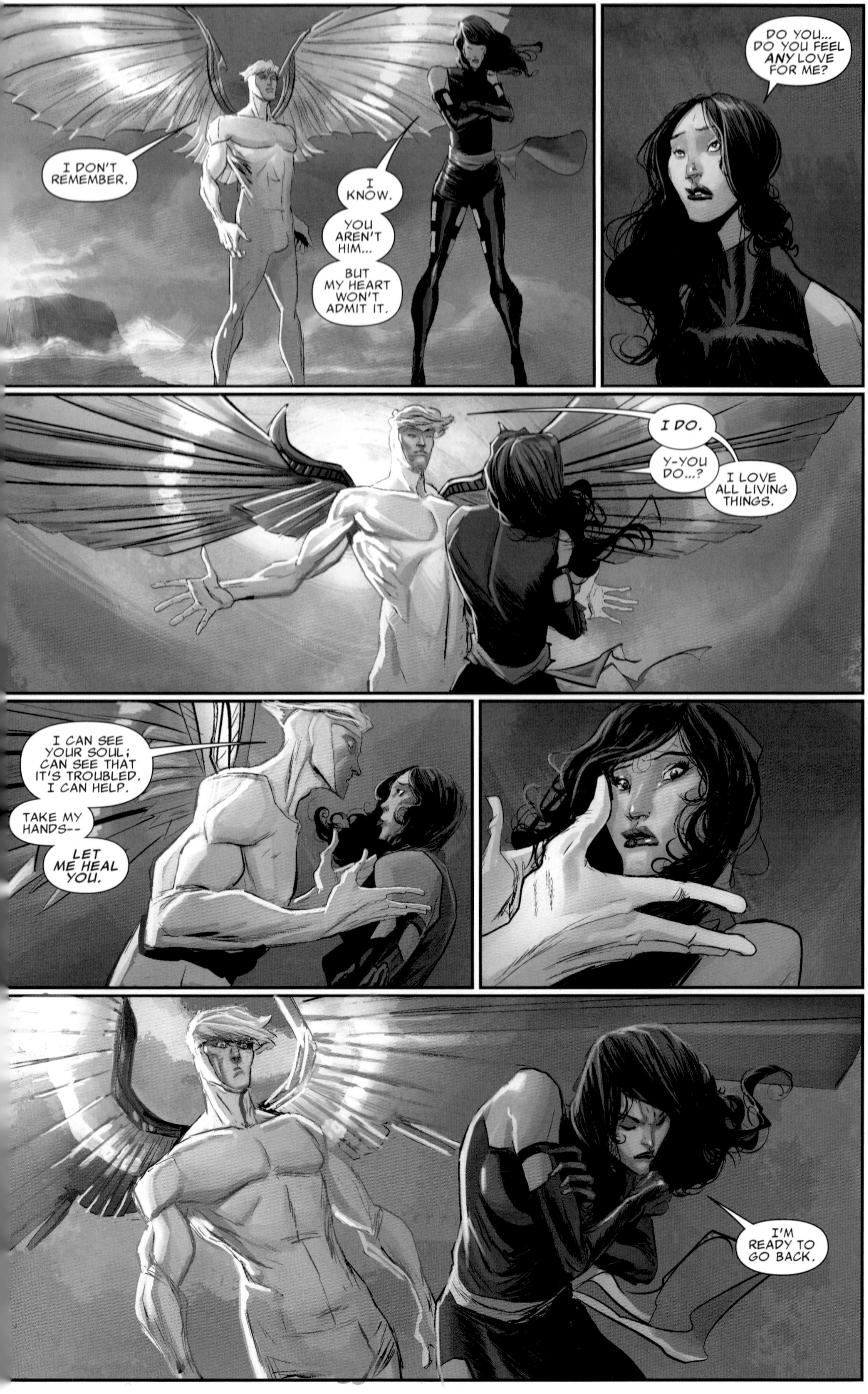
I DON'T REMEMBER.
I KNOW.
YOU AREN'T HIM...
BUT MY HEART WON'T ADMIT IT.
DO YOU... DO YOU FEEL ANY LOVE FOR ME?
I DO.
Y-YOU DO...?
I LOVE ALL LIVING THINGS.
I CAN SEE YOUR SOUL; CAN SEE THAT IT'S TROUBLED. I CAN HELP.
TAKE MY HANDS--
LET ME HEAL YOU.
I'M READY TO GO BACK.

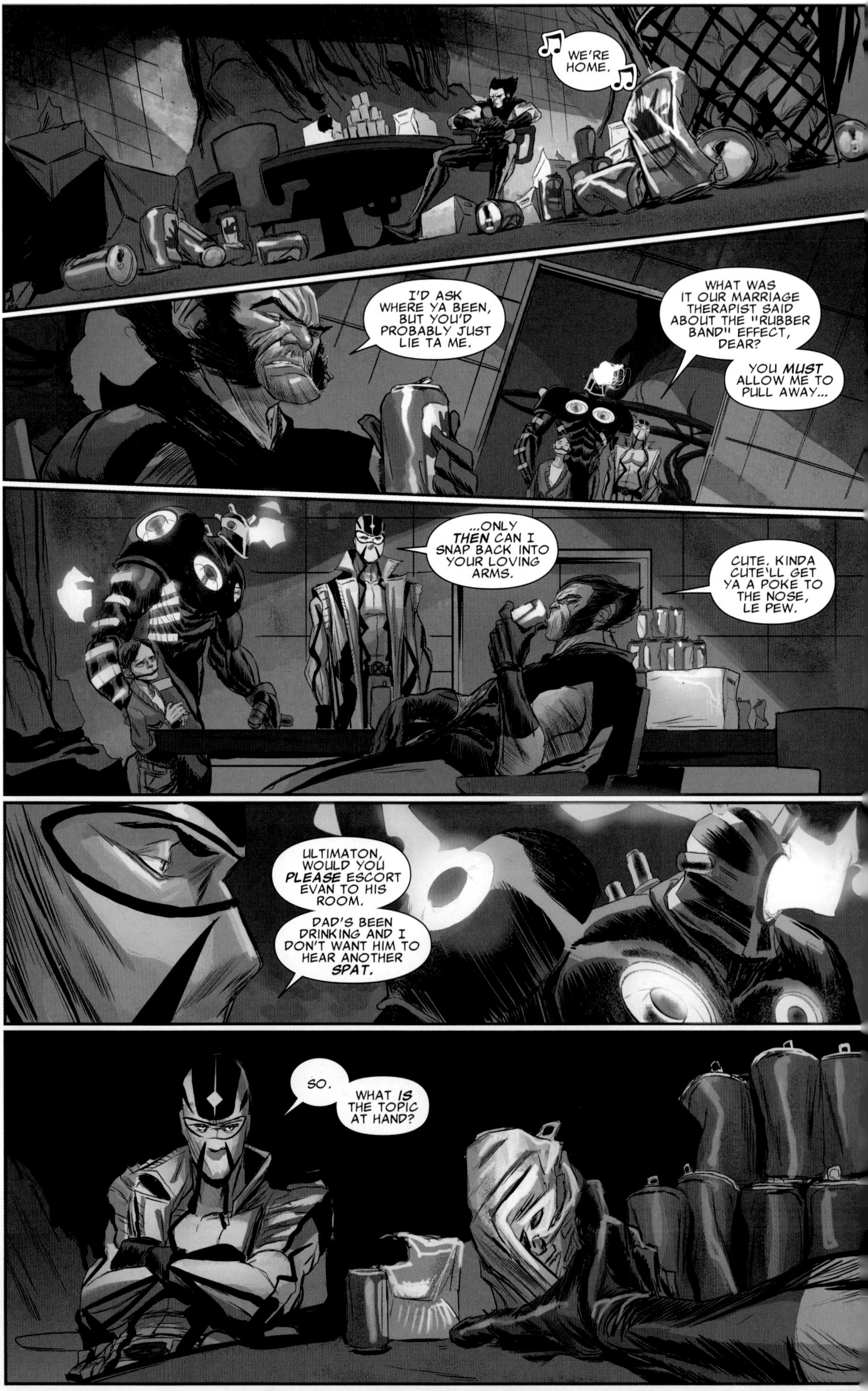
WE'RE HOME.
I'D ASK WHERE YA BEEN, BUT YOU'D PROBABLY JUST LIE TA ME.
WHAT WAS IT OUR MARRIAGE THERAPIST SAID ABOUT THE "RUBBER BAND" EFFECT, DEAR?
YOU MUST ALLOW ME TO PULL AWAY...
...ONLY THEN CAN I SNAP BACK INTO YOUR LOVING ARMS.
CUTE. KINDA CUTE'LL GET YA A POKE TO THE NOSE, LE PEW.
ULTIMATON, WOULD YOU PLEASE ESCORT EVAN TO HIS ROOM.
DAD'S BEEN DRINKING AND I DON'T WANT HIM TO HEAR ANOTHER SPAT.
SO.
WHAT IS THE TOPIC AT HAND?

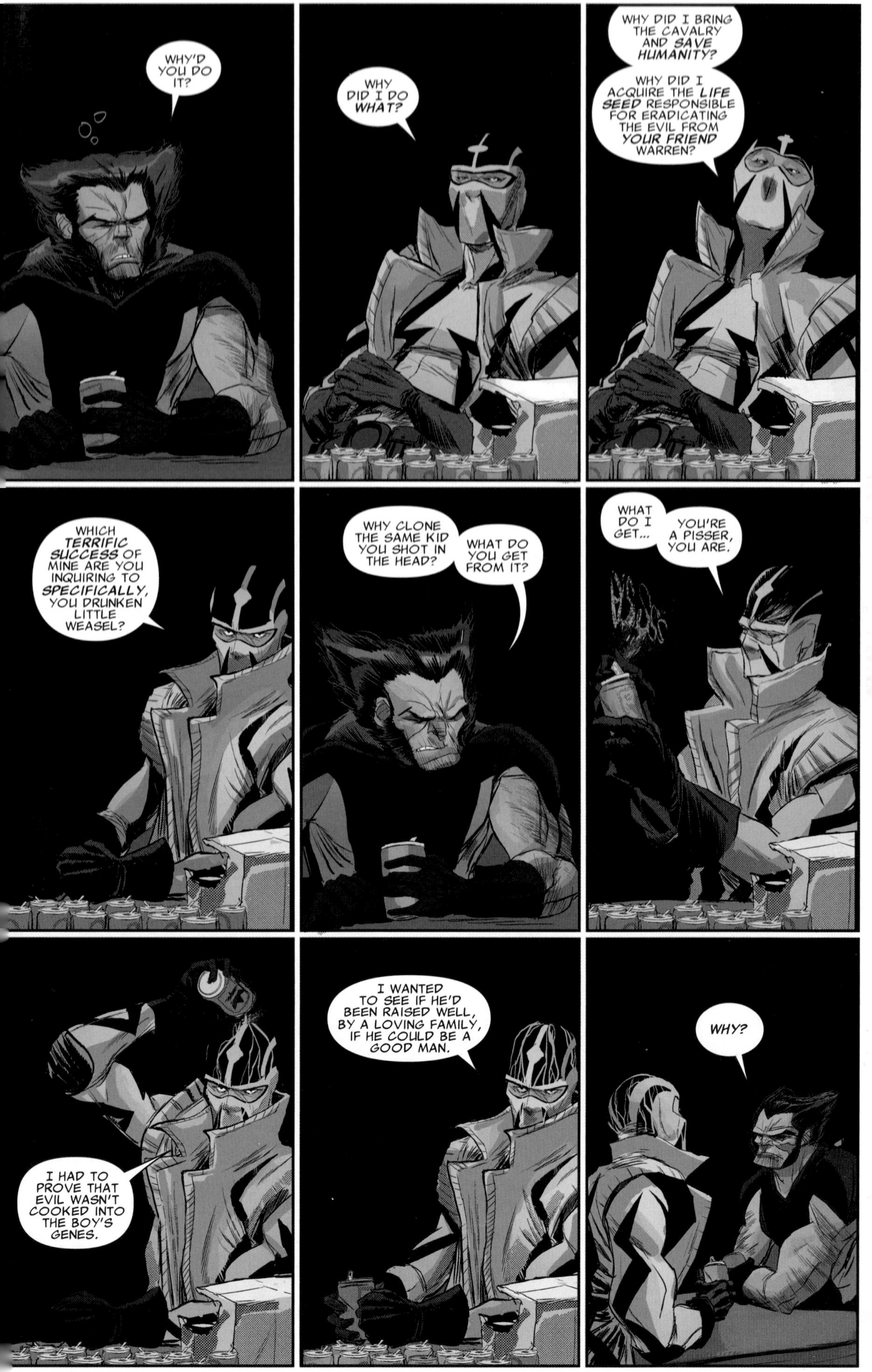
WHY'D YOU DO IT?
WHY DID I DO WHAT?
WHY DID I BRING THE CAVALRY AND SAVE HUMANITY?
WHY DID I ACQUIRE THE LIFE SEED RESPONSIBLE FOR ERADICATING THE EVIL FROM YOUR FRIEND WARREN?
WHICH TERRIFIC SUCCESS OF MINE ARE YOU INQUIRING TO SPECIFICALLY, YOU DRUNKEN LITTLE WEASEL?
WHY CLONE THE SAME KID YOU SHOT IN THE HEAD?
WHAT DO YOU GET FROM IT?
WHAT DO I GET...
YOU'RE A PISSER, YOU ARE.
I HAD TO PROVE THAT EVIL WASN'T COOKED INTO THE BOY'S GENES.
I WANTED TO SEE IF HE'D BEEN RAISED WELL, BY A LOVING FAMILY, IF HE COULD BE A GOOD MAN.
WHY?

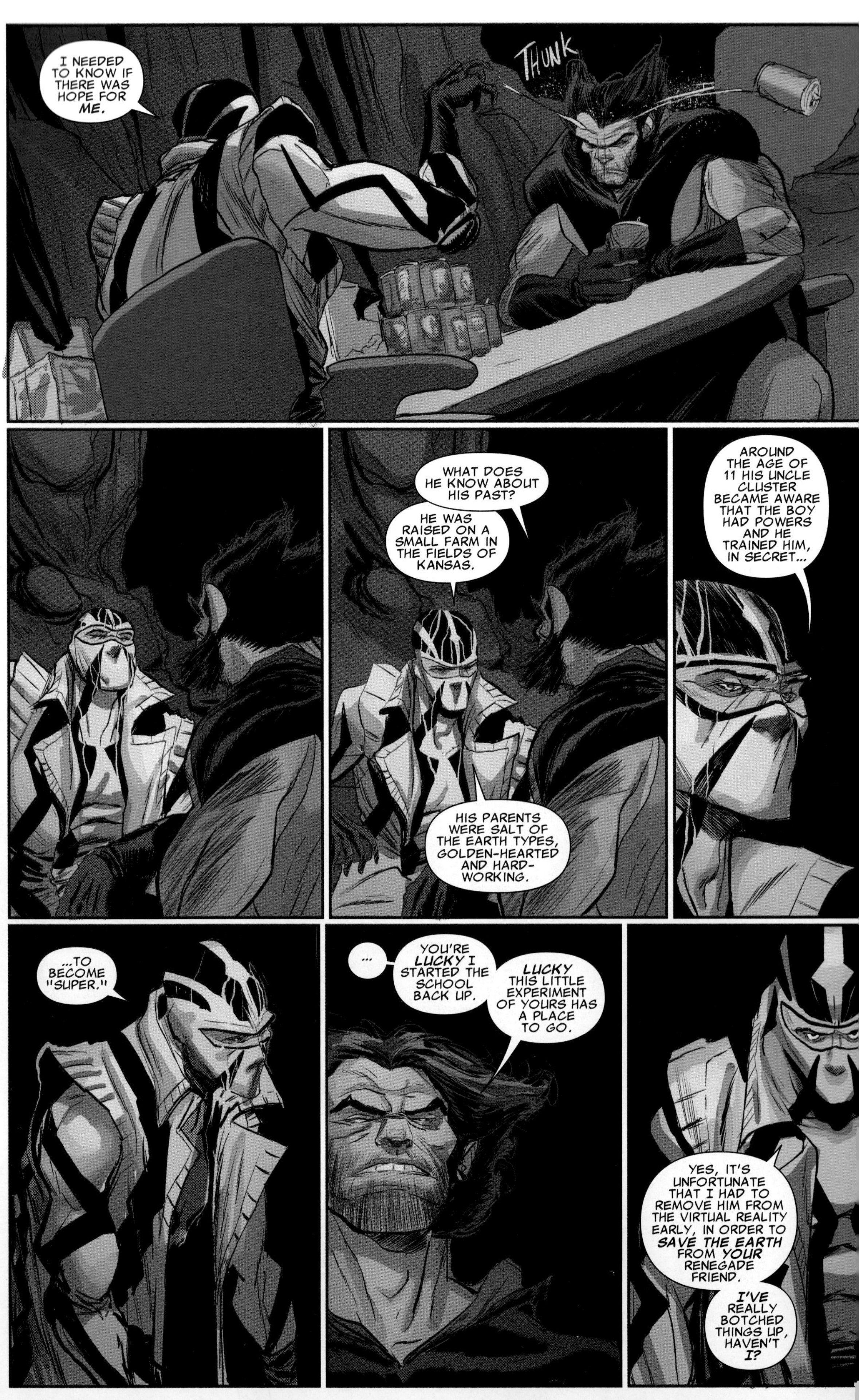
I NEEDED TO KNOW IF THERE WAS HOPE FOR ME.
THUNK
WHAT DOES HE KNOW ABOUT HIS PAST?
HE WAS RAISED ON A SMALL FARM IN THE FIELDS OF KANSAS.
HIS PARENTS WERE SALT OF THE EARTH TYPES, GOLDEN-HEARTED AND HARD-WORKING.
AROUND THE AGE OF 11 HIS UNCLE CLUSTER BECAME AWARE THAT THE BOY HAD POWERS AND HE TRAINED HIM, IN SECRET...
...TO BECOME "SUPER."
...
YOU'RE LUCKY I STARTED THE SCHOOL BACK UP.
LUCKY THIS LITTLE EXPERIMENT OF YOURS HAS A PLACE TO GO.
YES, IT'S UNFORTUNATE THAT I HAD TO REMOVE HIM FROM THE VIRTUAL REALITY EARLY, IN ORDER TO SAVE THE EARTH FROM YOUR RENEGADE FRIEND.
I'VE REALLY BOTCHED THINGS UP, HAVEN'T I?

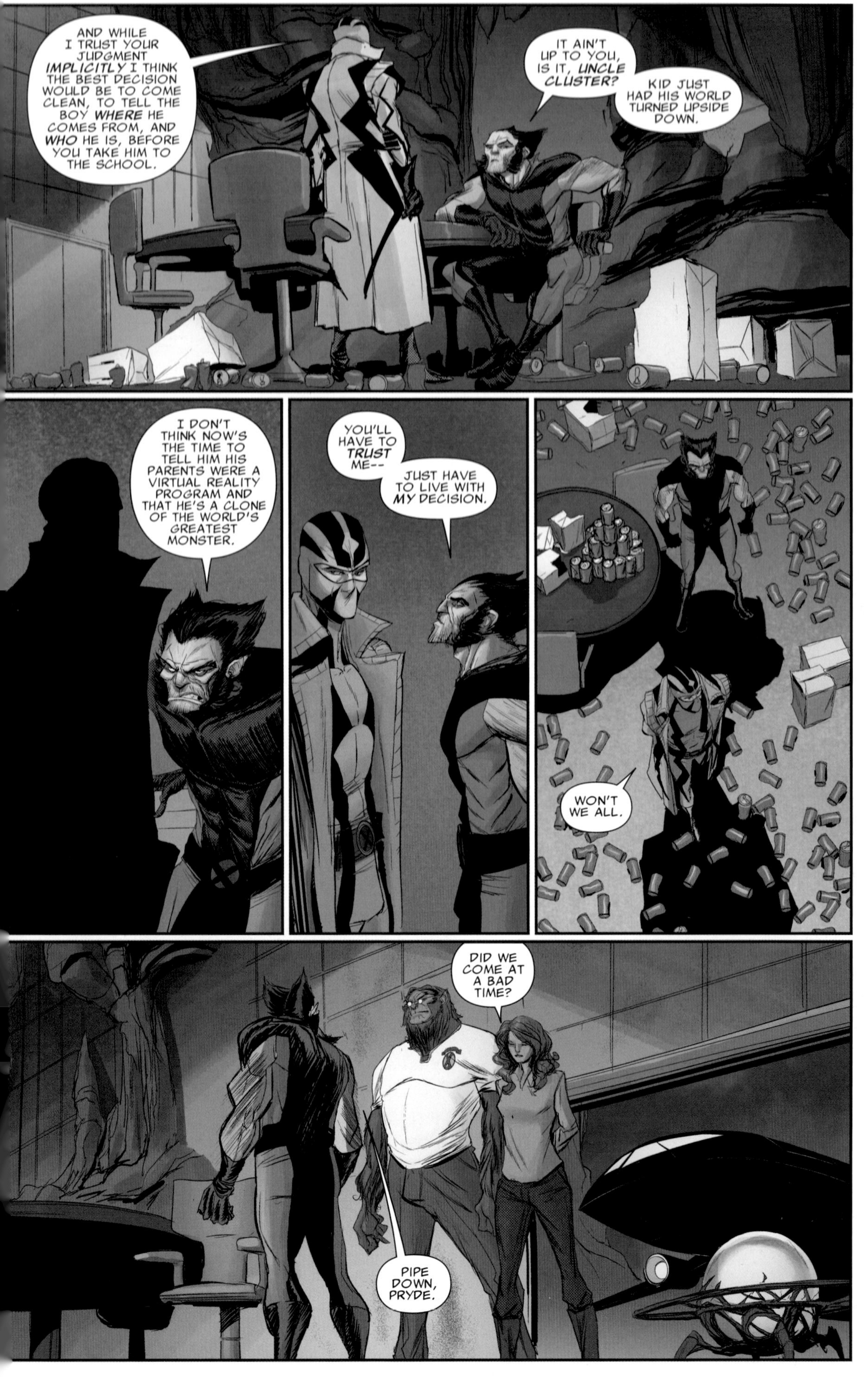
AND WHILE I TRUST YOUR JUDGMENT IMPLICITLY I THINK THE BEST DECISION WOULD BE TO COME CLEAN, TO TELL THE BOY WHERE HE COMES FROM, AND WHO HE IS, BEFORE YOU TAKE HIM TO THE SCHOOL.
IT AIN'T UP TO YOU, IS IT, UNCLE CLUSTER?
KID JUST HAD HIS WORLD TURNED UPSIDE DOWN.
I DON'T THINK NOW'S THE TIME TO TELL HIM HIS PARENTS WERE A VIRTUAL REALITY PROGRAM AND THAT HE'S A CLONE OF THE WORLD'S GREATEST MONSTER.
YOU'LL HAVE TO TRUST ME--
JUST HAVE TO LIVE WITH MY DECISION.
WON'T WE ALL.
DID WE COME AT A BAD TIME?
PIPE DOWN, PRYDE.

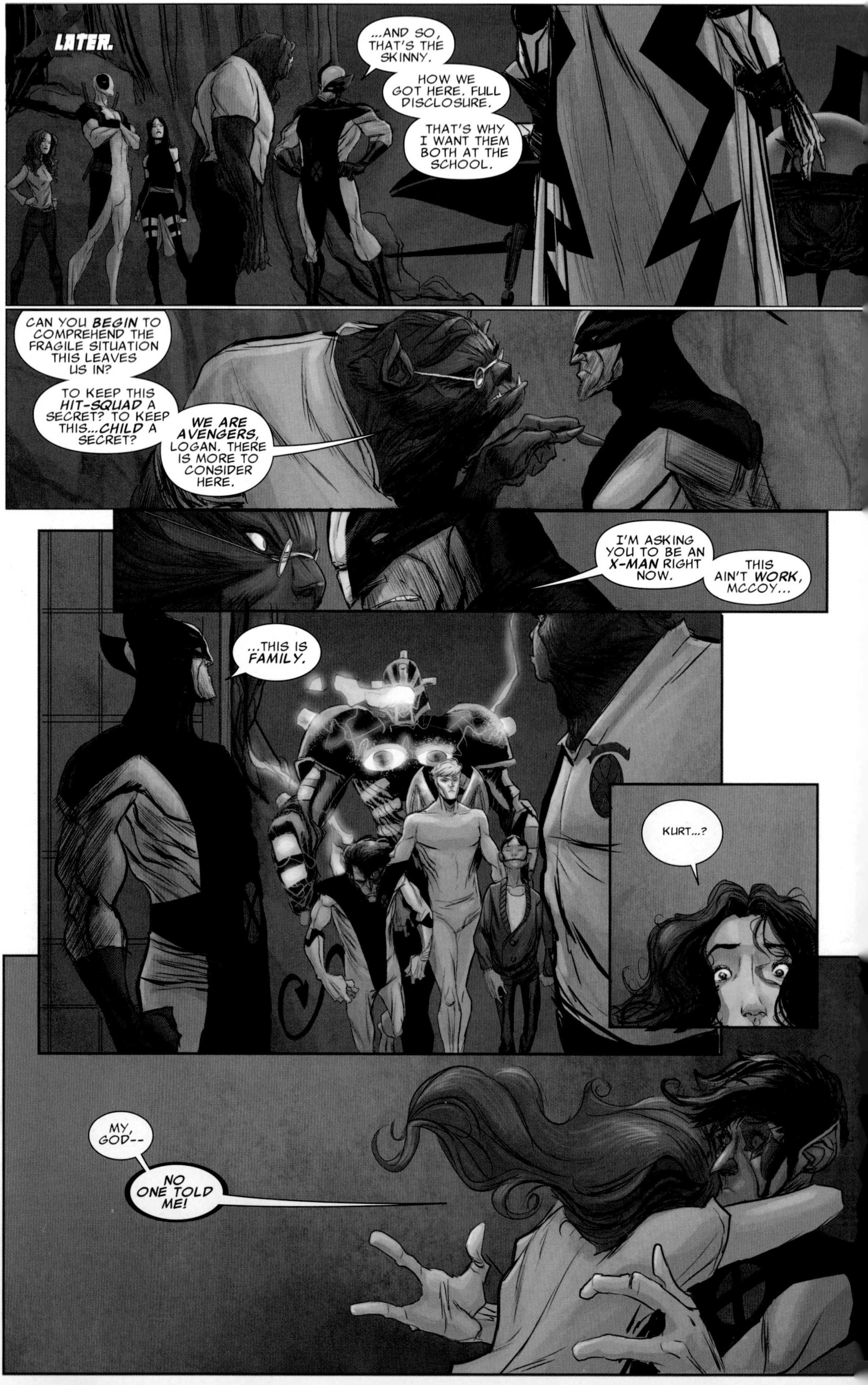
LATER.
...AND SO, THAT'S THE SKINNY.
HOW WE GOT HERE. FULL DISCLOSURE.
THAT'S WHY I WANT THEM BOTH AT THE SCHOOL.
CAN YOU BEGIN TO COMPREHEND THE FRAGILE SITUATION THIS LEAVES US IN?
TO KEEP THIS HIT-SQUAD A SECRET? TO KEEP THIS...CHILD A SECRET?
WE ARE AVENGERS, LOGAN. THERE IS MORE TO CONSIDER HERE.
I'M ASKING YOU TO BE AN X-MAN RIGHT NOW.
THIS AIN'T WORK, MCCOY...
...THIS IS FAMILY.
KURT...?
MY, GOD--
NO ONE TOLD ME!

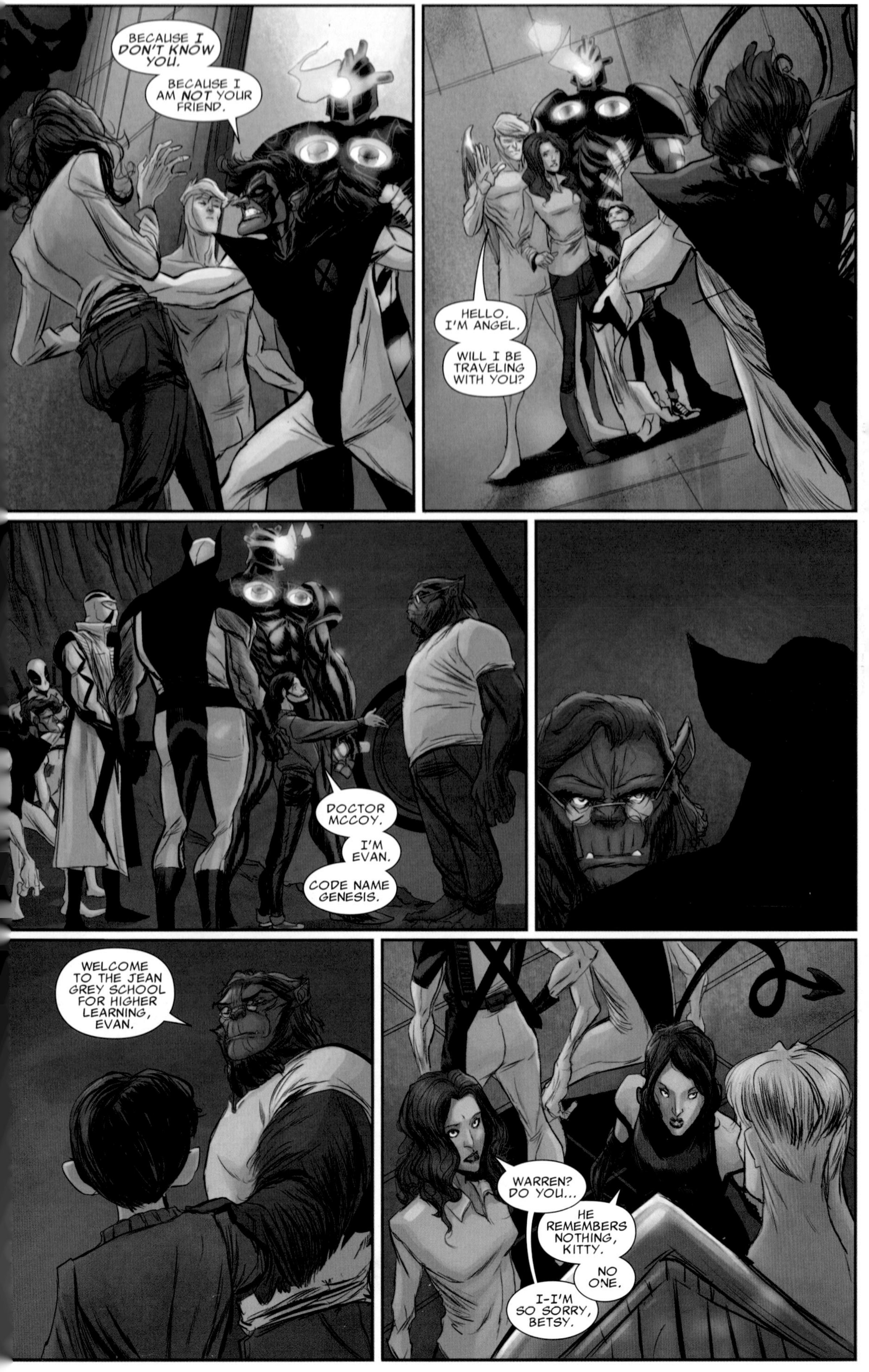
BECAUSE I DON'T KNOW YOU.
BECAUSE I AM NOT YOUR FRIEND.
HELLO. I'M ANGEL.
WILL I BE TRAVELING WITH YOU?
DOCTOR MCCOY.
I'M EVAN.
CODE NAME GENESIS.
WELCOME TO THE JEAN GREY SCHOOL FOR HIGHER LEARNING, EVAN.
WARREN? DO YOU...
HE REMEMBERS NOTHING, KITTY.
NO ONE.
I-I'M SO SORRY, BETSY.

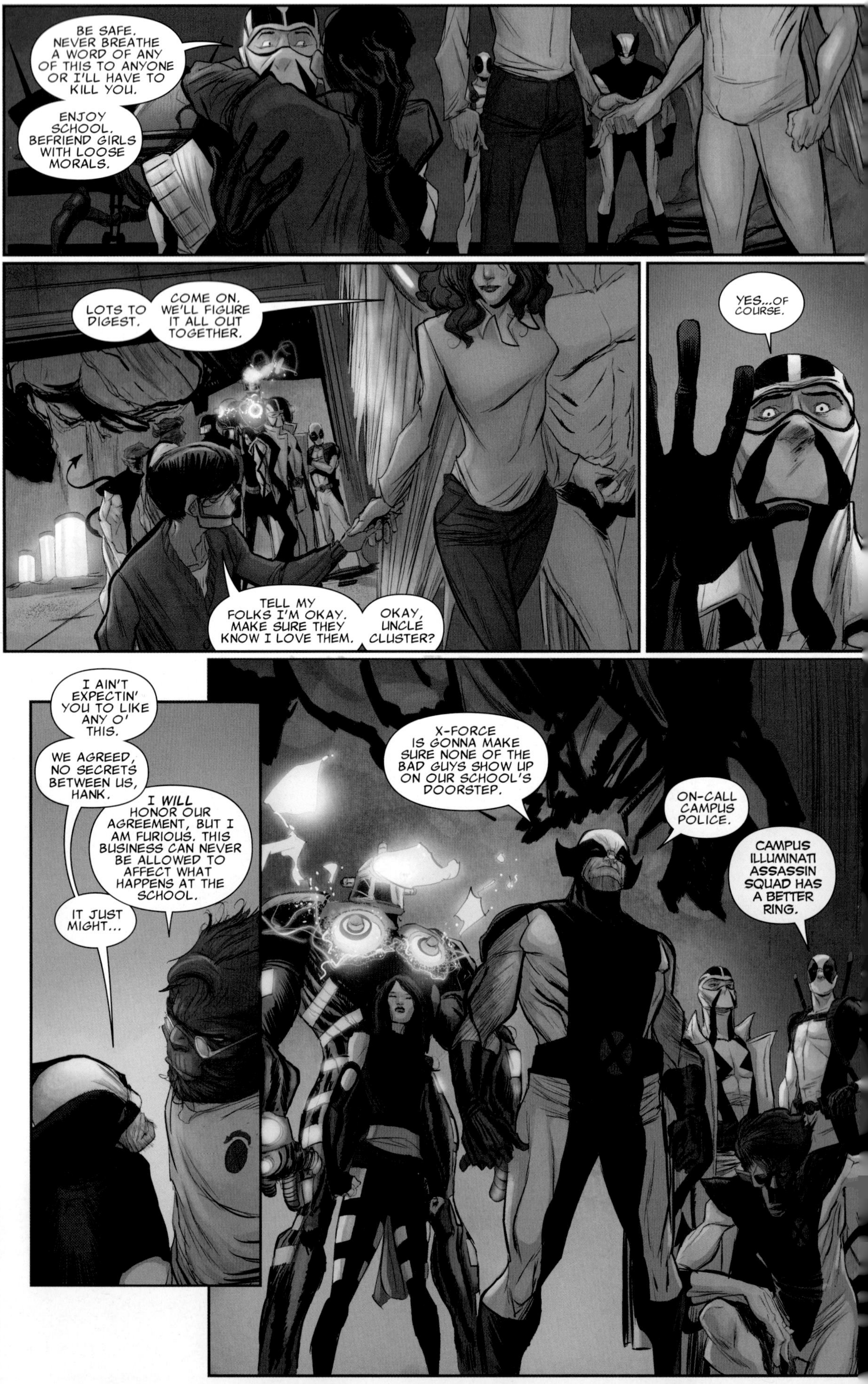
BE SAFE. NEVER BREATHE A WORD OF ANY OF THIS TO ANYONE OR I'LL HAVE TO KILL YOU.
ENJOY SCHOOL. BEFRIEND GIRLS WITH LOOSE MORALS.
LOTS TO DIGEST.
COME ON. WE'LL FIGURE IT ALL OUT TOGETHER.
TELL MY FOLKS I'M OKAY. MAKE SURE THEY KNOW I LOVE THEM.
OKAY, UNCLE CLUSTER?
YES...OF COURSE.
I AIN'T EXPECTIN' YOU TO LIKE ANY O' THIS.
WE AGREED, NO SECRETS BETWEEN US, HANK.
I *WILL* HONOR OUR AGREEMENT, BUT I AM FURIOUS. THIS BUSINESS CAN NEVER BE ALLOWED TO AFFECT WHAT HAPPENS AT THE SCHOOL.
IT JUST MIGHT...
X-FORCE IS GONNA MAKE SURE NONE OF THE BAD GUYS SHOW UP ON OUR SCHOOL'S DOORSTEP.
ON-CALL CAMPUS POLICE.
CAMPUS ILLUMINATI ASSASSIN SQUAD HAS A BETTER RING.

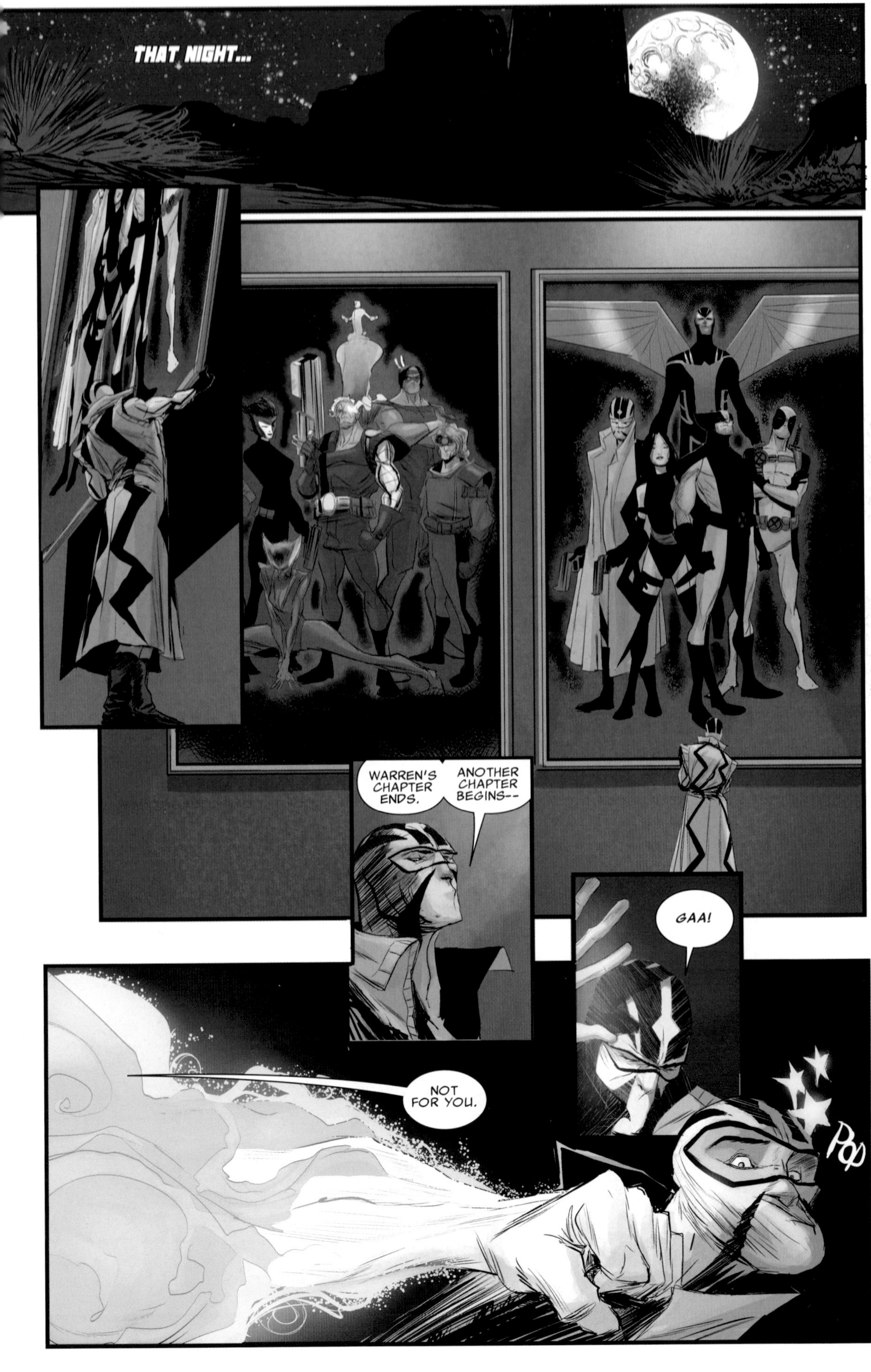

THAT NIGHT...
WARREN'S CHAPTER ENDS.
ANOTHER CHAPTER BEGINS--
GAA!
NOT FOR YOU.
POP

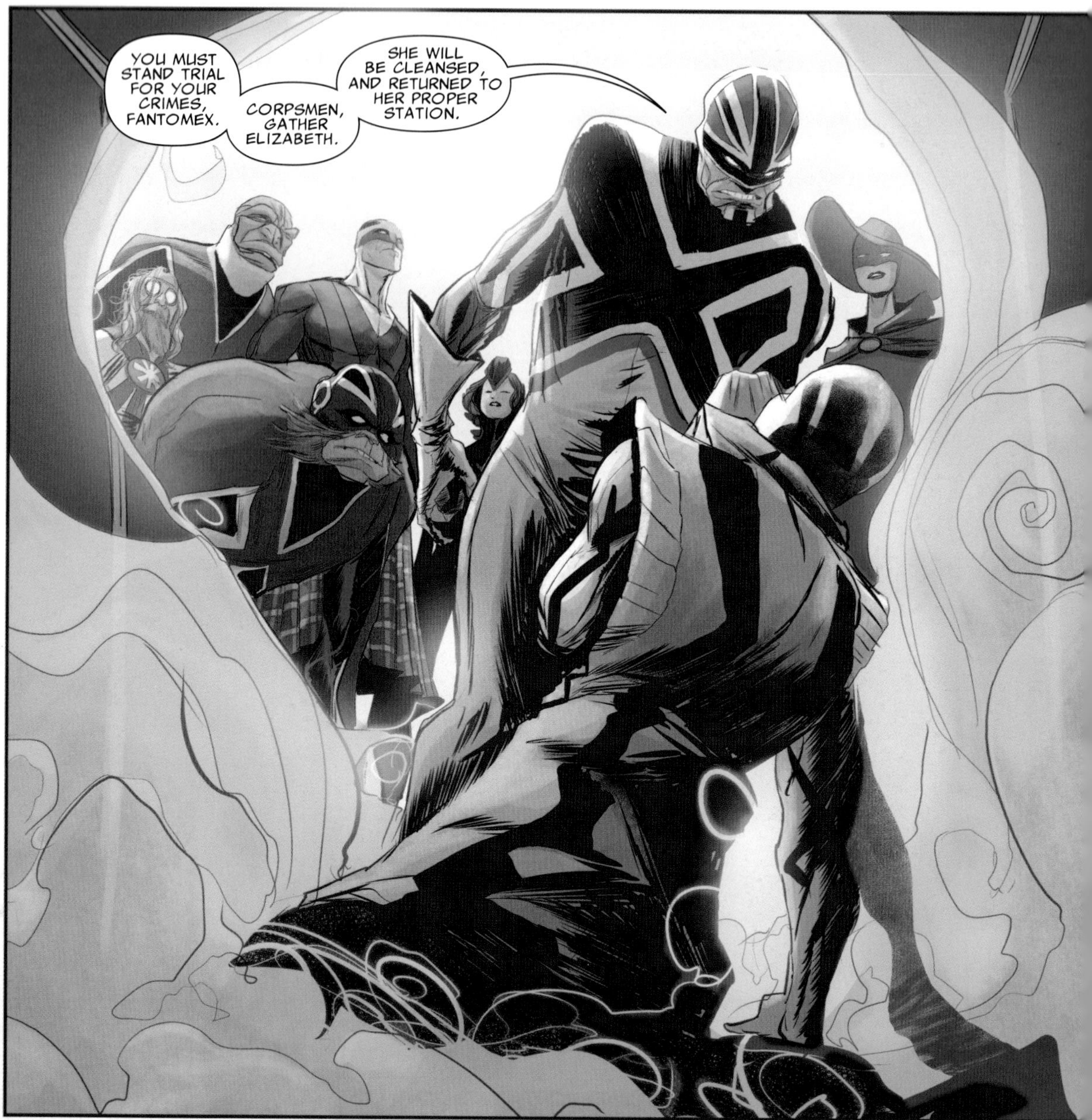
YOU MUST STAND TRIAL FOR YOUR CRIMES, FANTOMEX.
CORPSMEN, GATHER ELIZABETH.
SHE WILL BE CLEANSED, AND RETURNED TO HER PROPER STATION.

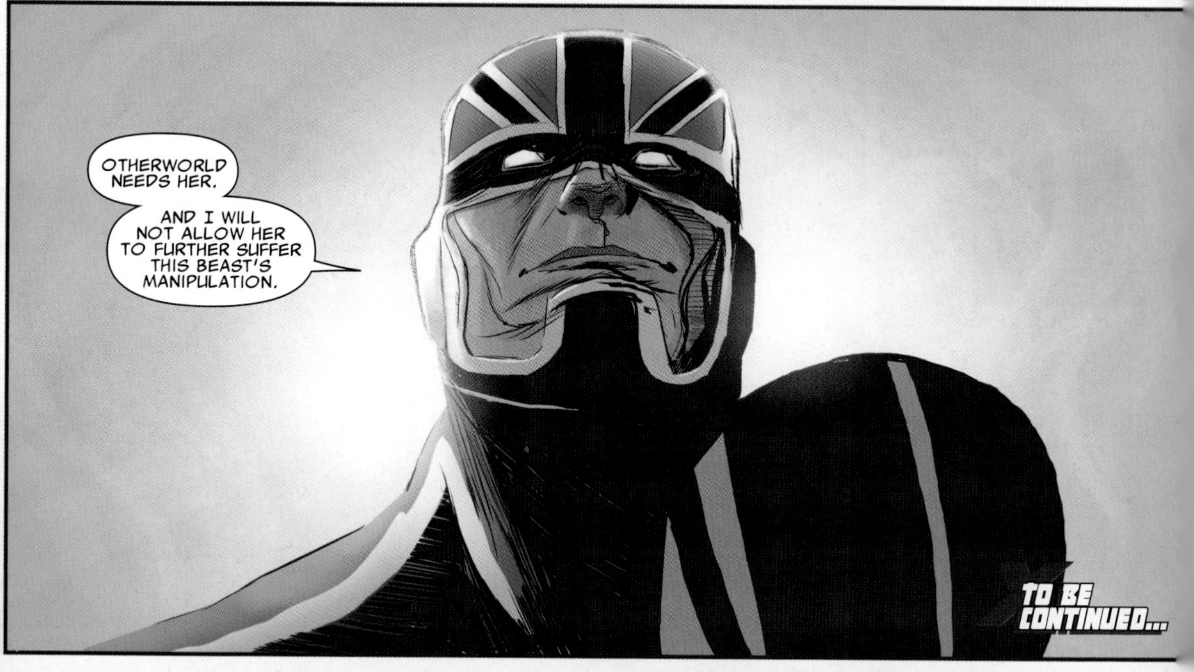
OTHERWORLD NEEDS HER.
AND I WILL NOT ALLOW HER TO FURTHER SUFFER THIS BEAST'S MANIPULATION.
TO BE CONTINUED...

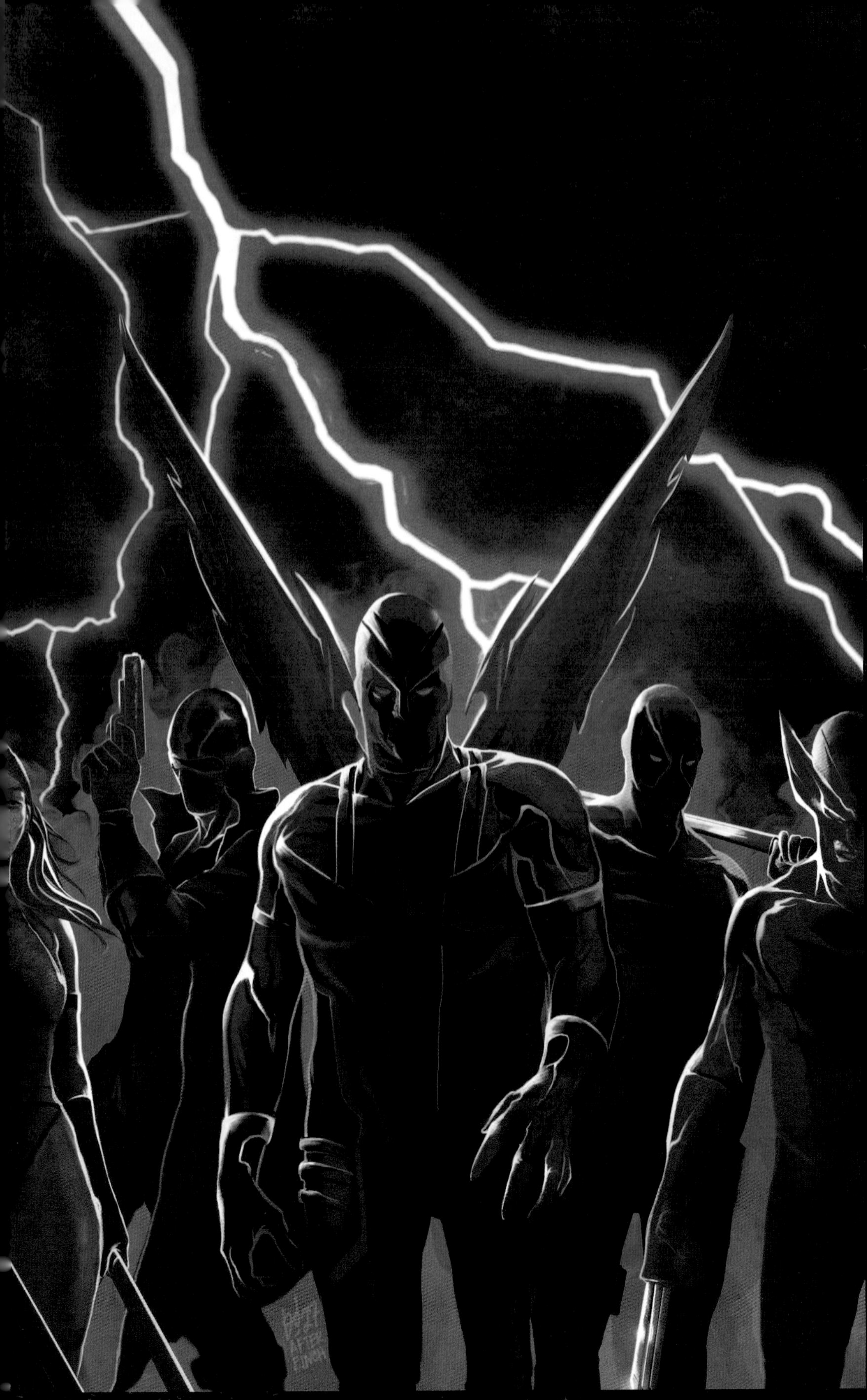

#16 MARVEL 50TH ANNIVERSARY VARIANT
by MICHAEL DEL MUNDO

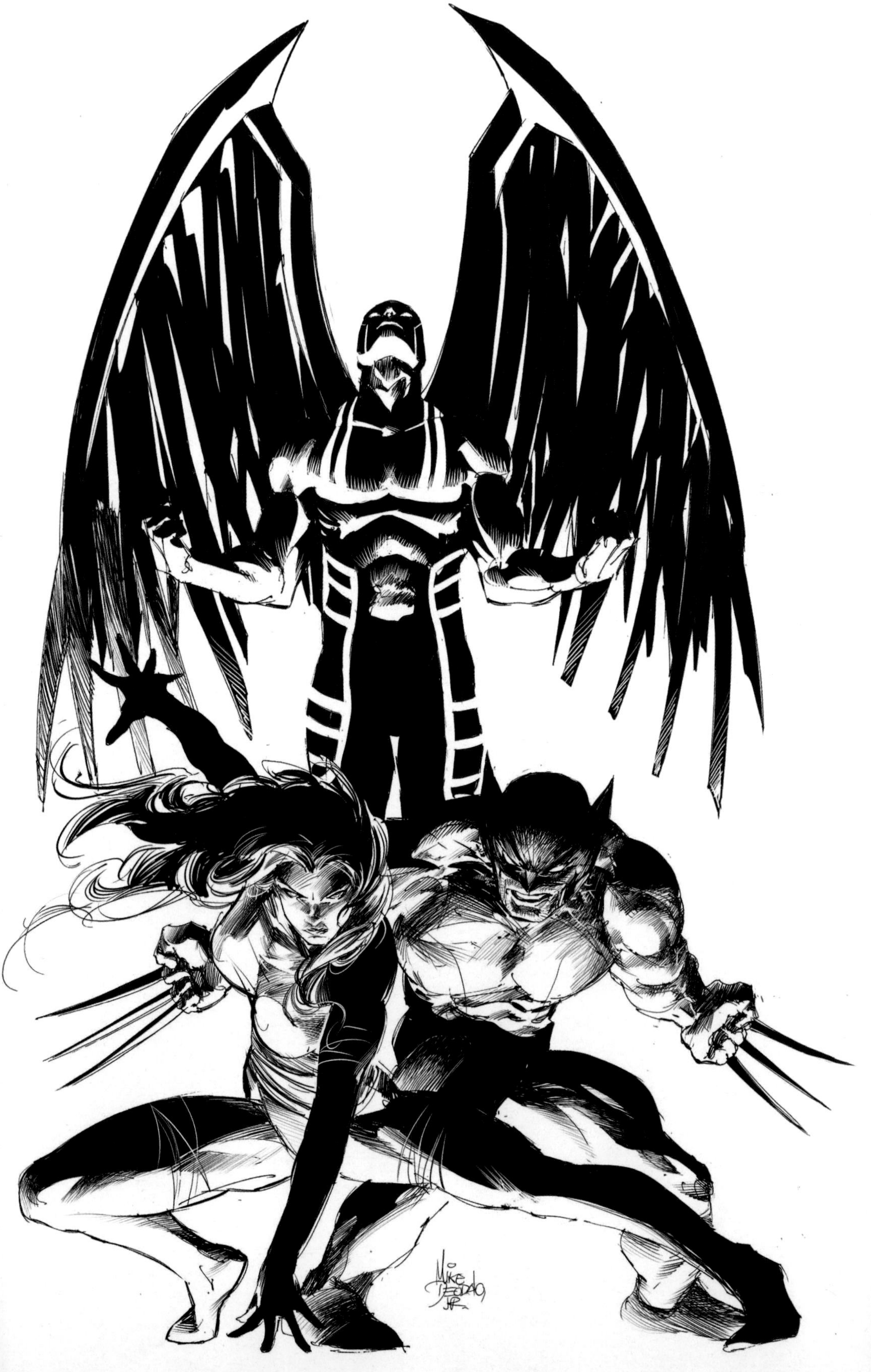

#15 ARCHITECTS SKETCH VARIANT
by MIKE DEODATO JR.

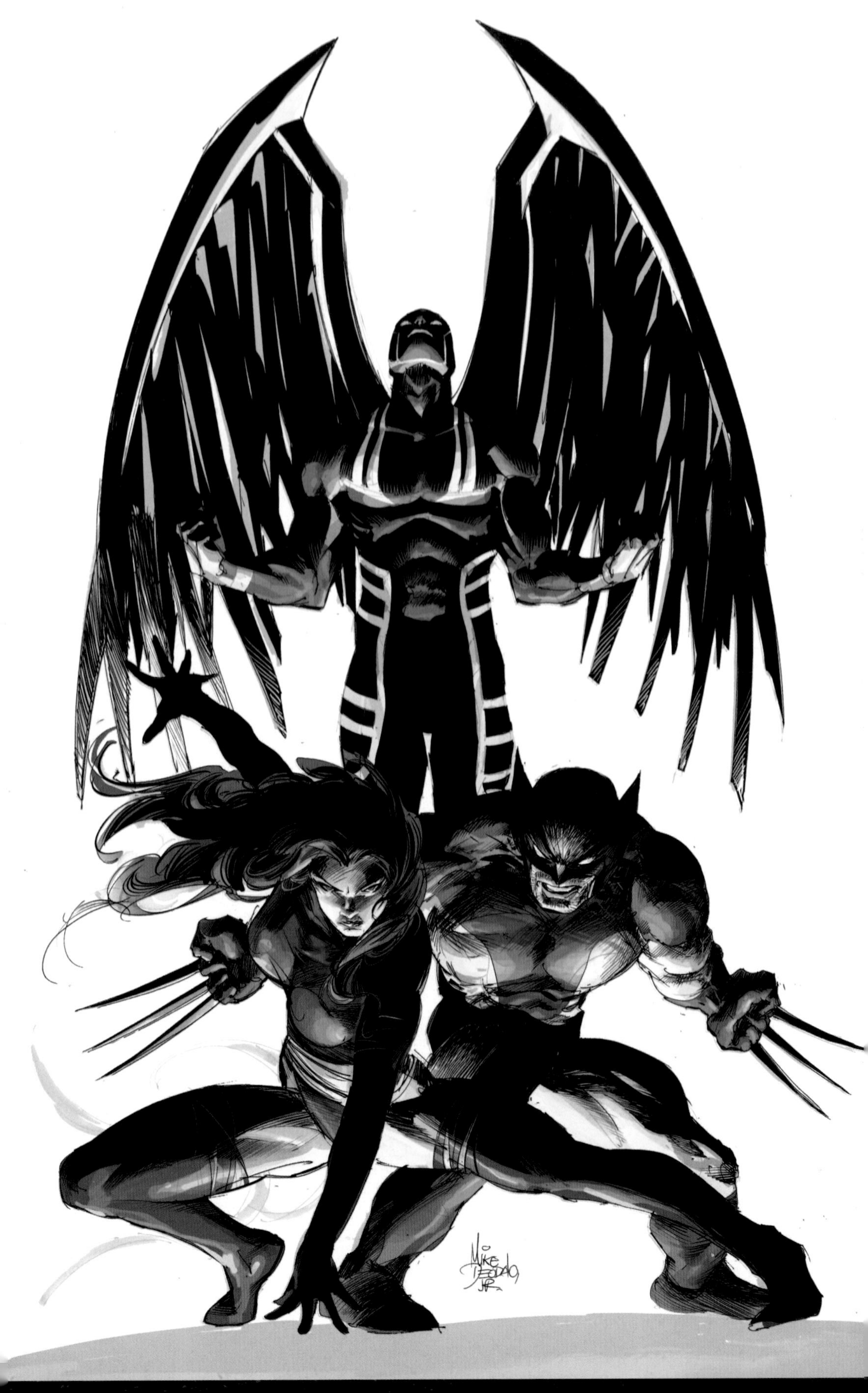

#15 ARCHITECTS VARIANT
by MIKE DEODATO JR. & RAIN BEREDO

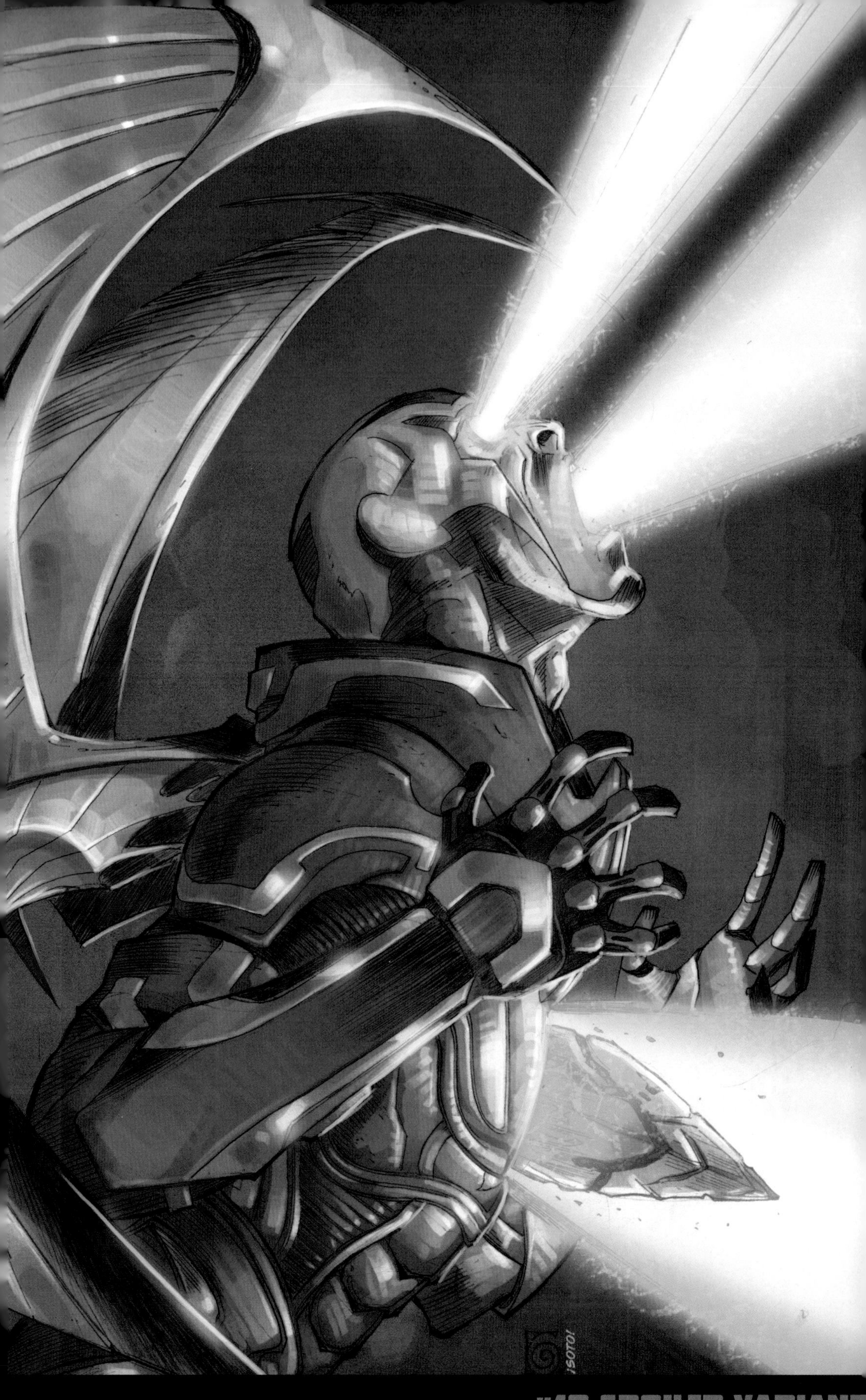
¡SOTO!

#18 SPOILER VARIANT
by RON GARNEY & CHRIS SOTOMAYOR

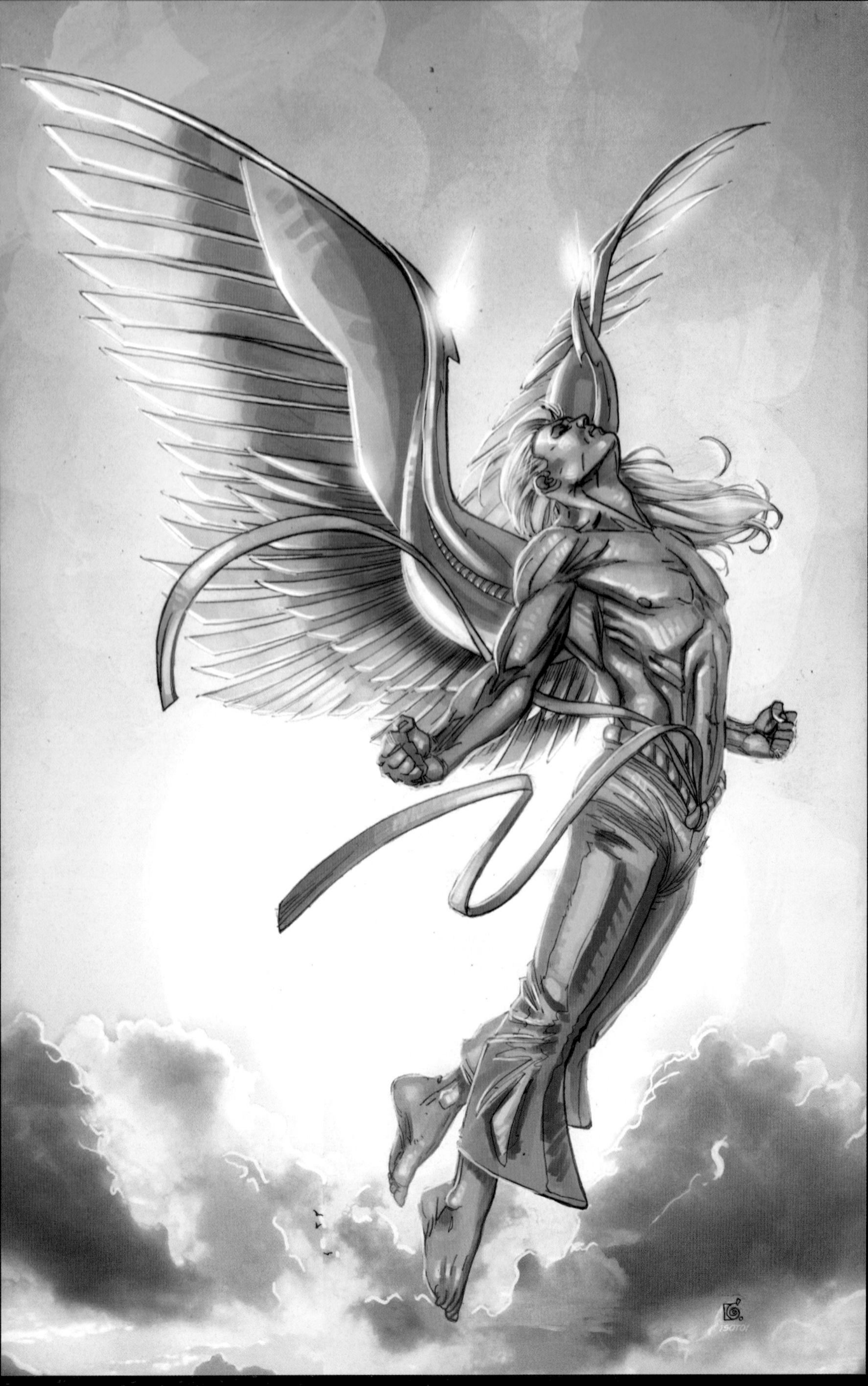

#19 SPOILER VARIANT
by RON GARNEY & CHRIS SOTOMAYOR

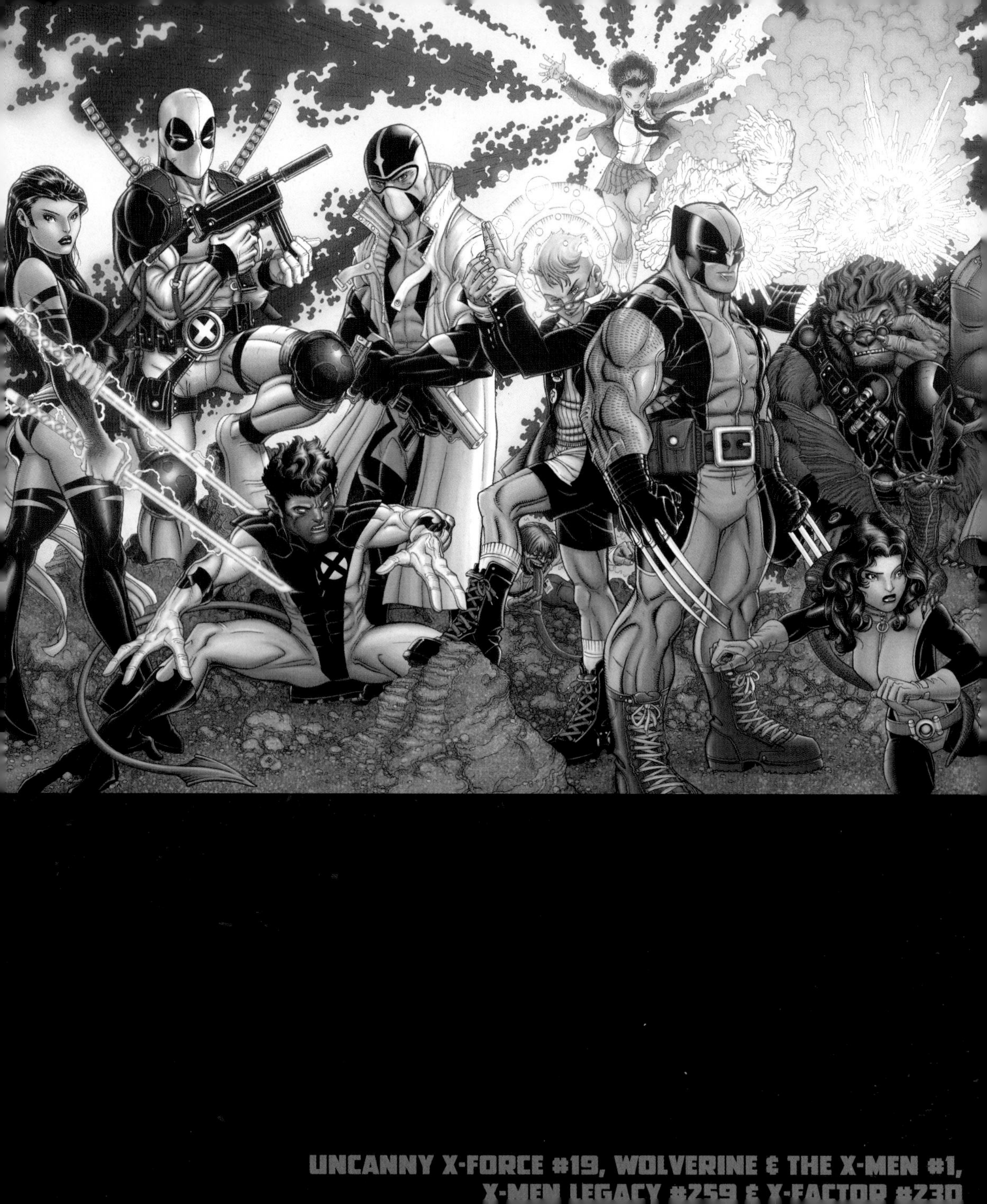

UNCANNY X-FORCE #19, WOLVERINE & THE X-MEN #1,
X-MEN LEGACY #259 & X-FACTOR #230

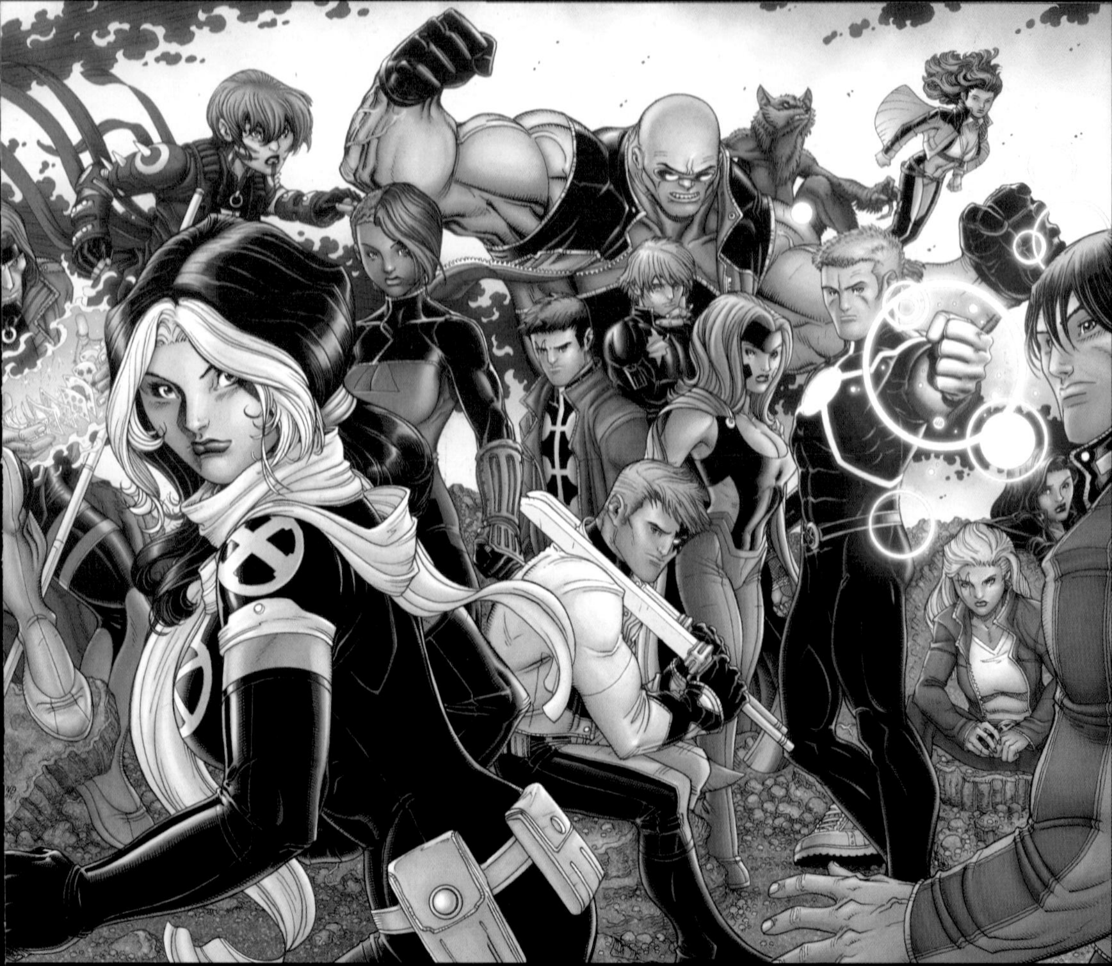

COMBINED VARIANTS
by NICK BRADSHAW & MORRY HOLLOWELL

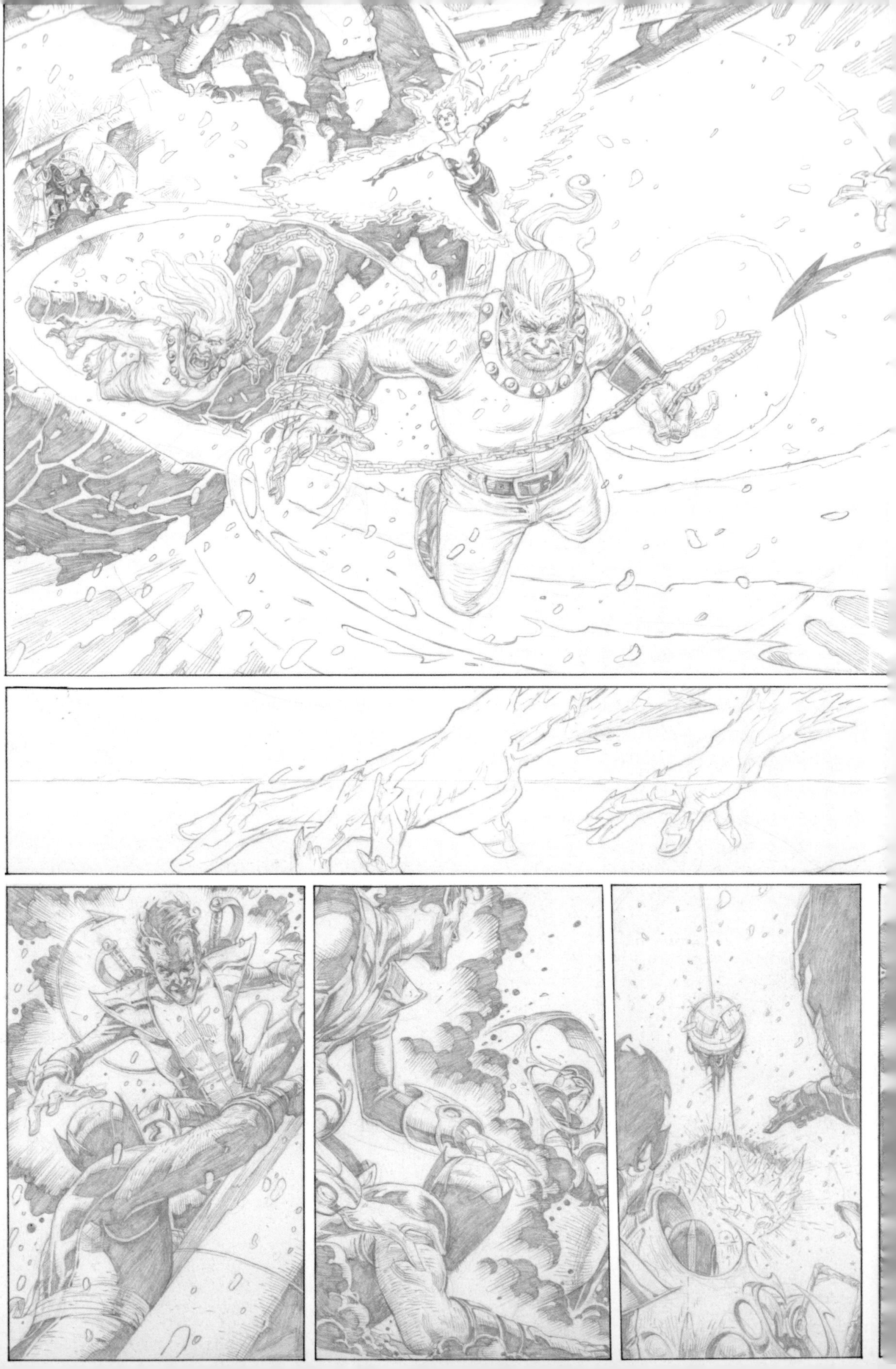

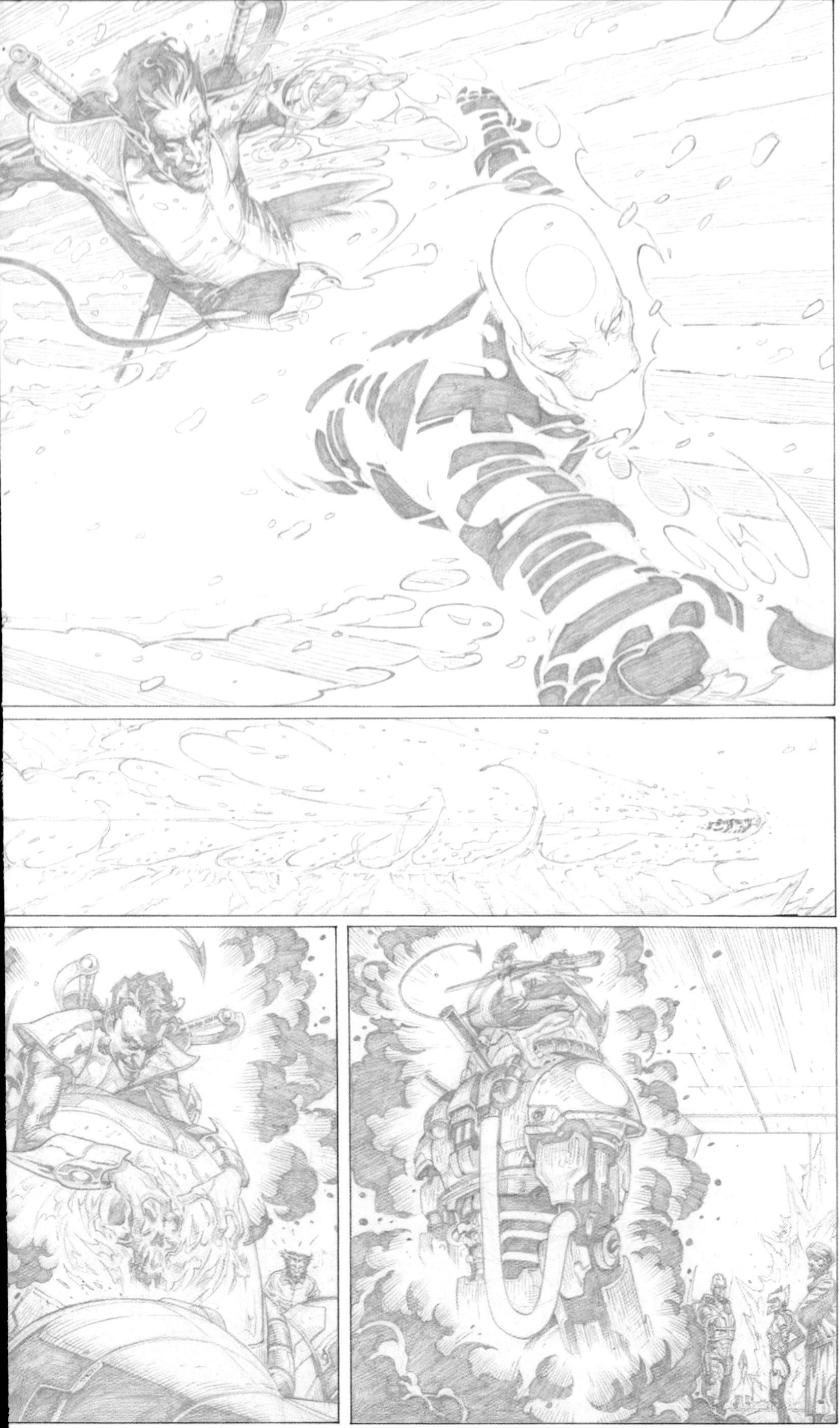

#17, PAGES 4-5 PENCILS
by JEROME OPEÑA

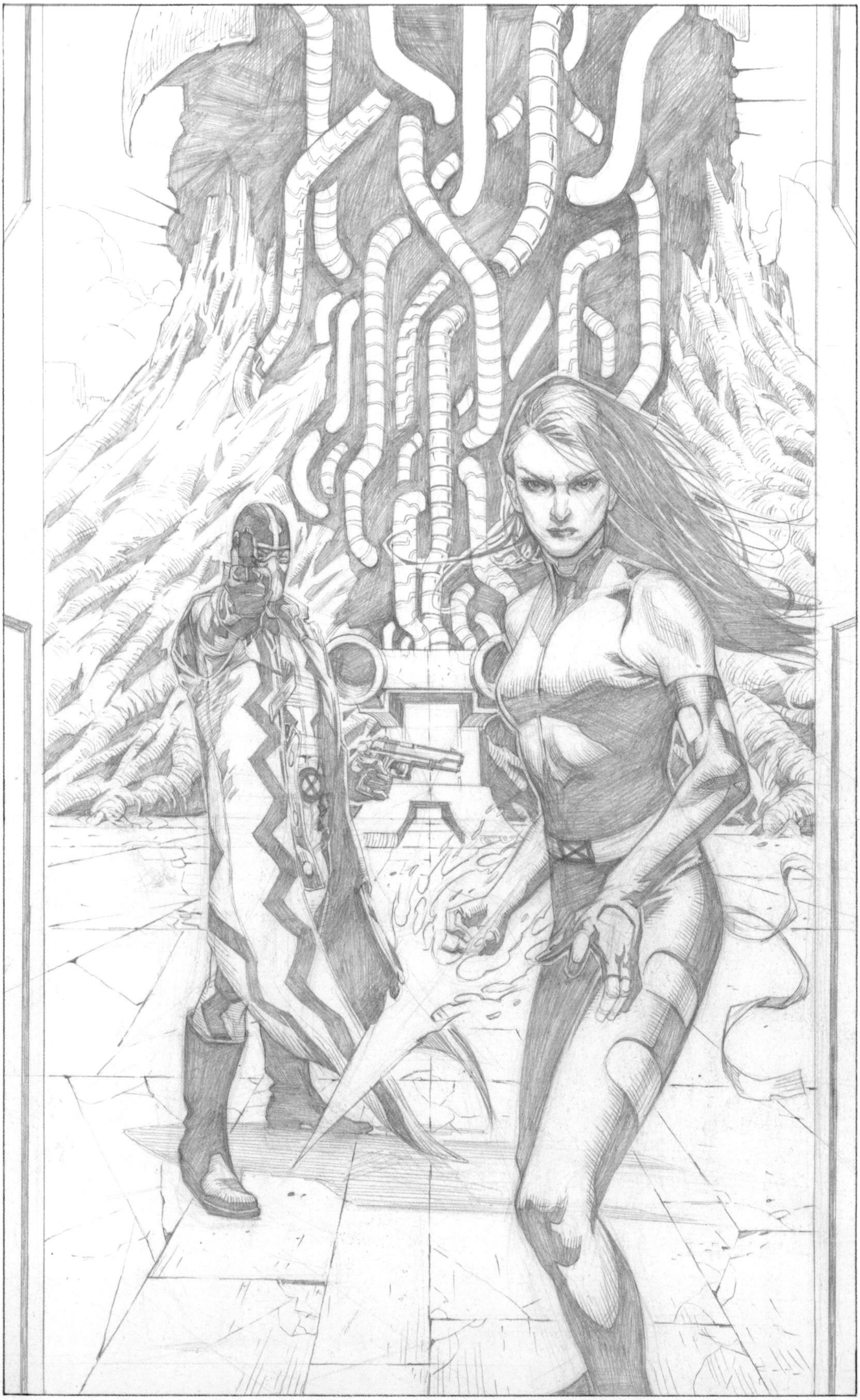

#17, PAGES 20 PENCILS
by JEROME OPEÑA